Praise for *It's a Boy!*

"*It's a Boy!* is a powerful guide to raising a son in today's world. Filled with stories from the front lines and practical advice, it is gentle and compassionate, yet also moving and beautiful. The heart of a boy beats in every page."
—MICHAEL GURIAN, author of *The Wonder of Boys*

"Michael Thompson has gradually earned his place as the Warren Buffet of child rearing, the real deal. His track record of uncanny timing, his hard-won knowledge, common sense, and humanism have resonated with parents everywhere. Now there is a desperate need to understand our boys more deeply; there is a palpable hunger to learn how to handle our sons better. *It's a Boy!* does both in a way not seen before. *It's a Boy!* will help your son to feel more loved, understood, and effectively guided by you—forever."
—RON TAFFEL, PH.D., author of *Parenting by Heart: How to Stay Connected to Your Child in a Disconnected World*

"Spectacular, extraordinary insight, enriched by countless poignant and telling stories of boys and their parents and teachers. *It's a Boy!* is an immensely helpful navigational chart for steering through the shoals of a boy's developmental stages."
—PATRICK F. BASSETT, president, National Association of Independent Schools

"Wise, sensible, accessible, useful—this is the must-have book that all parents of a boy will want and need to turn to as their child grows from a baby to an adolescent. Illuminated by Thompson's years of experience of working with boys and their families, this book is chock-full of new insights and the latest science about the ages and stages of boys' development. *It's a Boy!* is a book that parents, educators, health professionals, and policy makers will go back to again and again and each time come away with a deeper understanding and appreciation of why 'boys will be boys.'"
—ROBIE H. HARRIS, author of *It's Perfectly Normal: Changing Bodies, Growing Up, Sex, and Sexual Health*

"Bringing together the latest research and the most timeless knowledge and wisdom, this monumental book is unique, invaluable, and urgently important. Any person who cares about boys must own this book, as it addresses every relevant question and provides not only authoritative answers but also comfort, warmth, enthusiasm, and spark. What a truly amazing achievement, what a gift Dr. Thompson has given us all."
—EDWARD M. HALLOWELL, M.D., author of *Delivered from Distraction: Getting the Most out of Life with Attention Deficit Disorder*

By Michael Thompson, Ph.D.

Homesick and Happy

The Pressured Child, with Teresa Barker

It's a Boy!

Mom, They're Teasing Me, with Catherine O'Neill Grace
and Lawrence Cohen, Ph.D.

Best Friends, Worst Enemies, with Catherine O'Neill Grace
and Lawrence Cohen, Ph.D.

Speaking of Boys, with Teresa Barker

Raising Cain, with Dan Kindlon, Ph.D., and Teresa Barker

IT'S A
BOY!

IT'S A
BOY!

Understanding Your Son's Development
from Birth to Age 18

Michael Thompson, Ph.D.,
and Teresa H. Barker

Ballantine Books · New York

2009 Ballantine Books Trade Paperback Edition

Published in the United States by Ballantine Books, an imprint of
The Random House Publishing Group, a division of
Random House, Inc., New York.

BALLANTINE and colophon are registered trademarks of Random House, Inc.

Originally published in hardcover in the United States by
Ballantine Books, an imprint of The Random House Publishing Group,
a division of Random House, Inc., in 2008.

Photo Credits: page 3: © Lauren Giordano; 30: © Kristin Lake,
Look Out Art; 65: © Kristin Lake, Look Out Art; 105: © Joel Preston Smith,
www.joelprestonsmith.com; 146: © 2005 Jeff McCall; 193: © J. D. Sloan;
239: © 2005 Kelley King; 289: © Joel Preston Smith,
www.joelprestonsmith.com; 346: © J. D. Sloan

Thompson, Michael.
It's a boy! : understanding your son's development from birth to age 18 /
Michael Thompson and Teresa H. Barker.
p. cm.
Includes bibliographical references.
ISBN 978-0-345-49396-5 (hardcover : alk. paper)
1. Boys.   2. Child development.   3. Child rearing.
I. Barker, Teresa H. II. Title.
HQ775.T55 2007
305.231081—dc22   2007014205

Printed in the United States of America on acid-free paper

www.ballantinebooks.com

68975

Book design by Carol Malcolm Russo

To the memory of Tom Fuss, Andrew Sloan,
and David C. K. McClelland

CONTENTS

CONTENTS

AUTHORS' NOTE

WE ARE GRATEFUL TO THE HUNDREDS OF INDIVIDUALS WHO, THROUGH personal interviews, letters, books, research, and online surveys, have shared their stories, their expertise, and their insight in these pages. With the exception of professionals and a few other individuals who gave permission to use their names, all names and some personal characteristics of patients, parents, children, and others have been changed to protect their privacy. In some instances, some additional details have been changed for the same purpose. Any resulting resemblance to persons living or dead is entirely coincidental and unintentional. This book is designed to provide authoritative information in regard to the subject matter; however, neither the publisher nor the authors intend it as a substitute for professional care for any individual. For all matters of an individual nature, please seek appropriate professional attention.

INTRODUCTION

"Boys Really Are Different"

I HAVE BEEN TALKING TO PARENTS AND TEACHERS ABOUT BOYS FOR MY ENTIRE professional life, first as a middle school teacher, then as a high school counselor, and for the last twenty-five years as a psychologist. I have listened to parents in my office, consulted with teachers in school settings, and more recently answered the anxious e-mails of parents online. When I had a private office, 70 percent of my clients were boys and men. Now that I no longer have a clinical practice, I still work with boys every week, both at the boys' school in Massachusetts where I have been the consulting psychologist for fourteen years and also at the thirty or so schools I visit between September and June. Boys always inspire me. I see their great energy, compassion, and insight. I am witness to boys' devotion to their families, to God, to their loving relationships with their brothers and sisters, to their passionate pursuit of music, acting, and athletics. I watch them grapple with the challenges of school and problems in living and succeed. I love boy energy, enthusiasm, and humor. I also see that things are not easy for boys, and they are never simple.

Until very recently, we used to think—or want to think—that boys and girls were the same; or at least we weren't allowed to say, if we wanted to be politically correct, that boys and girls were different. Obviously, we've always known that we were raising children who had different bodies, genitals, and hormone systems; however, we assumed that boys and girls had more or less the same brains and that they needed mostly the same things from their parents to grow to become healthy adults. That is why in the past, the finest baby and parenting guides, such as those by pediatricians T. Berry Brazelton, Penelope Leach, and Benjamin Spock, hardly mentioned gender differences at all. They did not give different instructions for raising girls and boys.

Today, we are looking at our sons through two new lenses. One lens, the increase in our scientific knowledge about boys, is potentially enormously helpful to them and us. The other lens, our anxiety about and fear of boys, is quite destructive to them. Parents do their best to maintain a balanced perspective, but it can be challenging at times.

Moms, especially, wonder about their sons: *Is this normal? Should I be worried?* Boys tend to be much more physical and to take more risks than girls; they tend to get into trouble in school more, or take it less seriously than girls seem to. Much of this can be normal developmentally; sometimes, however, it can be cause for concern. My hope is that by understanding your son's development, you will be alert for those times when your concerns are justified, and know when you can sit back and enjoy your son's healthy boy-ness.

Let's take a moment to consider the new discoveries about boys. Recent research, in part the result of our ability to look inside the brain when it is operating, has demonstrated that the brains of girls and boys are more different than we have understood in the past. Steven Pinker, a professor of psychology at Harvard University, declares that there are sixty significant differences between males and females that have been discovered to date; some seem highly relevant to how we teach and raise boys.

When researchers give boys and girls the same language rhyming task and discover that different parts of their brains light up on a PET scan, we have to sit up and take notice, because it may explain so much about the differential performance of boys and girls in elementary school, and it may guide how we teach reading to boys in the future.

When neuroscientists can peer into the brains of boys with attention deficit hyperactivity disorder and see that their brains function differently than those of the majority of boys and girls, we have insight into the fidgety, distractible behavior of some boys.

When we understand that boys and girls differ in the ratio of gray matter and white matter that they possess in their brains, that boys' brains develop more slowly than girls' in some ways, and that boys may hear and see somewhat differently than girls, we may be unlocking the biological explanation for commonsense observations about boys that people have made for hundreds of years: they are immature in comparison to girls, grow up at a slower pace, and learn to read more slowly.

Researchers working with infants have shown that boys may be more vulnerable to disruptions in their early attachments to their mothers and fathers, and that their need for maternal and paternal "attunement" is just as great, if not greater, than that of girls.

Other scientists, studying traumatized and abused boys, have also begun to enlarge our view of boys, showing that they are not as "tough" or as "resilient" as our culture might have imagined. Writings by other clinician-researchers—and I like to include Dan Kindlon's and my book, *Raising Cain: Protecting the Emotional Life of Boys,* in this group—have brought back testimony from the consulting room and the classroom that speaks to the complex, inner life of boys that they may not easily share with adults. The combined evidence from neuroscience and from psychology gives us important information that can help a parent to raise a boy. This knowledge may also help you combat some of the destructive effects of adult misconceptions about boys that could negatively affect your son.

The new research keeps raising the question of how different boys and girls are. There is no easy answer to it, because scientists passionately disagree, coming at it from one side or other of the old nature-versus-nurture question.

As scientists discover more biological differences between boys and girls that are seen across all cultures, one camp of researchers—I'll call them the "essentialists"—are claiming that boys and girls are fundamentally and innately different physically, neurologically, and emotionally. There is research to support it.

On the other side, however, we have the "sex role/social learning theorists," who point out that we shape boys and girls with our cultural expectations right from the start. Girls gaze more into their mother's eyes than boys do, but not immediately after birth; they seem to develop that behavior after several months. Are we doing something different with our girl babies? That's possible, even likely. Is that training powerful? Yes, it is. And are girls much more "girl" after they have been treated like girls and have played with other girls from the age of three until ten or eleven? You bet they are! Gender-appropriate behavior is something that can be taught, and is taught, to every child in every culture. So while there may be biological differences, cultural training remains extremely powerful and still explains much about the reason boys are boys and girls are girls.

Then there is one final complication: if you are a woman—and thus were raised a girl—you have more of a "girl" brain than when you started out in life; similarly, if you are a man, you have more of a "boy" brain. Training and experience actually change the biochemistry of the brain. The brains we test later in life are never a product of just nature *or* just nurture, because nature and nurture are not mutually exclusive processes. Everything we see in our children is always the result of both nature and nurture playing off and influencing each other, shaping and reshaping our children, their brains, and their behavior.

I cannot resolve the scientific questions in this book; the debate is going to keep academics entertained for years, and as neurobiologists make more discoveries, much of what we now know will be updated. Personally, I am a centrist. I do not believe that any particular biological discovery will suddenly change all parenting advice, and so I have tried to keep this book in the center of the political debate. However, if the reader is going to take parenting advice from me right now, she or he is entitled to know how I think about the differences between boys and girls.

I have three bedrock beliefs that may, at first, sound contradictory. They are not. I like to think they represent three different levels of wisdom about the differences between boys and girls, which, taken together, can provide a sound basis for giving parenting advice. The first is that children are always more human than they are gendered and therefore their need for love, attachment, nourishment, guidance, challenge, and understanding is always more the same than it is different. That's why commonsense parenting advice has worked for years, even without the recent discoveries about boys and girls. When in doubt, I'll stick with experience and common sense.

Second, human variability beats gender differences. There is such variability in the human brain, temperament, and personality that individuality always wins. That is, if you are a profoundly shy person, that fact might make as much difference in your life as being a boy or girl; if you are a highly competitive athlete, that skill might shape your destiny profoundly, whether you are male or female. How can I not believe in the power of personality over gender when I am the parent of two children, one a girl who is a self-described "jock," played three varsity sports in high school, and now makes her living teaching tennis, and the other a boy who hates competitive athletics and loves art, drawing, theater, video games, and reading? There is nothing quite so humbling as being out on the speaking circuit talking about gender differences and coming home to a gender-stereotype-busting household.

In the end, however, I believe that gender really matters, and that's why I have written this book. Whether or not you accept Sigmund Freud's contention that anatomy is destiny, it is certainly very powerful. The average boy and the average girl *are* meaningfully different from each other, and those differences are played out in a million ways at home and school. Our sex is one of the most important facts about any of our lives and, along with race and social class and family, it determines much of our destiny. Knowing the sex of a child allows us to predict with some accuracy what toys he or she will want to play with and what his or her friendship patterns will be at age ten. It tells us what kind of problems a child is likely to encounter at different ages and how those developmental difficulties can be overcome.

So we should be talking about what boys do, how they react at different ages, what they like, what they typically do not like. We should be talking about the great variety of boys and what works for them all. The knowledge of gender differences, tempered by the wisdom that there are as many different personalities as there are children, should help to guide our understanding of our boys and the way we parent them. That is what I have tried to do in *It's a Boy*.

Family, friends, and neighbors used to reassure the parents of sons that they were in for a pretty easy ride. "Don't worry," they would say, "boys are easier than girls." I doubt that this was ever true, but people would offer it as comforting wisdom. "Boys are simple," grown-ups would sometimes say (boys still tell me that). What they meant was that boys were emotionally straightforward and easy to read; the feelings of girls, by comparison, were complex and mysterious. You could let a boy play outside without concern; a girl required physical and emotional protection. A boy could enjoy his driver's license and some backseat sexual experimentation in a straightforward way when he became a teenager; it was a girl who might feel exploited in that situation. If a boy got a good-enough education, there would be a place for him in the world; it was girls who would hit both visible and invisible barriers—closed doors and the glass ceiling—in the workplace.

Of course, boys were mischievous and would almost certainly get into more trouble in school, but hey, that was no big deal. Everyone in school understood the nature of boys. We trusted that they would grow up in time. We didn't need to do anything special for them when they were babies; they were pretty much the same as girls. If we loved them and were patient, if we had a sense of humor about them, if we used strong discipline, they would develop in a healthy way. If we gave them some space in which to explore and some meaningful chores around the house, they would turn out okay.

Who would say that today? What parent can feel sure that her or his boy is going to turn out to be "okay"? Boys in the United States are more at risk now than they have ever been for two reasons: their world has changed, and our view of boys has changed. First, the world in which our boys are growing up is different from the one we lived in. The biggest reason for this was the twenty-year epidemic of young male violence in the United States, culminating symbolically with the shootings at Columbine High School in 1999 and tragically reprised by the shooter at Virginia Tech in 2007. As a nation, we had to confront the fact that our sons had become the most violent in the industrialized world and that moving out of the cities and into the suburbs would not solve boys' difficulties. Violence isn't the only concern. We now hear on the news that boys are underachieving academically, that girls outperform boys in elementary school, high school, college, and graduate school. Forty years ago, 58 percent of college graduates were young men; in 2007 57 percent of graduating seniors are women, and soon they will be 60 percent of students on most college campuses.

There are profound societal changes under way that have had an impact on boyhood:

the epidemic of divorce in the United States, the loss of fathers in the lives of boys, the wide availability of guns, increased global competition, pressure for early performance in school and on the athletic field, the loss of male teachers, increased drug and alcohol use, and the rise of Internet porn and Internet gaming. Perhaps equally important, and the least mentioned in the United States, is the significant loss of safe places for our sons to engage in undirected, outside play throughout their boyhoods. That will be a theme throughout this book.

In this sea of change, from research findings to family patterns, it is natural that the concerns of parents have changed over the past three decades. Though we worry about all of our children—that's our job—in general we are now more worried about our sons' futures than our daughters'. For a variety of reasons, we seem to no longer trust boys and their natural growth. That loss of trust in boy development is my motivation for writing this guide to raising sons. I am hopeful that my experiences can be helpful to you as a parent.

As part of the research for this book, which included interviews with many teachers, parents, and boys, more than four hundred parents and almost two hundred teachers wrote in to my Web site, www.michaelthompson-phd.com, to answer long, detailed questionnaires about boys. A smaller number of boys over eighteen also wrote in to share experiences from their boyhoods. The answers to these questions provided a pool of wisdom, anxiety, and funny, loving anecdotes from which I could draw in illustrating the lives of boys. I believe they surround the reader with the voices of other parents talking about their sons that she or he might not otherwise hear.

The book is organized chronologically from a mother's pregnancy through the first eighteen years of a boy's life, or approximately the end of high school. The chapters break up boyhood into segments that range from eighteen months to three years. If you are a pregnant mother, if you have come home with that grainy black-and-white sonogram with a sticker proclaiming "It's a boy" and you're freaked out because you grew up in a family with three sisters, I hope *It's a Boy* can help you think about raising a son. You should start with Chapter 1, "Imagining a Boy." I hope you keep reading, to get the full boy story; but you may want to put it on the shelf and take it down at a later date. If you are the mother of an angry four-year-old who cannot seem to keep his temper under control, you should probably start with Chapter 4, "Wild Thing," which covers ages three and four. If you are trying to decide how to speak to your fifteen-year-old about his relationship with his girlfriend and about sexuality, you should turn first to Chapter 8, "Mystery Boy." I always hope readers will read back and forward from the present age of their boy. One of the compliments on *Raising Cain* I most cherish is when a mother comes up to me and says, "I loved going back and reading about what I should have done and saw that I had done it. It was so affirming."

You will find every chapter has three parts. The main text focuses on the major psychological issues of the age and profiles different boys and their struggles. A second section, boxed for easy reference, describes the achievements of that age along eight lines of developments, such as physical development, emotional self-regulation, and moral and spiritual development. This "Eight Lines of Development" section in each chapter provides a developmental backdrop for the story of boys' growth at every age. Each chapter also features sidebars that offer advice and go into depth on particular boy issues.

One of the differences between boys and girls is that boys don't talk to you as much, which makes it harder—especially for women—to understand what's going on in their lives. This book will help explain the normal developmental passages and milestones in the psychological life of a boy, including attachment and physical, social, academic, cognitive, and moral and spiritual development—and what some of the delights and challenges are that you can expect at each stage of development.

Loving parents want to do the right thing for their boys. They want to understand their sons, whether their sons are "all boy" or whether they run against the boy stereotype. Parents want to know that most of the problems they face with their sons are normal, and how to distinguish those from the ones that are truly worrisome. That is almost certainly why you are holding this book in your hands. I hope it is of help to you in raising your son. At the same time, however, I need to make a quick disclaimer: this book could have filled ten volumes. Any single age of boyhood, such as toddlerhood or the last two years of high school, could have warranted a book on its own; any single issue, such as sports or drugs and alcohol, could have justified a separate book. Indeed, books exist on all of these topics. For this volume, I have picked out the most important psychological issues at every age, based on my experience and the literature. I left more out of this book than I could put in.

I mentioned earlier in this introduction that we are looking at boys through two lenses: the lens of our new knowledge, which I discussed, and the lens of our fears about boys. I do understand that after so much male violence in the United States, and with so many boys underachieving in school, our worries are not totally irrational. However, our fears about boy life are not helpful to our sons. When we panic about the fact that they aren't reading in kindergarten, it demoralizes them; when they sense that we do not have faith in their development, it undermines them. They need us to see the promise in them; they need us to be excited about them as boys.

That's why I want people to know the story of boy development, because it *is* a trustworthy journey. As a parent, you can have faith in your son's biology and his psychology. They are reliable; he's reliable. He's built the way he is for a reason. The vast majority of boys fulfill their bright, shining early promise. They do get toilet-trained, they learn to read, they do (finally) get organized. (Never quite as organized as girls, perhaps, and their handwriting is never as good, but . . . after all, they're boys.) Overwhelmingly, boys grow up to be smart, loving, capable men who do their share of the work of the world. And on the way, they provide us with creativity, humor, dedication, imagination, and a thousand laughs. If you are raising a son, I would like to give you three words to help you: enjoy your boy.

IT'S A
BOY!

ITS A
BOY!

CHAPTER ONE

IMAGINING A BOY

What Were You Thinking?

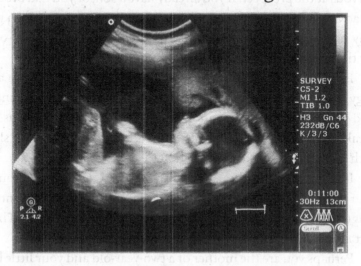

ANDREW'S PARENTS ARE GRAPPLING WITH THE ISSUES THAT OCCUPY THE mind of every loving parent. They aren't sure how to strike a healthy balance in their son's life between sports and academics, music and video games, friends and family time. Should they let him watch TV before he cleans up his room? When should they stand firm and when should they let their son decide for himself? They agree it's too early to think about college. But while they don't want to pressure him about eventual career choices, the family business does have his name on it. "We'll just take a wait-and-see approach," his mother says gamely as she pats her very pregnant belly. It is two weeks before Andrew's due date. As for Andrew, he mostly busies himself making wide turns in utero, the bulge of his tiny foot tracing an impressive arc across his mother's midriff.

Perhaps you, too, are expecting a boy. And if he is your first child or the first boy in your growing family, your curiosity and concerns about a boy's life fill your thoughts and conversations. You have heard other mothers say, "They really are different!" And, of course, they are. If they weren't, there would be no point at all in my writing this book.

"Boys are easier than girls," you hear. "Boys are an open book." "Boys love their mothers." But then what do you make of all those stories about boys being uncommunicative, behaving badly or struggling through school, stifling their inner life or losing themselves on the way to becoming men?

If this is your first foray into the intimate life of boys, you may be excited or nervous at the prospect. If you already have a son, or you had brothers, or you are a dad and remember your own boyhood, then your outlook on parenting a boy may have you feeling all the more confident and encouraged—or wary, bracing for the worst.

Perhaps you are the mother of a five-year-old boy and you are feeling a bit edgy about his interests. "My son really likes to play with guns," one mother told me. "I don't like them and I won't allow them in the house, so one day at breakfast he made a gun with his finger and his thumb and he 'shot' his brother with it! Why does he keep doing that?"

If you are that mother, you may be worried that, despite your great love for your son and the good home in which he is being raised, his interest in guns is a sign that he's going to grow up to be violent and dangerous. That's an uncomfortable feeling.

Perhaps you are the mother of a two-year-old and your little boy is suddenly beginning to seem different to you. He is starting to disobey you, to look right at you when he breaks a rule or touches something he's not supposed to touch. He laughs gleefully when you scold him. He seems so willful and defiant. Is that normal?

Or perhaps you are the mother of an older boy who has begun to pull away from you into a boys-only world that is clearly off-limits to moms. The goodnight chats are getting shorter and details of his day less forthcoming. You've heard that happens with boys, but you and your son have been so close—surely not him, not yet!

If you are a dad, perhaps you are not too proud to admit that you are a bit nervous about raising a boy, even though you were a boy yourself and you should, theoretically, know all about it. Maybe you had a hard time as a boy or have mixed feelings about your father, and you want it to be different for your son. Or perhaps you were a lucky boy and a lucky man, an enthusiastic dad who wants to get it right for your son. If you are a dad or father-to-be and you are making this effort to deepen your understanding about the life of boys, then your son is already a lucky boy, too.

IN THE BEGINNING:
WHAT MAKES A BOY A BOY

Though it may be surprising, genetically the female form is the "default setting" for human beings. That is part of the reason that boys have a more difficult journey toward birth and have more health complications at birth than girls do. The tendency toward the female form in humans is very strong.

The start is predictable enough. The sex of your child is decided at the moment of conception, when the sperm penetrates the egg. The mother's egg always contributes the X chromosome to the union; the father can transmit either the X or the Y chromosome, depending on which sperm completes the journey. If the egg receives an X from the father, the child will be a girl: XX. If it receives a Y chromosome, the child will have the genetic makeup for a boy: XY. Girls are better protected from certain genetic illnesses by having the XX combination. Even though an embryo may have the male XY chromosomal combination, an extra hormonal step is required to transform a fetus into a boy. If, for any reason, that extra step does not occur, the child will look like a girl, whether it is genetically XX or XY. For the first six weeks of life, then, an embryo looks the same whether it is going to be a boy or a girl.

If the Y chromosome is present, there is a gene on the short arm of the Y called the sex-determining region, which begins to transform the embryonic gonads into fetal testes. Very soon thereafter, the testes begin to produce a protein-like substance that blocks the development of the uterus and the fallopian tubes. The testes also secrete testosterone, the male hormone, and so development of a boy begins.

Not only must the male hormones be present to produce a boy, the fetal organs must respond to it. If they do, the tissue that might have formed the genitals of a girl, the labia, fuse together and become the scrotum of a boy. If you look at the scrotum itself, you can see that it looks as if it has a seam down the middle, as if it were sewn together out of two parts. That is because it could have been separate halves, in a female.

The tendency toward female development is very strong, and if anything goes wrong in the process of producing a male, it may result in miscarriage. We know that more male fetuses are spontaneously aborted during pregnancy and more boys have congenital defects or early respiratory problems at birth. Boys are more biologically vulnerable than girls from the beginning of life until the end of life.

BEYOND BURPING, BUMPERS, AND BABY GATES

Once you accept the miracle of a child coming into your life, once you embrace the humbling journey that parenting is for all of us, the question that drives nearly every conversation about boys, whether you are expecting your first or you have a houseful of them, is: *What makes boys tick?*

Development is the fundamental engine of a child's growth, the ongoing process in which nature, nurture, and sheer luck come together and a unique human being emerges. The biological story of growth and advice about prenatal health and the day-to-day care and feeding of infants and children are well covered in general parenting literature and medical checkups. We're here to focus on the psychological development of boys, the inside story of how a boy's inner life takes shape and progresses through infancy, childhood, and adolescence. It's a process that isn't always easy to see or understand, not because boys intentionally hide it (though they attempt to do so at times) but because they show it in ways that adults don't always recognize. But it's all there. In everyday life with boys they are always onstage, showing us what's new. Against that developmental backdrop, in the chapters ahead we'll examine the key issues of psychological development that dominate each stage because that is, for you and your son, where the greatest challenges and drama of childhood—and parenting—play out.

If pregnancy and parenthood have left you much time to think, you are full of expectations and wonderings about your boy. You are imagining your son as he will be in six months or two years or twenty years. You may be reading a lot of parenting literature and hearing advice from family, friends, and total strangers. And every day in the news there is another research finding about child or adolescent brain science and gender differences, but very little on their actual relevance to raising your son. How do you turn all that into intelligent, intuitive parenting for raising a boy? How do you begin to answer the two most important questions for the next eighteen years: *What do boys need? What is my son going to need from me?*

Those are questions we'll address in the pages ahead, but before we do that, let's look back to the time when your thoughts about boys first took shape long ago.

YOU HAVE BEEN IMAGINING A BOY FOR A LONG TIME

You may feel newly called to this deep exploration of the inner life of boys, but I want to suggest the surprising idea that you have been thinking about what makes boys tick all of your life, or almost all of it. Thinking about having a baby someday—and imagining that baby as a boy or a girl—is one of the most basic of all human thoughts. It starts early in life. As soon as they can talk and engage in imaginary play, children—boys as well as girls—begin to enact the role of parent, first by themselves and then alongside other children, imitating the actions of the mothers and fathers they love and watch intently every day.

Most of us don't remember what we played when we were three or four years old. That is why I want to remind you that you almost certainly did engage in some version of this domestic role-playing game, taking the role of a mom or dad, rocking a baby doll (or, if you were a boy, perhaps dismantling it or making it fly like a superhero or roll in the mud), and holding forth on what boys like and girls prefer. You "played doctor," asking bold, uncensored questions about body parts, making mental notes. You continued as a child to school yourself in a child's everyday version of gender studies, offering your expertise to any parent, teacher, or other child whom you felt was short on insight. From the age of five, when her younger brother arrived, my daughter, Joanna, objected to anything we did for our son, Will, that didn't seem properly masculine to her. "Mom, that's not for boys," she would declare about a toy or an outfit that was too androgynous to pass her gender test. She was afraid that we wouldn't raise our son in the right way.

In school, if you were a girl, you may remember complaining to a teacher about a bothersome boy—the noisy, pesky, clumsy, or fidgety boy, the boy who bugged you to distraction. Or you might recall disliking boys in a group, especially when they chased you and your friends on the playground or, perhaps in your teens, when you found them aggravating or baffling for different reasons.

If you were a boy, you remember how it felt to posture (or try to) around girls. You may have refused to play a game or do something someone suggested, protesting loudly, "That's for girls!" or "We don't want to be in reading groups with girls," a solid declaration of what eight-year-old boys like and what they hate.

These childhood examples of how we came to know boys or imagine boys' needs or wants may seem far removed from the adult reality of parenting a boy. They are not. Our childhood experiences form a huge reservoir of memories, thoughts, dreams, and feelings, many of them unconscious, that we bring to bear in parenting our own child. Whether we remember those moments or not, we have been coming to conclusions about boys our entire lives, and as a result, we have some pretty strong opinions—I call them imaginings—about what boys will be like, how easy or hard they are to raise, or what they might need as they grow up.

In the thirteenth century, Vincent of Beauvais, author of the *Speculum*

CIRCUMCISION: TO DO OR NOT TO DO?
THAT IS THE QUESTION

There isn't much about planning for your newborn son's arrival that is as private a matter and yet as publicly debated as circumcision, the surgical removal of the foreskin surrounding the head of a boy's penis.

It is a quick procedure that leaves an infant boy bleeding, breathless, crying, and, some people believe, terrified and overwhelmed. Others consider it a quick procedure from which an infant quickly recovers, both physically and psychologically. As for any traumatic effect, one mother told me: "Hey, being pushed through the birth canal is pretty traumatic, too."

Circumcision generally is performed shortly after delivery, or sometime within the next few days. In Judaism, circumcision is a religious requirement performed on the eighth day by a specially trained rabbi in a ceremony called a *bris*. Circumcision also is a religious custom among Muslims.

The results of a circumcision are, obviously, lifelong. Most boys in the United States are circumcised; most boys in the rest of the world are not. The puzzling discrepancy can't be resolved here, but it does mean that whatever you choose, there will be millions of boys and men who share your son's "look."

The medical pros and cons are something to discuss with your pediatrician and your spouse. Research suggests health benefits from circumcision, including significantly lowered risk among men for contracting HIV, the virus that causes AIDS, through heterosexual sex; a lower risk of other sexually transmitted diseases; and a lower risk of cervical cancer among women whose male partners are circumcised. That said, I don't think that medicine can provide us with a definitive answer on whether or not to circumcise boys. Let's be honest: circumcision is a cultural custom based on religious grounds, aesthetics, father-son similarity, and tradition. Either these things matter to you or they do not, and you decide accordingly.

Some people feel that circumcision gives the penis a more aesthetic look: cleaner, smoother, with a head like a rocket. Some women say they prefer it to the more complicated look of the uncircumcised penis. Many therapists and medical doctors suggest the father-son factor is meaningful. Parenting advisor T. Berry Brazelton, M.D., concludes that the father should have the last say in the matter. Most mothers, armed with information from the Internet and family tradition, have their own opinions on the subject.

What do men think? Fathers shared these thoughts:

> I am circumcised, and I have to say that it has never presented itself as a good thing or a bad thing—it's really a non-issue. My three sons are not circumcised, and we chose not to based on things we read as far as the procedure versus the need. The cleaning, if done right, is a pain . . . but it has not seemed to be an issue—no infections that we know of! It was a simple decision for us, as in the end the real question was "Do we really want our hours-old child to have part of his penis cut off?"

We agonized over the decision, endlessly. I am pleased we did it. When our son was growing up he would sometimes come into the bathroom and check out "correct form" when I was peeing. He sometimes liked to go simultaneously. I allowed this because I sensed that this was a becoming-a-person moment. I think it helped bonding that his equipment looked like my equipment. Also some of our friends who chose not to circumcise have had some negative health outcomes.

It was a simple decision. My wife and I both felt the boys would be more comfortable if they looked like their dad. We were a little more surprised at the open discussion of our decision. When she was pregnant with our first son, my wife was teaching at a Catholic women's college. I think she was a bit taken aback when the nuns there engaged her in discussions about our son's circumcision. Speaking only for myself, I think this simple medical procedure has become unnecessarily politicized in the United States.

We did *not* circumcise our first son because there seemed to be no reason, but we did just circumcise our second son because of a study that was mentioned in *Time* magazine about AIDS rates related to the toughness and openness of the glans. Either time, though, it was not a difficult decision for me. My wife found it difficult to have our second son circumcised because of the pain she perceived him experiencing.

For whatever reason, if you choose circumcision, you have the precedent of thousands of years of human beings who have decorated and cut their bodies for a variety of cultural or religious reasons. Just remember that when your son is seventeen and wants a tattoo, you'll have little credibility to say, "Son, I wouldn't want you to do anything permanent to your body."

As for the idea that circumcision is inherently traumatic and leaves huge psychological scars, I'm not convinced. In my experience as a therapist I've never had a man in my office complain about being circumcised or uncircumcised. One way or the other, boys and men seem to end up pretty satisfied with their penises.

Maius, the great encyclopedia of the Middle Ages, observed, "Woman is man's confusion." It seems to me that the obverse is also true: man—and thus boy—is woman's confusion. So, along with the general activity and demands of parenting a boy, mothers face that formidable gender gap and the unique, ongoing challenges and sweet rewards that come with it. And what about fathers, with the home advantage of gender affinity? Any honest father will admit that gender familiarity breeds its own kind of challenges and rewards—and sometimes no less confusion.

The sex of your child, then, is going to pull all of this out of you: your history as a male or female, your experience, your likes and dislikes. It will draw on your deepest feelings about your father, your brother, and, if you are a mother, everything that has ever gone on with your husband. The fact that your child is a boy is going to shape your life and change your psychology forever—and not just the way you feel about boys. Brain research shows that raising children shapes the way you think—neurologically—about them, too. Hormones and mirror neurons develop a sensitive biochemical circuitry that creates new connections and pathways in response to experience. We don't just experience parenthood; parenthood shapes all of our experiences. With this brain-mind-body linkage in place, and imaginings already in progress, it doesn't take much to push the "boy button" in your psyche and set all your personal preformed "boy" psychology into motion.

IS IT A BOY OR A GIRL?

Once you've got a baby on the way, the simplest question in the world—*Is it a boy or a girl?*—is fraught with implications. The question can set off a flood of feelings about boys that may include some positive ones, a number that are unhappy, and some that are ambivalent. A woman whose father had died when she was young told me she felt "both pride and intense anxiety" when she found out she was having a boy:

> I was raised, essentially, entirely by women in a family of women. . . . Men and boys always fascinated me, and I've always loved them, been fond of them— but they always seemed exotic, hairy, wild, noisy, unpredictable, with their big voices and big stories. Great fun, absolutely delightful—couldn't do without them. But also a little scary. The thought that I had to parent one of these was very intimidating.

Another mom described the chorus of concerns the news triggered for her:

> Panic mode! I had some anxiety about raising a male child myself. I am married to a wonderful man who is a terrific father, and it was not his capabilities I questioned, it was my own. "Old tape" is hard to stop replaying.

Each of us has "old tape" when it comes to boys, and parenting a boy—even just thinking about becoming the parent of a boy—pushes the play button. This mother felt she was "particularly sensitive to gender preference," but parents who say they have no strong preference about gender are nonetheless full of feeling about it, full of imaginings, as these mothers share:

> At first I was thrilled to learn I was having a boy, and then suddenly worried that he would have to go to war someday.

> I was shocked. I thought it was a girl. A boy? A *boy*? What would I do with a boy?

> I prayed for a son because I didn't want to go through the terrible turmoil my mother and I had experienced, especially when I hit puberty. But I also always loved the idea of a boy. A boy seemed like a child I could roughhouse with more easily.

What if, for any of a number of reasons, the thought of having a boy was close to unimaginable for you? One mother recalled that when she found out she was carrying a boy, she felt "a little worried because boys seemed so much more boisterous than girls." She also worried, she said, because "he would be an 'other' just by the very fact of him being a different sex than me. How would that be?"

Author Andrea Buchanan, in her introduction to a collection of essays by mothers of sons, wrote, "Long before I got pregnant, I began to fantasize about my imaginary daughter. I rarely imagined having a son. So a few weeks ago, when the ultrasound technician's pointer indicated my unborn son's rather obvious pointer, I was as shocked as I have ever been in my life."

As shocked as I have ever been in my life—that's saying a lot, and I think it speaks to the power of our expectations. How do you fall in love with someone, even a baby, who has so upset your expectations? How do you turn on a dime when your fantasies of the future have been so disrupted?

The mother of a young son, pregnant for a second time, cried when the prenatal test showed this child to be a boy: "I was saddened that I would never have a girl—a child in my likeness." Another mother described her attitude adjustment: "I had my heart set on having a girl and I cried when I found out it was a boy.... But by the time he was born, I didn't care one way or the other."

Rose and her husband, Nate, were the happy parents of two daughters when she became pregnant for the third time. When they learned from an ultrasound that this child was a boy, Nate's immediate reaction was to say, "We'll need to put up curtains with baseballs on them." His comment surprised Rose, and she later teased him because he had never mentioned curtains for either of their two daughters. Why did he think sports-oriented curtains were essential for a boy when he'd never imagined something like that for a girl? Confronting these die-hard stereotypes stirred up some of Rose's gender-equity sensitivities.

An even more personal historical conflict awaited Nancy. Nancy was a second child born eighteen months after her older brother died at age three from meningitis. She had never known him, but she knew very well that his death had, in some sense, destroyed her parents' well-being. "I was the replacement child," she told me. "I was born to heal and repair a wound. It was an irreparable wound; I never should have been asked to do that." After her older brother's death her mother had written to another family member, "This next child is our only hope for a cure." The problem was that the cure didn't work. Nancy couldn't fill the hole in her parents' lives. Ultimately, she had a terrible, unhappy relationship with her mother.

With a history like that, what did she wish for when she became pregnant? A boy. "I did feel, somehow, that having a boy would bring life back to my parents. That's not the reason you have a baby, but I was really glad that I could have a boy."

So giving birth to a boy stirs up feelings from the intergenerational history—and in Nancy's case, tragedy—of a woman's family. How did Nancy manage with all the history and ambivalence swirling around her? She found a personal reason for wanting a boy, one that worked for her alone, separate from the painful family history.

"I just celebrated his difference," she told me. "I am a feminine woman. I felt I could be more natural with someone who was different from me. Maybe having a girl might have meant competition for me, and I hate competition for me."

It is not just mothers who are full of feeling or who struggle with complex emotions over the prospect of a son. Practical issues are huge to men, especially since fathers are expected to be able providers and protectors. A father told me he had been "terrified" at the prospect. Another wondered: "How would I raise him? What to do about sports (I'm not a big fan), the military (I'm a veteran but didn't want my sons to be subjected to the military)? How to deal with the challenges he would face regarding relationships, alcohol, drugs, et cetera? What to do about the circumcision question?"

For Ed, the prospect of having a son was complicated by his own painful childhood. He couldn't imagine raising a boy who would be happy.

> I was hoping for a girl. I wanted a girl because I grew up as a boy. I had the crap beaten out of me in middle school, and I was molested by a teacher. I didn't want someone to go through what I went through. The disastrous part of all of this is that at eighteen weeks, when I learned we had a boy, I cried. I tried not to be upset. For me, it was emotionally hard. I just wanted to be happy that I had a child, and that it had ten fingers and ten toes.

But he found he couldn't; the idea of raising a boy still made him sad. He tried to pull himself out of it.

> I tried to focus on the fact that I'd always wanted a child before forty, and we did it five months before that date. But then seventh grade came back to me, memories of running out the door to escape, and I thought that was what was going to be in store for my son. Ultimately, I came to terms with the idea that I was being stupid about it. I have battled depression all of my life, and I had to realize that this child isn't a clone of me.

This child isn't a clone of me. It was precisely that thought that was so shocking to Andrea Buchanan and the other mothers who had been imagining raising daughters, not someone so profoundly different from themselves. For Ed the idea of raising someone exactly like him was deeply alarming. The idea of a son who wouldn't have to be a clone of him was a relief.

Linda, the mother of an older girl, wanted her second pregnancy to bring another daughter. She felt at home in the world of girls—especially shopping for cute girl clothes—and, she said, "I wanted a second chance to do a better job with a girl." Linda imagined herself becoming become the complete girl expert on her second go-round. It didn't turn out that way. When the doctor delivered the news from the ultrasound, her husband was "ecstatic" and called his father. As for Linda, "I wasn't thrilled. I really love him now, but it wasn't a happy pregnancy for me."

As every parent finds out sooner or later, you don't always get what you have imagined. You certainly don't get all that you wish for, and most of the time you don't get what you fear. And in time you find a way to make your peace with what nature has given you. When I visited Ed and Mary five weeks after the birth of their son, Sam, Ed described his feelings at the birth of his son: "It was unbelievable. I was so excited, I cried a little bit. I was just so thankful that we got through it all and that our baby was healthy."

What had happened to his fears of having a son, a son who might be condemned to a painful boyhood?

"I haven't given a single thought to any of the issues that we talked about before," Ed declared. Now, holding his son in his arms, it was all about having a healthy baby. "You know: ten fingers, ten toes, two eyes, one mouth, and all on the same head."

Linda eventually moved beyond her yearning to shop for cute girl clothes. And, pregnant with her son in her early forties, she remembered that in her previous career as a teacher she had always enjoyed working with boys in the classroom, perhaps because her younger brother was developmentally delayed and she had been his "protector" when he was little. When Linda learned she was having a boy, she reached down, past her desires and her fears, to become the best mother of a boy she knew how to be.

All of her instincts came into play—including yet more "old tapes" shaping her imaginings. To her astonishment, she finds she can't dress her baby boy in the yellow pajamas that his older sister wore, even if they fit him. The enlightened, educated woman in her is disgusted with her attachment to gender stereotypes. "I want to be able to put him in the yellow pajamas, but I can't. I hate myself for that, that I have such box-like parenting. You can have had diversity training up the yazoo and still you are what you are."

In other words, in the end you have to deal with the fact that you're having a boy, that the culture has many demands to make on you and your son, and that we're all stuck with an inner picture of what we imagine a boy to be. For Linda it is impossible to imagine putting her boy in yellow pajamas. For Ed it was originally impossible to imagine that he could give his son a good life. In his depressed feelings about his own boyhood, he didn't think that a happy boyhood was possible. Now, with Sam in his arms, he is ready to start shaping a boy.

"As for the boy stuff, I'm trying to introduce him to good music, to play on the bass guitar," Ed said when I visited him after Sam's birth. He pointed to a guitar in the corner. "Do you know what that is?" I shook my head. "A '76 Fender Precision." I looked at the handsome instrument propped in the corner, glanced back at the infant in his father's arms, and thought, *Of course, just what every boy needs,* because I know how important it is for a parent to have high hopes for his or her son. Not every parent dreams of his son loving a Fender electric guitar, but every parent has hopes for that child, and some fears as well.

IMAGININGS: A CLOSER LOOK AT OUR HOPES AND FEARS

The hopes and fears that parents experience about raising boys come from four sources. First and foremost, they arise from the history of a family over many generations and its many lessons, conscious and unconscious, about the nature and fate of boys and men. Second, they are the result of every person's childhood experiences with boys. Third, they come from the deeply embedded cultural expectations of boys. Fourth and finally, they stem from current images of boys in the news, the entertainment media, and advertising. All these powerful forces shape what we believe our boys will want and need, and whether we think we'll be able to provide it. They charge our sense of anticipation about this boy on the way and how we imagine he will take—or make—his place in the family.

What do the generational stories in your family tell you about the destiny and importance of men? Women have told me in therapy, "The men in my family haven't done very well," or "I come from a family of strong women," where the implication is that the men are weak by comparison. What if you come from a family where many of the men have been alcoholics? What if your grandfather was a notorious philanderer, or perhaps a fantastically successful businessman who was totally self-absorbed and uninterested in his family? What if you're divorced and your son's father has been a painful disappointment?

Alternatively, what if your grandfather was a hardworking, churchgoing father who was home every night, talking with his kids over the dinner table? What if your husband hails from a long line of honest, industrious, caring men? Or perhaps he is bucking a family tradition of men who weren't. There are many ways that men's character colors the family story, and most of us can find both inspiration and cautionary tales in the family tree:

My father was my hero when I was young and still is today.

The men in my family for the most part are emotionally distant, controlling, and often disrespectful of others' opinions.

All of them have made poor choices in their life (and they continue to on a daily basis). They do not learn from their mistakes, and they blame everyone else for their situation in life.

My father was the last of the great southern gentlemen. He was always respectful, well-mannered, generous, honest, and kind. I loved him dearly, but also saw him as relatively passive compared to my mother. I didn't have brothers and I did not see my father as a strong masculine role model, so I feel like I'm charting new territory.

Aren't we all charting new territory? Certainly. Yet as a child you would have heard stories about the virtues and vices of the men in your family over and over, and you have absorbed the lessons they teach: men are weak, men are reckless and die young, men are responsible, men sacrifice their family to their work, men sacrifice themselves to support their families. These lessons are inescapable.

We are all touched by the tragedies and triumphs of our families going back generations, and they propel us to want to raise a boy who will either match the historic triumphs of the men in the family or who will, at least, avoid the tragedies.

Euripides wrote, "The gods visit the sins of the fathers upon the children." The fuller truth is that it isn't just the fathers; it is the grandfathers and great-grandfathers as well. And it isn't just their sins that affect future generations; it is everything good about them, too. How can I escape the legacy of my great-grandfather, a Congregational minister who raised four children of his own, adopted two black children, and wrote a newspaper column about religion and family life? He died fifteen years before I was born, so I never knew him, but I knew that my mother had loved him and my whole family admired him. My life has, unquestionably, been influenced by the image of that patriarchal figure born before the Civil War began.

But that is no different from every boy and every girl who is touched, often invisibly, by the history of the men in the family, whether the details of their stories have survived the passage of time or are simply reflected in history: the great-grandfather who immigrated to America, served in the military, survived the Great Depression, or didn't. Whether your family legend offers a fully developed cast of characters or they have been lost to you for one reason or another, your mind reaches back to pick up the story line of the men in your family. Thus you mark the arrival of your son as one of them and begin to envision his future.

YOUR LIFELONG EXPERIENCES WITH BOYS

If the parenting experience can change your brain and fine-tune your mental reception for boys, the same can be said for other life experience with boys. Men themselves offer the most obvious evidence, taking in stride much of the routine boy behavior that drives their wives crazy. Wrestling? Pretend shooting with sticks and fingers? Dumb jokes about body parts? Men just don't see the problem, or they tend to have a higher tolerance for what they see as fundamentally normal for a boy. The father of two young sons confessed that he was amused by his wife's exasperation with such things. "The truth is," he said, "I probably tolerate too much burping and body noises because I like watching her roll her eyes at the testosterone imbalance in the home." A woman who has grown up with brothers or shared life with brotherly boys may have a similar comfort level with distinctly boy energy and expression.

Once at a workshop I ran for boys at an international school in Guatemala City, Guatemala, a teacher asked me, "Why do boys fight so much?"

"What boys, and what ages are you referring to?" I asked.

"My sons, they're eleven and nine," she replied. "They fight constantly."

"What do you mean by fighting?" I continued.

"Well, they compete about everything—who is first in this and who is first in that," she reported, both exasperation and concern in her voice.

"Do you consider that fighting?" I inquired, knowing from her worried expression that she certainly did.

"But they wrestle all the time . . . well, I don't know," she replied with uncertainty, because she saw that incessant competition and wrestling did not automatically qualify as fighting for me. "I didn't grow up with boys—I only had sisters," she said. "We didn't do that kind of thing." Of course not. Though sisters do fight and compete, they don't show their competitive fervor and desire to win in the openly exhibitionistic ways that boys do. They almost never wrestle.

Living side by side with brothers is like prep school for parenting boys. If you are a woman who grew up with a brother, then you may remember his obsession with baseball cards or bugs, his preference for books or TV shows you could barely stomach, his sloppy, careless way of sharing household space, or his seemingly limitless capacity to amuse or annoy you. One woman told me that her brother shot her in the legs with plastic pellets from an air gun, which hurt a lot. (He is now the president of a nonprofit foundation committed to humanitarian work.) Whatever indignities you suffered at your brother's hands, you have a ready-made frame of reference for becoming the mother of a boy.

Beth, who had raised an eleven-year-old daughter from her first marriage, was remarried and pregnant with a boy. She was quick to proclaim abject ignorance about boys. "I don't even know what to do with a boy," she said. "What am I going to do with him? I worry that he'll ruin my house."

But when I probed a little she immediately went back to her experience of her younger brother, Chris. She told me she wanted to build a separate playhouse in the yard so that her son could "trash the place, just like my little brother did." How much did she remember about her relationship with her brother? Not too much, she claimed. "Chris was just the baby—we all doted on him, and all the sisters spoiled him." She chuckled. "One time he set the woods on fire. And he was definitely a free spirit."

If you are going to raise a boy, it is helpful to have known a brother who burned down six acres of forest, and to have watched your parents manage the consequences. Beth knew that in order to preserve her house, she should build a playhouse outside that her son could "trash."

Or, as another mother shared, it is helpful to have grown up with brotherly boys on your block, "playing boy games—war, climbing trees, cowboys and Indians, baseball, et cetera," leading you to conclude, as she did, that "I enjoyed it . . . and enjoy boy characteristics and encourage our son to be imaginative and fun-loving." Or it is helpful to have had cousins like the ones that prompted this mother to write:

> I had no brothers. I had male cousins who were fascinating to me and also unbelievably wild. Wildly out of control. They'd come from Chicago to visit us and furniture had to be moved and things had to be locked up. Seriously. They'd have boxing matches and huge screeching fights. It was terrifying but great theater.

If growing up with boys acquaints you with the periodic forays into wild behavior, it also makes you familiar with their vulnerabilities and anxieties.

Watching your brother struggle with bed-wetting, night fears, or social isolation can help you prepare for the vulnerabilities that your son will display. "I paid attention to my younger brother a lot. I saw his pain in being misunderstood and getting in trouble all the time," one mother wrote. "I would sneak into his room after he got in trouble to give a hug of support. I guess all that and seeing the struggles my ex-husband had have made me have such compassion for boys."

If you had a brother who struggled with illness, you know how fragile they can be. "Despite our arguing," a mother wrote of her brother, "I always felt that he reached out to connect with me during insecure times. At bedtime he would knock on the wall of his room, adjacent to mine, and we would do our own Morse code before saying good night."

It is very common for boys to be shy, to avoid looking into the eyes of adults, to be reluctant to participate in the intense competition of town sports. If you are going to raise a boy, it is crucial to remember these things. Men may be tempted by the culture to remember their own boyhoods as heroic; it is helpful to remember the more tender truth. The memory of a weeping brother can counteract some of the cultural expectations of toughness for boys that I will be discussing shortly. It is useful for women, who don't have personal memories of boyhood, to recall that they shared a home with an anxious brother, or perhaps shared the struggles of another boy they knew well.

Even among women with a rich store of experience with boys from childhood, the lessons they learned and carry with them about boys vary enormously, as these mothers' recollections illustrate:

Having an older brother led me to like boys and to appreciate their impish, exuberant ways.

When I was a young girl, the few boys I knew were given to jokes about farts and boogers . . . not a great advertisement. The boys I was closest to in high school were the smart, nice guys. That is what I hope for in my son. ✿

Brothers? Terrible relationship. Angry, even dangerous at times.

I was fortunate to go to school with some very nice boys. This was helpful in that I knew that not all guys were violent like my dad. I knew that I wanted to raise a son that was different from the men my dad's age, and that is what I did.

Some women grew up around boys and learned to love them. Others grew up around boys and learned to fear, dislike, or distrust them. With or without brotherly boys, unless you went to all-girls schools, your assumptions about boys will be strongly colored by your early life with them in school and in your neighborhood.

CULTURAL IMAGES AND EXPECTATIONS OF BOYS

All of our hopes and fears for boys are shaped by the images and attitudes toward boys that surround us. Societal expectations for both genders are burned deep into our brains. The mother who could not bring herself to dress her eight-month-old son in yellow pajamas hated the idea that her reactions were so stereotyped, but her cultural training was so strong that she couldn't disobey it. If she had dressed him in yellow and taken him out in public, it wasn't just that she thought others would find it unseemly for him to be dressed in "girl" colors; she admitted that she found it unsettling, too.

We all have images of what boys are supposed to be and what they are going to like. Any nine-year-old boy will tell you: "Strong, tough, likes sports, doesn't cry." Many fathers, and some mothers, too, share that view. Even some who want their sons to live more fully expressed lives than the stereotype allows, often are unnerved by the thought that their sons won't grow up to be strong and tough. They are frightened to have a son who might not fit the cultural mold.

Whether it is success in baseball or hunting or repairing a car in America, or in soccer in Brazil, or outstanding academic achievement in Hong Kong or Israel, men all over the world immediately imagine that their sons will be strong and heroic in recognizable ways. They hope that their sons will live up to the masculine ideal of the culture. For the most part, we wish conventional cultural dreams for our sons, sometimes to our own disgust, because the culture has filled our minds with those dreams.

I have had the opportunity to observe boyhood in many countries, and have seen that there are significant variations in what a culture requires of a boy. In many countries it is enough to be respectful of one's parents and teachers and to be observant of the rules of your religion in order to qualify as a respectable boy. The cultural expectations for boys in the United States are comparatively narrow and cause many boys to struggle painfully with the feeling that they are lacking in some basic boy way because they do not enjoy what boys are "supposed" to feel and enjoy. It is difficult to be a boy in this culture because the demands for toughness and athletic prowess are so pervasive and many messages about being male are so mixed. Throughout this book I will address how to understand the pressures of cultural expectation and how to deal with them, especially if you don't happen to have a son who fits them. And most of our sons do not.

IMAGES OF BOYS IN THE MEDIA

It is a scary time to raise boys in America. There was a time when media images of boy life reflected the kinder, gentler themes of Norman Rockwell portraits. The worst of our media concerns were the violence and bad-boy imagery of men in movies, TV shows, and commercials.

Today it's not just the fiction of cinema, sitcoms, and commercials that delivers a disturbing picture of male life. Boys are in the news, making headlines that paint a grim picture of them as potentially violent or aggressive, self-destructive, disrespectful, impulsive, and problematic—a world of disaffected, alienated, lost boys seemingly mesmerized and mentored by screen violence and a hypersexualized pop culture.

The Internet now provides a place in which they express themselves as participants, creators, and correspondents on Web sites and in chat rooms and blogs; boys are eager players in sophisticated (but still largely violent) online, computer, and other video games. It's a disorienting picture for parents, an exciting but also disturbing one, with the easy availability of pornography online and the presence of sexual predators there. Boys show up as eager, masterful, and vulnerable in new ways.

In the more than seven hundred interviews and surveys conducted for this book, nearly every parent and teacher mentioned concerns about aggression or violence, sexualized media, or the disheartening negativity of male imagery in boys' lives today. Fathers and mothers alike voiced similar concerns:

> Men are too often shown as stupid or brutes or both. The lack of respect
> shown to men and boys by society in general I believe makes it very difficult
> for boys to feel good about themselves and about being male.

I worry about what our society teaches boys about being men. I worry about the violence portrayed in the media, I worry about the sex portrayed in the media—it's all over the place!

Incidents of boy violence in the news and the constant repetition of these themes can make you question the fundamental nature of boys and make you doubt yourself and your impact as parents.

HOW CAN I HELP YOU RAISE THE BOY YOU HAVE IMAGINED?

Let's return to the two most important questions you'll ask yourself for the next eighteen years or so: *What do boys need? What is my son going to need from me?*

To a great extent, the answer will vary from boy to boy and day to day; the combination of a child's individual personality, temperament, and experience of himself and his world presents anew each day. There are, however, some ways in which all boys' needs are the same and all parents can draw from the same well for wisdom. I want to offer the following four points as the foundation for successful parenting of boys. I think of them not so much as how-to tips, but as how-to-think perspectives for a parenting philosophy that continues to be relevant in different ways at every age and through every developmental passage with a boy.

First, you have to accept the reality that boys are different from girls. Second, you have to love the end product of a boyhood, that is to say, a man. Third, having acknowledged the gender of your child, you will need to step back and appreciate his uniqueness as a human being, because individuality trumps gender. And finally, you will have to surrender any lofty expectations of "making a man" of your boy. Nature will take care of that. You have an important nurturing role to fill in your son's life, but you are not in charge of his development; development is.

As basic and self-evident as these points may seem, they can be profoundly challenging for parents. Many parents, mostly mothers, have told me that the experience of raising a boy has brought them up against their deepest beliefs about the differences between the genders and has challenged some profound prejudices they possessed about men that they were not fully aware they held. Fathers struggle differently but equally with basic issues. Parents and teachers tell me that it is not always easy to figure out what is a gender trait and what is individuality, and above all, it can be tough to embrace the idea that development is in charge.

Let's consider these points one by one.

Accept That Boys Really Are Different from Girls

Obviously, what makes boys different from girls is their reproductive organs—the penis and the vagina, the testes and the ovaries—and the hormones that these produce, testosterone and estrogen. As the French say, *Vive la différence.* That is part of the picture, but not all. JoAnn Deak, a witty psychologist who has written about girls, proclaims, "The most gendered organ in the human body is the brain." She is right. Scientific research in the past twenty years has confirmed that there are many, many differences in how the boy brain operates and how the girl brain operates, on average. As a parent, you are about to raise a boy with a boy brain, and if you are a mother, it will operate differently than your own brain does. If you are a father, your son's brain may frustrate you in many of the same ways your own brain did when you were young. You cannot, even with single-minded effort and the best motives in the world, change a boy brain into something it is not.

That said, even though boys and girls have brains that operate in very different ways, children are children. When it comes to raising them, for the most part they need the same things: love, safety, guidance, challenge, understanding, and support. The brains may be different, but they are all young human beings. So if you are going to raise a boy, you have to remember that you are dealing with a boy brain, boy hormones, and a pace of development that is different from a girl's. But please do not let the idea of the boy brain make you lose your common sense about what young people need.

We'll look more closely at gender differences in the chapters ahead. For now, simply embrace the idea that you are raising a boy with a boy brain; welcome the reality and be open to discovering what that means, while never giving up your best, loving ideas of what a child needs.

You Have to Love the End Product: A Man

If you are going to raise a boy, you cannot just love him when he is little. You are going to have to like what he is going to turn into, namely, a man. I'm not saying you necessarily need to love your son's father or have him around. That's wonderful when it happens; however, there are a lot of single mothers in the world raising children without men to help them. Indeed, 35 percent of boys in the United States do not live with their biological fathers, and many of those mothers are doing a wonderful job without the daily help of a man. What I am saying, however, is this: if you are to be successful in raising a boy, you have to imagine the man he is going to become. Sometimes, with boys, that can be tough because on occasion it can be difficult to see the promise of the man in the boy.

One mother told me that when she first held her baby boy, she looked down at his body and saw "that he was such a perfect little man." Her take on it was that his body looked just like her husband's, she said, only smaller. And that made her happy, because she really loved her husband and admired the man he was. That's an ideal situation, and not all women find themselves in it.

Men, too, especially those with disappointing fathers or those struggling with difficult lives themselves, often struggle to envision a hopeful model of a man for their son.

However, it is always possible to reach into your memories and find a man you have loved and admired. Was it your father? Was it your grandfather or maybe a brother? Was it a teacher or a coach you had when you were in school? Perhaps a character from literature or film?

What quality did you admire? Was it his playfulness, was it his steadiness? Do you have a photograph of him that warms your heart? If you want to stay in touch with what you are raising your son to be, then take that photograph of your "best man"—whatever man you love—and put it up in your son's room. It will be a good reminder for you and a wonderful conversation starter for him as he's growing up: "Why do you have that picture up there, Mom?" "That's the kind of man I'd like you to grow up to be; he was strong and kind," or "He loved the outdoors and taught me to love it, too."

The legacy of good men, or even of flawed men's good moments, is lasting, as the mother we met earlier, whose father died when she was young, shared:

I am lucky in that I have many memories of him. I remember him playing goofy games with me and my sister—doing funny tricks, taking us places, showing us off at work . . . He seemed huge to me—and funny, smart, a little goofy, and very kind. I married a man just like him. It's only in writing this that I'm realizing how huge an impact my dad really has had on me—despite the fact that I barely had a chance to have a relationship with him.

The kind of man you want your son to be has already lived a good life. You knew him; he was in your family or in your school. Find him in your memories and let him help you guide your son.

Love the Son You've Got

So much of life in our competitive culture is required to be strategic and performance- or outcome-based, it is tempting to apply the same approach to parenting. With hopes of producing the best boy ever, we might set out to cultivate the best of traditional male attributes (smart, strong, steady, uncomplaining), but then perfect him by adding the quality of emotional literacy and subtracting violence and excessive aggression so he can be successful in life. Many caring parents speak about parenting as if it were a giant school project: if you just start soon enough, read the right research, and do the right things, you can get the particular end product you have in mind. One reason I don't like to hand out a lot of "do this, do that" advice is that the cumulative effect of all that advice is demoralizing when the child himself gets lost in the flood of helpfulness. With so much to "do" to make your son into who he "should be," when do you have time to let him teach you about who he is?

Your job as a mother or father is not to invent or create a better kind of boy who will develop into a more highly evolved man. If you try to do that, you will fail, and your son will resist you because he does not want to be your creation.

Whatever your imaginings about the boy on the way, your son is already busy becoming himself, expressing himself. If you are well along in your pregnancy and he is making himself felt, perhaps you already think of him as an active baby or a mellow one. That's fine. But stay tuned. Your job will be to welcome your son wholeheartedly into this life and wait for his temperament, his individuality, and his special gifts to emerge. At every age, the best thing you will ever do for him is to support those unique parts of him that you cannot even see yet.

Trust in Development

The textbook definition of child development is "the sequence of physical, cognitive, psychological and social changes that children undergo as they grow older." Child development is true interdisciplinary science that attempts to describe and explain everything we observe in children of different ages. It is the foundation of this and every parenting book. As sophisticated as developmental science has become, however many powerful theories it has developed, it does not yet have all the answers to the fundamental questions of what makes children grow the way they do.

We do not know, for instance—and you may find this hard to believe—exactly why boys and girls are different or how different they really are, or even whether parents are the most important influence in their children's lives. Researchers are still fighting over these and other fundamental questions. There is no absolute scientific answer to some of the most basic—and sometimes baffling—aspects of boy life. What makes it so hard for little boys to sit still, when little girls typically are able to do so? Is it a biologically driven behavior arising from male hormones? Is it the result of a difference in the amount of serotonin in the brain? Is it the result of watching too much television or a result of the kind of play boys engage in? We have theories, but we don't know for sure, so we have to trust that there is some wisdom at work in nature. We have to trust development.

Indeed, trusting boy development is the leitmotif of this book, a thread running through every chapter. Why do I urge you to trust development when neither I nor child development research can tell you for sure why something is happening? Because I have spent a long career as a psychologist watching development at work and I have heard thousands of children describe the story of their own growing up. Even if we do not totally understand it, it is a reliable process. More than that, it is an almost miraculous process, an intricate blending of biology, culture, family, and personal experience out of which arises a totally unique individual, a human being very much like all other human beings and yet completely different. And from the point of view of a psychologist, what is interesting is that every child—every boy—has a unique story to tell about his development and how he experiences his maleness, his parents, the television shows he watches, his hormones, the classroom he spends his days in, his troubles and his joys.

The most reliable person to tell us about his experience would be your son. Since I cannot personally talk with him, and because he will not always be able to explain things clearly to you because he is too young or inarticulate, I am hopeful that in the chapters ahead I can introduce you to boys whose conversations about their inner lives will illuminate some of your son's experiences and make them more understandable. And once you understand why boys, including your son, do things the way they do, you will, I hope, come to understand boys more deeply and trust in their development.

As a parent, it's often hard to trust development. You will want to make things happen that aren't yet happening because development is not ready. You will want to stop things from happening that are occurring before you are ready. You'll hear a lot about supporting development by trying to ramp it up—like SAT scores—with special developmental toys and activities. All this may give you the impression that you're in charge of development, driving it. You are not. Your son's development will be his own to live, his to manage, his to determine. Right now, as you ready your home, your family, and yourself for the arrival of your son, it's a good time to get used to the idea.

NOW IMAGINE YOURSELF: THE PARENT OF A BOY

Imagining is a full-time preoccupation for most expectant mothers and fathers, and it continues for the rest of your life with a son. At every age and at every turn, all your questions about your son's future will have you searching the tea leaves of your family, history, and culture. What are the signs that he will be a happy and successful man? Will he be a good husband and father? Will he have close friendships? Will he be close to his mother? And finally, how do you, as his mother or father, raise the healthiest, happiest, strongest—and I mean strong in character—son that you can possibly raise?

Antoine de Saint-Exupéry, the French poet, wrote, "To live is to be slowly born." Your son is going to be slowly born through the years to come. And you will have a front-row seat on the miracle of his development.

If you are expectant and taking good care of yourself, getting the proper nutrition, and avoiding alcohol and drugs that are known to affect fetal development, you are already being a good parent, supporting your son's healthy start. Once in the world, some of his development and his identity will be the result of forces in society, reactions to friends, television shows, and video games that you might hate. You will have a lot of control over these influences when he is very little; later on you'll just have to watch it happen. He may want to wear his blue jeans hanging off his butt with his boxer shorts showing—or whatever the fashion is sixteen years from now—because that's what his friends are doing. You can shut off the electronics when he is little, but at a certain point he can go over to someone else's house to watch TV. You will be sidelined over many years.

Some of what he is going to be will come from sources in the family: your parents, your in-laws, and of course your spouse. You'll have more say in this arena than in others, but you cannot always make your family do what you want them to do, can you? (If you can, please write and tell me your secret. My e-mail address is in the back of the book.) Many of the early experiences in his life will take place in school. He will fall in love with some teachers, hate others, pay too much attention to his classmates and not enough to his studies. And much of it you won't be able to see because it will take place behind the closed doors of school.

Finally, when all the other influences in his life, biological, educational, and social, are done, you are going to have a personal, intimate, one-on-one relationship with your son that is like no other. If you are a mother, I can assure you that it will be the most important relationship in his life except for the one with his father. And if you are a father, your relationship with your son will be the most important one in his life except for the relationship with his mom. Well, you understand—no one can ever quantify which is the most important relationship in a life except the child himself, when he grows up, but mothers and fathers usually head the list.

It would be a shame to miss the opportunity to be a huge and loving influence in your son's life. It would be a tragedy not to love him to the fullest extent of your ability and have him carry that love with him always. The desire to see your child thrive and have a good life has to be at the center of every parent's heart and fulfillment. You wouldn't be reading this book if you didn't feel that.

If you are going to be the parent of a boy, you might as well prepare yourself for an amazing adventure, as if you were a small child clambering onto the back of huge winged dragon. He—and I mean this dragon of a boy, of course—is going to take you places you never imagined going. He is going to bounce you up and down, and you may be a little frightened. When he steps onstage with his friends in front of the entire middle school to sing the rap song they wrote, when he gets absolutely terrified on a ride at Disney World that you imagined would be fun, when he makes a football team or strikes out in a Little League game, you may be sharing joys and sorrows you have never known in your own life.

If you are a woman on the back of this dragon, you will swoop down to earth and see things in an entirely new way, through the eyes of a boy. For a mother, raising a son is the closest you will ever come to crossing that unbridgeable gender line. When your little boy grabs his penis because he has to pee, when your eight-year-old rails angrily over a hurt as he tries to hide tears, when your thirteen-year-old lies right in your face, when your older teen who has been lifting weights at the gym strikes a pose to exhibit his muscular physique, you'll *get it*. Loving a son will make you empathize with boys and men more than you ever thought possible. All the while you are teaching him, by example, about women and how they think and feel, you will be learning a lot about what it is to live the life of a boy.

If you are a father, you are going to rediscover everything about your own boyhood from a different angle, and it will be disorienting to you. Your assumptions about what all boys love, because they were what you loved, will be tipped on end because he won't be exactly like you; he will be passionate about other things. At other moments you will know exactly what he is feeling and some old, terrible boyhood pain or thrill will wash over you. If you are fully open to the experience of fathering—that is to say, if you have some humility—you will, at times, respect him and doubt yourself. Your son will, at times, make you feel like a little boy yourself. He'll make you rethink who you are and everything you have done.

Our focus in this chapter has been on *imaginings:* all the ways you anticipate a boy and life with a boy, and begin to understand the developmental journey that lies ahead for him. But this time is also about imagining yourself as a parent, and your own developmental journey as a parent, specifically the parent of a boy. So as you witness your son's developmental progress, and some inevitable struggles, in the years to come, appreciate that you, too, are growing, from the parent of your imaginings into the parent you want to be.

An expectant mother wrote to me: "To be honest, I wasn't nervous about raising my boy until after I read your book *Raising Cain*! Ha—now I am aware of what happens with young boys, and scared of what awaits our family."

Please don't be afraid. It's *just* a boy.

Keep in mind this piece of wisdom shared by a mother who recalled her worry about having a boy. "I shared my fear with my mom, who wisely told me, 'You're not having a boy. You're having a baby. And boys love their mothers. You'll see.' She was absolutely right."

CHAPTER TWO

AN ESSENTIAL LOVE AFFAIR

Your Baby Boy: Birth to Eighteen Months

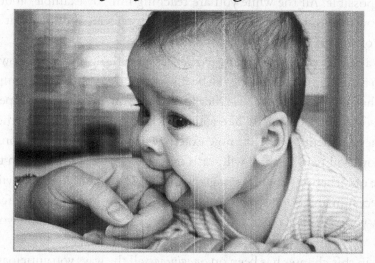

Although I was hesitant when I learned I was having a son, now I'm a complete convert.
I am so deliriously happy to have my boy, I can hardly remember what my hesitation was about.
I cannot imagine a deeper, more intimate connection than the one I have with him.
—Mother of a seventeen-month-old boy

EVERY PARENT HAS A BIRTH STORY, AND EVERY BIRTH STORY IS SACRED. YOUR son's story is the tale of his passage into life and the arms of family, certainly, but it is the story of your passage, too: your passage into parenthood with him. In the sweep of that story, you and all your rich imaginings tumble from the anticipation of a baby into the startling reality of the one you hold in your arms.

Because I adopted my children, my son's "birth" story is a bit different from that of most parents. For me and my wife it didn't involve a ride to the hospital, a midwife, a doctor, or the pain of labor. At least, we weren't there for that part. Our story does, however, have its own twists and turns. The beginning of "labor," so to speak, for my wife, Theresa, and I occurred on a Friday night in October some seventeen years ago when our adoption social worker called to say that a boy was going to be born at Newton-Wellesley Hospital on the following day and he was going to be available for adoption. Would we like to take him?

Absolutely!

I was the one who took the call, and I was stunned. Suddenly we were going to be parents of a boy! My son, Will, was born on a Saturday afternoon in Newton, Massachusetts, while we were attending the Ringling Bros. Barnum & Bailey circus at Boston Garden (hey, we already had the tickets). Seventy-two hours later, his birth mother signed the necessary papers waiving her parental rights and then asked to meet us. We met with her on a Wednesday morning in the offices of the adoption agency. Will's birth mother—he looks a lot like her—was a beautiful, gentle woman, who told us the details of his actual birth and gave us pictures that had been taken of him moments after he was delivered. She then presented us with her baby quilt, the one in which her mother had wrapped her as an infant. We cried and she cried. It was one of the most moving encounters of my life. We thanked her and then left to go pick up our son from a foster mother in Peabody, Massachusetts.

First, however, we had to pick up our five-year-old daughter, Joanna, from school so she could be with us when we went to get her new brother.

We journeyed to the home of the woman who took care of about-to-be-adopted babies from the time they were discharged from hospitals until the moment when their parents could legally pick them up. When she asked, "Who wants to hold the baby first?" Joanna excitedly volunteered, and positioned herself on the couch while the woman went to get our sleeping son from a crib in the back room. She handed our four-day-old son to Joanna, who held him on her lap for a couple of minutes with her mother sitting beside her. She then passed Will to his mother, and finally I got to hold my son, now a little bit awake. Even at four days old, my son was a model of truth in packaging! He was a peaceful boy in those first minutes, and he has continued to be an even-tempered boy for his whole life thus far.

As you hold your baby in your arms, it may feel like a quiet moment, a peaceful moment, even a sublime moment. But it is not a static moment, because you are searching his face and thinking: *Whom have I gotten here? What will he be like? What will he grow up to be?* You study your child's features for clues, and

> *There's nothing like the love you get from a baby. His face lights up when he sees me.*
> —Mother of four-month-old boy

you turn to others to say: *Isn't he handsome? Look at that hair! Isn't that a great head of hair?* Or *I think he looks like your family, don't you think? You can see it in his eyes!* We all took turns holding Will for the next ten hours (except for his time in the car seat), and when we arrived home we were met by friends who had delivered a baby girl just three weeks before. We all spent the evening holding our respective babies, trading babies, and talking endlessly about them.

Whatever we had imagined ourselves doing pre-baby was now totally banished from our thoughts. Will was now the center of the world and would be for the foreseeable future. Like all babies, he was extraordinarily compelling, and we were immediately drawn to him, as if by an all-powerful magnetic force.

Wherever your birth story begins and wherever it leads, through complications or comic moments, most of us eventually arrive at the same astonishing moment when we come face-to-face with our new baby.

"It was like a dream," Gwen recalled about seeing her baby boy for the first time. "I felt overcome with emotion. There was something so familiar about him."

A father described the moment: "I was proud, and I immediately felt myself 'consume the other.' It was a full embrace."

Mary reported that she was pretty wiped out by the end of her delivery of Sam, but she felt a connection to him immediately. "I felt like I recognized him from how he felt from the outside of my belly. I felt like I knew his bum and his feet." From that moment, her feelings for Sam were so intense, she said, "I feel I can understand the expression, 'I love you so much that it hurts.'"

And remember Sam's dad, Ed, the dad whose memories of a miserable boyhood had him dreading the arrival of a boy? The reality of little Sam in their arms helped Ed and Mary overcome the fears they had had during pregnancy, each one harboring doubt for different reasons about their capacity to develop a relationship with him. Sam arrived in good health and eager to eat, and Mary was able to breast-feed without complication. Five weeks later Mary mused, "I feel like this phase, the time I'm nursing, is just amazing. I had a lot of fears. Will we connect? Will there be that mother-son bond? He nursed in the first

A NOTE ABOUT NOUNS:
MOTHERS, FATHERS, AND OTHERS

Throughout this book I will use the word *mother* to describe the primary caretaker because they usually are, and a constant effort to refer to both mothers and fathers with each reference would grow cumbersome for the reader.

However, I intend no disrespect to fathers, who are equally capable of bonding with infants in their own way if they spend time with a child, and who will have a greater impact in the lives of their sons as the boys get older. Theirs, too, is a relationship that has just begun to be studied in any formal way, and it is one that deserves respect. The voices of fathers are represented throughout this book and include those of many men who are fully engaged as fathers—deeply loving fathers—and in the early months of their son's life are parenting as fully as a man can. My experience of loving fathers of this kind is that they are eager for information and not quick to take offense, and will read through any nouns or pronoun I choose to use.

hour and I felt so good about that. I know that I'm going to miss this so much when it is over."

When Mary says she is going to "miss this" when it is over, what is she talking about? Breast-feeding and the unique intimacy of that experience, certainly. But there is more to the profound "something" she senses that isn't unique to breast-feeding mothers. It happens to loving mothers everywhere, whether they breast-feed or not, and eventually it happens to loving fathers, too, and to adoptive parents as well as biological ones, as a baby stakes his psychological claim on us.

The mother of three young sons described it from the moments following the birth of her first, saying: "I remember instantly bonding and feeling love and joy that can't be described. We all swooned over how adorable he was and to this day feel that multiplied."

Long after your baby has left both breast and bottle, the bond you have formed in these early months will continue to deepen for both you and your baby. That bond, and the psychological security, or *attachment*, it makes possible, will nourish and sustain your son in different ways for the rest of his life.

The English pediatrician and psychoanalyst Donald W. Winnicott once made the startling remark, "There is no such thing as a baby," and then went on

> *There are so many things about him—*
> *I mean, I love watching his hair grow*
> *in. Silly, silly little things like that.*
> —Mother of four-month-old boy

to explain that we have to think of a baby and a mother as a unit. He was, of course, referring to the profound helplessness of the human infant. Of all mammals, human babies are among the least able to take care of themselves at birth. If they are not fed and cared for around the clock, they will die. They remain profoundly dependent—they literally cannot survive without a parent or parent figure—for at least six years, and in modern society, they remain partially dependent for three times that long. Every mother (or primary caretaker) knows this: she is undertaking the awesome responsibility of keeping someone else alive.

However, if the original purpose of mammalian mothering was to provide breast milk and protection to keep the baby safe, it has evolved into a much more complicated business in human beings. A mother enters into an intense relationship with her baby that lasts for years, and from the closeness and intensity of that early relationship a baby's adult personality is born. The way she responds to his neediness, his crying, and his smiles will have a profound impact on what he becomes as an adult. It has been said that the most important fact about the human personality is the way it is shaped over a long period of dependence.

Recent research in human attachment, however, shows that the baby's experience of the mother actually shapes his brain, and the experience of parenting will change the mother's and father's brains as well. We know this from research that shows that abused children may have traumatized brains for life and studies in mice and other mammals reveal that the structure of both maternal and paternal brains is altered by the experience of parenting.

This business of mothering is not a one-way street. It is very much a two-person operation. It is essential for a baby's survival that he be able to engage his main caretaker, usually his mother. He has to be able to call her and let her know what he needs; he also has to be able to please her and smile at her, rewarding her for the staggering amount of work she is undertaking on his behalf. Because he cannot speak and won't be able to communicate his needs clearly for years, she is going to have to focus on him to "hear" what's on his mind.

Simply put, she has to receive his message. She must, of course, provide food, comfort, and physical safety to keep him alive, but beyond that she has to create an environment of psychological safety and reliability. All mothers have an intuitive feel that what motherhood is going to require of them is to be available and reliable for their babies.

The essential job of all parents, of course, is to care for a baby. Infants are profoundly dependent on us; they can survive only if we feed them and keep them clean, safe, and warm. But you don't need a psychologist to tell you how to feed your baby, clip his fingernails, or change his diapers. What I would like to discuss is this growing relationship between a boy and his parents, a relationship that began when he was in the womb but which becomes extraordinarily intense the moment he is born, and in the months ahead becomes the cornerstone of his early psychological development: the love between parent and child.

FALLING IN LOVE WITH YOUR SON

I once interviewed a woman who was seven months pregnant with a boy. She was a restrained person, a self-confessed "neatnik," who was very focused on the physical details of having a baby. At the end of our conversation, we did not schedule any future appointments to talk, and I didn't expect to hear from her again. However, two months after our interview, she sent me a one-sentence e-mail with a photograph attached. The message read, "I'm in love." The attached photo, of course, was of her newborn son.

Through the first year and a half of your son's life, your most important "job"—and I am reluctant to use that word to describe this phenomenon—is to fall in love with him. His job, though he cannot possibly think of it that way, will be to fall in love with you. You two will need to spend thousands of hours getting to know each other and teaching each other about yourselves. You will become as closely attuned as possible. All of this will come naturally to most mothers; you won't have to plan it and you don't need much advice to make this happen. You and your baby boy are biologically prewired to have all of this happen. All you need to do is make the space—in your life, in your day, in your heart—to let this love grow.

> *He seems to enjoy learning about new things and picks things up easily. His mind is like a sponge, and he never forgets!*
> —Mother of a one-year-old son

The Eight Lines of Development

The Developmental Story Advances

Just as nature draws you into the loving relationship and secure attachment that is so essential to your son's early psychological development, other aspects of his development conspire to capture your heart and your attention. Here, and in the chapters that follow, we'll look first at the key developmental issues of the age, and then at the developmental backdrop that describes more general patterns of growth and change you will see in your son. We generally identify eight lines of development, along which all children travel at their own pace toward maturity and adulthood: (1) physical development, (2) the development of attachment, (3) social development, (4) cognitive development, (5) academic development, (6) emotional self-regulation, (7) moral and spiritual development, and (8) identity development. Although this breakdown can be a helpful way for adults to see development in progress, remember that your son—no matter how old—doesn't experience himself this way. He's busy living it all at once.

Physical Development

Infancy is the period of the fastest growth in human life. When you look back at the helplessness of the young infant and see how fast he progresses, it is astounding. In the first months of life, each day brings another advance that delights and surprises—not just you but your son, too. His physical movements are instinctive and allow him to find the nipple, to suck and look at you. His sense of touch is all-important to him. He waves his hands and feet in awkward, jerky motions as he tries to get control of his body.

Soon, however, he is trying to push up when he is on his belly, and he will struggle to sit up. By four months his physical coordination and ability to control his hands and legs are much better than just a few weeks before, and the fun begins. By seven months he can sit up and hold toys; soon after he is up and moving awkwardly and then crawling quickly and getting into trouble. He is pointing at things and grabbing them when he can. This allows you to play a large variety of games with him and have an ever-increasing amount of fun with him.

At nine months he is beginning to stand, and he needs you to stand by him, holding out your hands to steady him. He does not need you to hold him every second. He wants you to let go and trust that when he falls and cries, he is going to be all right. As he starts to explore, he is going to take risks. He wants to work on movement and to make progress must balance his need to hold on with his need to let go. He needs you to do something similar: balance your protective concern with your pleasure in his achievements, and learn to let go.

He is also going to insist on feeding himself by about nine months. Mealtime is an extravaganza of sensory adventures for your baby—color, texture, flavor—and, if you can brave the splatter, more valuable face time as he observes your expressive responses to his feeding frenzy.

Sometime around twelve months of age, he'll earn the rank of toddler, becoming suddenly (and forever) mobile and able to move surprisingly quickly. As dramatic as walking is, it is only one of a multitude of things he can do now, including pushing, pulling, and dumping things out. He can take off his hat, turn pages in a book, and flush toilets. Amazingly, he can walk holding an object in each hand but not quite get a spoon into his mouth reliably.

From a psychologist's standpoint, what is noteworthy about a child's physical development is the pleasure he takes in it. He doesn't need you to teach him these things; he only needs you to celebrate with him one stunning achievement after another. And he needs you to keep him from harm without being too anxious about his risk taking.

Attachment

In the chapters ahead, we'll follow the development of attachment as one of the continuing eight lines of development. However, since so much of this chapter is already devoted to attachment (see the main text and "Attachment Is Everything" on page 47), I'll simply say here that attachment is not only a key part of the developmental backdrop for the age, it is the backdrop, the foreground, and the defining focus of your son's early psychological development.

Social Development

Long before your son utters his first words, his smile will be his ticket to social engagement, beginning, of course, with you. For the first two months his attention will be almost exclusively on you, but his gaze will be unfocused. We know that babies recognize their mothers early on, but it takes them a bit longer to sort your face out from other faces. Though your one-month-old infant may smile in his sleep or at the end of feeding, the biggest moment is the emergence of the true social smile at around three months. Of course, it does not emerge exactly at three months, but in all cultures, the smile in response to a face is seen within weeks of the three-month mark. Now he smiles at your face and his father's face in a way that lights up the whole house. The social smile is the greatest reward you can receive for all the work you have done, and by six months he will be able to distinguish your face from any other face in all situations.

A baby's smile speaks a universal language and reflects a universal step in communication and social development. Having discovered the power of the social smile, your son is going to take it on the road. By seven months he will be smiling at everyone, as well as frowning and looking skeptical when the occasion requires.

You will be reading his face constantly and he yours, but he is also reading everyone else's. Babies of this age can look at a stranger over a parent's shoulder in the most penetrating way, either connecting with them or getting anxious about them. Because today's babies are so often in day care settings and have become accustomed to adults, many of them don't show the traditional stranger anxiety that used to be reported at nine months (and in any case, stranger anxiety was always less a fear than a manifestation of healthy attachment). By a year, he is a self-confident and friendly guy, waving bye-bye.

Just as naturally, your baby's expressive vocal repertoire of grunts, coos, and squeals will expand until—eureka!—his first word pops forth. By the end of his first year he'll have a vocabulary of four to six words you can understand. He can identify objects in a book, and he can build a tower of blocks. He will say "Hi" and "Bye-bye" soon enough. He should also be able to follow crucial one-step directions such as "Stop!" By eighteen months he will have an extensive vocabulary, somewhere between eight and twenty words. These first words, and the way they are used, are overwhelmingly social ("Mommy," "Daddy," "I want"), and a boy delights in being understood—despite continuing frustration at not being understood. Later on he will talk to himself, or make his toys "talk" as a way of practicing verbal thinking, but at this stage speech is a social act.

As for socializing, if your son is in a day care setting, he may find a friend as soon as he can crawl, but they can't do much together yet. They just like each other and they may smile a lot; sometimes they will spontaneously share objects, but mostly they'll tear toys out of each other's hands, causing their "friend" to cry. Consistent sharing is an achievement that comes sometime later, or it comes to the older one sooner than the younger one.

Some boys won't be ready for any kind of friendship this early; your son may keep his eyes glued on the adults, because he has transferred his attachment to you and his dad to these daytime caretakers.

Cognitive Development

In ways you notice and more you don't, your son will be tackling the wonders of his world with growing curiosity and contemplation, even if the focus of his attention is a pea gone overboard from his dinner tray. He is mastering concepts. Cognitive development is the name we give to the unfolding of the brain's capacity to solve problems. This is an inborn ability in all babies; unlike education, it is biologically determined and has a timetable all its own. All any parent can do is support it and enrich it; you can't make it happen and you don't need to. Your son will find all the problem-solving opportunities he will ever need in the world around him: in the house, at the park, going shopping with you.

Think of your little boy as a hardworking experimental scientist. For a newborn baby, exploring with his hands and mouth are pretty much the same. His interest is in exploring the world, and since everything is new to him, anything he does expands his knowledge of the way things work. Picking up things, putting them in his mouth, staring at them, trying to pull them apart, throwing them—all of these are cognitive achievements as well as physical ones, and they lead to an increased mastery of the world.

The thing to notice is that your son, once he encounters a problem, will work at it until he understands it. Two of the most important cognitive achievements of the first year of life are the discovery of the self in the mirror and object permanence, that is, discovering that objects exist when they are out of sight. Though they may see their image in the mirror, four-month-old babies don't recognize themselves. You will also notice that in the early months, your son won't notice when a tennis ball rolls out of sight. For him, it is out of sight, out of mind.

All of this changes around six to eight months. Your son may catch sight of his image in a mirror and be fascinated by himself. Peekaboo becomes his favorite team sport as he happily learns his lessons in object permanence. Practice makes patience in this game; the more he plays, the longer he learns he can wait and still expect the object to reappear. Now you'll see him search for the tennis ball because he has come to understand that something exists even when he cannot see it. What pleasure it will give him when he finds it!

Academic Development

Once upon a time we would have laughed at the idea of addressing academic development in a chapter about infants and toddlers. Today, emerging brain research, concern about boys' struggles later in school, aggressive toy marketing, superbaby images, and competitive parenting have combined to make this a topic of parents' conversations.

My advice: Pace yourselves. Don't get hung up on your baby's or toddler's academic development. Don't fall for the powerful marketing message that you can make a smarter, better baby by providing him with strategically designed "learning toys"—or that you need to, as if your love and his intelligence require aggressive enhancement to reach their full potential. They don't. Every moment your son is awake he is learning as fast as he can and in the best possible way.

He is doing it naturally, cultivating his intellectual curiosity and creativity through the joy of discovery. Your son is just as happy, and his neurons are just as happy, playing with a wooden spoon, shiny aluminum pie pans, colorful plastic bowls, or a clattering bundle of plastic measuring cups or spoons. Save your money—you'll need it for pizza a few years from now.

The best investment you can make in his early academic success is in your relationship with him now. There is no need to do flash card drills with your baby in hopes that you can give him an edge in preschool or even college admissions. Play Mozart when you put him to bed if you enjoy it; or take him to Kindermusic classes if you find them fun. If you're doing it to boost his IQ, groom him for optimal academic success, micromanage his development, or "make him" anything, don't. He'll get the message, and ultimately that kind of powered-up parental ambition is going to go hard on him. Babies teach themselves most things they need to know in their playful interactions with the world and with their parents.

The one exception I make to the rule of not formally educating your children in the first year of life is sign language. Teaching sign language to your son can be both fun for you and, if you stick with it, will enable you to communicate with him before he has a verbal vocabulary. Children between twelve and eighteen months can become intensely frustrated by their inability to say what they want. They are, however, able to develop a vocabulary of twenty or thirty signs from the American Sign Language vocabulary. (See more on infant signing on pages 99–102.)

Emotional Self-Regulation

One of the things we say to scold older children and even adults is "Don't act like a baby." We talk about acting like a baby when a child (or a grown-up) is not able to regulate his or her feelings, becomes overwhelmed by them, and does something that resembles a tantrum. Learning to control one's feeling states and reactions is one of the most important achievements of development, accomplished bit by bit over the course of childhood.

Your son's facial expressions are directly related to his emotions, and he can easily show you when he is frightened, surprised, sad, or angry. Every mother in the world reads her baby's facial expressions, because they are inborn and universal. What is not born into your baby is the ability to control feelings. You teach your son to calm himself and trust you that food is coming, to make the transition from waking to sleep, and to keep from being totally overwhelmed by his anger. You do it by comforting him, holding him, feeding him, singing to him, and reassuring him that the world is a more reliable place than it feels to him at that moment.

Your son's sleep patterns, and his ability to comfort himself upon waking, are a window into his earliest efforts to develop emotional self-regulation. In the first two months, as your son becomes more alert, he sleeps more deeply and wakes more decisively. He reacts positively to comfort and very negatively to pain. He careens between delight and distress. What discourages many parents is that after six weeks babies cry more, and they go through a period of what has been called "disequilibrium" at three months. You'll feel like you're going backward! Dads may feel the brunt of this in a special way, as it is often just about this time that they've gained more baby care duties, and so they may be blamed for the baby's fussing or feel responsible.

From four to six months, however, this transition will begin to smooth out and your son will become more comfortable and relaxed. He'll love to be cuddled and will become quite possessive of his mother and father right through nine and ten months. This classic phase of attachment means he will become quite distressed when separated from his parents in a way he was not at six months. From twelve to eighteen months he will remain vigilant about any threats to his relationships, protesting strenuously, for example, when his mother holds another child in her lap.

But as he grows he will become more self-conscious and will control his feelings in order to get the reaction he wants and because he is learning to trust your response. He will try to stop his crying if he sees his mother is attempting to respond to his distress. He will temper his own anger if he sees that his father disapproves. He will dance and show off and bask in the applause of his audience, demonstrating that he has high levels of self-control.

Moral and Spiritual Development

Before you can ever become a loving, empathic human being, you need to have someone show you love and empathy. I view infancy as a time when we pour love into babies in order to fill their cups to the top, thereby giving them a wellspring from which their later altruism and spirituality will arise. Thomas Lickona, the author of *Educating for Character,* says that the moral life of a child has three components: habits of the heart, habits of mind, and habits of practice. Habits of the heart, he believes, come from the experience of love and morality. When we care for infants, when we do our best to protect them from harm, when we say "Oh, poor baby" to a child who has fallen down and cut his chin, we are showing him empathy. That experience, repeated over and over and over, will not make him a deeply empathic two-year-old—that is out of his developmental range as yet—but it is teaching him the idea.

Protecting an infant is inherently moral behavior. When an eighteenth-month-old boy is kicking a fourteen-month-old boy, we intervene because the discrepancy in their size and skill is so great. The younger boy may not appreciate exactly what we have done by intervening; indeed, he may take it completely for granted. However, when he sees adults making the world a safer place for him, he is developing habits of the heart.

We know that babies begin to experience empathy for others around nine months. If a boy pulls on his mother's earring very hard and she yells "Ouch!" and shows distress, he will make a puzzled face, he will look concerned, and he may cry, especially if she is crying. He may even laugh, but don't take it as a sign of a callous child; if he feels confused or overwhelmed by your distress, laughter is a release.

The mother who observed that her seventeen-month-old boy so often shared her facial expressions added: "I am surprised at his generosity at this stage. He offers me and others everything—candy, food, toys. Also, if one of us is a little mopey, he will try to console."

That's the picture of perfect sync between parent and toddler: through his love—or, if you prefer, his impressionable neurons—he is learning how to feel the pain of another person. That is the beginning of a moral life.

However you spent the time before your son was born, whether on bed rest or meeting deadlines at work, you spent it with him, every minute of it. This may help explain his desire to keep things that way initially as he adjusts to his new postpartum living space. But his world has widened dramatically, and he is ready to expand his inner circle to include a doting dad, also a familiar presence if he has been patting and chatting with the baby along the way. Research—and simple observation of a caring, hands-on father with his baby—tells us that by eight weeks of age, an infant can discriminate between his mother and father and responds differently to each. Ample evidence also shows that fathers and infants bond in essential ways that have lasting benefit for both—and for Mom as well.

There is no strict timetable by which children become attached to their parents. Human infants, unlike geese, do not imprint on the first person they see when they hatch; they develop attachments over time, as the result of repeated holding, comforting, diapering, and feeding. That is why adopted children, even when they are adopted many months after being born, can and do develop powerful attachments to their adoptive parents.

So if in the first year of his life you and your son fall in love and become profoundly connected to each other, and if he also becomes deeply attached to his dad, then you will have helped him start to build the foundation of a secure personality, which he will have for the rest of his life. From the point of view of developmental psychology: mission accomplished.

ATTACHMENT THEORY: DR. BOWLBY AND THE CASE OF THE "STRANGELY DETACHED" BOY

Mothers have known the power of the mother-baby bond intuitively for thousands of years, but science and medicine have just begun to catch up, recognizing its role in healthy child development only in the past few decades. As recently as the 1950s, theories of the day held that cleanliness and getting infants on a proper feeding schedule were far more important than satisfying babies' emotional needs. This was considered the best medical wisdom of the day for babies and mothers from American middle-class families. Fathers had their prescribed roles, too, primarily as breadwinners and not as primary caregivers in any substantive way. So, too, at that time, the practice of separating hospitalized children from their parents was common, sometimes forbidding visits for weeks at a time.

But even during that era, there was a movement under way in both England and the United States to focus on the nature of the relationship between mothers—or primary caretakers—and babies. This line of research was led by an English psychoanalyst named John Bowlby, who had worked with boys who appeared "affectionless." One boy, a six-year-old named Derek, constantly stole things, even though he had come from a "good" family. He was "strangely detached" and nothing his parents did seemed to touch him, neither affection nor punishment. After studying Derek and other boys like him, Bowlby discovered that most of them had suffered from prolonged early separations from their mothers. Derek himself had contracted diphtheria at eighteen months and had been confined to a hospital for nine months without a single visit from his parents. When he returned home, his mother reported that he was like a stranger to her.

The discovery of the destructive effects of separation, including perhaps his own experience as a child, led Bowlby on a lifelong quest to understand human attachment and launched a fifty-year scientific effort to understand the mother-child bond. If your baby was put on your breast seconds after his birth; if you were

> *He's only seventeen months old, but he is very emotionally expressive. He has shown some expressions of empathy— he shows concern when another baby is crying. He also likes to rock and feed his baby doll. —Mother of a toddler son*

TV FOR YOUR BABY? DOCS SAY
TURN OFF THE TUBE

If you think TV viewing is harmless for your baby or that it might even offer developmental benefits, pediatric and public health experts want you to know otherwise. Their advice: wean him from the screen, and if you haven't allowed him to watch TV yet, don't. Play, walk, read, or just spend relaxed time with him instead.

A study at the University of Washington and Seattle Children's Hospital Research Institute found that a large number of parents are allowing their very young children to watch television, DVDs, or videos, so much so that by three months of age, 40 percent of babies are regular viewers. That number jumped to 90 percent of two-year-olds, based on the study's sample population.

This is in striking contrast to advice from the American Academy of Pediatrics, which has long advised parents to avoid television viewing for children under the age of two. "Although certain television programs may be promoted to this age group, research on early brain development shows that babies and toddlers have a critical need for direct interactions with parents and other significant care givers . . . for healthy brain growth and the development of appropriate social, emotional, and cognitive skills. Therefore, exposing such young children to television programs should be discouraged," the academy says in its recommendations for parents.

What can you do to avoid relying on the TV or reduce the amount of time your infant or toddler spends in front of the tube?

• If you want to occupy your baby or toddler while you're busy nearby, keep a low drawer or portable bin stocked with plastic dishes, wooden spoons, or other baby-safe items your son can play with to take the pressure off you.

• Read or just sit, talk, sing, or otherwise play in simple ways with your son—he'll thrive on the physical closeness and social interaction.

• If you're staying in due to weather, try a walk at an indoor mall instead. Many have mom-and-tot walking clubs or play areas where you can relax and enjoy your baby and the company of other parents, too—a boost for both of you.

encouraged to spend hours holding and handling a premature baby in an incubator; if your husband was encouraged to be in the delivery room—as most are these days—and was offered the chance to cut the umbilical cord; if your baby was given back to you the moment he was cleaned up and swaddled, and perhaps was allowed to room in with you during your recovery period—if any or all of this happened, it is because today's medical practitioners now recognize the power of early love between an infant and his mother and father. Research has established clearly now that this earliest bond and the continuing phenomenon we call attachment have lifelong consequences.

Why do you need to know all this theory? You don't. Mothers and fathers have loved, fed, and cared for their babies for thousands of years without ever hearing of John Bowlby or attachment theory or reading a parenting book.

I want to tell you a bit about it for three reasons. First, it may help you to better understand the needy, clingy, and totally exhausting behavior of your baby in the first years of his life. Some knowledge of attachment may make him more understandable to you and may give you a bit of patience when you might otherwise lose it. Second, there are still many people who believe that boys need to be "made into men," that boys need to be "toughened up" and that we cannot allow them to be as affection-seeking as girls. Once you learn about the nature of attachment, you will realize that nothing could be further from the truth. Third and finally, there is recent evidence that boys may be more vulnerable than girls to problems in attachment, so it's important for you to know that and to stay attuned to your boy. He needs you to be, especially in the first year of life.

YOU ARE THE CENTER OF YOUR SON'S WORLD

Many first-time mothers worry that they won't be able to connect with their babies, and the fact that the baby is a boy—someone so different from themselves—may give them extra anxiety. Your son doesn't see it that way. All babies, including your son, are born ready to love their mothers. Your son's most important survival instinct is to hold on to you, to cling, to cry, to suck, to smile, and to follow you, first with his eyes, then by turning his head, and then with his feet. All of this is standard operating equipment for the human species, developmentally speaking. Once a newborn realizes that "he" isn't "we" anymore, you quickly become the center of his universe and he spends much of the time in the first years of his life calling you, tracking you, and protesting when he cannot make you respond to him immediately. He will be the most ardent lover you have ever known. All you have to do is give in to his passionate pursuit and you will love him. It is almost impossible not to. Why? Because your instincts have prepared you to love him as much as his instincts have been primed to love you.

Most mothers are already so ready to fall in love with their babies that it happens quickly. For some it is love at first sight, or first thing after recovering from the stress of giving birth.

It doesn't necessarily go that smoothly for all mothers and babies, but minor complications and momentary setbacks don't appear to keep an otherwise healthy mother and baby from bonding and finding their rhythm in the first few weeks of life together. Nature and nurture conspire in their favor: a newborn is naturally intent upon nursing and sleeping, and a mother is naturally intent on providing both in loving arms. Nature and nurture conspire again in that although your son needs food to survive and he'll drink any milk to live, if he is given a choice he will prefer *your* milk, *your* smell, and the sound of *your* voice. By the eighth day of life, babies are able to distinguish the smell of their mother's milk—if exposed to nursing pads from two women, they consistently turn toward that of their own mother. In another experiment, newborn infants were given a specially wired pacifier that allowed them to choose what they listened to by the rate at which they sucked. They consistently sucked at a rate that permitted them to hear the recording of a human voice, and they preferred their mother's voice to any other.

Whether you breast-feed or bottle-feed your baby, you spend a lot of time looking into your baby's face, and he stares into your face, too. It becomes the most important sight in his life. Soon he will be able to read your emotions and you will be able to read his better than anyone else. He will come to recognize the way you hold him and bounce him, and you will come to know intuitively precisely the correct rate at which to rock him or bounce him. Though he may enjoy being held by other people, under certain circumstances you may be the only one who can calm him when he is crying. And there will be times, particularly in the first six weeks of life, when even you won't have the magic move that settles him right away. Patience is the only remedy.

What the two of you are doing is getting to know each other. You are dancing together; you are having a love affair at the deepest levels. You play with each other, you are fascinated with each other, you imitate each other. The two

ATTACHMENT IS EVERYTHING

On the island of Bali, tradition dictates that a baby is not allowed to touch the ground for the first three and a half months of his or her life. He is never put down alone on any surface. An infant is held by an adult or sleeps with an adult every minute. A baby is considered a god who is ready to join the world after about one hundred days. In a little ceremony, his feet are washed in water and then are allowed to touch the ground for the first time. There is, it seems to me, a lot of wisdom in this tradition. The Balinese recognize the profound dependence of the human infant and his or her need to be attached to the mother, and that early relationship is treated as a separate universe of experience.

There are countries in Western Europe where mothers are granted paid family leave for a year and fathers for six months. (In Norway, that most progressive and wealthy of countries, maternal and paternal leave are mandatory!) Universal benefits for mothers and fathers in the United States would do more to create a healthy, bright, resilient population of children than all the dollars that go for the programs and products devoted to crafting trophy children or fixing broken ones.

The demands of earning a living are real, and a psychologist cannot tell you how to balance your budget. What I can encourage you to do is take as much time as you can with your baby. Whether your occupation up to now has been in the workplace or as a busy volunteer, if you can, step away from that for at least three to six months and return when you feel it is right for you and your child.

Many parents cannot take that kind of time off in the early months of their baby's life. For them the process of getting attuned to their son takes place in the morning and evening, during nighttime feedings, and during the long hours on weekends. Babies are resilient, and though they prefer one single caretaker, they are able to attach to up to three caregiver figures in the first year of life. A mother who wants to be in tune with her son can be, even if she is not with him as many hours as she would like. Research suggests that what is important is the quality of attunement between mother and son, not the quantity of hours they spend together. As a practical matter, a mother should try to get the highest quality day care she can for her child, and ask for as much help as possible from family and friends to assist with the chores of life that might take her away from her baby, so that she can indulge in the timeless business of getting to know her son.

of you become a little comedy team, with your own routines. Why does this happen?

In your son's brain (and in every baby's brain) are "mirror neurons" that copy everything they see you do. When you smile, he wants to be able to smile, which he can do voluntarily and in response to you anytime he wants after he is three to four months old. When you frown, his face is likely to get more serious;

when you laugh, he will laugh. And, without planning it, when he makes a sound or a face, you will imitate him. When a four-month-old, for example, goes, "Da, da, da, da," a mother will almost immediately repeat those same sounds back to him. When a baby makes a spitting sound, a raspberry, most mothers will either do it right back or they will laugh, in which case their baby will laugh. "He is similar to me with his expressive facial expressions," one mother said of her infant son, surprised at the mirroring effect.

This intense imitative communication between mother and child is the foundation of a child's emotional life.

WAKE-UP CALL: BABY EVAN AND MOTHER ALICE

Baby Evan was asleep in his room when I arrived for a late morning visit with him and his mother, Alice, but in a moment we heard Evan crying over the baby monitor and Alice immediately got up to go into his room. She started talking to him just as she opened the door to his room, letting him know she was on her way. He was not crying hard, just little sputters and cries to let her know that his morning nap was over and that he needed to see her. Evan is a handsome boy, eight months old; when we came in he was lying on his back. She leaned over the crib and made eye contact with him. His fitful crying stopped momentarily; it was almost as if the sight of his mother took his breath away. He immediately raised his arms, and when she did not pick him up instantly he cried a bit again, as if to say, *Come on, Mom, pick me up.* She only hesitated because she wanted to look at his face, as if it were a long-delayed reunion. When she did pick him up she immediately began to rock her body back and forth in a soothing rhythm for him. (Suddenly, he saw me—the stranger in the room—and was slightly startled. Alice held him up over her shoulder so that he could see the stranger and yet feel completely protected by her body.) She then brought him back down, hummed to him a bit, and moved him to the table for a diaper change.

Changing Evan's diaper was an opportunity for constant talking, smiling, and changes of expression. Whether he frowned, looked worried, protested, or smiled and babbled, he got a mirroring response from his mother. When he looked worried, she asked, "Oh, so serious?" and her face looked serious, too, for a moment. Then she smiled and said, "We're going to go to the park. We're going to see all of your friends." Soon he began to smile as well. Alice and Evan negotiated several different moods together in the leisurely six or seven minutes it took her to change his diaper and put him in a new outfit. Evan successfully made the difficult transition from sleep to waking with the help of his mother's face, her voice, and her touch. When she lifted him off the changing table he was ready to face the day.

YOUR FACE TELLS YOUR SON ABOUT HIMSELF

Over time, your son starts to feel what he sees displayed on your face, and, equally important, your face tells him what he is feeling. If you give him messages of confidence, he takes those in; if you mirror his serious looks, he literally knows you are taking him seriously. You become the guide to his inner life. You are able to reliably give him the message "You are okay."

Babies are routinely overwhelmed with their feelings. When they get hungry, they can become wildly excited or angry and desperate. When they get frustrated, they can be utterly furious. When they are sick or feverish, they can be inconsolable. Infants may be small, but their feelings are huge. Of course, when you pick up your son to rock him, when you talk to him or sing to him, he is comforted by your presence. But your lack of panic and your understanding face also tell him that his feelings are not tidal waves that will wash him away; they are feelings he can manage, at first only with your help, but later because he remembers that his feelings come and go, and because he begins to form the idea that the world is an okay place.

SECURE ATTACHMENT: "WILL MY MOM AND DAD BE THERE?"

When you are able, over and over, to intuit what your boy needs, to calm him when he is in the middle of a storm of feeling, to play with him when he is in a playful mood, bit by bit he is going to start to get a picture of the world as a pretty reliable place. Fifty years ago, pioneering child psychologist Erik Erikson observed the early development of confidence in babies as well as the lack of it in disturbed children, and declared that the work of the first stage in life was developing trust.

We now know that a baby develops trust or confidence in life as a result of having two questions answered for him: *Will my mom and dad be there when I need them?* and *Will they pay attention to my feelings?* We now know that a baby learns the answers to those questions from having a secure attachment to his primary caretaker, usually his mother. It is the result of repeated experiences of being understood and cared for in ways that, for the most part, meet one's needs. If you bonded this way with your mother or father, it was because when you

FATHERS PARENT DIFFERENTLY— CELEBRATE THE DIFFERENCES

"Fathers do not mother," Kyle Pruett writes definitively, and indeed, there are some basic differences in a father's approach to an infant. We all know this from personal experience, and researchers have identified a number of gender patterns in parenting style. Some research has shown that mothers tend to be more soothing, fathers more exciting. Mothers, with their singsong voices and their tender touch, tend to make a baby's heart rate go down; fathers, with their bigger voices and their tendency to tickle and pounce on babies, make their heart rates go up. Sons and daughters alike will seek out the rougher play of the father, both during the first year and throughout childhood.

Children can distinguish their mother's voice and their father's voice by the time they are six weeks old, and, contrary to what you might expect, while a quiet infant is more attentive to his mother's voice, a fretting infant will calm more readily to the father's voice. Common sense and evolutionary psychology suggest that any child, boy or girl, benefits from the complementary nature of mothering and fathering. It guarantees a variety of experiences to grow his brain.

I do not want to overstate the differences between men and women; while there are differences in parenting, there are important similarities. Both mothers and fathers appear equally able to respond with love to an infant in distress, and they go about caretaking with equal amounts of planning and worry. There is no difference, for instance, between the physiological responses of mothers and fathers to crying infants. When a father is a single parent, his attunement to his children and his caregiving style are more important than the fact that he is a man, and his children are just as likely to have secure attachment patterns.

In the traditional family setup, with a mother at home and the father working to provide for the family, a father's impact on the child may be indirect in comparison to hers, but it is still substantial. When a mother feels that her husband supports her, she is more patient and emotionally responsive to her children and therefore more likely to be attuned to her child. The extensive literature on the unique impact of fathering suggests that the ideal situation for a child is a stable two-parent family and that a mother should take advantage of a father's ability to parent. He might do it a bit differently from a mother's point of view, but from your son's point of view it is all good.

smiled, someone smiled back at you; when you were hungry, you were fed; when you needed cuddling, you were cuddled; when you were furious, your mother tried to soothe you, but in any case she accepted your anger and didn't retaliate against you for it. She didn't ignore you and turn away. When a mother is able to do that for a baby, the baby gradually builds up a picture of the world as a pretty darn good place.

If, for a variety of reasons, a mother is unable to do this for her infant—if she is suffering from depression, if her life is terribly stressful, or if she cannot handle the demands of a colicky baby or three older children—she may be constantly presenting a face to her baby that is flat and unresponsive, anxious, annoyed, or frightened. Or their timing may be off. Some mothers do what they think is right for a baby without using any of the baby's cues. For example, when you play some variation of the "I'm gonna get you" or "creepy crawly little mouse" game with your son—the game in which you use your fingers to climb up his body and tickle his neck—you have to accurately perceive whether he is ready for the game. If he's not, he can become scared or upset. Sometimes babies want us to put our faces right on top of their faces and other times not. All of that takes reading the cues from the baby.

Every parent misreads her child's cues from time to time. There is no such thing as a perfectly attuned parent. However, when a baby frequently sees a flat and unresponsive face, or his mother forces herself or her schedule on him constantly, the effect can be to make him anxious. He develops a picture of the world as unresponsive to him. Researchers also have found that infants engage in "emotional eavesdropping," in which they watch the interactions between adults, and may modify their behavior in response to emotions they see the adults express. For better or for worse, the emotional interactions between parents register in a baby's mind. Even if he is not physically neglected or abused, if he observes too many upsetting interactions he may feel deprived of both the reassurance and responsiveness he craves.

Whether you manage alone, share the baby's feeding and care with your spouse, or find support from a reliable third caregiver, your baby boy relies upon you to protect and provide for him in three key ways: first, by ensuring that he receives adequate food, warmth, physical comfort, and caring touch, and is not deprived; second, by remaining patient, loving, and kind even when you are exhausted, so that you don't blow up at him or neglect him; and third, by

> *We go walking a lot. We go to the park near our house and cruise through there looking for birds and ducks. . . . He gets very calm in the outdoors. People would say put them in the car and drive them around to settle them down, but for him it's these walks. It's been a lovely treat.*
> —Father of a year-old boy

protecting him from too many changes in caretakers, or in other words, by trying to be there yourself for as much time as you can. When you must leave him in someone else's care, you try always to leave him with someone he knows and trusts, who will treat him in a loving way, as close as possible to the way you do.

Most mothers instinctively seek to keep a close protective proximity to their babies. Mothers often tell me they find it extremely difficult to be away from their babies for any length of time and they watch intently when someone else tends the baby for the first time, checking to see that the "stranger"—and that can be her husband, her mother, or her friend—is doing it right. It can feel unsettling to be away for long.

Rose wrote to me that when her son, Josh, was two and a half months old, she left him with her husband to accompany her older daughter to the theater. It was, she said, "the very first time I had been away from him for more than forty-five minutes." Is there any other relationship where you are never away from the other person more than forty-five minutes in seventy-five days? The mother-child bond is unique for its intensity.

Listen to how Jamie described her son on the day before he turned five months old: "I feel very close to him. He knows who I am. I don't feel like he's this 'baby' anymore." She meant he isn't a stranger, because now they are attuned to each other. She knows his moods, she accepts his negative feelings, and they are having a ball together. She went on:

I like to make him laugh—he's just hilarious! I love giving him a bath. He gets so excited. I love it—seeing his little naked butt. I just love him. I love him and I squish him and love him. I just show him that I love him.

Jamie has clearly entered into her son's world. They are engaged in long, reciprocal exchanges with each other in which she matches his intensity and tempo, and to which she adds variations and new ideas. What comes out of such a relationship? At first your son is just learning to regulate his biological life; through a synchronized relationship with you he forms a regular pattern of sleeping, eating, and eliminating. More important, over time he comes to control his own emotional life. He knows how to become aroused and how to calm down *on his own,* because he has practiced with you. For a child, the great thing about having a secure attachment is that it sustains him and it is portable.

Because of your good and responsive care, your son will come out of the first year of life with a secure base in his relationship with you. Your son will be most attuned to you and you to him, but he may also have a strong attachment to his father and to another caretaking person as well. We know that children who experience a secure attachment to their primary caretakers do better in almost every aspect of life, and the positive effects last for years. At six years of age they make friendships more easily, their health is better, they do better in school, and they have an easier time being parents themselves later in life. Psychiatrists and neuroscientists believe that early relationship shapes the brain for life. "Love, and the lack of it, changes a young brain forever," write Thomas Lewis, Fari Amini, and Richard Lannon in *A General Theory of Love*.

Securely attached children are able to sustain attention for longer periods, for example. Securely attached boys are bolder and more exploratory. Once they

ENJOY YOUR BOY

Above all, you should have fun with your son. Peer pressure among parents has intensified in recent years, just as the competitive environment has intensified for children growing up. Sadly, many parents today approach parenting in the same intense way they work at their jobs or studied in college. They consider it very serious business. But in the sea of information and opinion from books, magazines, newspaper articles, research briefs, Web sites, and blogs, it is possible to lose sight of the simple bond that nature designed so you and your baby can communicate, love, learn, and grow together. If you become too grim about parenting, your child feels it. Children read their parents' moods. I believe that your son will know whether you are, on balance, having some fun raising him or whether you consider it an endless series of chores or, worse yet, a project that must be done just right. Perfectionism is the enemy of enjoyable parenting.

I'd like to remind you of two of Donald Winnicott's powerful concepts: the child as a "going concern" and the "good-enough" mother. If a mother understands that she doesn't have to create her baby or make him grow, if she understands that he has the genetic and developmental program already inside, she can relax. And if she can trust herself to be a "good-enough" mother, she can stop worrying and just enjoy responding to his needs. There is also the "good-enough" father and the "good-enough" older sister and brother. A family does not have to be perfect to be wonderful for a baby.

start walking, they go farther from their mothers and are more secure with strangers than other children, as long as they can touch base with their mothers.

When a mother and baby cannot, for one reason or another, get exactly on each other's wavelengths, the baby may develop what is called an anxious attachment pattern. Sometimes it is quite subtle, but the mother cannot read her baby's desires and states of mind. She may become overwhelmed by his excitement or frightened of his angry reaction to her milk coming in slowly. If it makes her feel like a bad mother, she may become rejecting toward her baby, however unconsciously. Or tension may arise if she has a fixed idea of what babies need, a schedule or a goal in mind that makes her unresponsive to what her particular child needs.

Anxious attachment patterns show some variation as well, generally recognized as ambivalent and avoidant—both within the normal range, though not ideal—and disorganized attachment, which is considered more serious. Children with ambivalent attachments cannot seem to find the same level of reassurance from their relationship with their mothers that securely attached kids do. They become both very clingy, hoping to find comfort they need, and then angry when they fail to feel it. They alternate between clinginess and anger, and their parents alternate between anxiety and frustration. It is hard for mother and child to stay in sync.

Avoidant children often have mothers who won't accept their neediness or want to relate to them only when they are in a good mood. These mothers cannot accept a baby's natural distress. After a while the child figures that out and draws the conclusion, *I don't need you. I'll do it myself.* When there are too many separations, or a traumatic separation, in the early life of a child he can become avoidant. He may look good at ten months old, he may seem very independent, but there are times when his mother returns from having been out of the room and he doesn't go to her; if he does, he won't hold his hands up to her to be picked up, nor will he meet her gaze. He's avoiding the contact.

Avoidant responses occur, of course, in all babies at times. Mothers routinely have to coax and cajole a grumpy baby back into a positive mood and affirming relationship; that is a normal part of mothering. An avoidant child shows up as one who displays a persistent pattern of avoidance in situations where the vast majority of secure babies quickly warm to the relationship with their mother or caretaker. We imagine such babies feel, *When people don't stay around, what's the point of getting attached?*

When a child is adopted later in infancy—for example, at seven months or fifteen months—and has had inadequate or inconsistent care early in life, he can develop anxious or avoidant attachment patterns that will present challenges for his adoptive parents. Consistent, trustworthy care can remediate many difficulties in attachment. It is only when children have developed chaotic attachment patterns that it may be very difficult to heal their distress.

Children with a disorganized attachment style generally come from disrupted, sometimes abusive family environments where attachment stress can reach annihilating proportions. Such children just never know what to expect from a caretaker; their experience of their mother and father swings wildly from the loving to the neglectful, from soothing to sadistic. Their responses may reflect a desperate effort to get what they need, conditioned as they have become by an uncertain and potentially frightening environment.

SECURE ATTACHMENT AT FIFTEEN MONTHS

When can you be sure that your child has become securely attached? By fifteen months most children have developed an attachment pattern that is going to last. They will relate to their parents and other adults in much the same way at six years old, and perhaps throughout life. Though there will be opportunities for change throughout childhood and again in adolescence, these attachment patterns have proved to be long-lasting.

Johnye Ballenger, M.D., a pediatrician who teaches at Harvard Medical School, says that fifteen months is a crucial milestone for children she sees in her practice. Quickly sketching the attachment process as it shows up in a child's visit to the doctor, she says, "At four months they'll smile at anybody; at six months I want them to smile at me. At nine months I want them to be able to really connect with me; by twelve months I want them to be able to get two shots *without their parents crying.* And I think you should be able to teach a fifteen-month-old child anything. They love you and want to do whatever you do."

Dr. Ballenger is strongly suggesting that at a certain point you can trust the relationship that you have built up with your son. You can be separate enough at one year that you don't have to feel everything for him—that is, he can get a shot without you crying—and by fifteen months, if your child is securely attached, he will want to do things on his own. It would be detrimental if you keep doing things for him or remain intensely anxious about protecting him from everything. A boy who is secure only needs you to sit and be supportive from a distance, Dr. Ballenger told me, describing a mother who was connected to her year-old son as he got a shot but didn't act as if it were a tragedy. In another case, "I persuaded a fifteen-month-old to stand on the scale and weigh himself," she told me. "It took some time, but he did it." And he was clearly proud of himself.

The secure relationship is one that will bear some weight, so to speak, and it will allow a parent to ask her son to start imitating big-boy behavior, inviting him day by day to step into the bigger-boy world that awaits him. Securely attached babies also may cry on reunion, but that reunion cry is an expression of security: *I missed you, and I trust you want to hear all about it.* The goal of secure attachment is eventual independence, defined not strictly by separation but by a balance of separation and a maintained lifelong connection.

FIND THE VILLAGE IT TAKES TO RAISE A CHILD

"Family is the organizing theme around which our consciousness grows, from the earliest childhood stages of brain development," writes psychoanalyst Harvey L. Rich, M.D., in *In the Moment: Embracing the Fullness of Life.* "It is where we begin to define ourselves relative to others, and as part of the larger story of family, community, history, and humankind. At the deepest level, it is where we first discover ourselves. This family template for celebration of the individual, and of life itself, colors our experience in every other realm that follows—friendship, marriage, work, and community. Our ability to celebrate ourselves and others, to create meaning and find satisfaction in life, begins here."

Family and close friends support your best parenting and expand the world your son comes to trust. If you don't have that constellation of people in your life naturally, set about building your own "village" by tapping into others in your community. It might be a parent-and-babies play group in your neighborhood, or something as casual as the regulars you meet in visits to the park or playground. Seeing a lot of other parents and their babies gives you important experience in watching others struggle with the same problems you struggle with, and solving them in ways you might not have thought of. Also, seeing other children, especially children several months older than your son, will give you faith in development.

BOYS AND ATTACHMENT

Attachment is equally crucial for girls and boys, but it comes with some particular implications for boys. First, research suggests that boys are more vulnerable than girls to disruptions in attachment. Second, when boys have attachment problems, they tend to develop avoidant attachment patterns, and those are associated with later aggression and violence. If we're going to save our boys from being violent, I believe our work starts in the first year of life, by helping them become securely attached. Finally, I worry that some people still hold traditional notions that boys don't need as much loving and cuddling as girls, or that you have to do something early to "toughen boys up." There is some research that shows that traditional parents still get upset when little boys don't act in "boy" ways, and that is something I want to address.

One of the experiments researchers used to test the relationship between mother and child involved the use of a mother's "still face." In a lab setting, a mother would play with her child for two minutes, laughing, playing with, or tickling the four-month-old in a baby chair. Then, at the signal of the researcher, she would turn her back to her baby for a moment. When she turned around again, she would maintain a "still face" (also called a "poker face"), with no expression whatsoever. Researchers were interested in studying what babies did in reaction and how they tried to reestablish their relationships with the now-disengaged mothers. Though they hadn't been looking for gender differences, they were astonished to find that baby boys and baby girls had significantly different responses to the expressionless face.

Both boys and girls became distressed when they couldn't get their mothers to smile at them in her usual way. Many of the babies cried. However, after a period of time about two-thirds of the girls settled down and looked away from the mother, focusing on the lights of the lab or the design on the baby chair. It was a majority of the boys who continued to cry and were inconsolable. Some of them struggled against the straps holding them in, throwing themselves wildly from side to side, crying and angry.

If you watched tapes of these boys, you would come to the conclusion that little boys aren't tough at all. They are not as resourceful as girls; furthermore, as they lose contact with their mothers, they become increasingly distressed and angry in an effort to revive the connection. In my work with preschools, I often encounter four-year-old boys with whom teachers are struggling. They will describe a boy to me as angry, socially isolated, and hard to reach. He cannot make friends and he is headed for trouble. A boy like that often proves to be one whose history shows that as an infant he protested the loss of connection with his mother furiously but could not make her come back, and he permanently withdrew from all adults in frustration.

We know that avoidant boys are going to have difficulties in later life that securely attached boys do not. An avoidant boy may not, in adolescence, be able to make a relationship with a mentor, because he cannot allow himself to fully trust an adult. A fourteen-year-old boy who doesn't have a close relationship with an adult is going to be more susceptible to gang influences, and if he has a gun in his hand, he may not feel the same level of empathy for his victim that another, more secure boy would be capable of feeling. One important thing we, as a society, can do to prevent future violence is to provide our children with the attention they need to become securely attached. There are many factors at work in male violence, but early attachment is a significant one.

Having said that, I'm not suggesting you frantically glue yourself to your son in an effort to make sure that he is securely attached. Here's the best thing you can do: enjoy him, play with him, look at him, and fall in love with him. There will come a moment, however, when he will need you to let go a little more. Once he can sit up and play with a toy at seven months, he'll need to experience what it is like to be alone—to be in the presence of his mother without actually having his mother holding him or interacting with him. He will need to experience himself (safely) alone in the world for brief periods of time. Psychologically speaking, his sense of security will come from the close relationship he has with you, and knowing that you are there within calling distance. He may not look at you all the time as he once did, since the world will be an increasingly interesting place for him, but he has a sense of where you are all the time.

HOW BOYS ARE DIFFERENT: GREAT VARIABILITY AND SLOWER DEVELOPMENT

Sex differences become more pronounced as children get older. Beyond the obvious differences of the genitals, there are significant physiological and neurological differences between boys and girls that are present from birth and which are the result of the hormonal bath in utero. (See "What Makes a Boy a Boy," page 5.) Most of these differences, however, do not have much of an impact on parenting. If you haven't been the parent of a girl before you give birth to your boy, you are not likely to notice these differences because you have not had a basis for comparison. And even if you have already parented a girl, the individual temperaments of your daughter and son may be more powerful than the gender of your child from a parenting point of view.

Still, sex differences are apparent in infancy, and continue as boys grow. Boys are, on average, both longer and heavier than girls at birth. They have less fat and more muscle than girl babies, and this difference continues throughout life. They will grow up to be, on average, 15 percent larger than girls. Boys show greater strength in lifting their heads as they lie on their stomachs. They have larger hearts and lungs. They have a higher systolic blood pressure than girls and a slower resting heart rate.

Boys tend to grow up more slowly and have a greater variability than do girls. Height is a good example. We all know that girls reach puberty first and that they grow taller than boys in sixth grade. Boys don't catch up until late eighth or ninth grade, and then they keep growing for years after girls have stopped getting taller. By the time they are finished, not only are boys taller, on average, but there is a greater range of heights in boys, from short to tall, than there is in girls. This variability will be repeated in many other characteristics, from restlessness to reading ability. There is a great range of what is "boy," and when you give birth to a baby boy, you have to figure out what kind of boy you have gotten.

Perhaps the most important thing to know about boy development is that it is slower than girl development and it has a different trajectory. As a parent, you will have to learn to trust the arc and timing of boy development. If you do not, you will make your son miserable with parental anxiety, disapproval, or impatience over the visible differences, or when he isn't keeping up with the girl next door.

There are two issues here: one is the pace of development, and the other is the arc of development. It is easy enough to see that boys lag behind girls and that they eventually catch up in some ways, such as pubertal growth. However, like the arc of a novel, the entire beginning-to-end story of male development has its own logic, its own rhythm, and its own destination.

THREE IMPORTANT BRAIN DIFFERENCES

There are many differences between the brains of boys and the brains of girls, and no doubt psychologists and neuroscientists will discover more in the years to come. This is an exciting time for research on gender differences. We are

MEN, BE CURIOUS ABOUT YOUR OWN INFANCY AND TODDLERHOOD; MOMS, TAKE NOTE

Men are often short on everyday chatting skills, especially with their own mothers, and may avoid conversations with the womenfolk in the family for that reason. Fatherhood solves all that. Not only is sharing the details of your son's development likely to be a hit with your mother, grandmothers, and aunts, but your questions about your own infancy and early childhood will unearth a mother lode of information and insight that will help you understand your son, yourself, and the parenting practices that shaped your childhood.

What do you stand to gain from collecting stories from those who knew you as an infant and toddler?

• *Insight into your early temperament.* Is your son like you? Is he the kind of sleeper you were? Is he calmer or more irritable?

• *Management strategies.* You can get insider tips on how to manage your baby from techniques that your mother and grandmother remember using with you.

• *A way to connect with your child as an infant.* Dads often drift to the sidelines—or feel sidelined—during the baby days, feeling it will be easier to relate to older children. Learning more about your own beginnings will help you feel connected to your baby.

• *Something practical and positive you can do that everyone will appreciate, including your son.* Whether the conversations unfold over the phone, by e-mail, or around holiday dinners, they provide opportunities for deepening the experience of family and connection (and sometimes setting it straight)—a legacy you want to create for your son.

Beyond conversations, go for the evidence. Gather some pictures and artifacts from your childhood that will connect your early childhood to that of your son. It helps everyone—father, mother, and baby—if they can see him as the newborn heir in a long line of boys and men coming down through the family. Why do I think that is important? Because one of the most common things that happens in the lives of boys is that parents lose confidence in them, even if just momentarily. It helps to have reminders that every man started as a little, vulnerable boy. It will help you trust in your son's current and future development.

learning a lot about how men and women are different. However significant those findings may be in terms of biology, I don't believe that there are too many biological gender differences that, in and of themselves, compel us to give very different parenting advice to the mothers and fathers of baby girls and baby boys.

There are two reasons for that. First of all, the overlap between boys and girls on any trait is considerable. Boys and girls aren't two entirely different populations; whatever their differences, they are more human than they are gendered. They are more the same than they are different.

If you were to take the bell-shaped curve revealing the entire boy capacity for language, with a mentally handicapped boy at one end of the curve and a boy verbal genius at the other, and you were to superimpose that on the bell-shaped curve of girls' language ability, they would be largely overlapping, perhaps by 80 percent. In other words, both boys and girls speak and write, they learn to read, they master all aspects of language. How well they do that is affected by intelligence, by social class, and by the education of their parents. However, it is only out in the tails of the curve, the upper and lower ends, where significant gender differences appear.

So if you choose to talk about the genders as being very different, you will find support for your argument. If you choose to talk about the similarities between them, you will find very strong support for that as well. If you ask the question "Are boys really different from girls or very much like girls?" it is much like the question "Is the glass half empty or half full?" The answer is yes.

The following research is, however, fascinating and provides an illuminating window into the nature of boys.

Boys See the World Differently

Boys are interested in looking at different things than girls are. In a well-known experiment by Jennifer Connellan and Anna Batki, one-day-old babies at the Rosie Maternity Hospital in Cambridge, England, were recruited into an experiment of social perception. The babies were give the choice of looking directly into the face of a woman or a mechanical mobile that the researchers called "the Alien." It had all of the constituent parts of a face, but randomly distributed, so it did not look like a face. It had hanging parts that made it look more mechanical, and it moved. The researchers were not told whether the babies were male or female, but after the videotapes were analyzed and the sex of the babies revealed, researchers found that girls had spent a longer time studying the face, while boys had spent more time gazing at the mobile.

This confirmed earlier work by Svetlana Lutchmaya and Simon Baron-Cohen, who demonstrated that one-year-old girls looked up at their mothers more when they were playing than did boys, and boys preferred a movie of cars to a movie of a face. Leonard Sax concludes that "girls are born pre-wired to be interested in faces while boys are pre-wired to be interested in moving objects," and he believes this derives from the fact that the visual system is organized differently in boys and in girls. According to Sax, when it comes to the visual realm, "every step in each pathway, from the retina to the cerebral cortex, is different in females and males."

As a practical matter, these behavioral differences observable in day-old babies may provide evidence for a biological difference that explains why girls and women look into other people's faces more than men and boys do throughout life, and why adult women read faces better than men do. Differences in the thickness of the retina and the distribution of rods and cones in the eye may also affect the kinds of colors that boys like. After reading Sax's book, one teacher said to me, "For years I have been trying to get boys to use more colors in art class. I've gotten frustrated that they seem to just use black, brown, gray, and blue. Now that I understand that those are biological differences, I'll leave the boys alone and stop forcing them to use yellow and red crayons."

These research findings are controversial and the implications have not been universally accepted by scientists; they do, however, suggest that boys live in a different world, visually speaking.

Boys Don't Hear as Well as Girls

Infant girls hear better than baby boys, especially in the range of the human voice. In a study of 350 infants, Jane Cassidy, a professor at Louisiana State University, found that girls' hearing was substantially more sensitive than that of boys, and this allows them to discriminate speech more accurately. These findings fall in line with other research that shows that premature girls respond positively to music therapy that has no effect on boys, or perhaps the music that was used in these experiments—a Brahms lullaby—is not the right music for boys. This research is provocative because it suggests that the way baby boys hear the world and their parents' voices might shape their experience of being parented. Boys may rely more on cues other than voice. It also suggests a reason why boys don't pick up language quite as quickly.

Boys Don't Learn Language as Quickly or Use It as Effectively as Girls

Considerable research suggests that girls and women, on average, use language better and faster than boys and that these differences start early in life. Girls begin to speak earlier than boys. They are better spellers and readers. Women use longer sentences than men, their grammatical structure and pronunciation tend to be better, and they recall words more easily than men. Are these inborn, biological gender differences? There is evidence that they are because men and women use different parts of the brain for language tasks.

In a noted study by Bennett Shaywitz and his coworkers at Yale, when men and women were given a rhyming discrimination task, half the women showed activation of the Broca's area—an important language center in the brain—in both right and left frontal lobes. Men, by contrast, showed activity only on the left side. This exciting finding suggests that boys and girls may learn language using different areas of their brains. It also fits in with a large body of research showing that men use their brains in an asymmetrical way compared with women. That is, their hemispheres are more specialized and there is less crossover between the left and right hemispheres. Though scientists cannot absolutely prove that these differences are only biological and not the result of cultural training—being raised a boy does affect the structure of your brain, giving you a more "boy" brain—it is likely that they are, because these language differences are seen both early and throughout the life cycle.

DIFFERENCES IN PARENTS' PERCEPTIONS OF BOYS AND GIRLS

As much as we may learn about early childhood development and specifically about very young boys, what really matters to a boy is what we do with it: how the adults in his life perceive him, and how that influences their interactions with him. And the research on *that* suggests that our perceptions of boys—from infancy on up—are often gender-skewed, even when we feel we are being objective and seeing an accurate picture.

A number of experiments over the years have shown that parents perceive boy and girl babies differently and speak about them differently, right from the beginning of life. How could it be otherwise? We all have such powerful internal models of masculinity and femininity bequeathed to us by our culture that we are all going to project our gender expectations onto infants. When people pick up a baby girl they are inclined to say, "Isn't she sweet?" "Isn't she lovely?" and when they first pick up a newborn boy they say, "Isn't he handsome?" "What a big, strong boy."

Karen Adolph, an investigator of infants' locomotor development, asked parents to predict how well their child would do on a set of crawling tasks: would the child be able to crawl down a sloping ramp? Parents of sons were more confident that their child would make it down the ramp than parents of daughters. When Adolph tested the infants on the ramp, there was no difference whatever between the boys and girls, but there was a difference in the parents' predictions.

In another classic gender experiment, researchers found a difference in the way adult onlookers reacted to the crying of boys and girls. In the study, the onlookers allowed babies they believed were boys to cry longer before picking them up, and they comforted boys for a shorter amount of time than they did the babies whom they believed to be girls.

Our tendency to react to children based on our stereotyped perception of gender, rather than upon the needs of a particular child, is worrisome, because it opens us up to the possibility that we will miss the vulnerabilities of boys and underestimate the strength of girls. The most important thing about your baby is not that he is a boy but that you are attuned to who he is and what he needs. That dance of attunement between mother and child and between father and child is the foundation of a healthy personality. It would be terrible if our notions of strength and toughness for boys made us ignore boys' profound dependence in the first years of life.

Whatever new findings researchers turn up—and more come at us every day—it's important to remember that every boy already contains all the answers, every parent is on the cutting edge of research, and the truth about boys that we seek is all right there, unfolding before us, available to us, in the boy we've got. We don't have to wait for science to explain boys in order to be good parents for them.

CHAPTER THREE

BOYS IN MOTION

The Excitement of Being a Toddler: Eighteen Months to Three Years

Most of all, I enjoy getting to know him, which is an unending and constantly unfolding process, day to day, moment to moment—sometimes eating ice cream together, sometimes playing by ourselves in the same room, and sometimes snuggling together while we nap.
—Father of a two-and-a-half-year-old

I WAS WAITING INSIDE A HOTEL FOR AN AIRPORT SHUTTLE EARLY ONE morning—5:30 A.M., to be exact—and found myself standing with a group of sleepy adults watching a little drama between a mother and her handsome little boy, who was dressed in the height of toddler fashion: blue jeans with at least six pockets up and down the legs, a rugged gray sweatshirt, and a pacifier on a cord around his neck. He looked to be about twenty-two months old. I couldn't ask his exact age because his family spoke a language I didn't understand or even recognize, but I could read the boy's sturdy, confident gait; I could read his body English.

Julian in the Park

It was a sunny afternoon and I was sitting in the park with Kaylie and her son, Julian, age nineteen months, who was sitting on her lap. "This is Julian," she said. "He's a wanderer." By contrast, she noted, her three-year-old daughter wouldn't leave her side. "I don't know if that's a temperament difference or a gender difference. He'll go down the street and take a left or right."

Julian played around us briefly, then wandered away and headed down the path, stopping to stare at sights. He got forty feet away before he turned around to check on his mom. Then he played a kicking game with his feet. He kicked first with one foot and then with the other.

"He got his little hug at the beginning and now he's all set," his mother explained. He hopped on one foot and then both. "Are you doing the bunny hop?" she asked him. I asked her what she thought her job is. "I'm not a big chaser," she said. Julian started up a set of wooden stairs leading to the playground but turned around to watch his mother's reaction. He stopped, waiting for a sign from her that would tell him he could go up and out of her sight. She obliged and noted, "Julian wants to try everything out and figure out how it works for him."

He was out of sight briefly, but Kaylie saw that another mother she knew was keeping an eye on him as he ventured forth. In a minute or two he walked the forty feet back to Kaylie, sat on the bench next to her, and then almost immediately got up. "Waway," he said. He walked away again, explored a little farther, then returned. She watched him the entire time without getting up to follow him.

His attention was caught by a small Nerf football in the grass. He retrieved it and returned to his mom, handing it to her, then taking it back. "It's wet," he said. Then he walked away, turned around, and threw it at his mom. They threw the wet football back and forth for a while. She tired of the game before he did; she spotted his untied shoe and asked to tie the lace. He came over and allowed himself to be lifted into her lap, and she tied the shoe.

Kaylie wondered if she puts "less pressure" on Julian than she does her daughter, and whether she might have "less expectations for a male than I do for a female." What I saw is that she trusts her son; she has confidence in the relationship between them and feels comfortable watching from nearby and letting him explore the world on his own terms. She is his secure base, his emotional gas station to which he returns for refueling.

He had discovered that he could trigger the electric eye that would open the first set of huge glass doors, and that if he ran through them, he could set off a second electric eye, opening another set of doors, allowing him to run out onto the dark curb and toward the street. His sleepy, distracted mother was repeatedly surprised by his charges through the doors. She would jump to attention as the first set slid open and he rushed through, just in time to catch sight of him as he triggered the second set, which sent her chasing after him, grabbing his hand just as he reached the curb. Then she would walk him back through the doors and into the lobby, where she would speak to him in a serious voice, as if impressing upon him the dangers of the street and the need to stay in the lobby. I never heard him say a word in reply.

> I love how excited he is about things. I love reading to him and feeling his sweet, soft little hand on top of mine. And I love watching him figure things out patiently, tenaciously.
> —Mother of three-year-old boy

Following this talking-to, she would hold on to his hand firmly for about thirty seconds, slowly loosening her grasp to allow him some freedom to play nearby. He complied, beginning by making sweeping circles around posts in the lobby, glancing up occasionally to look at his mother. He seemed to sense the moment she relaxed her vigilance, seizing the opportunity to make a dash for the door once again. This happened four times in about twelve minutes, and though his mother seemed to grow a bit more exasperated with each headlong charge, she was never punitive. Indeed, she seemed resigned to this game. She must have known that once he had discovered his magical powers, once he understood that those doors were just going to open for him—abracadabra!—there was no stopping him.

As soon as your son can walk and run confidently, typically at about eighteen months, he is on the move. He is so excited about his new abilities, not just walking but climbing and running, that you have to keep your eye on him almost constantly. Linda described turning her back for several minutes only to turn around and find her son, Daniel, standing up on the stove! He had, in the wink of an eye, pushed a chair over and clambered up onto the cooking surface. Luckily, none of the burners was on, but this maneuver required his parents to be more strategic.

"Climbing has been the big change in our lives," she said. "We have gates all over our house. I feel as if Daniel sits and plots for a long time and then goes

BRAINS AND BUCKS, DOLLARS AND SENSE:
DO-IT-YOURSELF DEVELOPMENTAL TOYS

New brain research offers many intriguing clues about the way the brain functions, learns, and grows in early childhood. What also has become clear is that parents who want to support their child's healthy development have become the target market for a massive industry selling toys, games, and other materials advertised specifically as developmental boosters.

What you need to know is that a mud hole in your backyard, a squeaky old door hinge, cooking together, or taking a walk around the block offers many of the same development-enhancing qualities touted by pricey commercial toys (engaging the mind and the senses), and some added benefits—learning to be creative with time, situations, and everyday objects, for instance—that those toys can't provide.

Parents of grown-up boys—young men who have found success in their work and lives—share these tips regarding the kind of activities, play, and playthings that shaped their sons' childhoods (and their brains) from the earliest years, forward:

• Cooking, cleaning, and general housework and yard work (household repairs when they were older) *with* a parent

• Backyard play—kicking, throwing and catching balls; jumping games. Walks in the neighborhood, parks, or on errands

• Simple board games, puzzles, building blocks

• Books (read aloud, read alone, and audio for car time)

• Music and musical instruments; singing

• Family meals and conversation, bedtime chats, prayers

• Neighborhood events, volunteer work, or church or synagogue activities

• Caring for and playing with pets

and executes his plan. He always wants to move and go and be somewhere that he is not."

He is also expressing himself in powerful new ways, she said. The intense tantrums started at eighteen months. "He wants to walk everywhere, but never in the direction I want to go. When I pick him up he arches his back and screams and tries to hit my face." Are Daniel's attempts to hit his mother a part of every day? No, such outbursts didn't happen during the months of June, July, and August, when she was on vacation from her job as a teacher. She and Daniel had sweet times in the park when she could let him go his own way and she would just follow him. Then September arrived and so did his occasional tantrums. His outbursts coincided with her return to work and "the pace of our lives quickening," she said.

At this age, your son isn't sympathetic to your schedule. He's got his own work to do, his own agenda, and right now it's all about action. Remember how pleased you were when he reached those first developmental milestones? Remember the happy fuss you made when he took his first step? Held his own spoon? Said his first word? Well, now his psychology is dominated by his desire to use his new muscular equipment.

Eighteen-to-twenty-one-month-old children are, in the words of noted child developmental psychologist Louise Bates Ames and her colleagues, "unbelievably egocentric." Unrestrained childhood aggression also peaks at around two years, both in boys and in girls. While there are lovely, sunny periods in every boy's day, and variation in the degree of self-absorption of little boys between the ages of eighteen months and three years, the primary developmental drive in this period is toward independence and autonomy: Erik Erikson declared it to be the second stage of life and said it was characterized by "the will to be oneself." A child of twenty-four months may know very well that his mother wants him to do one thing, but he will look right at her and do something else. Why? Because he is physically capable of independent action and because he is rapidly developing a sense of himself as separate from others and their wishes.

The declaration of autonomy in childhood is a psychological revolution that gains speed as a baby approaches toddlerhood. Though there is no single point when he turns a cor-

> *I have no idea what normal development would be like, but he seems normal. Seems bright. And that makes me happy. —Father of a boy, two and a half years old*

The Eight Lines of Development

The Developmental Story Advances

An urban legend in parenting, one for which I've found no basis in fact or research, goes like this: Some developmental researchers hired a professional athlete to follow a toddler around and mimic exactly every physical movement that the toddler made. According to the legend, after two or three hours of trying to keep up with a toddler, the athlete was exhausted, but the toddler kept on going. Even as fiction, every parent recognizes the truth in it. Let's take a closer look at this moving target of toddlerhood.

Physical Development

Boys of this age are constantly moving. In the months after they turn one, they start losing their baby fat, slim down, and start to look like a young child. By eighteen months they walk unaided and are working on their balance. They walk up and down stairs alone (though not alternating feet yet) and soon they are running stiffly. They can turn corners and jump in place and, of course, climb up—but not down.

Two-year-old boys love to roughhouse. Nothing pleases a boy more than being able to jump on his father and wrestle with him. Often this is the activity that makes a father feel closest to his boys. Boys start to jump into their father's arms from the stairway; they love to be thrown high in the air. (When moms express unease about this, I suggest that they not watch!) Boys also love to run and throw themselves right at their moms. They want to be picked up, lifted up, and swung around. They can ride a tricycle and use a swing; early twos need help with the pedals and a push on the swing, but by three they can begin to pedal and pump with their legs.

Along with all of these achievements of gross motor control comes that one special achievement most welcomed by parents: successful bowel and bladder training. Most American preschools require that a child be toilet-trained by two years nine months, and boys are certainly capable of it, if you can get them to focus on it. All of the child-rearing guides recommend that you not become engaged in a power struggle with your child over toilet training, and I agree; such struggles can be very psychologically destructive. However, it is important to model, to request, to reward, and to challenge your son to learn to use the potty and then the toilet. There is a tendency to believe that you should wait longer to toilet-train boys than girls, but there is a problem, too, in not asking anything of your son. (See more on toilet training in the sidebar on pages 84–85.)

By three years of age your son can coordinate his arms and legs. He can kick, throw, and catch a ball. He is able to eat and drink independently and can even put on simple clothes, such as pants and a shirt that's not too tight. Your son is a pretty coordinated guy by the time he is three. Soon he will be using crayons with a correct grip!

Attachment

Attachment is discussed in some detail throughout this chapter. In the context of your son's overall development through this period, know that once an infant has a strong secure bond to his mother, father, and perhaps one or two other caretakers, he is well grounded. This is the secure base from which he now begins to explore the world, but he will also need to return to base for emotional refueling. Any stressor, such as illness or the birth of a younger sibling, is likely to produce clinging, crying, and constant monitoring of you. At times he may seem profoundly uninterested in you. At other times he will pad around the house after you, wanting to do every little activity with you. He may enjoy having his own set of dishes, pans, and implements to "help" you make dinner.

The toughest time may be when you want to go out in the evening. At two and a half, many children experience ferocious fears of separation and will display violent emotions and anger—even throwing up—in an effort to keep you home. These can be difficult to manage, particularly when you are trying to get somewhere. The best cure is a familiar babysitter with whom you can leave your son, crying pitifully with his arms waving helplessly, as you walk out. It is that same babysitter who will reassure you over the cell phone that he settled down happily moments after your departure.

Social Development

Friendship is important to two-year-old boys; they are just not very good at it. They are magnetically drawn to other children, both boys and girls (gender segregation comes later): they like the company, and being with other children fosters both language development and the development of problem-solving skills. However, true friendship requires the ability to empathize and to take turns. Two-year-olds are just beginning to develop the capacity for empathy, and they do not understand reciprocity.

When a two-year-old smacks another child, most of the time he does not really understand that he has hurt someone, and even if he does, he feels completely overwhelmed and aggrieved when someone hits him back. A boy may unthinkingly walk right over—stepping on top of—another child crouched low over her own toys in the sandbox; he may knock a friend down in the excitement of a hug, again unintentionally; and, of course, when he's really frustrated he may hit or bite someone. And this happens between *friends*!

Obviously, friendship among two-year-olds requires adult supervision. For starters, a group of two-year-olds will tend to wander away from each other when they're in a group, feeling the security of others and having no sense of danger. They also require adults to anticipate trouble and move in to separate them when necessary or divert them. If you provide both the boundaries and the supervision (and the diversionary tactics when needed), boys will develop close and affectionate relationships. They will greet each other, smiling and hugging, and then they will settle down for a good session of "parallel play"—that is, individual play in close proximity to one another. If you do all those things and keep them from killing each other, by the time a boy is three he will really value his close friends, refer to a few by name, and be eager to see them and miss them when they're not around.

By age three, your son will know how to share and he will be able to play with boys in a group, and that's when he and his friends will start to prefer to play with just boys. You may be quite invested in seeing your son play with girls, believing it guarantees that he will grow up to be a sensitive man with a healthy attitude toward women. He may do so with or without girls among his close friends in preschool. Meanwhile, don't get too attached to the idea of gender-balanced play. It doesn't last. Your son will spend a lifetime developing a strategy—and the emotional interface necessary—for a healthy relational style with girls and women. A preference for male playmates at this age is a normal, healthy piece of identity development and part of that progression.

The important thing to appreciate about the play of two-year-olds is that the "social contract" between a boy and another child—the terms and conditions of play in any given moment—is short indeed and has the potential to end explosively. The conflict that may erupt does not mean that the two children are not friends; they will be again in a couple of minutes, or tomorrow.

Cognitive Development

All children are scientists, in the sense that they are dedicated problem solvers. Between two and three, you can see that scientist actually conducting experiments in his mind. Where a four-month-old grabs something and puts it into his mouth and the twelve-month-old still has to handle things to understand them, an eighteen-month-old boy can group similar objects. Instead of trying to jam pieces into a puzzle, you can see a child of two and a half study the piece, observe the size of the opening, and make a match in his mind.

This ability to mentally experiment—to imagine the relationships between things—is also seen in play. Children now begin to engage in pretend play. When playing with a toy firehouse, for example, a boy will tell a story to go along with it and later find a plastic fire hat—as Tyler does later in this chapter—to wear while playing, just to complete the fantasy. He will make two toy dinosaurs fight over a cup that he pretends is the dinosaur's food. Children this age also understand that people are different from physical objects in the world. They know that people think and have intentions and feelings. What makes children this age different from adults is how much of their thinking is still magical. They can be certain there is a huge dragon under their bed, and just as easily be calmed when Mom waves a hand and "casts a spell" that keeps dragons away. Though they have observed the physical laws of the universe, they don't always believe that the laws apply to them. As scientists, their education isn't yet complete.

Academic Development

There are lots of colors in this world and lots of things to count. There are books to read and stories to be enjoyed. There are games to be played. Why would you turn all that fun into preparation for school? Enjoy counting, naming, coloring, reading, and playing fantasy games with your child. He is curious to know about anything you do. Cook with him, clean with him, walk in the park with him and identify trees and flowers and birds and animals. His vocabulary is increasing from twenty words to hundreds of words in this period. That natural pace of learning is something your son enjoys; it shouldn't be made into a chore. Teach him things every day, but please don't make it too serious. And don't use the television as a tutor (or babysitter) for your child. Research has found that stimulating TV for children under three years of age can lead to problems paying attention, restlessness, and difficulty concentrating in later years.

Emotional Self-Regulation

Learning to manage your feelings is one of the significant achievements of early childhood, and a three-year-old boy is much better at managing his moods than a two-year-old boy because he's had a lot more practice. He needs to master his fears of separation by surviving being apart from his mom for periods of time in the care of good people. He needs to master his fears by exploring the world and hearing your words of reassurance about bathtub drains, the dark, wild animals, and vacuum cleaners. He needs to master his frustration by living through it and seeing that his tantrums do not bring you to your knees.

Little boys who are frightened look into our faces to assess how realistic the threat is. What they need to see is your calm and confidence. It is hard on a boy when his mother or father is impatient with his fear. Not only does he not get reassurance, but he sees the disapproval. It matters to a two-year-old to be seen as "good" by his parents. He will be upset if he feels he has failed.

Moral and Spiritual Development

A two-year-old says "no" a lot, but he also says "I love you" and he is fundamentally a loving person. He is also trying to be a moral person. You can hear it when he says "no" to himself, to stop himself from doing something forbidden. When you see that, you are watching the beginning of internalization. You can see every aspect of a child's soul and spirituality in relation to his stuffed animals: his love, caring, and tenderness. The feelings he displays toward his teddy bear he will later display toward his best friends, his wife, and his God. He's practicing his spiritual development with a bear. Remember to keep your moral standards as those to which to aspire, not strict rules. "We don't hit in our family" doesn't really mean you won't see hitting. It means that you won't see hitting that is ignored; it will always be addressed with a reminder of the aspiration.

Identity

The fundamental achievement of this period is the discovery and assertion of the self. A boy knows who he is through saying what he wants and what he doesn't want. The "no" is an expression of identity; all boys use it, but "yes" is equally powerful as an assertion of interest.

Between ages two and three a boy learns that he is a boy and declares it proudly. He calls women "ladies" or "mommies" and he calls men "men," and though if shown a picture he knows the difference between boys and girls based on the clothes they wear, he may not be able to identify whether or child is male or female by the genitals. That part isn't so clear to him yet. Yet he certainly can identify them by what they do. When shown pictures of people doing tasks like driving trucks or taking care of babies, he'll always put them in the sexual stereotyped categories. He only wants to do boy things, and though he imitates both his mother and father, as he approaches three years of age he is likely to articulate his identification with his father.

ner and starts to demand independence and declare that he is his own self, eighteen months is the traditional beginning of that new phase, because a child this age is physically capable of running away from his parents—and knows it— and he begins to use language to demand things he wants. Dealing with this new "independent" child requires something very different from parents.

TYLER: WILLFUL AND DETERMINED

I watched Tyler in his day care center when he was twenty-one months old. His day care companion, a fifteen-month-old girl named Cindy, walked right between Tyler and the day care teacher and stood there, apparently oblivious to him. Whether she meant to or not, she was occupying the limelight. He kicked her twice in the leg. She didn't collapse or protest strongly—indeed, she only looked uncomfortable—but the teacher immediately remonstrated with him: "Don't kick Cindy, Tyler! It's not nice to kick people." Before the words were fully out of her mouth, he had kicked her again, just for good measure. You could see that he did so because he knew he was going to lose this debate with an adult sooner or later. In the meantime, he just wanted to register that he was an independent actor. He kicked because he could kick. It was a demonstration of will, pure and simple.

After being scolded a second time, Tyler walked away as if the matter were settled, but he quickly circled behind Cindy with three sets of adult eyes on him and kicked her very gently two more times in slow motion—almost a mime kick. Here was a demonstration of both willfulness and self-control. It was hard not to smile. At the same time, I could see that his mother and his day care teacher were concerned: *What if he continues to kick people? That wouldn't be good.*

Remember that an infant younger than a year cannot consistently experience himself as separate from his mother because he needs her so much and because she interprets his needs, his moods, and his yearnings for him. She is constantly mirroring what he wants, reflecting back his excitement for him, empathizing with and attending to his pain. He has biologically predetermined jumps in physical independence, such as crawling at seven months and walking at a year, but as a psychological matter he is too helpless and needy to express more than brief moments of anger and independence. Even after he starts to walk, he needs someone nearby to hold his hand so he doesn't fall, and his mother is almost always there, watching him, holding her hands out to him, picking him up and dusting him off. He and she together have created a partnership so intimate that they are almost one person, the two of them. However, at some point, that intimate partnership begins to separate slowly, and sometimes painfully, into two individuals, because he now begins to interpret and articulate his moods and needs for himself, often with the use of the word *no*.

Traditionally, this stage has been called the terrible twos, a time when children discover their own (negative) power. Most parents bracing them-

> *He's quite defiant and I'm not sure if or how that will develop as he gets older. He is not concerned with our so-called consequences of bad behavior.*
> —Mother of a two-and-a-half-year-old son

selves for this allegedly terrible period are surprised to find their children are rather sweet and loving at twenty-four months. Eighteen to twenty-one months can be tough, of course, because children are so impulsive and determined to go their own way, but parents feel mostly okay about it because it has a new and experimental feel on the child's part. The oppositionality, aggression, and anger that emerge again at two and a half seem more deliberate, willful, and "in your face." And it is all played out on you, the parent. No day care teacher or babysitter seems to get the same intense reactions from a child, especially the unhappy feelings, that parents do, particularly mothers.

How you react to the high activity level and autonomy strivings of your little boy matters a lot. Parents often get angrier at little boys than they do at little girls. Abuse statistics confirm that boys are at greater risk of being abused and even killed by their parents than are girls. Why is that? What is it about boys that triggers a different reaction from parents and caregivers?

MANAGING BOY ACTIVITY AND ASSERTION

Boys have higher activity levels than girls, they lag behind girls in language development, they become more easily frustrated (largely because they lack early language), and because they are so focused on their play and do not check with adults as much as girls do, they do not appear to care as much about the reaction of adults. All of this can be frustrating for parents. Little boys, on average, seem to show more flashes of temper than little girls do and provoke angrier reactions from parents in return. There are going to be many potential flash points in the life of a toddler boy.

In early infancy, level of activity is determined more by individual temperament than by gender. However, from as early as ten months, some gender trends are visible: boys, on average, tend to be less compliant than girls. This small discrepancy between the genders seems to increase between the ages of one and two, and it will grow until school age, when a majority of boys are more active, regardless of temperament, than any girls. This is not true of *every* boy and *every* girl. You may have a very calm and even-tempered boy, and there are, of course, many hard-charging girls, but on average, boys are more oppositional with adults than girls at this age. Boys in groups have more quarrels, they have more difficulties adjusting to situations, they express more tension, and they engage in more biting, thumb sucking, and masturbating. They appear more intense and focused on *what they want*. This singular focus of boys requires parents to move from simply responding to their needs to managing their activity levels.

RUSTY: ALL ACTION

When I visited Rusty, his mother, and his grandmother in his nana's downstairs rec room, he was all smiles. A strong, sturdy boy of twenty-three months, he spends most weekdays at his grandmother's house while his mother works, but this was a summer weekend, and he had the attention of his mother, grandmother, and a visitor. He immediately grabbed a large green exercise ball and started to pound on it, saying, "Huh, huh, huh," in rhythm with his pounding. After a while, he left the ball and began "dancing" (as his grandmother calls it) in a powerful jumping-up-and-down motion that clearly delighted him. He kept it up for more than a full minute until he flung his feet forward and landed on his bottom, cushioned by his diaper and the rec room rug. He repeated the whole dancing sequence while two adoring women watched him . . . and set limits for him.

At any moment, Rusty's activity level could suddenly become a problem. He ran up to the lighted screen of my laptop computer, full of curiosity; his fingers practically itched to touch it. He stopped suddenly and said, "Don tah," which clearly meant "Don't touch." His mother explained that "don tah" was Rusty's name for all computers, because he had heard that phrase so often when he tried to touch them. On two occasions, again fascinated and full of temptation, he approached the computer again, only to repeat, "Don tah." The fact that he had the language to express the thought meant that he was beginning to be able to control his own impulses by using words to remind himself of what he should do. However, a little while later, he threw a tennis ball—and I mean really winged it—from across the room with such force that it hit the computer screen. (The screen was not damaged.)

Rusty's throw reminds us that a boy this age is strong enough and sometimes accurate enough to do some significant damage. A toddler does not have the capacity to understand the relationship between cause and effect. Because he can't foresee the consequences of his actions and he is so impulsive, he could break something that is important to an adult, or he could stick his hand into a barbecue grill or a pot of hot water. Parents have to protect boys constantly from their own capacity to cause mayhem. They have to try to anticipate everything, both to save the glassware and china and to protect the goodwill and good mood between a boy and his parents.

Rusty's grandmother, Pam, was doing an admirable job on that score. Everything in the cellar rec room that could be broken had been removed or was placed up high and inaccessible. Rusty had easy access only to the carpeted floor, the couch, and several plastic bins of toys. The situation was not perfect because with his strong throwing arm he was still capable of hitting something breakable on a high shelf, though under the preemptive guidance of his mother and grandmother he was protected from his own destructiveness. The design of the room and the anticipation of his mother and grandmother had limited his ability to break something and potentially infuriate them.

The concern is that our perceptions and preconceptions of boys may color our understanding of their intentions and lead parents to see them as defiant and deliberate in their destructiveness when they are not intending to be. Of course, they can get angry and they can be destructive. Like Daniel, they can try to hit their mothers in the face, and they do kick their little friends in day care, even when adults are watching. I had friends who called their sweet little toddler "the Terminator" because he was so physically quick and his impact on the house was so destructive. In my PBS documentary *Raising Cain*, we captured a spectacular scene in a day care center of two little boys throwing blocks over a wall at two other boys. The blocks were flying in both directions and the boys were shouting and laughing their heads off. It was only a matter of time before a child was hurt by a falling block. However, the intention was not to hurt the others. The fun was in throwing the blocks.

But children in day care also punch, scratch, and hit each other. Not every day, but sometimes. Richard Tremblay, a Canadian researcher, writes that uninhibited human aggression peaks at two years old and is slowly and gradually brought under control in the years after that. That is to say, human beings are readier to hit and attack each other when they are two than at any other point in the life cycle. Thank goodness that two-year-olds aren't six feet tall and 180 pounds!

Let me repeat: boys between eighteen months and three years do not understand much about cause and effect. They cannot foresee the consequences of their actions. They can, however, express their independence, whims, neediness, frustration, and magical thinking. When they grab for things, throw things, disobey us, or, worst of all, look right at us and still kick someone else, they do so because they haven't yet developed the ability to resist their sudden impulses. Most of the time, however, they are simply being active and exploring.

> We've had a couple of close calls with cars, complicated by his natural independence and our desire to foster it. There's just no question that he's going to be one of those boys you're at the emergency room a lot with.
>
> —Mother of a two-and-a-half-year-old son

At other times, of course, a boy's actions are motivated by frustration and real fury. They become angry or greedy simply because they are overwhelmed with angry, greedy feelings. At those moments, any parent can feel her own anger rise in response. Mothers write:

> I find it hard when he does not get his own way and he gets extremely angry with me, sometimes to the point of pinching me really hard and screaming. My immediate reaction is to shout or pinch back, and I sometimes have to remove myself briefly from the situation to stop this from happening.

> When my boys cry, I want to encourage them to express their emotions. However, I do not want to create a monster that flies off the handle because "that's just the way he expresses himself." So I struggle constantly to find the balance between self-expression and a brat.

Dads, who may empathize as former boys, can find this behavior equally exasperating:

> Much of my frustration seems to be around irritating but developmentally appropriate issues—impulse control, fine motor development, insatiable curiosity, and screaming and yelling, particularly when the event is insignificant or unimportant in my eyes. On occasion I have a difficult time appreciating his perspective—that a flip-flop falling off his foot really is upsetting.

> Most challenging? Handling his angry outbursts, which is to say that I have a difficult time handling my reactions to his angry outbursts.

GENDER DIFFERENCES AND PENIS PLAY

Beyond obvious sexual characteristics, the physical differences between girls and boys become more apparent during the toddler years. Boys have more muscle and bone than do girls, they tend to be about two pounds heavier on average, and they are just beginning to show the higher activity levels that will distinguish them from girls. However, temperament still dominates in small children, so whether your child is outgoing or shy, fearful or fearless may be more important in defining his or her behavior than whether she is a girl or he is a boy. All of that will change once he becomes a regular member of a boys' group between ages three and four.

Boys discover their penises when they are babies and often touch or tug them. Thirty-six percent of one-year-olds were reported by their mothers to play with their genitals, and the incidence was higher among boys than girls. Prior to two, however, finding and playing with the penis is often a hit-or-miss affair; perhaps because of the diaper a boy may not have access to his own penis. But starting at two he becomes very interested in his own genitals and curious about the genitals of others, both boys and girls. That curiosity is normal.

Holding their penises in an anxious way is a common habit for boys. Though most people—even psychologists—scoff at Freud's ideas, it is still the case that a boy's first theory about the difference between boys and girls is very much what Freud described, namely, a castration theory. Once he has seen a girl's body, a boy is likely to believe that a girl had a penis like him and lost it somehow—maybe someone cut it off—and that tends to worry him. Also, he finds it comforting and pleasurable to hold on to his own penis. Mothers report that more than half of children engage in some exploration of their own genitals or those of other children during the preschool years. Sex researchers believe that the actual number is probably a good deal higher than that; some mothers are worried or self-conscious about their child's touching himself and reluctant to report it to researchers.

It is the job of parents to understand that little boys do not know any better; they cannot choose to restrain their anger. They need discipline, but never retaliation. Too often, physical punishment of small children comes out of retaliatory impulses in us. The term "terrible twos" can remind us that this is just a phase, that it is not unique to any one child, that it arrives on a developmental schedule and will depart for the same reason. It is crucial that we see this stage as a developmental bridge to important adult qualities. As one father said, "I see him as similar to me. Strong-willed, but also an observer." Your son needs you to have some courage and challenge him; he needs you to support his real independence. And true independence for a child is getting rid of the diaper, taking some risks, saying no, getting some time-outs, and coming back strong. One mother wrote to me, "I guess the time-outs aren't working. Now he looks at me, does something wrong, and puts himself in a time-out." Well, I think that's terrific. He's the criminal, he's the judge, he's the jury—and he's the comedian! In the old days people called that a boy with "spirit."

One father told me that he was relieved that his son was openly expressive at this point, "that he is willing to scream when he really is angry. I never did that as a child, or at least at some point I stopped out of fear."

It won't be long before these young boys will, as a developmental matter, be able to control their impulses better than they can in toddlerhood. They will do so because they love us and they have repeated experiences with their parents restraining them, holding them, picking them up, reminding them, and scolding them. All parents need to provide such limits and boundaries for their two-year-olds.

It is important for us to understand that though their feelings are often very strong indeed, their intentions are not evil or cruel. Toddler boys are just experimenting with their independence or they are momentarily angry and impulsive. "Stop," "No," "Don't do that," or the diversionary "Oh! Look at this!" are better words to use with our toddlers than "you're a bad boy." There is no such thing as a "bad boy" between eighteen months and three years. There is only a toddler trying out his will to be himself.

ATTACHMENT: THE SECOND ACT

I have been describing a hard-charging, mobile boy full of impulses. What happened to the close, intimate, rarely-out-of-sight relationship that a boy had with his mother, his father, and perhaps some third caretaker in the first eighteen months of life? The highly attuned responsiveness of mother to child is now replaced by a coming-and-going partnership. A child can tolerate longer separations. The intense feelings of love and reciprocity are still there, of course; they just take some different forms. One mother wrote, "I love it when I have been out for a few hours and on returning we are both so excited to see each other. He runs to me saying, 'Hugs, cuddles, and kiss.' I melt every time."

The differences between what a twelve-month-old child needs by way of reunion with his mother and what an eighteen-month-old boy needs are dramatic. Alan Sroufe, the respected attachment researcher from the University of

Minnesota, said, "If you think about it . . . eighteen-month-old babies are more like you and me than they are like twelve-month-old babies." He describes how a year-old baby after a separation of even a couple of minutes wants to be held for some time when his mother returns. He crawls to her, he cries, he climbs up on her legs, and when at last he is in her arms, he "hugs in and holds on." An eighteen-month-old boy, by contrast, wants to be picked up briefly. Soon he is wiggling out of his mother's arms and sliding down her body to put his feet on the floor.

Toddler boys just need to know they can touch base with their moms, dads, and other caretakers when they need to. After a moment, they want to climb down to resume playing. Their play may include their moms, but it is more often now in a symbolic way—for example, pouring pretend juice for her. What is important to note is that the invitation to the mother now comes from the child. Rusty would play with his trucks alone, almost oblivious to his mother Leah's presence, and then he would include her by zipping a truck over to her. "Rhumm, rhumm," he would say, and then let fly with a car to Leah. She would receive it, turn it around, and send it back. They might do this several times, and then he would continue playing as if she were not there. He was in charge of the play.

We know from research that boys tend to check less with their mothers when they are playing. When girls are playing near their mothers, they make more eye contact and solicit more approval than do boys. Does that mean that boys have less need for their mothers than girls do? Absolutely not. They still need their mothers or caregivers close by. After all, they are little and there is much that they cannot do yet. But they no longer require the constant interaction with adults. They are becoming more interested in solving problems on their own, and they need to experience themselves as being on their own to do so.

At one point when I was observing Tyler at day care, I saw that the plastic fire hat he had left on the table had fallen off and was wedged in a hard-to-reach space between the back of the table and the wall. Any strategy for recovering the hat was going to be awkward, but Tyler chose absolutely the hardest way to go. He stretched and wriggled across the bench seat toward the small opening between the seat and the surface of the table, where he clearly expected to be able to reach down, grab the hat, and pull it up. But the moment he grabbed for the hat, he lost his balance, and he found himself dangling at an awkward angle, unable to go forward or backward. All three adults who were watching him wanted to make suggestions. You could see both his mother's hands and his day care teacher's hands fluttering, as if they wanted to show him how best to approach the problem. But he did not ask for their advice, and if he perceived that they wanted to help him, he didn't take it into account. He was going to solve the problem in his own awkward way.

Toddlers often want their mothers to participate in their play, they want them to appreciate everything they do, and at the same time they want their independence. They may make frequent trips to you, bringing you their toys and piling them in your lap, and then suddenly run away, trusting that you'll keep them from going too far. At the beginning of this chapter I described a boy running through the automatic doors of a hotel. That was exactly what he was doing: exercising his independence and reassuring himself that his mother was paying attention and would keep him safe. It can be a maddening combination, but it is the age-appropriate way for a child to show his attachment needs.

One researcher wrote that caretakers need to be a "supportive presence" during this period. That's easier said than done. You are constantly shifting between being interactive with your child and standing back and supporting him from a distance. The normal, securely attached boy is gripped by a constantly changing wish to push his mother away, cling to her, and then push her away again. The intensity and mood shifts can be exhausting for both child and parent.

Some mothers become overwhelmed with a child's demands and start to withdraw. This makes a toddler wild with neediness; he may become babyish or begin to have a tantrum. It is his only way of telling you that he needs you to be more involved. Other mothers cannot stand to be pushed away and close in on their son, not allowing them to separate. A father often responds to these rapid fluctuations with anger, as if his son had challenged him. What happens when parents cannot meet the attachment and independence needs of their child in the way he needs them met?

DARRYL: A PASSIVE BOY

The director of a preschool consulted me once about a boy, two years eight months old, whom she apologetically described as a "Baby Huey." "He's overweight and immature and completely passive," she told me. "He can't relate to his peers at all. He doesn't seem to know what to do with them." She also said that he sat with his legs splayed out in a W formation, with the legs out to the

TOILET TRAINING: NATURE IS ON YOUR SIDE

"One day I came home and found someone had peed his name on the side of the garage," the mother of three adolescent sons wrote to me. "I asked him, 'Did you pee on the side of the garage?' Of course he denied it. I said, 'Why would your brother pee your name? Next time you pee on a wall, don't sign your name.'"

Since I have known boys who would have peed their brother's name on the side of a garage to get him in trouble, I'm not so sure how this mother knew which of her sons was the culprit. But it doesn't matter. I mention her story for two reasons.

First, because it illustrates the casual pleasures of peeing that boys find so entertaining. This distinctly male art form ranges from "crossing swords"—two or more boys bringing their streams together in just such a way—to assorted styles of target practice or writing their names in unorthodox places (one realm in which boys' writing skills surpass girls' at an early age). The term "pissing match," generally used as a metaphor to describe a pointless contest between two opponents simply attempting to outdo each other, derives from the authentic version that is precisely what the words suggest: a contest in which boys see who can urinate the farthest and the longest. If you don't see the fun in this, you clearly are not a boy and never were one.

My second reason for sharing this mother's note with you here is that her tone conveys a certain good-humored pragmatism I admire and recommend.

If you are the mother of a boy who is not yet toilet-trained, you may be stressing out over this, and I want to encourage you not to do that—for your sake, but especially for his. Be assured that it is a rare little boy of two or three years of age who will resist toilet training because he prefers to pee in a baby diaper and wear that cold, soggy mess, when instead he could be doing target practice into the toilet bowl and earning praise and M&Ms from you. Nature is on your side in this regard. Every boy wants to be manly, and baby diapers are one of the first things to go.

You can trust development as an ally in your efforts to toilet-train your son. Not only will your son naturally come to want to take control of his bladder and bowel movements somewhere in the neighborhood of ages two to four, but you can use boys' natural physicality and kinesthetic (action-oriented) learning style to engage their interest and boost their success. For a boy, toilet training is hands-on learning at its best. And even the most wildly active boy can sit still long enough to take care of business. So relax.

How do you tell if your son is developmentally ready to take charge? Most are ready to start toilet training between ages two and three, and you'll know it because they'll start to want to imitate what a parent or older brother does. A few boys may be in their fourth year before they're ready to start. Boys tend to start later and take longer than girls, so don't use his sister's or another girl's experience as a guide. Some cues:

• He is staying dry for several hours between diaper changes. This means his bladder and bowels have developed sufficiently to be up to the task.

• He's showing an interest in staying dry and clean. He may complain about a wet or soiled diaper, or even announce it's time for a diaper change.

• He likes the looks of those Spider-Man briefs you've brought home. Think incentives!

The step-by-step technique you choose will depend on personal preferences—whatever seems the most promising fit for your son, you, and your setting. You can obtain detailed instructions from conventional sources, including friends, your child's pediatrician, and the Internet. The key thing is to ask something of your son when you see the signs that he is ready and able—children do like to be challenged in their development—without getting into a power struggle with him.

Whatever approach you choose, it can take several months for any child to master the practice. Try not to pressure him. Be supportive, generous with praise and rewards, patient with accidents, and never, ever critical or demeaning. Try tailoring your efforts to appeal to the developmental strengths of little boys. Some boy-friendly strategies:

• Boys prefer action over talk. Explain the concept, but keep it simple and short. I've seen boys tug their mothers toward the bathroom faster than they could find the words to say they needed to go. The point is to give your son a way to communicate his need, not to require that he necessarily master the language first. The urgency of the moment may make that difficult.

• Boys look to emulate other boys and men. Accompanying his older brother or dad into the bathroom or men's room will give him the idea more effectively than discussions about it.

• Boys like bathroom humor and goofy picture books such as *Everyone Poops* and *The Gas We Pass: The Story of Farts*. There are other excellent children's books that make the case for using the toilet in language and imagery that boys love.

• Give him some time to play at home without pants or diaper and with a potty nearby. Encourage him to sit on it. The floor might get wet, but the more time he spends out of diapers, the faster he will learn.

• Make it fun. Mothers have told me about putting a few Cheerios in the toilet bowl for their sons to use as targets.

• Back off for a while if it becomes a power struggle, then start again.

> *My son loves to talk. He talks about Thomas the Tank Engine and friends, family, Thomas, friends of the family, Thomas, favorite foods, and Thomas.*
> —Mother of a two-and-a-half-year-old son

sides and bent behind him, a developmentally immature way of sitting more appropriate to a one-year-old than to a two-and-a-half-year-old. He didn't move much at all. When the school director talked to the mother about him, the mother insisted that there were no problems with Darryl. She said that he wasn't passive at all. "He's smart and creative at home," she said. But the school staff did not see those qualities in Darryl and insisted that he get some evaluation because they weren't sure what was going on.

Darryl turned out to have above-average intelligence, and his language development was average for his age. There were no health reasons that accounted for his developmental delay and emotional immaturity. He did have below-average muscle tone, but there did not appear to be a neuromuscular basis for that. Perhaps he simply wasn't getting any exercise. The staff was stumped, and finally asked the mother to spend an hour with him in the preschool setting so they could observe and videotape mother and son's play together. They wanted to see the Darryl that his mother did when she was with him.

What did the videotape show? It showed a boy whose mother was constantly, relentlessly conversing with him. She outtalked him by a ratio of ten to one, laughing too hard at anything he said, praising him as "clever" and "funny" and "just the best little comedian in the world." More worrisome, she was unable to read the cues he was giving her that he wanted to play by himself. When he moved to the left to find a toy for himself, she would move to be in front of him and insist that he relate to her; when he turned and moved the other way, she would block him in that direction. Finally he just gave up, sat down, and passively reacted to her, trying to please her while looking sad and trapped.

It was clear that she thought talking and language-based games should be the center of a child's experience. The constant verbal interchange, her many questions and comments, and Darryl's occasional desultory replies reassured her that her son was getting plenty of mom time and lots of language development. The truth was that he was getting far too much time with his mother and had no experience of himself, literally no time to spend with his own individual self experimenting in the world. It is possible to delay a child's growth by not letting him explore, the preschool director noted, adding, "These days everyone is looking at boys through the lens of special needs, and we search for a physical explanation such as sensory motor deficit, but sometimes it's just that the child hasn't been allowed to do what he needs to do."

Darryl's parents were divorced and his father absent. His mother was devoted to him and, perhaps out of love or guilt or both, spent every second with him when she wasn't at work. She believed that a child develops confidence and competence interacting with his parents, and thought she was doing what was best for him. It is true that a boy wants and needs interaction with his parents, but that need is different for a seven-month-old baby than it is for a two-year-old. At two, he needs to be out making his mark in the world.

BUNNIES, BLANKIES, AND TEDDY BEARS

I want you to engage in a little visualization exercise with me. Picture your favorite professional football team or your hometown baseball team. Imagine all

---

HOUSEHOLD CHORES: INVITING A HABIT OF HELPING

Boys like to feel useful. They like to make a contribution. From the earliest age, when you're working in the kitchen, you can ask your son to help you—not busywork, but actual work that needs to be done. If you ask a boy for help, he's likely to give it to you and he learns it's not such a big deal.

When you enlist your son's help, you are educating him. In Chapter 2 I mentioned author Thomas Lickona's *Educating for Character,* in which he says that the moral life of a child has three components: habits of the heart, habits of mind, and habits of practice. When you develop good character, you have a desire to help (habits of the heart), you recognize situations in which help is needed (habits of the mind), and you follow through and actually provide the help (habits of practice). Chores are what Lickona would call habits of practice. You're giving your son an experience of helping, but also giving him the chance to feel useful in a way he typically cannot in school.

And it's easy to find jobs they like to do. Maybe it is mashing potatoes. Digging a hole. Helping you with pliers or a wrench.

With little boys, of course, you have to be there supervising the task. The trick with chores is to know when your son is ready to do it on his own or still needs you to monitor—not to micromanage, but to witness his work, his contribution. And yes, thanking him is important. That's not just for little boys. Longer than you might imagine, boys like you to acknowledge their help, and they will always appreciate a thank-you.

of those large, muscular, athletic men standing shoulder to shoulder in their uniforms. Now picture them all holding teddy bears, toy bunnies, and blankets. If you want, you can visualize them all sucking their thumbs, twiddling their blankets, and holding their bears up to their cheeks. Why do I ask you to picture this? Because most men did suck their thumbs, and almost all of them once owned stuffed toys that meant everything to them. If at age two they were separated from their special companion toys, they went nuts. These big tough ball players might not like to be reminded of that vulnerability, but that attachment to that bear—what psychologists call a "transitional object"—is part of what made them the strong and independent men they became. Every child finds one—be it a bear, a bunny, or a blanket—and though the relationship may last for years to come, age two and a half is the peak of a child's attachment to a comfort toy.

If you are the parent of a two-to-three-year-old, by this time you are very familiar with all of the things that younger children do to calm themselves, including thumb sucking (usually with a finger stroking the nose or some accessory toy or blanket), pre-sleep rocking, head rolling, constant pre-sleep demands, and masturbation. Children have trouble regulating their tension because they cannot identify the sources of their distress and they cannot articulate what they need. They do find ways to soothe themselves, however, and as young as four months they can systematically use their hands as a comforter. So you will see a baby with a fist in his mouth. Later, you will see him try his fingers and ultimately settle on his thumb. Some boys suck their thumbs for many years, especially at times of stress, causing their parents to worry about them deforming their teeth. But in due time he may come to settle on a toy, customarily an animal or a blanket.

One of our favorite characters from children's literature is just such a toy. Do you remember meeting him? He belonged to a real English boy named Christopher Robin, whose writer father, A. A. Milne, made the boy-bear relationship immortal.

Here is Edward Bear, coming downstairs now, bump, bump, bump, on the back of his head, behind Christopher Robin. It is, as far as he knows, the only way of coming downstairs, but sometimes he feels that there really is another way, if only he could stop bumping for a moment and think of it. Anyhow, here he is at the bottom, and ready to be introduced to you. Winnie-the-Pooh.

The father's genius was to capture the exclusivity of the relationship between boy and bear as well as the way in which a toy becomes the focus for a boy's imagination. It is, in fact, a relationship that has been written about a lot, because children love those stories and some theorists believe such comfort items are enormously helpful to a child as he strives to develop an independent sense of self.

A special comfort toy is a child's first sustained, independent creative act. What do I mean by that? Though we buy the toys (and probably too many of them), the child chooses the one that is going to be special to him, and he breathes life into it. He begins to treat his bear or bunny as a loving companion, a reassuring presence, someone who works for him. Though parents may try to introduce such a toy into their son's life, he doesn't always pick the best-looking bear, nor does he necessarily love the one his grandmother bought for him. He loves the one bear or blanket that he loves. He may even fall in love with a hard object like a little toy car, not at all like a soft bunny. That's his choice. Parents have to go along with it.

Soon his comfort toy becomes the first living thing in the world that both can comfort him and *is totally under his control.* I say "living thing" because the bear or comforting blanket has been given magical life through the boy's love and wishes. This is how it feels from a child's point of view: *Because I have a bear to love who also loves me back, I don't need my mother as much as I used to. Moms and dads aren't always reliable—sometimes they don't pay attention, sometimes they frustrate me—but my bear is always here for me. He warms me, he cuddles with me, I stroke him and bang him around; I mutilate him by pulling at his fur. I am in charge of my relationship with my bear; therefore, I am a little bit in charge of my world.*

Girls with difficult temperaments use their toys to calm themselves more than easygoing girls. In contrast, easy boys use them more than high-strung boys; sadly, the boys with more difficult temperaments tend to aban-

> *I am most concerned that he can melt my heart instantly. He gets away with more than I let my daughter get away with.* —Mother of a son, two and a half years old

FEAR NOT FEAR ITSELF

Whether it's fear of bugs, drains, toilets, or particular foods, kids develop fears and they get over them. What can you do to be most helpful to your son?

• *Do not panic.* (And you thought this was going to be about your *son's* fears!) If you get anxious about his fears, then he thinks, "Whoa—this really must be something worth getting anxious about!" Your son will pick up on your anxiety and it will make his fears worse.

• *Try to see it from your son's point of view.* One of the gifts of having children is the opportunity to see the world through fresh eyes. If your son is fearful of drains, for instance, look at a drain with "first-time" eyes and you will see it is a startling, gurgling black hole, sucking everything down into inky darkness, and you don't know where it goes and or who's in charge down there!

• *Understand that fear is reasonable to a child.* It is a product of his immature cognitive ability, lack of experience, and magical imagination.

• *Fight magic with magic.* Use a positive attitude and "magic" rituals to engage your child's sense of magic to help him calm himself. Make an elaborate show of carefully searching for hidden monsters under the bed or peering down the drain and ascertaining that all scary things have been successfully banished.

• *Don't worry about "giving in" to his fears.* Sometimes parents feel that if they acknowledge a boy's fears and respond to them, they are "giving in" and will only reinforce an irrational fear and make it grow bigger. This assumes there is no developmental process at work. There is, and your son will most likely outgrow his fears. What he'll remember is how you've treated him at a time when he was frightened and vulnerable.

• *Be brave and be kind.* It's your attitude toward the fear—both your acceptance of his fear and your lack of fearfulness—that will help your son conquer his fear. Comments such as "You don't need to be afraid" are of limited utility. Attempting to talk a child out of his fear is not really helpful. Be accepting and re-assuring without being dismissive.

• *Treat every fear as temporary.* Share the wisdom: "This too shall pass."

don the toys or transitional objects when under serious stress. Researchers believe that because girls are more cognitively mature, they can make better use of a toy during a stressful separation.

If a boy loves his toy or blanket so much, why does he treat it so badly? Why did Christopher Robin walk down the stairs with poor Pooh's head bumping on each step? Why does a boy allow his blanket to become so unbearably dirty and smelly, and why does he fight you when you want to wash it? He is, of course, upset to have it away from him and being tossed around in the washing machine. More simply, from a boy's point of view, his bear is the absolutely perfect companion exactly the way it is because it absorbs all of his love as well as his anger and neglect. A toddler understands that he has the capacity to hurt his mother both physically and emotionally; he knows he can make his father mad, and that's pretty scary. The greatest fear for a child of this age is that he will anger his parents and they will abandon him. In this arena, a toy bear is far better than a mom, because you can do whatever you want to it and it stays with you all the time.

A toy can become so emotionally important to a child that he is willing to have a tantrum and display rage against his mother when it is misplaced; even she cannot console her son for the loss. Her love is a help, but he has to have his bear back. The power of a child's reaction to the loss of his comfort toy is a measure of how important it is to him from a psychological point of view.

I know a mother whose son's beloved baby quilt disintegrated to the point that it was nothing but smudgy strips of shredded fabric. She had tried to replace it with other quilts, but he refused to accept a substitute. She waited as long as she could, but by the time he was three there was almost nothing left for her son to hang on to. Her solution? She went out and bought some identical fabric—it was quite a search—and made a new quilt for him. On the side of the new quilt she sewed a pocket, and into the pocket went the scraps of the beloved quilt. He could open the pocket anytime he wished to view the sacred relics of the original. Suspicious at first, he finally accepted the substitute and allowed it to comfort him.

Most parents see and understand a son's need for self-soothing and try not to have a war with him about thumb sucking or animals. Loving parents intuit how important that first beloved toy is and what it means for their son's independence and sense of safety. They honor their child's love for it, even if keeping track of it, packing it in the right suitcase, and retrieving it is sometimes a total pain in the neck.

One mother told me the sad tale of her family's return home from vacation, only to be told the airline had lost their luggage—with her son's little stuffed tiger inside. It was his nighttime sleeping companion, she explained, and that night as bedtime approached he asked for Tiger and she had to explain what had happened. She suggested that perhaps for one night he could sleep with Mouse, one of his other stuffed toys. "Initially he was not very sure about this, but eventually he relented," she said. "The good news is they found our bags the next day, and now he sleeps with Tiger *and* Mouse!"

Does every boy have a comfort toy? No. Some boys—and I was one of them—stick with their reliable, not-easy-to-lose thumbs; other boys seem to find different comforting rituals sufficient to soothe themselves; still others use a succession of toys—some choose a different one every day, or even have a special item of clothing—for company without ever developing the powerful relationship that I have described. However, a majority of boys develop this powerful relationship with a comfort toy sometime between one and three years and then, gradually, the intensity and passion of this first love relationship fades away. The bear spends more and more time on the shelf, or is just available by the pillow for nighttime comfort.

I always hope that parents will understand that a bear or blanket, even one that a boy holds on to visibly until he is six or eight, or sometimes even older, is not a sign of immaturity or weakness. I consult for an all-boys camp in Vermont and almost all the boys there, right up until the age of fourteen, bring a childhood toy with them for their first (and second and third) sleep-away experience. When a boy is far away from his parents for four or eight weeks, it naturally revives the wish to have the company of that comforting companion who first helped him to be independent. At morning inspection the counselors make the rounds of tents. Outside are the twelve-year-old boys, standing at attention. Inside the tents are all the beds with sheets tucked, blankets pulled taut, pillows straight, and teddy bears and bunnies leaning up against the pillows.

LANGUAGE: DIFFERENT TIMETABLES, COMMON FRUSTRATION

There are two things that make a toddler-age child feel independent from his parents: his physical mobility and his language. The ability of a boy to express himself is enormously liberating because it means he doesn't have to have his

"USE YOUR WORDS . . . NO, NOT THOSE WORDS!"

There is something naive about the ever-ready instruction "Use your words, not your hands." It ignores the fact that words can be hurtful, too. It assumes that children can simply convert angry impulses into nice words. And it invites us to sidestep the issue of real feelings that boys are often trying to express when they choose words we don't like. An embarrassed but also somewhat proud grandfather told me this story about his grandson, Logan, who found himself in just such a bind.

Logan, who was three and a half at the time of the incident, was having a playdate at his friend Don's house. He was playing with a blue plastic baseball bat when suddenly Don yanked it away without any warning. Logan responded by hitting Don with his fist. Don's mother, who was nearby, did just the right thing. She went first to Don, who had started the contretemps, and said, "Don, you don't just grab the bat away from Logan. If you want to play with it, you have to ask him, you have to take turns. You shouldn't have grabbed it from him like that." Next she turned to Logan and said, "Use your words, not your hands."

Without hesitation, Logan turned, looked directly into Don's face, and said, "Fucking dog!"

Boys don't always use the words we were hoping to hear. But when you think about it, what was Logan supposed to say when told to "use his words"? Could he have said something like: "Don, it wasn't very nice of you to take the bat away from me. I'm very disappointed in you"? Not likely. For Logan, the angry moment was not over just because an adult had intervened. There were still things to be said. Boys are often blunt and to the point.

Of course, we have to train boys of any age not to swear and not to insult people in any and all situations. I believe in a civil society and an educated society. We cannot go around calling each other "fucking dogs" all the time. For that reason, growing boys often disappoint us with their word choices. They are often blunt and coarse and angry. It is possible to get completely hung up on their language and react only to their word choice without acknowledging that they are also honest, in their fashion.

If you are going to raise a boy, even a nice boy, you cannot constantly jump on his choice of words and ignore his feelings—especially if he has done what you have asked and used his words. That baffles boys. We come across as hypocrites, because what we're really saying is not "Use your words" but "Use nice words," only we're not really saying that clearly. And then we complain, "Boys don't express their emotions." Well, they do.

When your son of any age, from three and a half to eighteen, is angry and expresses it honestly, you have to acknowledge the sincerity of his sentiments. If you are raising a son, you can't be squeamish—you can't wilt just because of a little rough vocabulary. You have to acknowledge the ferocity of your son's feelings. After he says something tough, pause, receive the message, then look him in the eye and say, "I know you're angry. You have a right to be angry, but can you say that in another way?" He probably will.

Q&A: PLAYING WITH TOY GUNS

Q: *Your* Raising Cain *documentary on PBS was a great relief for me. It made me feel my boy is normal and helped me understand him and his behavior much better. Nevertheless, most mothers of toddler boys I know tend to judge very negatively little boys who are allowed to express their aggressive behavior by playing with weapons, telling stories, or wrestling. How should I handle mothers (or parents) who do not allow their boys to express their aggressive behavior and are critical of my son?*

A: When another mother glares at your son for shooting with his finger or a toy gun, you might turn to her and say, "I see that worries you. Do you think that childhood play leads to violence?" If she is honest, she will probably say, "I don't know. It just makes me uncomfortable. I don't like shooting of any kind." Or she might say, "Maybe. If boys play with toy guns, perhaps it will make them want to use real guns when they are older." You might reply, "I understand your discomfort, and I used to worry about it myself, but after I talked to so many peaceful, responsible grown men who acknowledged that they had engaged in pretend gunplay when they were young, I stopped thinking that it was going to lead to real violence. Now, as long as they aren't poking each other in the eye with the guns, I just think it is play."

Don't get defensive when she glares at your son; all you can do is acknowledge the other mother's discomfort and then reassure her that you have thought through the issues. What I know for certain is that she doesn't have any research on her side that connects normal boy play with later violence. All she has is her fears, and you can help her let them go if you are willing to address them directly.

mother or father right there to interpret his needs for him. He can say what he wants, he can make himself understood by other people, and he can say no. There is great power in language. There is also a lot of frustration.

When children come to language is very much a matter of individual development. Children vary widely in when they master language. There are also gender differences; girls tend to develop language earlier than boys. Some girls may be using fluent "jargon" at fifteen months and be speaking in understandable three- and four-word sentences by two years. Some boys, too, are early talkers, while other boys may still be pointing, not speaking, at two years of age and may not say much at all until two and a half. That's a huge developmental range, and it leaves lots of room for parental worry.

By the age of eighteen months, the average child uses ten to twenty words; by twenty-one months he certainly has twenty words or more, including people's names, and is beginning to put together two-word combinations. For instance, Rusty referred to the computer as "Don tah," or "Don't touch." By two years he may be combining three or four words in a sentence and starting to use pronouns such as *I, me,* and *you.* Typically, however, the use of pronouns comes later, and for the time being he will still call himself by his name: "Rusty wants juice."

It makes parents nervous when their boys don't develop language as quickly as girls, or even as quickly as other boys. We all want our children to grow up on schedule, so any slowness in development that a parent thinks is a delay is likely to be unnerving. But for boys in particular, the issue of slow language development is fraught with meaning, because many parents are aware that boys are much more likely than girls to develop conditions such as autism, and that the first sign of autism is a significant delay in the ability to communicate in words.

Watching Rusty (age twenty-four months) play for ten minutes or so, I heard him use only one distinct word, *truck.* When I asked his mom, Leah, about his language development, she answered, "He's got about fifteen words," with a slight hint of worry that it might fall short of what it should be. I asked for a list of his vocabulary and found he had a list of mighty boy words: *truck, ball, duck, tractor, train, milk, banana, dirt, rock, dump truck, Pooh, Tigger, Elmo, Mum, Dad, Nana, Papa,* and *baseball.*

The moment Rusty heard our recitation of his vocabulary, he was all smiles. He pointed to the big green ball and said, "Ball." He pointed to the wooden duck decoy high on a shelf over the TV and repeated, "Duck." He clearly enjoyed the mastery of words. However, his attention didn't last long, and sometimes he would point and lapse into using his all-purpose generic word, which sounded like a soft grunt, a "huh." He didn't struggle with the names of things; he looked to grown-ups to read his intentions and supply the words.

His mother had an explanation. "He only spends time with his grandmother and me and his aunt. I think we've provided all his words for him!" Was

I recognize that this age is precious. I feel closest in the evening when everything is winding down, when I can sit with him in my lap, or we turn out the lights in the room and sit by the Christmas tree or count the cars from the bedroom window. —Mother of a son, two and a half years old

DON'T PANIC OVER RAMBUNCTIOUS BOYS!

It is no fun watching your son bop someone else on the head in a playground; it is hard to see and embarrassing to have to break it up. But that should be punishment enough. My wife, Theresa, says that she vividly remembers sitting in the park and listening to a Greek chorus of mothers of girls comment in whispers on the behavior of others mothers' sons, particularly when the boys were impulsive, aggressive, or momentarily out of control. There is a lot of competitive parenting going on in America, and too many parents, sadly, are willing to judge others rather than provide support. The social pressure brought on mothers who "don't control their boys" is real and it can make them feel terrible.

It is helpful to have a friend, preferably the mother of an older boy, who can realistically assess your son's behavior and who can support your parenting of him. You should not have to feel that your son's impulsiveness or activity levels are either (1) your fault or (2) signs that he is growing up to be an ax murderer. He is almost certainly not. If play-fighting and whacking another child (and I don't mean that in the Mafia sense of the word) on the playground were signs of future aggression, then most men would be murderous adults, and they are not. Don't let people make you think that two-year-old aggression is necessarily a sign of future aggression.

When you are dealing with your son's high level of activity and his occasional anger, you should hold three things in mind to keep yourself from panicking.

• Constant activity at this age is not a sign of future criminal behavior; you do not have to worry that it is going to turn into something bad.

• Occasional outbursts of temper and aggression are also normal, and with time and understanding, and with your help, they will come under your son's control.

• Your son needs you to distinguish accurately between activity, which should be celebrated, and aggression, which needs to be met and managed with a steady hand. If you can't separate them, then he will not be able to tell the difference, either.

Your two-year-old will become civilized if you ask him to be. It is hard work to get him to control his impulses, but he really wants to be a good boy for you. You have all the leverage in the world, if you use it. A child's world needs to be consistent when he is younger so that those expectations are firmly set at this, the wildest, most aggressive time in life.

she worried about language development? "Well, his cousin, who is only four days older, can count to eleven!" Clearly there was some competitive pressure in the family. "Then again," Leah said, "he's been in day care for a long time, and Rusty's just been at home with his nana."

I asked whether she had pursued her worry about his language. "Well, I spoke to the pediatrician about it," she said. "He told me that I could call the early intervention language clinic at Children's Hospital, and I did, but they couldn't make an appointment for three months. And then, of course, Rusty started talking so much more in the past month." She shrugged. "Actually, the pediatrician predicted that by the time I got an appointment Rusty would be on track with his language. The doctor said, 'It will come in time.'" And it did. Rusty's language development was under way, even if Rusty wasn't counting to eleven like his day care veteran cousin.

Every parent worries a little bit if he or she has a son with below-average language development; the problem is that the nature of development doesn't allow you to meaningfully measure what is below average and what is above because things are changing constantly. Every worried parent has to decide whether or not to pursue some early intervention option or simply to wait. Or, as in the case of Rusty's mother, you schedule an appointment for a language evaluation and then cancel it because by the time the appointment rolls around three months hence, your son's language development has kicked in.

PROBLEMS IN LANGUAGE DEVELOPMENT: AUTISM AND SPEECH PROBLEMS

Autism, a serious disorder of communication and connection, afflicts five times more boys than girls, and it is on the increase (currently one in 250 births). It is between the ages of eighteen months and three years that pediatricians begin to identify children who may have an autistic spectrum disorder, the third most common developmental disability after mental retardation and cerebral palsy. Boys who use language in a stylized way or repeat words and phrases; boys who insist on sameness, who resist change and prefer to be alone, who don't seem to want to be cuddled by their parents or anyone else, or who don't appear to experience fear or feel pain; and boys who make little or no eye contact and are obsessed with objects need to be brought to a doctor's attention because early diagnosis of autism is crucial. Early intervention can make a significant difference in the life functioning of an autistic child.

Many parents believe that a child who speaks fluently and early is not going to be autistic. And they are mostly right. However, fears about autism are a worry for parents. The problem is that all children love routine and resist change at one time or another, and there are many moments when a toddler resists being cuddled and wiggles out of your arms. At times, most little boys avoid eye contact and can be obsessed with toys, so a nervous parent who is looking for signs is likely to find some things to worry about in her son's behavior. Indeed, some characteristics that we later come to think of as male are seen in autistic children. Simon Baron-Cohen, the English autism researcher, argues that autistic people just have a very bad case of maleness. That's why it is important to remember that some boys develop language later than girls and other boys. Delayed language development is not, in and of itself, sufficient to diagnose autism.

Between the ages of two and three many children experience problems in articulating speech and are hard to understand. Some may stutter. These are normal problems, and typically if we just wait, their speech will clear up and become steadier. There is a gender difference, however, in stuttering. Girls are more likely to outgrow it than are boys.

BOY FRUSTRATION WITH LANGUAGE: AT A LOSS FOR WORDS!

There is a mantra that must be used a hundred times a day in every day care center in the United States: "Use your words, not your hands!" It is said as a day care teacher pries two children apart. But what do you do if you don't have words yet? Or if your tentative grasp of words disappears when you are very upset? And how do you feel when other children do have words? When the most developmentally advanced girls begin to talk more fluently between fifteen and eighteen months, most of the boys don't really notice. As long as they have their basic vocabulary of ten words and their mothers can decipher and anticipate their needs, they are okay when they are at home. In a day care setting, however, the situation is very different. The children with more mature language skills can get their needs met more easily and are able to boss around the children who are developmentally tongue-tied. As children become both more physically active and more assertive, conflicts between children are inevitable. And many times—most times—a child doesn't have the language ability to resolve the conflict.

When my son, Will, now sixteen, was eighteen months old, we put him in a in a large, lovely, day care setting with big rooms, high ceilings, a vast collection of toys, and a favorable teacher-to-child ratio. He was fine for the first six

TAKE IT OUTSIDE: CULTIVATING THE NATURAL BOY

The out-of-doors is a two-year-old boy's friend. It is big enough for his energy and filled with things that he cannot hurt. He is a natural scientist. Take him out as much as you can, summer and winter. Let him walk as far as he can with you following him; allow him to explore, pick up sticks and leaves, shred them, throw them. Let him get dirty. Strollers can be convenient for parents, but they restrict a child from walking and exploring. Once a child is able to walk and run, a stroller should be used only to get him somewhere and bring him back or when he is really tired.

Peter, a friend who is the father of a toddler, explained why he has taken young Noah outdoors as often as possible—and barefoot—from the beginning, despite his wife's initial concerns. "I'm averse to putting shoes on his feet. He's running around and she's worried about what he's going to step on at the park, but I want him to have that live tactile contact first. People have said, 'Where are his shoes?' and I say, 'He's being Huck Finn today.' I want him to feel a sense of trust in himself and his ability to navigate through the physical world, and have a real strong contact with the physical world through his hands and through his feet."

months. However, after he moved to the two-year-olds' classroom, he encountered problems. Will was somewhat delayed in his speech. He couldn't speak very fluently and he could not make himself understood. He had words that we, his parents, could recognize, but in stressful situations he froze and was unable to speak. He was a good and gentle boy who, when another child grabbed a toy out of his hand, could not speak and could not protest, but he could strike out. He began to bite.

Though we began cooperating with the day care administrators immediately after they brought his biting to our attention, the truth is that when your child is biting at preschool, you are in a race with time—or development. We began to have Will evaluated. We went to meetings to discuss his speech delays, and he was sent to a speech pathologist. It was not enough. One day he was involved in a conflict with an assertive little girl and he scratched her on her face. Our son was expelled from preschool.

Many parents have written to me with similar stories. A frustrated, impulsive boy with not enough words to express himself is going to have a hard time in many preschool settings. I asked Michelle Anthony, M.D., the coauthor of *Signing Smart with Babies and Toddlers,* to tell me what kinds of parents seek out her infant sign language classes.

FATHERS: GET INVOLVED IN THE NITTY GRITTY

Fathers who sincerely want to be involved in their sons' lives sometimes find that even if their commitment to work does not take them out of the game of parenting their boys, the close bond between mother and son seems to exclude them in the first eighteen months of their son's life.

It is important to remember that a young child can be profoundly and lovingly attached to a number of people. Not an endlessly large list, but three central figures—usually mom, dad, and another grown-up—in the first year of life and then a growing number of people in concentric rings of relationship. The inner ring usually includes mom, dad, and a caretaker or a brother and sister. It gradually enlarges to include all his brothers and sisters, aunts and uncles, family friends, and then teachers. The important thing to remember, however, is that your son likes to be in charge of the list. Once he is past infancy, once he can walk, he wants to elect his main attachment figures, and he wants to both promote and demote them according to his whim.

Typically, it is around the age of eighteen months to two years that he wants to demote his mom temporarily and elect his dad, or discriminate between how he uses his mom or his dad. Why? Because he is old enough to do so, because it is part of his declaration of independence from his mother, and because he has discovered his identity as a boy and he has started to identify with his dad in a whole new way.

Dads, this is your big chance. Your son wants to imitate you and he wants to identify with you. This is a time to build on that impulse in him. The human brain is designed to learn by imitating, and two-year-olds imitate everything. When we are very little and we see someone else pick up a cup and drink from it, our hands and lips involuntarily start to imitate the motion. As we grow, we censor the urge to imitate others, though it is still inside us.

Leah writes about Rusty and his dad: "Tonight, my husband was coughing and clearing his throat. Rusty immediately started doing the same. He also likes to stand next to his dad in the bathroom and pretend he's shaving or combing his hair. And when he's at my parents' house, he likes to sit with my dad and pretend he's reading the paper or correcting papers."

Rusty is an equal-opportunity imitator, his mother notes. If he sees her brushing her hair, he'll get his brush and do the same. He copies words and phrases from both parents. But over time he is going to increasingly imitate his father and his grandfather. If a dad welcomes that imitation, if he makes a ritual out of it, then he is going to be creating a bedrock foundation for himself and his son. The son's primary identity experiences will be: I know who I am because my mother loves me, and I know who I am *because I am just like my father.*

I have treated and interviewed so many fatherless boys in my career that I am profoundly convinced that every boy yearns for a father after whom he can model himself. This is the age, eighteen months to three years, when that identification accelerates. Boys want to be like their dads in every possible way.

One father of a three-year-old boy told me, "We have developed a ritual. My son wakes me up every morning and wants me to get out of bed so that we can 'cross swords.' " For those of you who don't know what "crossing swords" means, that's when two males urinate into the toilet at the same time crossing their streams of urine. What fun for a boy who has just started to urinate standing up!

You cannot become a powerful figure early in your son's life unless you get involved in the big-deal issues of his universe, which are in fact the nitty-gritty issues of bladder and bowel training, controlling his impulses, sorting out right from wrong.

A dad should help with toilet training by harnessing a son's wish to imitate and to please. Have him sit on his potty when you're sitting on the toilet. What your son does, right or wrong, should matter to you.

Unlike your father's generation, you may find more men getting involved as you are in hands-on parenting. The father of a three-year-old boy told me that he has enjoyed being so involved in his son's care, but it's been lonely. He wishes more men like himself were interested in sharing notes on children's sleep issues and potty training, for instance, as mothers traditionally have done with other mothers. Whether or not you find camaraderie among other fathers right away, your son will welcome your attention and conversation and, over time, will become good company and an expressive consultant on what he needs from you.

"Parents who know about sign language for babies usually start before one year, around eight to ten months," she said. "Then there are the 'panic' families, mostly families of boys, who start flooding in around fifteen months because they see how smart their child is and yet he's not talking!" He's frustrated and they're frustrated.

She said that mothers often come after their sons have been involved in incidents of social aggression in their play groups: hitting, biting, throwing things, and tantrums. In addition to concerns about their sons and the welfare of other children, the mothers are socially embarrassed. "You've got the chatty little girls who are all playing and the boys who are hurting each other," Anthony says. "You don't have as good control as a parent, and that can be embarrassing."

In her ten-week course, Anthony tries to teach a child twenty-five American Sign Language signs, some that are relevant for the child, such as "ball" and "fan," and other words that the parents want them to have, such as "milk," "finished," "bed," and "stop." She can also teach a child to make a little pointing sign with his hand, turning it toward himself to indicate "my turn" and toward

CREATE OPPORTUNITIES FOR INDEPENDENT PLAY

Every boy needs to learn to play by himself. Play is the most important activity of childhood; it is absolutely the best way for children to learn. These days we tend to think of play as social or organized or something you do with your parents. It is not. In its purest form, play is done by a child alone creating his own special world of pretend. But for a child who has been so dependent on his mother, the transition to solo play can be, at moments, a bit lonely and even momentarily scary. He'll look up suddenly and feel abandoned, or need to come and show you something. How then can you teach him to play by himself? You cannot. He has to learn it through experience. All you can do is create a context in which he can be alone in your presence.

Since an eighteen-month-old boy needs his mother or caretaker so much of the time, and since you are worried about the safety of a two-year-old, you have to be nearby, but you should not always be interacting with him. The best possible situation for a boy is a room where you can sit doing your work (reading, cooking, paying the bills, or working on the laptop) while he plays nearby. The initiative rests with him, both to design his own play and to call you when he needs you. If the room is pretty safe, so that you don't have to be intervening to protect objects all the time, so much the better. And if there is no television, his capacity for playing alone will continue to grow slowly and steadily.

If you want a five-year-old who doesn't interrupt you constantly, if you want a ten-year-old who is dedicated to a hobby, if you want a twelve-year-old who can sit and do his homework on his own, the best preparation is giving him a chance to be alone with his own play at this age. At the deepest psychological levels, he is developing the feeling "I'm okay when I'm alone. I can find things that interest me. I'm a strong and creative guy."

another child for "your turn." If a mother sees her son signaling "my turn" to another child, the other toddler may not be able to read the sign, but she can anticipate that conflict is coming and intervene.

Anthony believes that at this age you can see every behavior problem as a language problem. I don't think that is completely true, but it certainly is the case that once a three-year-old has command of a good vocabulary and his speech is clear enough to be understood, the temptation to hit his mother, to have a tantrum, and to clobber other children in day care is much reduced. If a boy with an average vocabulary who can make himself understood is still trying to hit people after the age of three, it's time to talk with his pediatrician and consider a more formal evaluation.

At this early age, a boy's excessive aggression may be successfully addressed with family therapy or with "play therapy," in which the therapist uses play as a medium through which the boy can express feelings he can't articulate, says psychologist Lawrence J. Cohen, author of *Playful Parenting* and a family and play therapist. Cohen is an energetic advocate for parent-child play and free play in children's lives, and points to the special importance of it for young boys.

"Play is the way kids connect with other people, and play is the bridge for children between feelings and language," Cohen says. "Play is the way they express themselves, especially about deeply emotional things that they can't yet put into words. Before they are able to 'use their words,' they can express themselves symbolically through play. Even boys who are very verbal often lose their verbal abilities when they are stressed, frustrated, or angry—right when they need it most."

GIVE A BOY PERMISSION TO BE HIS INDEPENDENT SELF

One of the hardest transitions for any parent is the transformation of a loving, sweet baby into a willful two-year-old. But for mothers of boys, the onset of defiance, willfulness, and even hitting is sometimes deeply shocking, even disorienting. Why should that be so? Haven't most mothers read about or heard about the terrible twos? Why do they take it personally when their boys become unreasonable for developmental reasons?

I suggest there are three reasons why it is upsetting to have a child become a little tyrant, and two of them are amplified in boys. First, the growing independence of the child is an abrupt change in a loving relationship. Second, a misbehaving child opens you up to social embarrassment and comments from other people. The remarks of other mothers are likely to be more critical if you have a son. Third, because overt aggression is not usually an acceptable part of a woman's repertoire or identity, the explosion of "aggressiveness"—or is it impulsiveness?—in a boy is often difficult for a mother to understand and accept. Your philosophical approach to your son's independence will shape how you manage this crucial period of growth.

The relationship you have had with your infant is in some ways perhaps the most completely fulfilling love relationship in life. You are the center of his world and he is the center of yours. While his needs for care are constant and exhausting, his need for you and his adoration of you are also total. What brings it to an end is customarily not your readiness to have it end; it is your toddler's announcement that he is no longer in love with you in the same way he was. It is a declaration of independence. And whether that is expressed in the physical act of running away or by hitting you, it is in some sense as shocking as the American Declaration of Independence was to the British, because it is a revolution in the relationship and it is always accompanied by angry feelings and sometimes by angry action.

Whether your son's revolt is expressed through tantrums or through dangerous and oppositional behavior, you have to accept that the underlying reason for it is right. You also have to see it from his side. He believes he has to fight against a bigger power to gain his independence even though he is smaller, needier, and more erratic. And finally, he's going to hurt your feelings and make you feel helpless. Parents don't like to feel helpless, and sometimes they make the mistake of reacting harshly or perhaps withdrawing their affection. Both are hurtful and confusing to your son.

It is possible for you to crush this revolution. You can suffocate a child's desire for independence. You can turn his love for you against his own autonomous strivings by constantly frustrating his wishes for independence.

Even when you have to grit your teeth and say quietly to yourself, "He's only two," allow him some space for his independence. And when he starts to get into trouble, pick him up in your arms with good cheer. Divert him, redirect him, laugh with him. Let him feel your adult power and control, not your constant disapproval.

A mother told me: "Raising a son is definitely the hardest challenge I've faced, but also the most rewarding. Everything about him amazes me."

Take the challenge. Be amazed.

CHAPTER FOUR

WILD THING: POWERFUL LITTLE BOYS

The Three- and Four-Year-Old Boy

As mad as I was, I almost laughed out loud when he shouted, "You're not the boss of me!"
—Mother of a four-year-old boy

I HAVE ALWAYS THOUGHT OF MAX, THE LITTLE BOY IN MAURICE SENDAK'S *Where the Wild Things Are,* as being somewhere between three and five years old. Dressed in a wolf suit and making mischief to the limits of his mother's patience (we're never told exactly what the infractions were, but every parent knows), she orders him to his room. Defeated but defiant, he threatens to eat her up even as he retreats to his time out. Boys at this age are experimenting with their power, and sometimes they can come close to eating their moms up with their defiance and ferocity. A three-year-old boy is going to push your buttons because that's what he does and because the terrible twos aren't over when a boy is two or two and a half; they reappear at three and a half and again at a number of stages throughout childhood. Parents need to be psychologically prepared for these

> *My son is just beginning to develop and express an active imagination. I have found lately that entering into and participating in this imagination has been wonderfully fun and magical.*
> —Father of a boy, two and a half years old

times of challenge. The great English pediatrician-turned-psychoanalyst D. W. Winnicott summed it up when he wrote:

What is the normal child like? Does he just eat and grow and smile sweetly? No, that is not what he is like. A normal child, if he has confidence in father and mother, pulls out all the stops. In the course of time he tries out his power to disrupt, to destroy, to frighten, to wear down, to waste, to wangle and to appropriate. Everything that takes people to the courts (or to the asylums, for that matter) has its normal equivalent in infancy and early childhood (and in adolescence), in the relation of the child to his own home. If the home can stand up to all the child can do to disrupt it, he settles down to play; but business first, the tests must be made, and especially so if there is some doubt as to the stability of the parental setup and the home (by which I mean so much more than house). At first the child needs to be conscious of a framework if he is to feel free, and if he is to be able to play, to draw his own pictures, to be an irresponsible child.

What does that "normal boy" look like? As these parents describe their three- and four-year-old sons:

Talkative, bright, curious, and outgoing, with a very keen sense of justice.

Easygoing and rolls easily with change. People and relationships are very important to him. He is not overly sensitive, but he is empathetic. He's not a worrier and I am. It is so alien to me. He tells me to relax and reminds me to be patient.

When he gets angry, he'll hit or throw a tantrum.

He doesn't like surprises, and when he gets an unexpected response or disappointment, he panics and cries.

Stubborn and quick to anger. He is also very happy and loves to play play play!

Sometimes when I read Winnicott's quotation to audiences of parents, I translate it from fancy English into plain American words: your normal child is going to lie, cheat, steal, cause chaos, and push all of your buttons, many times over. If you do not "stand up to all the tests" and provide the sense of framework he needs, you will become frightened of him. And if you are overwhelmed by him, he will become terrified of his own impulses. He will feel unsafe. No boy wants to be stronger than his mother, even though he is fighting all the time to be strong and autonomous. If he thinks he has become more powerful than his mother, he becomes terrified and aggressive, searching for someone who can reassure him of the "stability of the parental setup."

DERRICK: TYRANT OR TESTING?

Derrick, a handsome, brown-eyed three-and-a-half-year-old boy with curly hair, played quietly on the pediatrician's floor with several toy cars and some little plastic toy characters. He was absorbed in his play, at times lying on the floor as if he wanted a nap, but he was listening to every word the adults said. Harvard Medical School pediatrician Dr. Johnye Ballenger had invited me into her office to meet Derrick's parents. Derrick had been giving his parents a hard time for the past year, and when I arrived, Dr. Ballenger was already deep in discussion with them.

"I was just telling the father: no more televised football on Sundays!" declared Dr. Ballenger. She was laughing, but her voice carried a sense of command. Dr. B., as she is also called, introduced me to Derrick's parents, Richard and Melissa, adding that Richard had been a professional football player. She made it clear that it was perhaps understandable that father and son would be watching so much football on TV since the father had played the game, but it would not be good for the boy. "All Sunday afternoon is *way too much television,*" Dr. Ballenger proclaimed.

Was television the problem that had brought them here? It turned out that something bigger was at stake. Derrick's day care center had complained that he wasn't participating in circle, wasn't learning anything, didn't know his colors, and refused to do much of what was asked of him. There were also conflicts between Melissa and Richard about how to discipline Derrick. Dr. Ballenger

When my oldest was three, we went to Legoland; he wore his hula skirt, and some of the comments from the other parents were rude, to say the least. I wanted to scream at them, "He's three, leave him alone," but he was mostly oblivious and I didn't want to bring his attention to the comments.
—Mother of two sons, three and five years old

took it all on, first wondering aloud whether he had some problems with color blindness (far more common in boys than girls) and testing him on the color of various crayons. He didn't know orange. Melissa was surprised. "I just assumed he'd know his colors. He knows an iguana from an ostrich." She suggested that they could use flash cards with him.

"I'm not big on flash cards at this age," Dr. Ballenger said. "It's more natural if you work on colors and numbers while doing everyday activities. You can name colors and count carrots when you are preparing dinner." Then she changed topics. "What about sleep?"

Derrick's sleep time, from 9:30 P.M. till 6:30 A.M.—with a two-hour nap each afternoon—met with Dr. Ballenger's approval.

"What about eating?"

"He eats everything in sight," his mother said.

"Terrific. As long as they are healthy choices," said Dr. B. She was watching Derrick play on the floor. "Well, he has good imaginative play," she observed.

"He loves *Star Wars*," his mother continued. "He's obsessed. He loves Yoda."

Derrick looked up at the mention of the name. "Yoda. It's a lightsaber," he said, reciting a line from the movie.

"Books?" quizzed Dr. Ballenger.

His mother shrugged, "I think he may be ADHD."

"It's too early to check for ADHD," Dr. B. replied. Still watching Derrick, she said, "He's dextrous. He needs to focus on books. TV is too passive."

His mother returned to the troublesome issue of the day care center. Though she liked the day care center because it was so diverse and there were other African American children there, she was concerned because the staff seemed intimidated by Derrick; they avoided confrontations with him because he was likely to have tantrums.

She herself had trouble disciplining him, she explained. "I try to discipline him and he doesn't pay attention." Worse still, she said, was that in the car, he refused to wear the seat belt on his car seat. He knew how to unbuckle it and would do so when they were driving, or would refuse it from the start and make a scene.

Dr. Ballenger became quite serious at this point, looking directly into the young mother's eyes and speaking bluntly to her: "There is no *discussion* about seat belts with a child."

"But he keeps taking it off," Melissa said. "And whenever we get into the car he *has* to open the car using the unlock button. If I don't let him, he throws a tantrum. And then he *always* has to put the key in the ignition."

"No, he doesn't!" Dr. Ballenger commanded.

Derrick's mother continued in a confessional tone: "He thinks the harder he kicks and screams, the more I'm going to do what he wants. He falls to the floor in the grocery store when he wants M&Ms." She admitted that although she used candy as a reward for Derrick *not* having a tantrum, something didn't feel right about it. She felt manipulated. Other than the candy as a behavioral incentive, she said, "we reason with him."

Dr. Ballenger pulled her chair up close and zeroed in. "No, you can't reason with him. You have to choose one or two behaviors that are dangerous and think of appropriate, natural consequences. Consistent, loving limits are what this doctor orders."

Both Melissa and Richard were nodding. As I was to learn later, Derrick obeyed his father but not his mother, and that was making trouble in the family.

Dr. Ballenger carefully addressed Derrick's dangerous behavior of removing his seat belt. She instructed Melissa to pull the car over and turn the motor off, telling Derrick that they would drive home once he put his seat belt back on. She then went on to tell Melissa about how to use a therapeutic hold to help calm Derrick when he was having a tantrum. She demonstrated how she should wrap him in her arms and hold his legs with her legs, firmly but gently. The point is to help regain control and to help him regain his composure. The therapeutic hold is never used as punishment or to show a child who's boss. The therapeutic hold can be dangerous if done angrily.

All the while, Derrick was playing and watching and listening. Nothing was lost on him. How would he react to the changes in his mother's disciplinary style?

Two weeks later I visited Derrick and his parents at home. He greeted me at

The Eight Lines of Development

The Developmental Story Advances

Your son is now a person, and he knows you are a person, too. He knows what he likes and what he doesn't. He is steady on his feet and confident in himself. He can delight you and infuriate you: his choice. He is also very much aware that he is a boy. He is interested in the differences between girls' bodies and boys' bodies.

During these two years your son is going to cultivate his boy identity. Like all children, he hopes that his parents see him as a "good boy." At the same time, however, he will be gripped by the idea of "bad boys" and what they do. He and his friends will spend a lot of time talking about superheroes like Superman, but they will also discuss their evil counterparts, "Bad Superman" and other villains. He is grappling with the reality of his own internal impulses and what society is going to ask of him as a boy. If you, as a parent, stand back, you can watch your son and his friends work at becoming more "boy."

Physical Development

Your son is nature's original action figure. He thinks with his body; if he arrives at an open space, he will start to run. At the age of three or four your son runs, climbs, tests his balance, and is beginning to successfully coordinate small and large motor abilities. He also competes in whatever game he finds himself, often boasting about his achievements: "I'm the fastest." Even boys who know that they are not going to win cannot help joining in the race.

If your four-year-old has older brothers, he is going to do everything in his power to compete with them, taking risks and dissolving in frustrated tears when he is unable to keep up.

Some boys of this age are rapidly becoming athletic. Boys will begin to imitate athletes they have seen, role-playing them just as they play Power Rangers and Spider-Man and other superheroes.

The competitiveness and athleticism of the age do not, however, mean that boys this age are ready for organized sports. Running around with friends and free play is sufficient for them because at four the majority of boys are not yet ready to focus on the drills that are part of practice. Drills make fathers feel better because they think they are preparing their sons for sport, but very often it makes the children anxious by suggesting that what is going on is more than just play. They also may not be ready for the frustration and possibility of losing that is part of organized sports because they will take those failures to heart.

Attachment

After the age of three, a securely attached boy does not have to see his mother all the time. He has internalized the image of her in his mind and does not have to have the constant reassurance that she is there. That's what makes it possible for him to attend preschool, even if separations from Mom in the morning can be upsetting. What is most notable is how a boy can bring other adults into the inner circle of attachment figures: teachers at his nursery school, a regular babysitter, an aunt or uncle. He is in charge of electing or rejecting the important big people in his life and sometimes transferring his attachment needs from a parent to a teacher. He may also open himself up to the possibility of finding a corrective and healing experience. An anxious or avoidant child may make a relationship with another adult who reads his rhythms and needs better than his parent does. Attachment research shows that while attachment patterns, both secure and anxious, are stable for the majority, they can change in a minority of children, often in a healthier direction.

A boy of three or four also continues to use his teddy bear or security blanket. Every boy described in this chapter had a reliable, portable companion and was proud to show it to me, without the slightest embarrassment.

Social Development

The excitement in friendship is a hallmark of preschool. At three, boys love the idea of having a friend, and some, like Martin and Frank (see page 129), really form a strong bond that endures from week to week. Many others, however, will play with whoever is at hand, so a teacher can still pair up two four-year-olds with the words "This is your friend; he wants to play with you" and have the boys accept it. That will not be true much longer.

Boys always need other boys who can help with a project. Fantasy play of any kind—running a play farmstand, for example, or a Power Rangers battle, and most especially a major block construction project—requires a group. You will see a group of boys begin to build a block city, a racetrack, or a complicated marble slide. Initially, they cannot coordinate their efforts, and they may shout instructions and objections at one another: "No, the garage doesn't go there." Gradually, however, leadership emerges and they settle down into a quieter, more goal-focused work team.

As they move from three to four they do not exclude ("You can't come in," "Go away") as quickly or as casually as they used to. Boys of this age identify strongly with the group. Preschool teachers use that capacity to rally children to a common task.

Cognitive Development

The most striking thing about the cognitive development of three- and four-year-old boys is their astonishing heroic imaginations and the way they start to integrate their fantasies with reality. Walker's dinosaur play had all these elements in it: the imagined ferocious opponent, his heroic attack, a constant running narrative combining real facts from paleontology and fantasy from movies. A boy's imagination can be employed in any scenario. In some ways it is the most fluidly creative time in all of life.

Two other cognitive breakthroughs are worth mentioning: the intense curiosity that drives a boy to ask "Why?" over and over and over, and his awareness of past and future. He begins to grapple with the concept of time and tries to master it.

Academic Development

Three- and four-year-olds are learning every moment; there are major achievements in academic development even if they are not in any kind of preschool setting. They are learning to count and recognize some letters (you can do an eye test using letters, especially the ones in his name). By four some boys, especially the older fours, are able to write some letters and perhaps their entire names in large capital letters, and they will boast, "I can write." Boys can order blocks from the longest to the shortest or from the heaviest to the lightest. They remember an astonishing number of facts. All of this should be fun and spontaneous; don't push academics. A boy knowing all of his letters and numbers at three or four does not signify brilliance and does not predict future academic success.

Emotional Self-Regulation

The fluid imagination of a boy this age is mirrored in his up-and-down and side-to-side emotions. Louise Bates Ames describes boys of this age as "out-of-bounds": first laughing, then crying, often quiet and then incredibly noisy. Boys move rapidly from one emotional state to another. That said, there are important temperamental differences in all boys. Your son's cautious temperament will mean he is on the quiet side of out-of-bounds; his gregarious nature will put him on the wild end of out-of-bounds. Adjust accordingly. One father captures the range of his son's day: "He battles Darth Vader all day, then at night holds my hand and hugs the stuffed raccoon he's had since birth."

The continuing advances in language mean he will be able to control his emotions better and better, producing the quieter, more serious five-year-old he is going to turn into very soon. However, there are some boys for whom anger and frustration outpace their language ability, and the result is continuing tantrum behavior. All boys, however, not just those who have a tendency to tantrum, are starting to get the message that a strong boy should hide his feelings. Therefore, a boy who blows up is going to be getting a lot of strange looks from his friends, and he will want to pull himself into line with their expectations if he possibly can.

Moral and Spiritual Development

Three- and four-year-olds are capable of great empathy, moral thought, and spiritual yearning. They are fascinated by right and wrong and who is hurt by the world's cruelty. One four-year-old cried when he saw the results of a forest fire. Another watched intently as the nightly news anchorman reported on a family tragedy, then asked his mother: "How is he saying that and he isn't crying?" A three-and-a-half-year-old boy scolds his parents if they fight, saying, "It's not nice to talk or act like that."

A father wrote, "My family goes to church every week and we speak about God in our everyday conversations. And so my son will often thank God or Jesus for the day or for something. I love the moral and spiritual development I am seeing in him."

And what better realm for an articulate four-year-old boy to express the trinity of his heroic imagination, his developing identity, and his own brand of moral goodness and spirituality, as this mother describes: "Most of all, we build a home where kindness is the most important thing. We talk about God from time to time. Ben believes that God is the superhero of all superheroes, more powerful than even Batman and Superman, and invisible to boot! Religiously, he describes himself as 'I-wish.' That is, half Irish (Catholic) and half Jewish. He discerns the differences in almost encyclopedic/historical terms."

Identity

You don't have to go too deep inside to find out about identity formation in a three- or four-year-old boy. A lot of a boy's conversation is about who he is ("I'm strong" or "I'm the fastest") and who he wants to be a second later ("I'm Luke Skywalker"). He takes on so many identities in his play that one might think it is all about identity formation, and of course it is. He also imagines what he might be when he grows up ("I'm going to be a fireman").

Three and four can be a disconcerting time for some parents if they have a son who seems to be interested in being a girl rather than a boy. One father wrote to me, "He dresses 'fancy' during dress-up time. By 'fancy' I mean flamboyantly effeminate by my standards—cape, sequined headband, wand. I have to remind myself that he is one of the most 'boy' boys I've ever known, but I draw the line at him wearing sequins in Red Lobster."

Is this boy trying to communicate something about his underlying sexual orientation or is he just playing in the fluid way of four-year-olds? One cannot really know at first, because some boys of this age are just drawn to great costumes that can be used in imaginative play—is a Darth Vader mask any less outrageous than a sequined headband and a cape?—while others are really not sure that they want to be boys.

No parents ever imagine they will have to tackle the issues of gender identity and sexual orientation with a four-year-old, but some do. Almost every time I go to a preschool or elementary school, the teachers ask me about a boy who is absolutely determined to play only with the girls or to dress only as a girl, or, more rarely, who declares that he is a girl. In general, teachers accept that there have always been boys like this and they imagine such a boy is likely to grow up to be gay. The vast majority of teachers to whom I have spoken seem to accept that such a boy was "born that way."

In a recent *New York Times* article on such "gender-variant" children (the older terms were "sissy" boys and "tomboy" girls), Dr. Edgardo Menvielle, a child and adolescent psychiatrist at the Children's National Medical Center in Washington, said that about three-quarters of the boys who display such behavior in early childhood grow up to be gay, one-quarter are heterosexual, and a tiny fraction become transgendered, that is, they actually claim an identity as a woman. There is controversy in the field about whether to try to make a child conform to his biological gender or allow him to express his own variations as he pleases and try to protect him from the expectations of society. Most school districts basically require a child to have a clear male or female identity.

The subject of gay and transgendered children is a complex one, and we will tackle it again at puberty, when gay boys acknowledge their homosexuality to themselves and begin to act on it. Having seen a significant number of effeminate boys of preschool age, I find it hard to believe that they choose to act effeminate. They just do; that appears to be just who they are. My experience leads me to conclude that they are driven to act effeminate or question their male identity by some yet unexplained biological underpinning of gender identity.

the door of their lovely old frame house, thirty miles outside Boston. Derrick immediately wanted my attention, and we sat together at the table. He showed me his letter cards and identified the pictures on them. From his point of view, the only problem with the evening was that he wanted me and his parents to devote all our time to him. That's normal; however, I was there to find out why he was able to intimidate his mother but obeyed his father. What was the difference in their approaches to a three-and-a-half-year-old boy, and had things changed since they heard Dr. Ballenger's advice?

Two weeks after hearing Dr. Ballenger's advice on setting limits, Melissa and Derrick had turned a corner. When he had insisted on opening the car and putting the key in the ignition, she had said no; he had, she reported, "flipped out." She decided to use Dr. Ballenger's therapeutic hold method, and so she wrapped her arms and legs around Derrick and sat on the ground in the parking lot for close to twenty minutes. She told me, "He was like, 'What is this woman doing? What has happened to this woman?' "

It worked. "He hasn't asked to open the car since," she said.

And when he took off his seat belt she pulled over and refused to drive home until he allowed her to refasten the belt; they sat by the side of the road for a long time. Now, when he is tempted to remove it, he tells her he's about to, and she warns him, "Do you want to sit in the car?" He stops.

BOY POWER: SCARY FOR PARENTS, SCARY FOR BOYS

Derrick highlights the central difficult issue for boys between the ages of three and five: getting control over their yearnings for power and their displays of aggression. The tendency of children to tantrum for their parents and behave well for strangers is well known. The ability of boys to frighten their mothers while obeying their fathers is also familiar. Even so, the degree to which Derrick had been able to completely manipulate his mother and his day care teachers with his intransigence was notable. There were two reasons for this. First, Melissa had fallen totally in love with her son—that's good—and she was not ready when he changed from a baby to a formidable little guy. Second, she did not come from a family where consistent discipline was practiced, and so she had no experience from which to draw as a new parent. "I basically thought I couldn't control him," she admitted. "I loved him as a newborn; they eat, sleep. One and a half wasn't so bad. Everybody said it was the terrible twos, but he wasn't that bad. But after that, he figured out right away who was the sucker and who wasn't."

Richard had grown up in a family very different from Melissa's. Though Richard's family was close and loving, his father, a minister, was a disciplinarian. He used tone of voice, spankings, and a belt to discipline his children, three boys and a girl. As a father, Richard said, he wasn't going to "do the belt," but he did believe in spanking. When Derrick was being deliberately disobedient—

> *He is still attached to my husband and myself, but I love that he is becoming an independent person.*
> —Mother of a three-and-a-half-year-old son

"when he looks right at you and does something bad"—Richard said he asked his son to hold out his hand, and he slapped it.

"You hardly slap it at all," Melissa said, but she clearly admired the fact that her husband had some disciplinary method that Derrick respected. She knew that if Derrick was misbehaving for her, he would straighten out when he heard his father's car in the driveway. That she hadn't been able to discipline Derrick between the ages of two and a half and three and a half had been demoralizing for her. She had needed and welcomed Dr. Ballenger's advice, and I could see that she was starting once again to feel powerful in the life of her son.

In my experience, parents sometimes become immobilized by a boy's misbehavior for two reasons: they have no model for effective discipline, or they become confused precisely because the misbehavior comes from a boy. If you didn't have discipline in your own life, it won't come naturally to you. So if you, like Melissa, have the chance to marry someone who did have that, it can be a plus if your expectations of your son and your parenting styles are compatible. If neither of you knows how to discipline, you can look for that wisdom from friends and neighbors, from teachers, or even from books. I know many teachers who have said to three-year-olds who have just hit their unnerved mothers, "You cannot hit your mother. I won't have it!" The voice of authority the teacher uses with children shows the mothers that you can effectively manage a three-year-old.

But sometimes parents get confused about boys. Why do parents hesitate to discipline boys? Or why do they make the mistake of disciplining them too harshly? They do it because they are shocked, ashamed, or confused—shocked because they cannot believe that their loving baby boy is suddenly so oppositional, ashamed because they feel inadequate and afraid that they really are raising a male monster, and confused because they cannot figure out how much "aggressive" behavior is tolerable in a boy. The last point is a fascinating and difficult one. How much activity and aggression should parents tolerate in a boy? And how can you tell the difference between activity and aggression?

ACTIVITY, PLAY AGGRESSION, AND REAL AGGRESSION IN BOYS

The most common question that mothers of young boys this age ask me is, "Why is my son so aggressive?" I immediately ask, "Would you describe what you mean by 'aggressive'?" because so often the behavior a mother describes is the normal active, power-hungry, impulsive, independent play of a four-year-old boy. However, to a worried mom her son's behavior is a sign that his play could lead to aggression in real life, and she wants to make sure that doesn't happen. Brenda described her four-year-old son Asher's play:

> Everything becomes a weapon. I have established with my kids that we don't buy toy guns, swords, or any other kind of weapon, period. They have essentially grown up without watching television, so it's like, "Oh my gosh, where is this coming from? They 'kill' people on a regular basis!" And everyone with boys says boys just do that, it's just normal, they shoot at people they love. This makes me frantic inside.

Her concerns are understandable. The United States has the highest rate of young male violence in the industrialized world; TV is full of it, and everyone worries about the impact of video and computer games. No mother wants to raise a boy who cannot manage his aggressive feelings, and by three and a half or four years of age, they clearly are capable of a lot of anger and intentionally aggressive acts. At the same time, they may be loving, cuddly, and eager to please most of the time. How do you sort out the "good" activity from the "bad" aggression? It is tough to do. Let's go back to Brenda, above, and hear the rest of her description of Asher:

> Asher-dasher-crasher-smasher, I call him. He's all about motion. He is an overwhelmingly affectionate and snuggly kid, but he's also on or off, running at full blast or sleeping. His eyes open, his mouth starts, and he's out of bed and *going*. He doesn't take a nap. On top of that, he's the epitome of a little brother—he likes to antagonize his sisters, and he's finely honed those skills.

Brenda wondered how to handle Asher's incessant motion, some of which seems aggressive but may not be. "I don't think he sees a difference between hugging and kissing, on one hand, and jumping on your back and climbing up your body, on the other," she noted. "In his mind it seems to be one and the same." She must sort out his real aggression against his sisters, which has him breaking their things, from his pretend aggression, played out with guns. What is normal and acceptable for boys and what is not?

These are tough questions to answer, because there are wide variations in what different societies and different communities define as "natural"—and acceptable—boy behavior. When I visit international schools in the Middle East they tell me that elementary-school-age Yemeni boys are particularly hard to manage in the classroom because their families believe that masculine boys are naturally restless, wild, and a bit disobedient, so the parents do not curtail them much when they are little. They are a handful in the classroom. Korean and Japanese boys, by contrast, are asked to demonstrate high levels of obedience to teachers and personal self-control at young ages. An American mother living in Paris told me that she had sent her son to a preschool class at age three, and when she arrived to pick him up at the end of his first day he was sitting quietly on a bench with all the other children. When he saw her he did not run to her as she expected, not until he had looked up at his teacher and she had silently released him with a slow nod of her head. "I don't know how she did that!" the mother exclaimed.

There is some reason to worry about the high levels of aggressive behavior among American preschoolers. Researchers have shown that by age four, American preschoolers engage in more aggressive acts when they meet in a playground than do French children, and our boys and girls are significantly less physically affectionate. French children hug and kiss each other more. Researcher Tiffany Field suggested this is the result of different child-rearing practices between America and France, particularly that French families touch their children much more than American parents do.

Cross-cultural studies suggest that American parents may have a paradoxical approach to boys. We worry a lot about our boys' aggressiveness, we tolerate higher levels of it and thereby unwittingly encourage it, and we do not spend time doing the calming, peaceful things that, for instance, French families do, including frequent caring touch and quiet reading. The paradox sends a confusing message to boys and leaves many parents confused about what constitutes reasonable expectations.

Linda Dahl, a second-grade teacher with more than twenty years in the classroom, offers this uncomplicated standard:

"I WAS RAISED WITH THE BELT"

When I visit schools and speak to parents at PTA evenings, I am often asked about my position on spanking and corporal punishment. One father said, "I was raised with the belt, but I'm trying not to use it on my son. Still, I sometimes spank him. What do you think about this?" I told him that I was not in favor of corporal punishment of children, for a variety of reasons. Another father told me, "I've only used the belt on my son twice, but it sure got his attention like nothing else. There is nothing I do that is quite so effective." It was clear that he was challenging me to come up with some alternative as effective as "the belt."

Most American parents have spanked or swatted their children's bottoms on occasion. It is what their moms and dads did to punish them when they were growing up, and they repeat that parenting practice with their own children. It is almost impossible to raise a child without, at the very least, experiencing the impulse to hit him when he does something impulsive, defiant, or deliberately disobedient. If a child runs into the street suddenly and we pull him back, we often strike him because what he did was so dangerous, it made us feel so helpless, and *we don't want him to do it again*. When a child is extremely oppositional, it seems as if he is challenging the basis of our authority, and we feel intensely provoked. We want him to respect our power. If a child engages in some premeditated act of disobedience, we naturally want to increase the punishment to fit the crime, and that might mean a spanking or "the belt." These reactions are completely human and understandable.

If the parental reaction to swat a child is so normal, if it has been done for so many years, why do I recommend that you not spank or hit your son? Why have all the countries in the European Union outlawed corporal punishment, even in family life? Why have a majority of states outlawed corporal punishment in the schools? In *Raising Cain*, Dan Kindlon and I pointed out that parents rarely hit children as a first choice; they do it when they are frustrated, are out of good ideas, or have lost control. Hitting boys, we said, is the product of an "exhausted mind." Most parents do not feel good about themselves when they have hit their sons. That's what they say. They wish they had found some other way, and I agree.

There are many good reasons not to hit boys, especially not boys under the age of two.

• *Spanking may not teach your son the lesson you want him to learn.* When you hit a boy, his fear of your anger and his fear of being hit may so completely overwhelm him that the lesson you are trying to teach is lost. All he remembers is how angry and out of control you were, not the "right" or "wrong" of it.

• *Children under the age of two do not understand the relationship between crime and punishment.* Babies and toddlers are too impulsive and not yet cognitively well developed enough to make the connections between cause and effect. They don't understand why they are being punished.

• *You are teaching your son hitting as a solution to problems.* When you hit children, you model hitting for children as a solution to problems, and even though they may obey you in the short term, in the long term they are likely to imitate your behavior by hitting in school or at recess. Boys especially imitate their fathers, so fathers who show self-control have sons who demonstrate self-control; fathers who blow up, get angry, and lose it often have sons who do the same thing.

• *Once you use "the belt" you drain power out of other types of punishment.* Once you start relying on physical punishment, anything else lacks punch. A boy may not believe you when you raise your voice or threaten to take something away from him. He knows you are serious only when you get out the belt. So you have reduced the number of tools available to you to deal with significant misbehavior.

• *It may hurt the relationship between parent and child, especially father and son.* Though spanking or hitting may cause your child to obey you in the moment, in the long run it results in a son's resentment of your power. You get short-term obedience and long-term disrespect. If you had listened to as many boys in psychotherapy as I have over the years, if you had heard how many boys are just waiting for the father to "try something" when they are sixteen and eager to retaliate, it would give you pause.

• *Reliance on physical punishments can escalate and lead to physical abuse and trauma.* If you start to hit your child and both of you get accustomed to it, it may lose its power for both of you. You'll have to up the ante to make your point, and that can lead to abuse.

There are many other ways you can get children's attention when they have been impulsive or disobedient. Boys, no matter how active and mischievous, want their parents to love them. If they see how upset you are at what they do, if they see your anger, they are going to feel frightened and try to obey in the future.

1. *Set up your house so that small children can stay out of trouble.* You can help children avoid being destructive or disobedient by locking drawers and closets and by putting breakables out of the way.

2. *Supervise, monitor, and anticipate.* You can head off a lot of disciplinary moments with a smaller boy through your alert anticipation of trouble.

3. *Use your voice, your anger, and your moral outrage—not physical force—to communicate the lessons you want your son to learn.* You have powerful tools at your disposal.

4. *Use time-outs, loss of privileges, loss of playtime with friends, and loss of TV and video games as forms of punishment.* There are lots of things you can do. Over time, as you get to know your son, you will figure out what punishments are most effective.

5. *Remember that redirection, praise, and guidance are the best disciplinary tools.* The original meaning of the word *discipline* is to make someone your disciple. Your son wants to follow you and earn your respect. You don't have to hit him to make him want that.

You may have to give yourself a "time-out" when you have the impulse to hit your child. That's okay. One man told me that his parents always took their time with him in disciplinary situations: they always said, "We'll see about that," and came to a decision slowly. He said those were painful, agonizing moments for him. As parents, we have great power with our children, as long as we remember that we do.

I know boys tend to be more active, but there's a difference between being active and being mean. And being active and being obnoxious. And when they're obnoxious they need to be called to task. Little things you can work through. You can look the other way at some things, so you don't get after them for childish, impish things, but when they're stepping on somebody else or hurting somebody else, they've got to stop. If you don't take that to the mat, then you don't get respect.

Boys who are going to be overly aggressive tend to display that behavior by the time they arrive in kindergarten; boys who are going to be more peaceful tend to be more self-controlled when they arrive in kindergarten. Partly that is because of temperament; some boys are just hard chargers and some boys are more laid-back. However, temperament alone is never the full answer. Some combination of developmental maturity, parental expectation, and disciplinary style has produced a child who by age five can, for the most part, control his impulsiveness and aggressive feelings.

What can we learn from parents who successfully rear their active, sometimes aggressive little boys to become well-adjusted older boys?

First, they recognize that time and development are going to help their son mature. A boy of three can be completely overwhelmed by his feelings of defiance and anger, as you see when they tantrum. The natural course of maturity

> *I worry that his playfulness, his silliness, which I adore, is not tolerated much, either in school or outside. I'm not ready to squeeze the sillies out of him quite yet!* —Mother of a boy, four

suggests he'll be a peaceful five-year-old because five-year-olds are generally more controlled. You do not have to discipline them ferociously to get them there. Excessive force simply creates new problems.

Second, they understand that a boy of three and a half or four years is a motor person par excellence and the vast majority of his behaviors are driven by a desire to move and show off his muscles, not by anger. He wants to run and jump and kick and shout; he moves quickly. He wants to test his balance, new muscles, and improved coordination. He wants to prove how "tough" he is by taking risks. All of this is natural boy.

Third, they are sufficiently well attuned to their son that they can read his anger and frustration early and find some way to acknowledge it before it becomes extreme. It is not nearly as easy to divert a furious four-year-old as it was to divert a two-year-old, but because he has more sophisticated language, he can tell you what is upsetting him. Though he may not like what you have planned for him, he does not have to cry about it or fight you. He can tell you. If you give your son time to express himself and you really listen, you will get through most angry crises.

Finally, they distinguish between play and real violence. Playing with toy guns and lightsabers is not dangerous aggression; it is play. Could someone get hurt if boys are swinging plastic swords around? Of course, but does that mean that you should stop all potentially aggressive play between boys? No, because a lot of such play is at the heart of what all boys do. It is between the ages of three and five that boys begin to form social groups and develop distinctive patterns of interaction that will characterize boy play throughout childhood and adolescence.

BOYS IN GROUPS: FINDING THEIR PLACE IN THE PACK

The moment I walked out onto a New York City school's rooftop playground to observe recess for the three- and four-year-olds, I spotted the distinct groupings of boys and girls. Like many urban play spaces, the playground was so small that thirty children filled it up, and a casual spectator might have concluded that all the children were playing together. Of course, they really were not. Six children on tricycles, three boys and three girls, rode by in front of me through the narrow space between the wall and the climbing structure. They looked, momentarily, like a group. It was an illusion. Once they had negotiated the narrow straits and space had opened up, they split into two factions, with the girls circling around the play structure and the boys making a reverse loop, with two boys following the fastest biker, the three-year-old "leader of the pack."

Indeed, the more I focused on the play, the clearer it became that the boys and the girls were playing together in mostly gender-exclusive groups. Five talkative girls occupied the downstairs level of the play structure in the center of the playground, occasionally hanging from the rope netting. A few boys were playing soccer and occasionally wrestling with each other. A rectangular shed with benches was staked out by girls sitting in a row, along with one boy. The only other mixed-gender group was composed of three children, two boys and a girl, running around the top level of the play structure. With the exception of the boy who was sitting with the girls in the rectangular shed, all of the boys were involved in something physically active.

What I was seeing was the beginning of the separation of the sexes for purposes of play. This process of separation, which has been happening slowly up to this point, suddenly accelerates as children near their third birthday. By age three girls have begun to explicitly state that they want to play mostly with girls. "Boys are too rough," they report. By the age of four, boys become the biggest advocates of boy-only play, and they will continue to be the more ferocious enforcers of gender-exclusive play. "We don't like the same stuff," they declare. "Boys don't play with girls."

This strong boy opinion is sometimes upsetting for parents. Moms, in particular, may have gotten attached to the idea of boys and girls playing together in harmony because that was what they appeared to do at eighteen months and two years. For many of them, the coed collaborative play of that earlier period foreshadowed a peaceful relationship between the sexes in the future. The sudden split in play seems abrupt and arbitrary. What causes boys to want to play with boys and girls to play with girls? It is a question that has been much researched, and we have some theories.

A BRIEF HISTORY OF GENDERED SOCIAL PLAY

Babies, of course, play mainly with their parents, and they choose toys that attract them, without reference to whether they are boy toys or girl toys. By one year, a girl is more likely to pick up a baby doll than is a boy, and a boy is more likely to pick up a truck. Such sex-stereotyped toy choices are locked in by the

FATHER-SON RITUALS

For many years, I have conducted fathers-only discussion nights at schools because men talk more openly about their parenting struggles with their sons when the resident experts—mothers—are not present. I always conclude these evenings by asking the men to tell about a favorite ritual they have with their sons. Most such rituals are natural, easy, and fun for both a boy and his dad.

Some fathers with young sons include them in morning rituals like shaving (boys love to lather their faces and run an empty, bladeless razor across their face like Dad), reading the comics in the newspaper, or making pancakes on a weekend morning. Others find their moments at the opposite end of the day, with bedtime reading, TV, or a chat about the day. There are the hiking, camping, hunting, and fishing trips. Chess or card games. Season openers for their favorite sports teams, or a pause to refresh on the way home from a son's game or music recital.

The answers aren't surprising, but they are a reminder of the remarkable range of ways fathers and sons can connect, and the value of even the "smallest" such rituals in a boy's life. More important than the detail of what they do is the way it makes them feel: it makes the father *feel like a really good father* and the son *feel like a really good son*.

And for a boy, feeling like a good son in the eyes of his father means everything. Men can attest to it, and to the simplest ways it can happen.

A ritual of shared time is often something easy and fun between father and son, but it is important to remember that many men looking back value times with their fathers that were not at the moment either easy or fun. Times when their dad insisted they work together to fix the roof or repair a car. When duty called and they were expected to show up alongside Dad for family or church obligations.

There are times when a father requires something of a son that is annoying or burdensome to a boy and the boy will resist precisely because it *isn't* fun and he'd rather be playing video games. But as he becomes engaged in the task he feels more competent—he's actually driving the nails, helping out in some real way, or even simply accompanying his dad into his father's world, whether that is at work or beyond, and he can see that his father is pleased with his contribution.

These moments of apprenticeship have an enduring impact on the psychology of boys. A boy needs to feel useful and appreciated, but it it's a very special thing to feel useful to your father, and appreciated by him.

age of two, with nineteen out of twenty boys choosing a truck or similar traditionally male toy as their favorite. Toy choice does not seem to be the reason for gender-exclusive play, however. Boys and girls who are friends may play side by side with their respective toys, engaged in parallel play. They do not really play together, because they are not yet developmentally able to do so.

You may observe a boy and a girl of eighteen months standing at a sand table, each shoveling sand into a funnel that trickles down onto a moving wheel. Standing shoulder to shoulder, they make no effort to coordinate their play. They will occasionally call out to each other—"Look!"—and draw attention to their own play, hoping to impress their companion. There is no doubt that they enjoy each other's presence. They might make brief efforts to coordinate play (or annoy a companion by trying to dump a shovelful of sand into the friend's funnel), but for the most part they cannot merge their fantasies long enough to sustain any story line. Their only reciprocal play takes the form of hunt-and-chase play or rolling the ball back and forth. Gradually, they will develop the ability to play out a shared fantasy, with either a same-sex partner or one of the opposite sex. Being able to coordinate play with another child is a singular developmental achievement, and most parents are deeply touched by the sight of their child playing *with*, not beside, another child.

A matter of months after achieving the ability to coordinate play, however, boys and girls split into two groups, and by and large they play apart for the next seven to eight years. The separation is so complete that by age eight, they are living in entirely different social worlds. Eleanor Maccoby, author of *The Two Sexes*, cites one study of elementary school children ages eight to eleven that found the "median percent of social time spent with children of the other sex was zero." Zero! And programs designed to get the genders to mix at recess and playtime have only short-term effects. Anthropologists have found that children of all cultures, races, and social classes show this same preference for same-sex play.

Indeed, the draw of gender-exclusive play is so strong that it tops race and social class. If you observe a school playground filled with elementary-school-age white and black children, you will find them grouped by gender, not by race. Poor and rich boys will find a game to play together before either will choose to play with girls from their own social class.

Why is this so? Science does not have conclusive answers; however, researchers have theories. So do children. Around the world, if you ask children the question, they venture a variation on the same answer: "Girls have cooties!" "Boys have cooties!" That is, there is something objectionable, weird, and different about the other gender. Why do they develop that prejudice? Is it that they don't like each other's toys? Is it that they have stereotypes about the other gender? Is it hormonal? Is it that their parents influence boys to play with boys and girls with girls?

Studies show that parents do *not* systematically steer small children in the direction of same-sex play. On the playground, mothers tend to say to their boys and girls, "Go play with the other children." Research also shows that children enjoy gender-exclusive play before they have developed gender stereotypes, so it cannot be that they have an idea that makes them discriminate against each other, though such stereotypes will come into play later. So it isn't parents and it isn't stereotypes. What is it? Any boy will tell you: "It's more fun to play with the boys."

Apparently, boys are drawn to boy play because there is something attractive about the nature of the play itself: it is rougher and more exciting for them than girl play. Eleanor Maccoby reports that boys are stimulated to "bursts of high activity" in the presence of other males. This means that a very quiet boy at home may suddenly become a wild guy when he is with other boys. It is easy to see that many boys light up with excitement when they start to play with a group of boys. Why? Maccoby's conclusion is that there is some kind of "prenatal hormonal priming" that predisposes boys and girls to respond differently to different kinds of social stimuli. That is, the male hormones that have washed the brains of boys in the womb produce a different style of play in boys three years later. The experimental proof for this theory is that when unborn female chimpanzees (our closest genetic relatives) are injected with male hormones at a critical point during their gestation, they tend to wrestle and roughhouse more than other female chimps. Under the effect of male hormones, girl chimps act more like boy chimps.

Once preschool boys begin to play exclusively with boys, their world changes dramatically. Though research shows that over time about 25 percent of play on preschool playgrounds is mixed, the vast majority of a boy's life is spent in boys' groups with boys' rules, and there is no escape. An athletic "tomboy" girl can play with the boys, but boys taunt any peer who wants to consistently cross over and play with the girls. While this effect is first seen between three and four, it is slowly reinforced over the years. I asked a kindergarten boy why boys always prefer to play with other boys, and he said, "I don't know. They just like to play with boys." As it happens, that's very close to a social scientist's explanation of the phenomenon.

When my son, Will, was a first grader in a mixed-age Montessori classroom, he came home one day and said, "Dad, I can't play with girls anymore." I was upset for him, because I knew he sometimes liked playing with girls.

"Why not?" I asked him.

"Because Mitchell says so," was his answer, and his voice told me it was conclusive. Mitchell was a second grader and the biggest boy in the class; what he said was law.

So, whether he is shy or extroverted, athletic or not, a boy plays with other boys and, over the course of time, he becomes more "boy." Girls congregate in smaller groups and tend to choose indoor spaces; boys gather in larger groups and prefer the out-of-doors. Boys play hunt-and-chase games, they engage in more competition, and when they are riding on tricycles, they are much more likely than girls to play "ramming" games where one boy runs into another boy's tricycle. They shout, they yell, they wrestle, they make machine-gun noises, they throw sand at each other, they shoot each other with their fingers and fall dead. All of this is done in a great good spirit by boys all over the world, and more than anything, it is what turns a boy into a boy.

If boy play is naturally rougher than girl play and it sometimes puts boys on the edge of aggression, how should adults respond to it? Should they see it as normal or dangerous? Can schools tolerate it or not? Let's go back to a rooftop playground in New York to focus on two boys whose behavior raised issues about competition and aggression for the teachers and parents.

MARTIN AND FRANK: SOCCER, WRESTLING, AND BITING

At the end of the rooftop playground was a small plastic-frame soccer net occupied by a middle-aged woman teacher defending against the kicks of two boys. Martin is a thin, redheaded boy; the other, a slightly larger, more square-built dark-haired boy, is named Frank. Both boys, just a couple of months short of their fourth birthday, were excellent kickers. Martin, in particular, seemed unusually coordinated for a boy his age. The two boys kept collecting the balls that the teacher returned, and moved to new positions for their shots.

For seven or eight minutes the boys kept shooting pretty steadily. After that, however, there were times when a returned ball would get by them and their attention would waver from soccer. At those moments they would completely forget about retrieving the soccer ball. They would run toward each other and start to wrestle, each bending at the waist and extending his hands in the classic Greco-Roman wrestling pose, stepping forward, feinting, circling, and finally grappling. Whenever they started their wrestling, the teacher would emerge from the goal and, in a cheerful voice, urge them to resume kicking.

"You've forgotten about the soccer balls," she would call out, and after several repetitions of her reminder the boys would stop wrestling, retrieve the soccer balls, and begin to kick again.

After several such losses of attention, the teacher suggested to the boys that they stand in the net and defend against her kicks, which they did for a while. Anytime she stopped kicking the ball, they would lose focus, start to hang on the netting of the goal, and eventually fall on top of each other and start to wrestle. When the teacher saw them at it, she would again encourage them to get the soccer balls and start to play the game with her. It was evident that she was more interested in soccer than they were and that she had been assigned to keep an eye on them and keep them on task. I was curious and later spoke to the director of the school about why one teacher was monitoring two boys so closely.

It turned out that about three weeks prior, Martin had pinned Frank to the ground in a wrestling match. Finding himself in the more powerful position, Martin had not relented, even as his friend struggled and struggled underneath him. Martin enjoyed his superiority for too long; eventually Frank reached up and bit him on the face. That worked. Martin got up and the incident was over for the boys, but it had only begun for the adults. The director of the school called both mothers. Martin's mother was upset and requested that her son be prevented from playing with Frank. Frank's mother felt bad about the biting but refused to apologize because her son had been provoked. The school could not negotiate an end to the parental stalemate and so had designated a teacher to keep these two friends from wrestling. That's why she was trying so hard to keep them focused on soccer.

As I watched Martin and Frank, it was perfectly obvious to me that they were the best of friends. They clearly loved playing together. Furthermore, they were the two most capable athletes on the playground. No one else could keep up with them. Whom else were they going to play with? When a curly-headed blond boy tried to play soccer with them for a short while, he gave up quickly because he could see that his skills were not anywhere near theirs (they were not mean to him). The two of them were competitors, however, and could not stop themselves from testing each other's skills and ability. Not skillful enough to test each other as kicker and goalie, they were going to test each other in that most elemental boy sport: wrestling.

And if their penchant for grappling had resulted in one boy biting the other because there was no referee to separate them at the crucial moment, what of it? Could they ever settle the issue? Could they resolve the conflict on their own? The mothers thought not and escalated the incident with their own reactions. The request that the two boys be kept separate was clearly irrational, especially given their friendship, but the teachers felt compelled to appease the parents.

The dilemma of Martin and Frank is similar to one that many of our boys face today. Adults don't trust their play, we don't trust their friendships, and we cannot allow them to work things out because our tolerance for the physical aggression of little boys is so low, and that is because we think it is the forerunner of adult violence. For my PBS documentary special, *Raising Cain,* I interviewed the anthropologist and educator Joseph Tobin at Arizona State University. He showed us tapes from a Japanese preschool in which one boy punched another and then stepped on his hand. The teacher, who saw the entire incident, never moved. She allowed the "victim" to cry and to be comforted by some caretaking girls in the class, who warned the boy not to play with the aggressive boy because "that always happens" with him.

Professor Tobin said that American teachers are shocked by the Japanese teacher's nonintervention. The American belief, he said, is that if we allow boys to wrestle and fight, especially fighting that results in someone getting hurt, it will lead to their developing habits of hurting others. We believe we must stop them so they do not become accustomed to solving conflicts in this way. He questions whether that is the only possible outcome of an incident of hurtful conflict between two boys. Could it be that they learn from such an encounter *not* to hurt each other?

If the teachers could allow it, would Martin and Frank have worked things out on their own over time? Could they have reached an agreement about how long Martin could sit on Frank without enraging him and causing him to bite? I believe that they could have. Indeed, I predict that they will do so, as long as their mothers don't conspire to keep them apart. What a shame if the parents do succeed in overmanaging the boys' play and keeping them from having weekend playdates, because these boys are friends. You only have to watch them to see that. However, boys solve conflicts in ways that are not necessarily verbal and may involve force.

It used to be that we accepted physical competition as a given in boy life. It used to be an American ideal. In *Tom Sawyer* Mark Twain has Tom meet a new boy on the street, a boy who is "a shade larger than himself."

If one boy moved, the other moved—but only sidewise, in a circle; they kept face to face and eye to eye all the time. Finally Tom said:

"I can lick you!"

"I'd like to see you try it."

"Well, I can do it."

"No you can't, either."

"Yes, I can."

"No you can't."

"I can." . . .

So they stood, each with a foot placed at an angle as a brace, and both shoving with might and main, and glowering at each other with hate. But neither could get an advantage. After struggling till both were hot and flushed, each relaxed his strain with watchful caution, and Tom said:

"You're a coward and a pup."

But this, of course, is the beginning of a friendship.

Though Tom Sawyer is probably between ten and twelve (Twain never specified his age), this archetypal confrontation is not so different from the one I have described between Martin and Frank, though they are only four years old. Boys test each other's strength, they compete, and most of the time they are still friends at the end. They will test each other another day. And the time when this begins is around age two. When boys are younger than two and they hurt another boy, it may be simply the case of a boy expressing autonomy and anger; his friend got in the way. At age four they will test each other, or at least two athletic, ambitious four-year-olds such as Martin and Frank will. Other boys their age may not be ready, but they will be soon enough.

Can we allow them to do so? Perhaps it would help if we understood the purpose of boy competition and their aggression. Evolutionary psychologists believe that boys compete and wrestle and fight as a way of establishing a hierarchy of strength and leadership that will reduce conflict in the years to come. Once boys know whom they can beat and whom they cannot, they settle down to play.

I would like to finish this discussion of boy play, boy aggression, and boy conflict—boy competitiveness—with a little story that also occurred on that same rooftop playground. As I was sitting there with my laptop, recording the behavior of the children, a little boy and a little girl walked up to me and stood about a foot away. "Who are you?" the boy asked.

WATCH OUT FOR NONSTOP
ANGER AND AGGRESSION

One thing that is not normal is a chronically angry boy: a boy who is constantly aggressive to other children, who cannot tolerate frustration of any kind, who explodes in fury or really tries to hurt people. Nothing I have said in support of boys playing games of hunt-and-chase, playing with make-believe weapons, pretending to be superheroes, or wrestling means that it is okay for a boy to constantly blow up emotionally. If you have a boy with a hair-trigger temper who has everyone, including you, walking on eggs around him, that is a problem. The question that needs to be answered is whether the problem is with the boy or with the context or some combination of both.

Preschool boys who viewed violent TV programming were found to be at significantly higher risk for later aggressive or antisocial behavior between the ages of seven to nine, according to a study by Christakis and Zimmerman. The study included 184 boys and 146 girls ages two to four, but the link to later aggression was found only among the boys, for reasons not yet understood, the authors noted. The connection is significant because the toddler and preschool years are when most children learn alternatives to aggressive behavior. If they don't, they're headed for later trouble. Sometimes the boy may be troubled, even depressed, and need psychiatric help. Under the age of ten, depressed boys outnumber depressed girls (that switches at adolescence, when there is more girl depression). Sometimes there are social and cultural factors at work.

The director of a preschool evaluation team spoke to me about a "gorgeous, sparkling, intense" boy from Costa Rica named Francis who had been thrown out of two day care settings by the time he was three and a half years old and was in danger of being excluded from yet another. She described him as "impulsive and aggressive" and recounted numerous incidents where he disrupted the play of other children or hurt them. "He was so fast and smart and aggressive. If I hadn't seen it I wouldn't have believed it. He got three kids at his snack table. He perceived that other kids were taking things from him."

His mother spoke Spanish with him at home. At two and a half his English-language skills were tested and found to be weak. Everyone had concluded that his behavior was bad because his language skills were bad, because he didn't seem to understand enough English to follow directions. The director disagreed. "We had him tested and there were no cognitive deficits and a little language delay. He's only three and a half. He doesn't need sophisticated language in day care." She sensed there was something wrong.

His mother, perhaps because of her self-consciousness about language, would not go to see the behavior consultant the team asked her to see. The early intervention group worked with the teachers to make their discipline more effective with Francis, but discipline did not seem to be the answer.

In this case, help came from an unexpected source: a college student majoring in child development who needed an internship. She applied to the early intervention team, and they assigned her to spend time with Francis, ninety minutes twice a week. Happily, she spoke some Spanish.

After she had spent a lot of time side by side with him, he finally told her that he was worried that the white people were going to kill him. Where had he heard that? Was it something his mother had said or that he misinterpreted? No one knows, but it was clear that he believed it and was acting on it. "He was in survival mode all the time, but he did not have the language to say it," the director told me. Once he had confessed his secret fear to his aide, his behavior calmed down enormously. She talked to him about his anger being like crying; they discussed how other kids cried when they were scared, whereas he became aggressive. The interpretation helped him. The director of the early intervention team quoted the noted child psychiatrist Stella Chess, who said, "Ninety minutes twice a month can change a life." In this case, some careful attention and understanding rather than discipline and expulsion were what Francis needed.

I answered, "I'm Dr. Thompson. Who are you?"

"I'm Adam," he announced, "and this is Marta. What are you doing?" he demanded with some force.

"Writing a book about children," I replied.

"Well, my brother can beat you up," he declared, taking me aback.

"Oh? How old is your brother?" I asked this confident three-and-a-half-year-old boy.

"Sixty-one!" he replied, and I tried not to laugh.

"Really? Sixty-one? Well, that does make him older than me by a year," I said. "Maybe he *could* beat me up. Is he really sixty-one?"

Adam looked confused and consulted his knowledge of numbers.

"I think he's six," was his reply, and he and Marta abruptly turned around and walked away.

A WONDERFUL, EXUBERANT, MAGICAL AGE

So far in this chapter, I have focused so much on boy impulsivity, the need for appropriate parental discipline, and the aggressive elements in boy play that I may have failed to convey what a sensational, imaginative, and funny presence a boy can be between the ages of three and five. A four-year-old boy loves to be praised, loves to show off, and loves to boast: "I can jump high" or "I can count."

He is expansive, he's curious, and he lives in a larger world than he has lived in before.

He also believes that he can create the world through his thoughts and wishes. He does not yet understand the laws of cause and effect and he does not yet accept the constraints of reality, so he lives in a world of magic, living dinosaurs, tall tales, imaginary companions, and big fantasies. One mother, who worried a lot about being "too intense," said about her four-and-a-half-year-old son: "I have much more fun in my life because of who he is."

It would be a shame not to enjoy a boy's imagination at this age. What stops many people from fully enjoying their son's unique play and creativity is that they feel the need to teach him about reality, or they misinterpret a boy's magical thinking as lying. The answer to those concerns is that your son will come to understand reality in time as he matures. In the meantime, let him construct an exciting world in his head.

One year my daughter, Joanna, was the babysitter for a lively four-year-old boy named Walker, whom she often brought over to our house, accompanied by his equally lively and engaging three-year-old sister, Ruthie. I always looked forward to their visits and sometimes allowed myself to be lured out to play when I didn't feel too consumed with work. When we went to the park we always went hunting in a magic world of dinosaurs. All I had to do was turn myself over to Walker; he would introduce me to the characters and dangers of his imaginary world. Over the course of several months I watched Walker try to integrate his love of facts about dinosaurs with his imaginary world.

Perhaps one of the reasons that boys of this age so love dinosaurs and pirates and superheroes is that they do not regularly see them on the street or in preschool. Therefore, they do not have to deal with the reality of a living thing. Instead, they can appropriate for themselves the power of dinosaurs or pirates. Brenda, mother of Asher-dasher-crasher-smasher, said, "He's really into Spider-Man. I'm not sure where that started, but at this point it appears he was born to be a superhero."

Boys love to be able to make stories come out the way they imagine. This preference for the imaginary over reality is hard for some parents to bear. It is reassuring for them to hear their children say reality-based or school-appropriate things, as if that were evidence that their child was growing up in a developmentally appropriate way. But grasping reality too soon is not a sign of

Hunting Dinosaurs with Walker: Entertaining Fantasy, Facts, and Fun

Walker, four, and his younger sister, Ruthie, were excited that I could take a break from work to play, and as we walked to the car to drive to our favorite nearby park he started talking about dinosaurs right away and continued as we drove. He had a blue and red model of a *Tyrannosaurus rex*. It roared, and he wanted me to hear that right away. Then he showed me the teeth.

"How many teeth does he have?" I asked.

Walker immediately started counting. He got to twenty-one with no problem, but after that he kept repeating: twenty-two, twenty-three, twenty-two, twenty-three, twenty-four, twenty-two. He is a smart four-year-old, very smart, but he has his limits. When he got to twenty-four, I asked him if that included both the lower and upper teeth, but he could not answer. He preferred to show me the roar again right away. I was duly impressed and stopped my teacher-like questions.

As soon as we got to the park he started seeing dinosaurs. His younger sister, Ruthie, was doing the best she could to keep up.

"They're up there," he said, pointing to a small hill. We headed for it.

"They're behind that rock," Walker said.

Ruthie joined in, trying to spot the dinosaurs. "He's over there," she said.

"No, he's not. He's there," claimed Walker, pointing in a different direction. His sister could not possibly see the dinosaurs; he was the authority. He informed us: "They live in the Great Valley and they come from the Mysterious Beyond."

We clambered up hills and over rocks. Walker identified dinosaurs just ahead of us, and we charged them, but I was the only one who actually stabbed them. Though we charged together, Walker could not bring himself to stab thin air, so for him they were always moving ahead or slightly out of reach. Walker was on the fence between his magical thinking and his realistic thoughts. He imagined dinosaurs everywhere, but he didn't feel credible to himself when he was stabbing at nothing, so the dinosaurs of his imagination kept moving ahead of us.

"They're flying over us," he yelled. "There's one!"

We hid behind a large rock, hoping that the dinosaur would not be able to spot us from the air.

"He sees us!" Walker cried, and we ran away through the trees. I guided Ruthie and Walker away from the poison ivy.

Menotomy Rocks Park in Arlington, Massachusetts, is a wonderful park, quite civilized on one side of the big hill, with a pond, playground, and picnic area, and quite wild on the other side. There are places where you cannot see any houses and it feels as if you are deep in the woods. In these areas, Walker was on his guard. Luckily, all three of us had big swords (sticks) for warding off danger.

We spotted another dinosaur, but it ran away as we attacked.

"They're scared of my shirt!" cried Walker, pointing to the Batman logo on the front of his superhero shirt. He threw out his chest and charged off again. If you were in any doubt about why your four-year-old absolutely needs a Batman shirt, here is the answer: he needs it to scare away dinosaurs.

We spotted a large boulder with a small depression on the top filled with water.

"That's their drinking bowl," Walker declared. We climbed the boulder to investigate. Ruthie started to stir the brownish-green water with her stick, flicking a clump of algae onto Walker's pants. Ordinarily, Walker is pretty fastidious, but not when he's hunting. He simply took his stick and removed the algae, leaving a wet, green mark on his pants. No time to wash up—there were more dinosaurs to find, and we did locate a few more. Only Ruthie and I stabbed them.

Coming down the hill into civilization again, we were tired. Walker was talking about dinosaurs, mixing facts from books with animated movies and questions: they lived millions of years ago, they lived in the Great Valley, some could fly, they were killed off after a meteor hit the earth, they had different kinds of body armor. He talked about a particular dinosaur with a bulb at the end of its tail, and he mentioned that the velaciraptor was the fastest.

"What's your favorite dinosaur?" he asked me. I know enough about boy questions to know that I should turn it around.

"I'm not sure," I said. "What's yours?"

"My favorite is the triceratops, because he has three horns for fighting."

"Why not the *Tyrannosaurus rex*?" I inquired. "He's bigger."

Walker paused. He had to choose between *his* favorite and the universally recognized champion carnivore, *T. rex.*

"The triceratops," he repeated, sticking with his original. "Because of the three horns."

healthy development. Playing endlessly with his own creative imagination is the work (and I don't even like calling it work) of the four-year-old. As one mother said, "He is quite bright intuitively; he sees shapes in the clouds." When was the last time you stared at the clouds? Enjoy your son's imagination at this age. A huge dose of reality, in the form of school, is coming soon enough, and that will be the subject of our next chapter.

TAMING EVERYDAY DRAGONS: UNDERSTANDING BED-WETTING, NIGHTMARES, THUMB SUCKING, AND MASTURBATION

Your four-year-old is going to do his best to present himself in public as a strong little guy. Indeed, four-year-old boys often characterize themselves as "tough" and go to great lengths to show it. Though your son may cry when you leave him at preschool, he will try to pull himself together as quickly as he can and will have an active, fun day. He is, after all, a big boy now . . . except when he isn't. You, his mother, know the inside story. He may still wet the bed many (or most) nights; he has scary dreams that wake him. He whines a lot, he often comes into your room wanting to sleep with you, he still sucks his thumb, he can be picky and inflexible about eating, he may masturbate in public, and he can become terrified of dying. And you and his dad are the only ones who see *all* of this.

All of these things are normal for threes and fours because they need the chance to fall apart for some part of each day. The technical word for the phenomenon is *regression,* and children mostly do it with their mothers because they feel safe and understood by them. You understand this as your son's being tired, or cranky, or overstimulated. After all the progress of the day, they need to regress, and this regression serves the purpose of signaling to you or your son's caretaker that he needs to go home, to go to bed, to do some quiet activity.

You will learn your son's style and how to soothe him. One mother writes that she struggles with her son's whining. "I can't stand whining. I don't like it when he says 'I can't.' I prefer 'I don't want to.' When he cries too much I close the door and walk away. It's especially hard for him to cope when he's tired. My husband's always around to do it, though. He's a wonderful husband and father." Another mom told me that when her four-year-old comes home from prekindergarten in an upset frame of mind, she knows it because he immediately goes to get his bear, which ordinarily he does not use until bedtime. He needs his calming companion.

BABY MAKES THREE: SIBLING RIVALRY

The mother of three sons told me that when her youngest was born and his big brother, who was all of about six years old, held him for the first time, he whispered in awe, "He is a miracle!" For most young boys, a new baby in the family is more of a mixed blessing. In fact, to almost every older sibling a younger sibling seems like a bad idea.

Sure, there are some perks—an eventual playmate, some status in the family as a helper and role model, maybe a big-boy bed. But those are abstract ideas as far as benefits go. The practical downside can be steep.

A new baby cuts into the availability of your number one resource: Mom. A child very soon figures out that he's going to have to share the most important resources in the world: his mother's love, his mother's lap, and his mother's time.

A new sibling creates doubt and competition in the mind of an older child. Imagine it in a marital context: your spouse announces to you that because he loves you so much, he's going to get another of you. What would you think? Nothing good, I can tell you. Every child is thinking, *Wait—I should be enough! I'm a full-time project, and if you think you need another one, maybe it's because I'm not good enough.* Just thinking those (regressive) thoughts makes him feel babyish, and that doesn't feel good, either.

It stirs everyone up. That's simply what babies do. Everyone gets stirred up by the exclusivity of a mother's relationship with a baby, and it's easy for an older child to feel bumped out. Even dads get jealous sometimes.

That said, a boy also can embrace the inherent uncertainty and possibility a baby introduces, and find some delight and new opportunities in the role of older brother. To foster this bright-side adaptation:

• *Prepare your son for the new arrival while you're pregnant.* Let him know a baby is on the way and involve him in preparations so he can try on the new role of helper and responsible big brother.

• *Acknowledge his mix of feelings, including the negative ones.* Tell him you know it's going to be hard sometimes but also fun sometimes, too, and that it's natural to feel both happy and grumpy at times. Be open with your appreciation when he is helpful, kind, or understanding. Let him experience the new dignity and pride that go along with his new role in the family.

• *Don't say don't, as in "Don't feel the way you do."* When he says he hates his baby brother, don't say, "Don't hate your baby brother." Say, "Yeah, it's not easy to have a baby brother. Sometimes they can be demanding and a pain in the neck," and then take time to hear him out.

- *Watch out for the whacks.* The temptation is for any small boy of two or three to give the baby a whack every now and again just to let him know who's boss. It happens in every home, and it is not because the older sibling is a bad child. You'll need to keep an eye on the baby and help the older boy develop self-control. By the time an older sibling is six or so, he is more likely to be developing that self-control and experiencing himself favorably in his new role.

- *Show him you're still 100 percent in love with him.* A mother told me that she herself had had misgivings about her capacity to love two children equally—she couldn't imagine loving another child as much as she loved her first son. To her delight, she discovered she was quite capable of loving them both deeply, and noted that she simply had loved her firstborn longer.

- *Keep your connection strong.* Make time to be actively engaged with your older son—play, cook, read, or weed in the garden together. The activity will help him feel his connection to you, and because boys tend to be more emotionally accessible in the context of activity, it may provide a comfort zone for him to share his feelings and be open to your encouraging words.

I don't want to dismiss all of these symptoms with a wave of my hand. They still need to be managed. It is not a good thing to have a three- or four-year-old coming into bed with you every night, because he may come to believe that he cannot ever sleep in a room by himself and he may become more afraid as a result. That's a problem. You will need to accompany him back to his room, talk to him for a little bit, sit with him, and help him to return to sleep. It isn't good to have a boy constantly masturbating in public; it is upsetting for people, and if he cannot stop when he is reminded gently, it is probably a sign of excessive anxiety that needs to be attended to. No expert has ever offered advice that has stopped a boy from masturbating, but your son should be encouraged to do it in private, and if it is constant, you may need to address whatever threat is causing his constant anxiety.

It is worth noting that most psychological symptoms—the things that psychiatrists and psychologists worry about—are simply ordinary regressive behaviors with the volume turned up. So it isn't always easy to figure out what is temporary regressive behavior and what is more worrisome, because children of this age do go through phases where they are afflicted by fears and bad dreams. They need to be able to fall apart, and they need to be able to pull themselves together. In the end, you have to trust your judgment, be able to share your concerns with your spouse and your son's pediatrician, look for the nuances of development at work, and stay open to insight that comes from thoughtful observation and deliberation—not rushes to judgment.

SAVOR THE TENDER, TUMULTUOUS TIME TOGETHER

For mothers especially, during this time you are still the center of your son's world. Though your son ranges farther afield than he ever did before and may be in a preschool setting all day, his sun still rises and sets with you. He will never again find you as funny a companion as he will in these two years. He wants to joke with you and engage in silly word play; he wants to read with you and play board games. He doesn't want you to leave him and he doesn't want you to change. He will study you and critique what you are wearing, even your earrings, but only because he wants you to be his.

If he is in love with you, no doubt you are probably totally in love with him. A mother declared, "My son loves me and I love him. We have our own unique connection. I really enjoy figuring out who he is as a person. You always know where you stand with him because he gives you so many direct clues." One mother said that the most satisfying aspect of her relationship with her four-and-a-half-year-old son was "the pure love. There are no expectations from him." Well, of course there are expectations from him, but much of the time they are for closeness and attention and praise.

Another mother told me, "All three of my sons seem to think I am central to their general well-being. They like to hang out in my bedroom and read near me when I read in bed. They seem to think I know how they feel." And what age boys was she speaking about? In case you are worried that you will lose contact with your sons in the future, she is speaking of her four-year-old, of course, as well as her ten-year-old and thirteen-year-old sons.

This chapter began with a ferociously demanding boy who threw tantrums when he did not get his way and who seemed quite willing to hurt his mother's feelings. Here, I am talking about enjoying your connection to a devoted boy who is totally in love with his mother. It seems a contradiction, but it is not. They are two sides of the same coin, because your son is becoming more complex. He wants to hold on to you fiercely, and he wants to grow away from you. He wants to please you, and he wants you to admire him. He wants to respect your authority, and he wants to possess it himself. These are inevitable human contradictions.

Once you have solved the problems of discipline by developing a natural authority and some techniques that can stand up to his challenges, the two of you can settle down to have a great time, and you will. By the age of four many boys are little commentators who will give you a nonstop narration of your life together. By the age of four his vocabulary has grown from the twenty words he had at age two to fifteen hundred words, and soon, at age five, it will be more than two thousand. He can understand what you say, and he will converse with you about the many things you do together.

I think of this as a time when you have him mostly all to yourself and he has you all to himself. He can be a great companion. Freud thought that at this age a boy was in the Oedipal phase and wanted to possess his mother and compete with his father. It is a dubious theory if you take it literally; four-year-old boys don't want to have sex with their mothers. But Freud was not wrong about the passionate possessiveness that they display at this age. There are many three-

MAILBOX Q&A

Q: *My son wasn't even one year old when his father left. I worry that if I say things like "Your father was very good at that" or "He was really interested in that," my son will long for him more. I worry if I don't say anything, he'll feel it is not all right to discuss his father and ask questions. I worry about the effect of a child being raised by only one parent. Up to this point, I have only told my son, "Your father wasn't ready to be a father." I wonder when I should tell him the truth.*

A: I don't know what the "truth" is that you speak of. Probably he doesn't need to know it right away if the truth is ugly. What he does need to know is that, despite his father's absence, there were good things about him that he passed on through his genes. Whenever your son does something good that reminds you of his father, you should mention that to him. "Oh, your dad was strong like that. . . . Wow, you throw a ball like your father. . . . You're a sensitive guy like your dad." He needs to hear that he came from a living, breathing man and that that is a good thing in your eyes. Later on he will ask why his father left, and when he does you can give him a short, honest answer to the question; if he follows up with another question, give him more information.

Your son will have men in his life, and he will get a lot of what he needs from them, as well as from other boys. Will it exactly make up for not having a father? No. Will it be enough to make him a good man? Absolutely yes, as long as you see in him every day the man he's going to become.

and four-year-old boys who declare to their mothers that they're going to marry them when they grow up.

A friend whose job allows her to work from home tells the story of her son at this age, having grown accustomed to seeing her only in her jeans and T-shirts, being startled one day to see her wearing a dress and heels to go to a client meeting. He asked her why she was dressed that way. "This is what women wear when they go out someplace special," she said, to which he offered a completely egocentric and loving reply: "But you're not a woman—you're a *mom*!"

FATHERS: A DEEPENING COMMITMENT . . . OR NOT

Every father has to choose and choose again how involved he will be with his children. Why does he have a choice when his wife does not? There are multiple pressures, social and biological, that force couples with small children into more stereotyped gender roles. If mothers breast-feed their infants—and the vast majority do—they become tied to the well-being of their children in a biological way and get to know the temperament, rhythms, and quirks of their infants and toddlers. They tend to spend more time with the children than do fathers. Even couples who intended to share child rearing equally find themselves falling into traditional caretaker-breadwinner roles. A father is then presented with a choice when he comes home from work: interacting with children or reading the newspaper and watching TV. Research shows that a majority of dads choose the television; working mothers spend more time with children when they come home than do fathers.

Not all fathers, however, want to opt out of all the chores or the fun. They have promised themselves that they will be involved fathers. When they make that choice, it often has a lot to do with their disappointment in their own fathers. One father wrote to me, "My father was not very warm and loving when I was growing up. He just didn't know how. He was never unkind or authoritarian, just aloof. He doesn't know this, but the one time he ever took me fishing I had overheard my mom scolding him to do it: 'Your son is going to grow up and you won't even know him!' "

Another father of two sons, ages three and a half and one and a half, said, "My father was an aggressive and abusive alcoholic, and that has totally shaped the kind of father I want to be for my sons. I want to be their caregiver. I want them to come to me for anything and everything. I want to do fun things with

> *When he gets very physical with his friends, I get anxious. I don't want anybody to get hurt. But it's usually just mutual boy play. I am worried how he will transition to kindergarten.*
>
> —Mother of a boy, four and a half

them. I want to show them and tell them how much I love them. I want to *be there* for my children."

Even when a father has made a commitment, it can be tough to make it a priority and to deal with the feelings of being the backup parent. One dad, asked to describe the hardest thing about fathering, said: "Finding time after work. And I get my feelings hurt easily by the younger one's preference for Mommy." Another said, "My work takes a toll on my moods and energy, and sometimes when I come home I have little psychic energy left until after a 'self time-out.' My sons don't understand this."

But the payoff for spending the time is enormous. The man whose own father was an abusive alcoholic wrote, "I feel very close to both my boys. I feel it a lot when the workweek begins again and I can't see them as much as I would like to. But I also feel it when I am with them. I am always thinking about my family and how much I love them."

Dads Play, Play, Play

Researchers have found that the nature of a mother's bond to her children is different from that of a father's. Mothers, on average, tend to be more emotionally in tune with their children than dads. In one videotaped study, fathers tended to interrupt the flow of their children's interests when they wanted to influence the child's play. Mothers watched, waited, and used the child's natural curiosity in order to redirect their play. If mothers are spending more time with children and are more in tune with the children, then what are the special contributions of fathers? There are a number, and arousing play is chief among them.

Both mothers and fathers engage in more chasing, rolling, tickling, play-boxing, or wrestling with boys than they do with girls; however, it is easier for fathers to engage in such play. Fathers of preschoolers orient toward any play that involves large motor ability, and boys, in particular, respond to it strongly. One father in my survey described the things that he and his son do together in the evening: "He loves it when we play with his toys, run around the house, wrestle, dance, and read at bedtime." Another dad's list included "biking, watching trains, going to the park, going for ice cream, reading to him, going to

FROM THE DADDY DIARIES: LIKE FATHER, LIKE SONS

Paul, the father of four-year-old twin boys, offers a pragmatic perspective on parenting:

"My sons seem to be typical four-year-olds. They're wild and fun. They have great imaginations and play with their toys and friends all day long. They get mad and sad and hurt. They sing out loud to themselves and dance when they're happy. They love to read books with me and my wife. They are best friends with each other but also struggle with competition and sharing between them.

"My mom says I was 'a big noise covered with dirt'—a little rascal, always dirty and noisy and getting in trouble and pushing limits, a little social bug in class and always disruptive. My sons are the same. I encourage it. I like to see them pushing their own limits, and the rewards are noticeable. They fearlessly explore their surroundings, getting bruised and cut in the process sometimes, and when they succeed, their self-confidence grows noticeably. I think they'll probably be school-smart, too, but I don't know yet. I'm not pushing that. I want them to play. They're learning numbers and letters anyway just because they have their tape measures for when they're playing 'construction man' and from asking about the books we read.

"We get loud and obnoxious together, we wrestle and play chase, we go to the beach and play. I participate in their games. I dream up fun things that are unusual; we sit on my longboard skateboard like a toboggan and ride down the gently sloping sidewalk together till we're going pretty quickly by the end of the block, then do it again.

"We sing 'Twinkle Twinkle Little Star' and about three or four other songs together at bedtime, just like my mom did with me. We read books before bed. They help with raking or pruning; I've taken them carefully up the ladder onto the roof to clean the leaves off. They like pounding nails into boards or wearing my motorcycle helmet around the house. They definitely like helping with fixing things or just doing the chores.

"We've given our sons basic tools for successful interactions with others and remind them of those tools when needed, but I find if I intervene too much, they don't learn. If I hang back and let them thrash it out, they often surprise me with the way they get things worked out. Only when they really go brainstem and start physically hurting one another do I have to step in.

"It keeps getting better and better. How could it get better than this? Four years old is pretty cool. I hope I can say the same at sixteen."

church, going for hikes and walks, making birdhouses, doing Christmas rituals like cutting down the tree and going to the Santa parade."

Wrestling is not the be-all and end-all of the father-son relationship, however. That same father who emphasized going and doing said that the most satisfying things he did with his sons were "holding them, telling them I love them, and hearing it back."

Be Sympathetic with His Fears

One of the things that a preschool boy looks to his father for is admiration. We have already seen that by four a boy wants to be seen as "tough"; he uses the word a lot to describe himself, and he hopes that he can live up to that ideal. Of course, he cannot be so strong, at least not all the time. He gets frustrated, he cries, and he often feels little and incompetent. He also has a lot of fears: of the dark, of strange places and things, of crowds, of being left alone. Sometimes dads become embarrassed by the natural fears of a little boy; mothers seem to understand them and accept them more easily than fathers.

When my son was three we went as a family to Disney World. We had arranged in advance to go to two "character breakfasts" where the well-known Disney movie characters were played by adults in costumes: Aladdin, Chip 'n Dale, Snow White, and of course Mickey himself. The person who played Aladdin must have been well over six feet tall, and when he came cheerfully up to our breakfast table, our son, Will, took one look and shot under the table, refusing to emerge in spite of Aladdin's blandishments and reassurances. Two days later Will was still not ready to go up and hug Mickey, as so many other children were doing. He watched cautiously from a distance.

I do not remember being embarrassed by his fears, but I do remember wishing that he didn't feel them so acutely, partly for him—it is not fun to feel scared—and partly because . . . well, why? Why did I need him not to be afraid of a Disney character? I think it is because I, like all fathers, in my gut am likely to draw the incorrect conclusion that a fear at three or four years old might remain a fear at eight or fourteen. Nothing could be further from the truth. Fears are part of development; they come and go. Between three and five they are so powerful because of the vividness of the preschooler's imagination. If, for them, dinosaurs are real and potentially lurking around any corner, then an immense Aladdin figure is not to be trusted. Who knows what he'll do?

We can laugh gently at the fear of a three-year-old or four-year-old, but boys are acutely sensitive to being

He is like a present that I unwrap every day. —Mother of a four-and-a-half-year-old boy

shamed, and they care deeply about what their fathers think of them. It is important that a father understand that his son's fears are normal and not necessarily indicative of similar fears in the future. Is it the case that there are boys who are temperamentally bold

> *He pushes me out of my comfort zone and teaches me to be a better parent.*
> —Mother of a boy, four and a half

and others who are temperamentally cautious? Of course, and such traits continue throughout life, but even the boldest boy can be easily frightened when he is a preschooler.

No Need to Toughen Him Up

One of the things that mothers talk to me about with real pain is their husband's attempts to make their sons tougher. A mother will tell me that her husband is more controlling or uses harsher disciplinary techniques than she does, or especially that he seems uneasy with her attempts to console the boy when he is upset. "You're babying him," a father will say when the mother is just comforting her son. Research shows that fathers, on average, use more controlling discipline, and they can, of course, rely on their larger size and deeper voice. Many fathers are also proud of the fact that they don't rush to their son's aid quite as quickly as their wives do. "She wants to protect him from falls, bumps, and bruises, and I want him to fall occasionally and learn from the small pain," wrote one father.

I have no objections to one parent—and it isn't always the father—asking for more self-reliance from the child and the other being more sympathetic. I do object to fathers who believe that little boys, who are acutely sensitive to their father's opinion of them, need to be toughened up with harsh discipline or tough lessons. Life will toughen up all boys; their experiences of being in social groups, of competing, and of trying to measure up to their ideals will provide plenty of tests. If a father tries to toughen up a preschooler, either by frightening him or by humiliating him, the fear of the father that results may last for a long time. There is no better foundation for a strong, "tough" boy than the understanding and love of both his mother and his father, no matter what.

CHAPTER FIVE

READY OR NOT,
HERE COMES SCHOOL

Your Son, Five to Seven

The hardest thing for him seems to be his energy, and the difficulty that creates for him in school.
Sitting still and writing and coloring are what's called for at school right now,
but he would rather be moving, jumping, rolling.
—*Mother of a six-year-old boy*

NICK, WHO WILL BE SIX IN A MONTH, SHOWED ME AROUND HIS SMALL KINDER-garten classroom, part of a cozy community preschool located in an eighty-year-old building behind the church where his family worships on Sundays. Nick is a tall blond boy with a serious face. His mother told me that he has an "old soul"—"Everybody says so," she commented—and he was living up to that description.

He took his time, leading me on a careful tour of the room where he spends his days in a group of ten children, seven boys and three girls. It was late November. Three months into the school year, he was clearly proud of his school and felt at home there. He had been ready when he started kindergarten, perhaps more than ready. He was five years eight months old when he began and he had started reading on his own that summer.

His mother said she had had him repeat prekindergarten because she felt strongly that he was not ready for kindergarten, even though he was clearly strong enough academically. "He wasn't good at transitions," his mother reported, "and he liked home so much."

Nick was furious about her decision because his best friend, who was only four months older than he was, moved up to kindergarten and left him behind. He went on strike for the first three months, refusing to make friends with the pre-K crowd; many days in the fall, he stood at the window watching the kindergartners at recess. He was a bit distant from the teacher and openly angry at his parents. He told me that pre-K was "boring, the same things every day." Now, however, he is at peace and close to his friends in kindergarten. "This is my mailbox," he told me, pointing to one open-ended section in a wooden honeycomb of twelve openings. I asked him what kind of mail he gets.

"Our school mail. We get a poem of the week. Pictures that we might draw. Homework."

"Homework?" I asked. "What kind of homework do you get?"

"Hmmm . . . stuff that we do. It's the letter *s* this week. We write the letters and we have to come up with our own *s*-word."

"It's not so tough," his mother, Jean, added. "Usually two or three pages."

"Sometimes five," Nick corrected her, and it wasn't clear whether he was boasting or just trying to be an accurate reporter. We stopped in front of the newsprint pad at the front of the classroom where the teacher had written four sentences about Thanksgiving. Nick read three out of the four sentences accurately. I sensed he had memorized one of them, but it was also clear that he could sound out the three syllables of *Thanksgiving*.

> *They tend to compare my son with the girls in the class and conclude that he is diagnosably hyper; in fact, my son is eager to please and will focus endlessly on projects that seem to blend imagination and action. Adult women seem quick to suggest ADHD, while adult men smile and remember their boyhoods when they deal with him.* —Father of a six-year-old son

> *He is very active and athletic. He jumps over ski jumps, hikes, and runs. In truth, I've never seen him out of breath.*
> —Mother of a seven-year-old son

We continued our tour over to the farmstand, where children were playing at selling vegetables; the listening center, where two children could listen to books on tape through big earphones; and a sand table covered with green nubby platforms on which children build their Lego structures. "We only do the sand sometimes," Nick said, implying that sand play is rare indeed. "You can see some down there." He pointed under the table.

Then he took me to the back part of the room, to an extraordinary structure about a foot tall, a dome-shaped "jail" constructed out of sticks and green duct tape. "This was the dungeon that we built," Nick told me, his voice and eyes brightening. "Mike, Ken, and Todd. I built it, too. Mike and Todd started it. When they were building it I helped. We tried to tie something with string, but it wouldn't work. Then we tried clear tape, and it wouldn't work. The top was okay but the bottom was slipping. So we found the green tape and it was good. And I figured out how to put the stick at the bottom so the bad guys couldn't get out."

Of all the things Nick had showed me so far, this dungeon that the boys had built together was clearly the most exciting thing in the room for him. Teamwork, creating something with other boys, the excitement of "bad" guys who needed to be put in jail—it was all embodied in that stick-and-green-tape creation. On this one quick tour of his classroom, Nick had unwittingly introduced me to all the aspects—and conflicts—of kindergarten: work versus play, the "letter of the week" versus a homemade dungeon, reading sentences versus sand play. Nick was clearly ready to do it all. What made him ready for school? Was it his advanced age, his early reading ability, his capacity to cooperate with others to build a dungeon, or his even, mature temperament?

If Nick could be the poster child for kindergarten success, why do so many boys, including boys Nick's age, present such a different picture? What shapes a boy's journey through his earliest years in school—kindergarten through second grade—and how does his experience shape him? How do these earliest school experiences come to define him, not only in school but in his relationship with his parents and his beliefs about himself?

DEVELOPMENT MEETS ITS MATCH—OR MISMATCH

Parents who describe their sons at kindergarten age often paint a poignant picture of a little boy who is loving and vibrant, eager to learn and eager to master his world. Depending on the fit between a boy's development and his school program and teachers, their son's transition to kindergarten seems either to open his life up in new, exciting, and sometimes challenging ways or to close it down in a struggle that comes to overshadow every part of his life. A mother described this before-and-after picture of her five-year-old son:

> He was very emotionally aware, sensitive and empathetic, until school started. Now he seems angry, hostile, and frustrated. He used to share his feelings, but now in kindergarten he seems really mad at me a lot. It's hard to take—the disrespect, sass, faces. Kindergarten has thrown a wrench into the works.

Another mother summed up the concern parents often express:

> My biggest worry is that his energy level and physical expressiveness will be a source of shaming for him—and that he will be mischievous in order to differentiate himself, as well as get into power struggles with authorities because of his need to be in charge.

Finally, the struggle can exhaust parents as well as their boys, and shake their confidence in their son, themselves, and the future. A mother described what impresses her most about her six-year-old son: "I love that he feels passionate about a lot of things. I love that he is a different character all the time. I love that he imagines. I love that he is a good artist. I love how he loves people and animals and even things. I love that he is smart and has an excellent memory. I could go on and on." She then, however, expressed her hopelessness over her son's continuing difficulty at school and with teachers:

> I feel he is drowning—he is misunderstood and just felt to be stupid by his teachers—and I wonder what I can do to help him. I wish he could have more male teachers. I wish I could find an all-boys school. I wish he could just grow up normal and happy.

The Eight Lines of Development

The Developmental Story Advances

"He runs at extremes," said the mother of a five-year-old boy, going on to describe the physical and emotional whirlwind of boys this age. "He loves me and shows it, leans on me when he needs it with no care for where we are. Still likes to twirl my hair for comfort, as he did as a baby when he was nursing." At the same time, she is distressed by power struggles that occur "when I need him to do something and he refuses and is unable to tell me why, or what he'd rather do. The revving up that happens with him in unstructured settings. The difficulties he has keeping his hands to himself, either acting out impulsively physically toward other kids or accidentally pushing into or tripping over them without always stopping to say sorry." Let's see why.

Physical Development

By the age of five, the average boy can run faster, jump higher, and throw a ball farther than the average girl; boys excel at physical activities that involve power and force. Girls excel in fine motor skills, such as drawing or writing, or in gross motor skills that combine foot movement and balance, such as skipping, so boys can seem clumsy next to girls, and boy handwriting is usually immature and illegible in comparison to that of the average girl. What is true for both boys and girls is that they work hard at the things they are good at and tend to lose interest in the things they are not as good at, so the gender gap in throwing a baseball and in handwriting, for instance, is going to grow over the coming years.

There is a huge range of athletic ability in boys from five to seven, from the dazzlingly athletic to the uncoordinated and cautious. In the world of boys a big split opens between boys who are ready, even impatient for organized sports and those who wish to avoid them. Boys who are not very good will still claim that they are close to the top in sports in their group. It is hard to tell whether they are self-deluded or lying; what is clear is that athletic status is very important.

When there was more neighborhood play, boys could move in and out of games, with the less talented gaining acceptance for simply filling out a team and making the game possible. With town sports occupying more and more of the life of suburban children in the United States today—82 percent of children in the United States participate in town sports—a boy and his family are forced to confront a number of questions: Is he an athlete or not? Once he has made a commitment to a team, does he need to see it through? Does he have the emotional resilience to withstand the competitive intensity of other boys and the possibility of losing? If he decides to leave organized sports, is he a failure?

Like it or not, boys are always defined by their athletic ability or lack of it. Because you can never be sure how boys will react to the competitive pressures, I tend to want to protect boys from competitive sports for as long as possible, unless you have a son who is literally dying to get into them and can handle them. One father wrote me that his son is "terrible at sports. He was the only basketball player on his team to stand in one spot and attempt to use Jedi powers to win the game, and he's targeted by rougher kids for bullying at times." I would like to see the majority of boys play on recreational teams of mixed ability, protected from a system of select teams with cuts until they are closer to ten years old, but the social pressure to join teams when every other boy in the class is in them can be overwhelming.

Attachment

A mother may feel that her son is moving away from her as he becomes more independent between five and seven; it only seems that way because he is forging stronger relationships with other adults, namely, his dad and his teachers. At this age, a father might feel that he has a new, more dedicated companion who shares his interests. I know a father who saved all of the comic books from his childhood to give to his son, and started to do so when his boy reached kindergarten. His wife was baffled by comics and put off by what she regarded as the violence in them. The son was thrilled to share what his father had once loved as a boy. Becoming closer to his father also allows a boy to resolve whatever disappointments he has left over from the Oedipal phase of the four- and five-year-old boy we met in the previous chapter, who was so in love with and possessive of his mother.

Your son now has a lot of new adult women in his life, mainly his teachers, some of whom he dislikes ("She's mean") and some of whom he adores ("She's nice"). If boys in kindergarten, first grade, and second grade have a teacher who likes boys—and they figure that out in no time at all—they bring to her much of the same love and energy they share with their moms ("Mrs. Jones, look what I made!"). And if they have a teacher who does not understand boys or is punitive toward them, they act toward her like angry, disappointed lovers.

Social Development

By the ages of five to seven, boys have been each other's companions and playmates for some years, and the rules of boy society are well known to all: exclusive boundaries for the boy group, no playing with girls, cooperation in group projects, individual competition in running, boasting, and showing off, and close, empathic (but unadvertised) relationships between some boys.

That boys do not talk as much as girls about having a "best friend" is sometimes confusing for moms, because it is often such a feature of girl life in kindergarten and first grade. Mothers, who remember the power of such friendships from their own lives, often wish it for their sons. Close boy friendships do occur, and sometimes, when the families are close as well, two boys can be as close or closer than brothers.

Popularity in boys' groups is based on fulfilling the ideals of masculinity, and boys compete about this in highly public ways: by boasting about their athletic accomplishments, by wearing jerseys for their favorite sports teams and athletes, and by retelling exciting parts of movies they have seen.

Cognitive Development

The biggest change in these years is that children grow out of the magical thinking of years three and four and become far more logical and connected to the concrete properties of objects. The brain is coming under the control of the frontal lobes, and that manifests itself in the more realistic attack on problems demonstrated by children of this age. One of the key cognitive achievements of this age is labeled "conservation." Psychologists test for this achievement by showing a child two beakers of the same size containing equal amounts of liquid. Once a child has confirmed that the two beakers contain equal amounts of liquid, the contents of one of the beakers is poured into a third, taller, thinner beaker. When they see the taller column of liquid, younger children react to the superficial difference and say the taller one contains more than the original beaker. Only when a child is capable of understanding that the amount has not changed, even though the superficial look of it has been altered, has he mastered the principle of conservation.

This experiment is known to every psychologist, and though it may not seem to have practical implications for parenting, I think it is important for parents to understand the powerful changes in the thinking of a boy at this age. The five-to-seven shift will transform your boy from a magical thinker into a true scientist, and he will then be driven to master the world as it is. This age sees not just the explosion of scientific inquiry but also a burst of creativity. Boys at this age imagine many things and want to create and build them.

Academic Development

The central academic achievements of the years from five to seven are managing the transition to school and its demands, tackling reading, and coming to grips with numbers. Readiness for school is crucial to a boy's academic success, because if he is ready for kindergarten, then he is likely to transform into the "young scholar"—as one first-grade teacher described it—that many first and second graders become. Academic success for a boy depends on his readiness for school.

Emotional Self-Regulation

Between five and seven, boys gain an enormous amount of control over their feelings. You see far fewer outright tantrums in boys of this age, and the occasional meltdowns—an inevitable part of childhood—are more circumscribed. It occurs in part because children become self-conscious in front of other children. A kindergarten boy who cannot tolerate any frustration is going to see the impatience and exasperation in the faces of his classmates when he interrupts play with his demands, and other children are going to start avoiding him. The threat of exclusion is as effective in helping a boy bring his behavior under control as any adult intervention. Precisely because peer pressure is so powerful, when a boy remains unaffected by it and continues to blow up, boast, lie, and have tantrums, he is signaling that he is unusually angry because of his family situation or possibly that he has a diagnosable mental illness such as oppositional defiant disorder, conduct disorder, or severe ADHD.

All boys try to control their crying once they are in a classroom with other boys. It is not that a boy is censured each and every time he cries; a group of boys makes an instantaneous evaluation of whether or not any boy who is crying had a good reason to do so (and thereby reserve for themselves the right to cry for cause should they need to).

Learning to manage emotions and emotional outbursts is an important part of growing up for all children. But when boys are pressured to avoid crying at all costs, anywhere and everywhere, they pay a high price. When crying is declared off-limits for a boy, he is shut off from an essential part of healthy emotional expression. If he can't cry to release the emotional tension—the pain, the sadness, the anger—it takes a huge amount of mental effort to keep from crying. As time goes on, the pressure of unresolved hurt and unshed tears grows, and it takes even more effort not to cry. Talking about emotions in any way might open the floodgates, so it often seems better not to talk at all, or to shout angrily or strike out physically, instead of talking from the heart.

Play therapist Larry Cohen, whose clients also include men, said that when he asks men in therapy how they managed not to cry when they were boys, their stories are heart-wrenching. "Even when abandoned or neglected or abused or bereaved, these men had to maintain stoicism and toughness at all costs, even as little boys. They remember deliberately closing off, turning to violence or pornography, pushing themselves in sports or other areas beyond where they felt pain, throwing themselves into their work. Sometimes all it takes is for men to finally tell these stories in order for the tears to come tumbling out, at last."

Healthy emotional self-regulation for a boy allows for tears and talk and time to reflect on life's hardships, gather his wits, and move on.

Moral and Spiritual Development

School is a great moral crucible because all children are sharing the scarce resources of the classroom: the teacher's time, first place in line, free-choice time in the block corner (there isn't room for every boy). Issues of justice and cries of "That's not fair" become central to classroom discussions in the early grades. If an adult hears these discussions only as complaints, he or she is missing the powerful moral debate that goes on among children of this age. They are trying to define for themselves what is "good" and what is "bad," and then trying to live up to the definitions.

Much of this sounds like scolding or tattling, and adults sometimes react against children who are using their adult-like voice on classmates—it can get tiring—but the underlying impulse is the desire to know what is moral and live up to it. Every boy wants to be a "good boy." If his impulses or his temper gets him into so much trouble in school that he cannot see how he will ever be thought of as good, watch out: he'll fall into despair or adopt an angry, outlaw identity.

Many boys of this age pray. A Native American father wrote that his six-year-old son prayed on occasion but that the prayers tended to be a "superficial list of thank-yous." On the other hand, his son's imagination was deeply engaged by certain Ojibway traditions, and he would tell his father what the blowing trees were saying and what the colors of the sunset wanted him to hear. He also participated in blessing ceremonies involving the burning of sacred plants such as sage, cedar, and sweetgrass, which symbolize cleansing. The father noted: "This also works to eradicate monsters, by the way."

Nick's mother reported, "He has a picture of my mother and father holding him when he was a baby, and he thinks about them being with God," but he told her that God should be a girl. "He wonders whether animals have the same heaven. I say, 'I don't know. What do you think?' Sometimes he likes to imagine what heaven looks like." Nick's mother takes him with her when she visits elderly, house-bound members of her church, a number of whom have since died. When his own grandfather was dying, Nick stepped out the back door, looked up at the sky, and shouted out, "God, get ready for Grampa!"

Identity

Between five and seven years a boy's identity becomes solidified; he knows that his gender, name, and skin color are all permanent. Gender now matters to boys more than it ever did before. Many things are decided on the basis of whether an activity is a boy thing or a girl thing, and much of your son's public identity depends on his asserting his boy-ness. This includes a lot of boy humor, laughing about farting, potty talk, and the beginning of sex talk. You cannot stop it; all you can do is set limits on it.

However, boys at this age often define themselves by what they do not like, and after three years in school, there is plenty of material to draw upon for an unhappy worldview. Many parents find their seven-year-olds to be gloomy and full of stories of suffering: how the other kids at school "hate me" and how the teacher "hates me" and how unfair everything is. Many caring parents who declare proudly that they believe what their child tells them may find themselves baffled by the onslaught of negativity in the seven-year-old. The seven-year-old with his complaints stands in stark contrast to the scattered, imaginative five-year-old and the triumphant, purposeful six-year-old, but it is just a momentary regression on the way to three of the most focused years of childhood: eight, nine, and ten.

WHEN IS A BOY READY FOR SCHOOL?

No matter how much preschool a boy has had—and more than half of American children have had some preschool experience at least a couple of days per week—the transition to "real" school, to kindergarten, is an important moment in a boy's life. It is culturally important because it marks his transition from the protection of the family to being a citizen of a wider world. It may be the longest separation he has ever had from his mother. It might mean that he rides a big yellow bus, alone, for the first time. It might be that he is given something called "homework" that he must remember to take home and which his parents will take seriously. It might be the first time he feels that he is being evaluated and compared with other boys outside his home.

The age at which a boy starts kindergarten, his developmental readiness, and the experiences he has there will affect him for the rest of his school career, and perhaps for the rest of his life. In his first three years of formal schooling—kindergarten through second grade—he forms a view of himself as a successful boy or a failure. Research confirms what most parents and educators see every

> *I swear he'll either end up in the Olympics or end up comatose in a hospital bed. Part of me is proud of him; part of me worries. Fortunately he is very coordinated.* —Mother of a seven-year-old son

day: that how well a boy performs in these earliest years of school affects his self-image and later performance. Many boys who struggle eventually find (often with help) a strategy that enables them to "do school" and survive with psyche intact, but it is a monumental task for them, and for their parents. Parents know this intuitively and do not want to start their sons in school too early. At the same time, they want them to be challenged at the appropriate developmental time. Some parents, for economic and work reasons, need for their boys to start school as soon as possible. They may not want to pressure their sons by putting them in a situation where they might fail, but they have no choice.

What is it that makes a boy ready for the responsibilities of kindergarten? Fundamentally, his readiness is determined by developmental changes in his brain and body. Many years ago, Sheldon White, a psychologist at Harvard, described a series of transformations that have since come to be called the "five-to-seven shift." The brain changes dramatically in these three years; it becomes more coordinated and coherent, more efficient, and capable of a greater attention span. The process of myelination, which provides the axon of the cortical neurons with an insulating sheath and improves the transmission of nerve impulses, accelerates. There is also a pronounced growth spurt between five and seven, the only such phase of rapid growth between infancy and puberty.

As a result of these biological changes, psychologists observe radical shifts in children's command of grammar and in their cognitive development. They can, for example, distinguish more clearly between fantasy and reality. They now understand that Sesame Street isn't a real place and that the characters on television cannot hear the people who are watching them. They are emotionally steadier and more serious. They are capable of getting themselves dressed, running errands, and paying attention for much longer stretches of time.

It should also be noted that all those biological changes and the emerging command of language are put to use by boys in ways that may or may not be welcome in the classroom, as first this father then a mother note:

He is physically active, always moving, always making sound effects with his mouth, struggling to grasp the complexities of an effective knock-knock joke.

Once they're five, *everything* is about the penis. I can't even tell you the last time we went without a day of some type of bodily function being discussed—everything from how come "it" is hard when you get up in the morning to all the butt, fart, pee, and poop talk.

At Nick's preschool, described at the start of this chapter, I sat with Mary, the mother of four, talking about her twin sons, Jack and Will, who had just turned five a few days before. They were running around the playground at the end of their day in pre-K. Jack was clutching the penguin he had just received as a birthday gift. One of the boys' friends is just four but already more mature in his speech; some boys her sons' age are already in kindergarten. But Mary understands well that chronological age and developmental age are different and that pre-K is right where her sons need to be, developmentally. She is neither afraid nor defensive. She sees that her boys are on the young side, and she has faith. Jack came over to his mother and idly twirled the penguin in her lap. But he was also looking past her, cautiously watching the older boys running and ramming each other with trucks; it was apparent that he had retreated to his mother's side because their activities made him fearful. Only eight months separate Jack and Will from Nick, but it is a critical eight months.

KINDERGARTEN HAS CHANGED, BUT BOYS HAVE NOT

Parents today are aware that kindergarten is no longer the "children's garden" that the original German name suggests. Due to the pressures of state testing, the almost universal college expectations for today's high school graduates, and the increasing demands for homework in early elementary school, this first year of school is a more academic place than it has ever been. One kindergarten teacher wrote to me saying that the challenges for her children were "being ready to read fluently, write with legibility, and problem-solve real-life mathematical situations." Wow!

The universal trend in American education has been to start academic preparation earlier, both to give disadvantaged children the early academic experiences that long have provided a strong foundation for middle-class chil-

HOW TO HELP YOUR SON THROUGH KINDERGARTEN TRANSITION

Most countries have a little ritual celebration when you send a child off to kindergarten. In Russia they have a whole induction ceremony for new kindergartners in an assembly. Going off to kindergarten is a special day, and it's much anticipated and talked about. To mark the moment and support your son through this special transition, look for ways to familiarize him with the idea and the place, and recognize it as part of growing up.

• Talk about it in advance, but don't overdo it. Often parents' own anxiety over their son's start of school finds its expression in too much talk. Visit the school so your son can get some hands-on time on the playground or in a classroom, if possible. Many schools welcome visits at scheduled times. Have your son talk or visit and play with boys who are already in kindergarten.

• Many boys are excited to be starting kindergarten. Don't assume that episodes of the jitters mean he's school-phobic.

• Once he starts, develop a reliable routine for getting to school in the morning. Make sure it allows time for him to get dressed and ready without feeling hurried. Be upbeat in the mornings.

• If possible, walk to school or encourage some activity—it will help your son manage his energy for the demands of the school day.

• Take cues from his teacher or other parents and children about goodbye rituals. If you have any concerns about his ability to settle in, ask the teacher how he is adjusting.

• Talk with your son about his day, or allow him to talk about anything *but* his day if he prefers. Listen to his fears without soliciting them. Express confidence in him no matter what, and use your tone of voice to reassure and encourage.

dren and to better prepare children for the testing that looms on the horizon, in second grade or fourth grade. These efforts to beef up the curriculum have changed the nature of kindergarten and altered the experience for boys, who lag behind girls in the development of the reading, listening, and small motor skills that are so helpful in school. The same kindergarten teacher quoted above who wrote about the necessary academic skills also said: "I think the boys who come to school with fine motor struggles are telling me that they still need to work with Legos, blocks, trains, and building materials and are not ready to spend time on detailed fine motor activities."

Kathleen Fraser, the longtime director of the preschool evaluation team in Arlington, Massachusetts, has strong feelings about the matter of the right time to start boys in kindergarten: "For twenty years, I said that children should go to kindergarten on the young side, when they were just four years nine months or early fives, and I continued saying it in hopes that the fact of having younger children would keep kindergarten a social place. But I have stopped. Kindergarten has changed for good; it is much more academic. So now I say, 'When in doubt, keep them out!' "

Jane Katch, for thirty years a gifted teacher and author of compelling books about kindergarten children at play in her classroom, agrees with Fraser's assessment. "When I started teaching kindergarten, most kindergarten classrooms had a lot of play. They emphasized social development and verbal development and some ABC's." The assumption of that day was that children would learn to read in first grade. There was very little pressure on kindergartners; the classrooms were filled with "big blocks, woodworking, sand, and water."

She remembers the change that occurred in the late 1980s. She was teaching at the University of Chicago Laboratory School, founded by the great American educator John Dewey as a showcase of progressive education. Suddenly Katch was required to give reading and writing tests in kindergarten. "It was really weird for the kids. Paper-and-pencil tests! The students in my class thought they were supposed to help other children. Now they had to sit down and they couldn't talk."

Over the years Katch has come to believe that today's more academic kindergarten "doesn't work for boys. What happens is that they come into school thinking they are okay and they immediately discover that the things that are valued by the teacher are the things they are worst at: fine motor coordination, word/sound discrimination skills, hearing the beginning, middle, and end of words. They can't come up with them

> Because I am a woman and an only child, watching him grow is like observing a foreign creature—he seems so exotic and eccentric to me somehow. His boy energy is (mostly) fun to be around and I appreciate it immensely.
> —Mother of a seven-year-old son

or recognize them. They will in six months, but they can't now. They aren't as good at coming up quickly with answers to questions, so they don't raise their hands. It is much harder for them to sit still, so they're told they're restless."

With passion, Katch continued to talk about the bind in which school puts boys. "And we've cut out everything that they are good at. Boys at this age have terrific skills at making big things happen together, as a group—cooperating, communicating, being a constructive group together to make exciting things work." She went on to describe how that morning the boys in her kindergarten had all gathered in the block corner of her classroom and had built a double chute for marbles. The bottom was a ramp with several lanes the marbles could go down and different numbers at the bottom for scores that depended on which lane the marble ended up in. The boys wrote big numbers such as 100 and kept score—"Not that they can add," Katch mentioned—and they cheered each other's good shots.

Katch does not teach reading to her kindergartners. Why not? She is more interested in getting them to tell their own stories. That's what every child does in her class every day: they dictate their stories to her, she reads them out loud to the class, and then they are acted out by the children. Her children learn to be authors before they are readers.

"The first-grade teacher is pleased that my kids love to tell stories and aren't afraid to put them on paper," Katch said. "Kids from other schools who come to her class may know more about letters and sounds, but they sit in front of their blank paper and won't put anything down on it because they might make a mistake."

> *The way to get him to tell me things is just to hang out with him and just have it quiet with lots of space, and he brings things up.* —Mother of a five-year-old boy

HOW THE CHANGE IN KINDERGARTEN AFFECTS BOYS

The developmental discrepancy between the average girl and the average boy in kindergarten is not a secret to anyone. Children know it. As a six-year-old girl once told me, "All the girls in kindergarten can read, and not all of the boys can. Some of the girls can read chapter books"—she could—"and *none* of the boys can!" A first-grade boy explained to me, "Boys are the ones who always get in trouble." Children intuitively pinpoint the key developmental discrepancies that teachers and research tell us predict a boy's early success or struggle in

"WHAT REALLY MATTERS": A MOTHER'S LETTER

Dear Dr. Thompson,

Our seven-year-old son, Tim, from the time he was a toddler, was incredibly active and got into just about anything. Additionally, as a young child, he was diagnosed with language delay and not only was delayed in speaking, but he would (and sometimes still does) use idiosyncratic words to describe things.

I used to worry that something was incredibly wrong, with him being so fearless, active, and all. The combination of this and his language problems made us wonder if he had some sort of learning difference or attention disorder. I was afraid for him, so I am embarrassed now to admit that I wasn't always the kind and patient teacher that I should have been. Reading your book *Raising Cain* and hearing you speak at a school program was an eye-opener for both myself and my husband. In so many ways, I had absolutely no idea how different boys were from girls.

Our way of teaching Tim began to change. We wrote letters in the sand and taught him to count by jumping. We learned not to tell him that he couldn't go over ski jumps, but rather we told him that he needed to learn to go over small jumps before he attempted the big ones. We learned not to push his development, but to start kindergarten at six years old.

We don't yet know if he has a learning difference, but it is now less important. I know what matters the most is raising a kind and empathetic person, and I've learned to appreciate and admire him for the person that he is.

We joke that we may not be able to take our boys to fancy restaurants, but they can hike, ski, and climb like no boys you've ever seen!

school: reading (cognitive development), self-control (the development of emotional self-regulation), and the capacity to make the shift to the community life of school and the shared learning expectations that form the structure of a school day and school learning (academic development).

Because reading, sitting still, and taking school seriously are so strongly developmental, the boys on the younger end of the development arc are most at risk for difficulty or failure in an academic kindergarten, although all children are shortchanged by a curriculum that pressures them to move forward too quickly.

The question "Should we hold our son back?" is one of the most common queries I get from parents and it is not a simple one to answer, because there are so many factors involved, both developmental and economic. (See pages 184–85 for a readiness checklist.) Some parents, such as Nick's mom and dad, can afford not only to keep their child out of school for an additional year before starting in kindergarten but also to pay tuition for a small, private kindergarten. They can afford to say, as Nick's mother did: "He was young. He wasn't good at transitions. He needed more time at home." Most families, however, cannot honor a child's need for more home time. As a result, their sons may suffer in kindergarten from being too young, surrounded by more developmentally mature girls and significantly older boys who are likely more developmentally mature as well.

Two Scandinavian countries, Finland and Norway, whose test scores are among the best in the world, do not traditionally start school until the age of seven. Though Norwegian and Finnish students are behind their European and American counterparts in academics when they start school, they soon catch up.

For many boys, kindergarten is a time for them to gain control of their feelings and their behavior and to learn how to interact socially with other children. It is a place where they grow up and come to terms with the reality of school. Whatever family finances dictate, and whatever rationale policy makers use to front-load kindergarten with academics and eliminate the traditional play-based year, these adult priorities do not eliminate boys' developmental need for it.

JEFF AND IAN: THE CHALLENGING PACE AND FACE OF CHANGE

Jeff, a stay-at-home dad, was worried about his son, Ian, a five-year-old now in kindergarten. Even though Ian was on the older end of things at five years ten months when he started in kindergarten, "he definitely did not want to go." His father thought that the biggest challenge for Ian was going to be "submitting to structure." "He's rebellious," said Jeff, who sees himself in Ian. "He is *all* about imagination and fire. School has very little to offer him at this point that he is interested in."

Ian also had tools to fight back against his parents: he is extremely strong-willed and was willing to pout, hide under the covers, and actively resist.

"I'd put on his shirt and you couldn't get him dressed the rest of the way," Jeff said. "I'd come back and he'd be naked."

And Ian wouldn't talk about his fears of kindergarten. When his parents tried to bring it up, he would change the subject. "It was denial and avoidance," Jeff said.

Both Jeff and Ian's mother, Anita, were in tears the first morning of school.

"I'm sure he picked up a lot of our anxiety," Jeff acknowledged. It was only the sight of another set of crying parents rolling their son's bicycle home empty that made Ian's parents finally laugh at themselves. Sending their son off to school was not, after all, a life-and-death matter. But for Ian it may well have felt that way, being yanked from the comfort and competency he felt at home and, with nothing more than a parting hug and a kiss, dropped into the abyss of Kindergarten: The Unknown.

Despite the rough start, by midyear Ian was adjusting pretty successfully, as do most boys. In fact, Ian was having a typical challenging kindergarten experience. He had to manage being away from his parents for a long school day, five days a week. He had to share the teacher with many more children than he did in preschool. He had to learn how to survive social conflicts, deal with the stress of being with other children all day, and master the art of cooperation. He had to learn how to survive hurt feelings and discouragement and how to conform to the schedule of school and the expectations of the teacher. Most especially, Ian had to learn emotional self-control. Kindergarten can be a tough place, particularly for a high-energy, immature boy.

Ian struggled, but by early spring his parents were relieved to see him making noticeable progress in the skills of negotiating with friends, learning what it means to be someone's friend, and figuring out what it means to be part of a small group and a large group.

"The first time Ian had indoor recess it was a disaster," Jeff said. "I was there watching, and he became extremely upset because the gym teacher was yelling at the kids to make them line up in a circle. He could not tolerate the coercive discipline and was begging me to take him home. Today he has adjusted to it. He actually likes that same teacher who had him in tears at first. He has become hardened to the small violence that is school discipline."

He stopped fighting going to school, too. "It's down to two to three days a month of rebellion," Jeff said, crediting the school's developmental rather than academic curriculum. There are no goals for reading as such by the end of kindergarten. His class is working on word sound families—*bat, cat, mat*—and Ian is on pace with the rest of the kids.

And Ian's social skills have developed dramatically. "At the beginning of kindergarten he had no friends in the class," Jeff said. "He has four now and a playdate after school almost every day. At the beginning of school, he would melt down if a friend wanted to go play with someone else. Now he may not be

Q&A: SIBLING RIVALRY BETWEEN YOUNG BROTHERS

Q: *My six-year-old son has always dominated his five-year-old brother, but since his younger brother has started school, the six-year-old's behavior has become more mean. He often tries to gang up on his younger brother when they are on group playdates. He also likes to tell my younger son how much better he is than him at various games, sports, and so on. I've tried time-outs, taking away toys and activities, and explaining how hurtful this is to his younger brother. When I ask him why he does this, he simply says, "I don't know." My older son doesn't exhibit this behavior at school with his classmates, only some gentle teasing. What should I do?*

A: The closer in age two boys are, the more intense the sibling rivalry between them. When your older boy was in school and his younger brother was not, the older one could feel more grown-up, and he could imagine that he had his own territory. Now he has to share school and share his friends. It is vitally important to him to be older and "cooler." I think he's showing off for his friends. That's what is making him meaner.

The question I have for you is whether your younger son is being crushed by all of this. You use the word *dominate*. I take that seriously. Does that mean he is getting punched and hit and is constantly getting the worst of it? When the older one boasts, does it hurt the younger one's feelings, or does it just make him more competitive? Does your younger boy like to provoke his older brother? Does he ever land some blows, either verbal or physical? Most important, does he keep seeking out his older brother's company? Do they play cooperatively when it is just the two of them? If the younger boy does have some power in the relationship, the "domination" may not be as harmful as you believe. Indeed, the younger brother may often enjoy testing his strength against the older one.

If they really are at each other's throats every day after school, for a period of time try to arrange some separate playdates for your younger son at someone else's house when his older brother has friends over, or vice versa. I bet they will miss each other, and when they ask to be together tell them, "I can't let you play with each other when friends are over because it gets so mean that I cannot stand it." See if the older one will clean up his act a bit when he understands that you are prepared to separate the two of them.

Q: *How can I get my sons to listen when I'm asking them to do something that is pretty reasonable—without yelling? For example, if my seven-year-old son is sitting on his five-year-old brother who is screaming for him to get off, I can calmly ask him to please get off his brother, and he just ignores me. I'll ask him again in a firmer voice, and he stays sitting on his little brother. Finally, I'll yell, "Get off now!" And then, of course, he'll get off. I don't like to yell and I'd like to figure out a way not to.*

A: Most parents yell at their children now and then because the situation absolutely demands it—for example, when a boy is doing something dangerous. However, most yelling by mothers occurs because a mom gets taken by surprise by some misbehavior, or is feeling exhausted and impatient. Parenting is hard; everyone should be forgiven for occasional yelling. The difficulty comes when a parent gets in the habit of yelling and then nothing else but yelling seems to work. Either it starts to lose its power and you have to up the volume and intensity or you have to rely on it exclusively. That's when you need to change strategies. But first, a word about boys and yelling.

Some experts on boys claim that because boys don't hear the mother's high-pitched voice as well as girls do, you should yell at boys. I grant you that boys of all ages (husbands, too) seem to have the capacity to tune out the female voice. Whether that is a hearing difference or psychologically motivated I cannot say. Perhaps a boy doesn't "hear" what he doesn't want to hear. That's probably the situation when one brother is sitting on top of another. He doesn't want to give up his hard-won, triumphant position, so he tunes out the maternal intervention in order both to savor the moment and to make the point to his brother that nothing scares him—not even his mom.

But what about the good, old-fashioned threat, delivered in a quiet, determined tone of voice? You might say: "If you don't get up off your brother, you are going to lose television for two days." You could say, "If you don't get off your brother, you are going to have to come into the kitchen and cook dinner with me." Another suggestion: try counting down from ten in a serious tone of voice. "Ten, nine, eight, seven, six . . ." Very few boys want to find out what is at the end of such a countdown.

Sometimes, just standing in silence can be the most effective thing. If you get very close and just stand over him while he is on top of his brother, he will become confused by the fact that you aren't yelling and he'll get off. Finally, and as a last resort, you could get physical in the way that effective dads do: tickle him, grab his foot and tug his sock off, or place your hands firmly on his shoulders—as if you were going to give him a massage—and give a gentle squeeze, not a hard one, but in a way that he is going to find extremely distracting. Do all of this without raising your voice at all. These are male kinds of things, and they don't come naturally to mothers. However, if you are going to get off the yelling track you are going to have to do something unexpected. Surprise them.

P.S. I hope you don't always respond when the younger brother screams for help. Younger brothers (I am one and speak from experience) can be quite manipulative about starting fights with the older brother and then yelling for a referee. Most of the time when brothers are fighting, unless you have reason to be concerned from prior experience, the best technique is to find that you are also having a problem with hearing their yelling. If you don't intervene all the time, they may find a way to resolve many of their own conflicts.

happy about it, but he takes it in stride and asks if he can play his video game when we get home."

He also has developed insight about cooperative play and his place in the social milieu, Anita observed. At the start of the year, Ian insisted on calling the shots in any creative play activity—for instance, making up a story line for a game of make-believe. If he didn't get his way completely, he often would burst into tears and refuse to continue with the play. "He would get furious when they didn't go along with his dramatic plot exactly as he saw it playing out," Anita said, adding, "Now, I see much more give-and-take on evolving plots, and if a friend insists that a *Star Wars* character would act in a particular way or has certain attributes that Ian disagrees with, he'll protest a few times, but an impasse won't derail the action as it once did. And later he'll report to me what the friend said about *Star Wars* and why he disagrees. He's obviously seeking confirmation that he's right, which he usually is, since he's seen those movies so many times. But he's mature enough to let an argument like that slide in favor of continuing play."

The changes have unfolded slowly but steadily, Jeff said, and he concluded: "I see it going in the right direction incrementally."

Childhood development is precisely that: incremental. Especially as boys start formal schooling, development can show up as slow or uneven, inadequate in a setting that calls for fast and uniform. Coming on the heels of the dramatic growth and developmental advances of infancy and toddlerhood, the growth we see in kindergarten through second grade can seem glacially slow to us. Parents often see it more clearly only at the end of the year if they think back to the boy to whom they said goodbye on that first day of school and compare him with the boy running out the door into summer.

DEVELOPMENTAL SELF-REGULATION: LEARNING SELF-CONTROL AND COOPERATION

Suky Werman, an art gallery owner in Lenox, Massachusetts, collected and preserved all of the three-by-five cards sent home by her son Daniel's kindergarten teacher charting his daily progress. She published them privately in a small book entitled *Notes from Kindergarten*. They are printed as they were written by the teacher, in colored marker, along with little smiley or frowning faces. Reading them gives you a flavor of the challenges a boy faces in meeting the demands of this first school experience:

Daniel, you had a difficult morning—you talked during morning rug time and hit Michael A. after lunch. [frowning face] Your afternoon was a little better but Gar said you were running during music.

Daniel, you had a hard day. You were sent off the rug for talking and at your desk you put a pencil in your ear to make everyone laugh. At recess you called Jonathan an idiot something and at lunch you kicked a soccer ball into Oliver's face. I remind you to behave but you seem to forget.

Daniel, you had a great morning! [smiley face, "GREAT" sticker, and star] Your afternoon was good except you got a little too excited and loud when you did the ten questions game. You did a good job at music rehearsal!! [smiley face]

And then, one day, a serious note to his parents:

Just wanted to let you know that Daniel was using inappropriate language and gestures today at school (f—— and his middle finger). He lost five minutes of recess today. I told him next time he would be sent to the office. He wanted me to tell you that he was a good snack helper today.

When I interviewed Daniel's mother, she told me he wasn't the only boy in class to get such cards. "There was a little posse of them," she said. His friend Oliver received one card from the teacher that said, "Oliver peed on Daniel today." "They were in the bathroom and fooling around," said Suky, laughing at the twenty-year-old memory.

These collected cards reflect the struggle that every boy in school undertakes in his first year to control his impulsiveness. You can hear the patient exasperation of his teacher in her remark "I remind you to behave but you forget." The book is touchingly dedicated to "Daniel and his teacher," suggesting correctly that this business of a boy learning to manage his impulsiveness is a two-person dance going on between boys and their teachers in kindergarten classrooms all over America.

By school age, three-quarters of the boys in any classroom are more active, more impulsive, and developmentally immature in comparison to girls of the same age. What happens to a boy like Daniel, who started school at the same

TRUST BOYS' PLAY AND THEIR MANAGEMENT
OF AGGRESSION

One mother told me that she and other mothers of the boys in her son's kindergarten class had consciously trained themselves to turn their backs and converse among themselves when their sons played in a field after school. If they didn't watch the boys, they weren't tempted to intervene constantly in their sons' play. It is important that parents trust the play of boys. When you see boys engaged in free play, let them pursue it, even though the nature of the play seems potentially aggressive to you, as long as the boys are known to each other. Why do I say that? Because boys need the experience of free play to work out their issues of strength, skill, and hierarchy in order to create a stable boy society where there will be less aggression.

On one sunny school holiday, I sat and watched four six-year-old boys playing in the park without any apparent parental supervision. One of the boys was wearing a karate uniform and was armed with a lightsaber. He was obsessed with it and would spin wildly trying to hit the other boys. At first it was a lot of fun for them. All three boys would take turns jumping in close to him and would then leap out of the way when he swung at them. The "karate kid" was boastful and aggressive, and his swordplay had a driven quality. He kept it up too long, and the other boys became bored or annoyed with him. After a while they took fewer and fewer turns jumping in to provide him with an opponent.

Eventually, the two most athletic boys moved into the trees quite far away from him. He tried to entertain himself imitating classic sword moves, but it wasn't the same as having playmates, so he went after the third boy, who was obviously more cautious and timid than his two stronger companions. He didn't like being attacked, but because of the rules of boy life (tattling is strictly taboo), he was not allowed to say so. But he cleverly glanced over his shoulder and saw an adult woman he knew—perhaps she was the one who had brought them to the park—supervising her four-year-old daughter swinging on the swings, with her back to the boys. By systematically backing away from the swinging lightsaber, the cautious boy cleverly lured the myopic swordsman into close proximity to the mother and her four-year-old. As the swordsman swung close to the legs of the mother, who hadn't yet seen him, the cautious boy called out, "That's dangerous. You shouldn't do that!" And, of course, the mother had to turn around and scold the swordsman.

This was a brilliant example of the management of one potentially aggressive boy by three others. They played with him, and when he could not read the cues of their disinterest (or dislike), two of them ignored him and the third brought him cleverly to the attention of an adult. What allowed it to happen was that the boys had the space, the time (the whole process took twenty minutes), and the lack of adult attention to work things out on their own. If, right at the beginning, a parent had said, "That's dangerous; don't swing that sword," the boys never would have been able to test out the game and the swordsman never would have had the all-important feedback from his peers that what he was doing was boring and self-absorbed. Would this swordsman learn the lesson from just one such occasion? Probably not, but he will learn the lesson of limiting his bravado and aggression far more effectively from his peers than from an adult.

Boys of five, six, and seven are able to assess the risks presented by one boy's insistent aggressiveness. They can decide better than any adult how close to get and how much or how little of it they want. And they are capable of arranging a just punishment for a boy who does not read social cues. Boy justice is justice, and the management of behavior by friends is, most of the time, more effective than management by adults because the lesson "Grown-ups don't approve of this" is not nearly as powerful or long-lasting for a boy as the lesson "My friends do not like this." Adults reflexively react—and overreact—to displays of boy aggression, but if they react too fast they deprive boys of the chance to manage their own fears and administer their own justice. If your son is in an unfamiliar situation, with boys he doesn't know, you are likely to be a bit more vigilant. Fair enough, but watch without intervening too quickly. If you want your son to develop leadership skills and to become socially resilient, you need to trust the play of boys when they are with their friends.

age as Nick (five years nine months) and was clearly on the active end of the boy spectrum? Daniel was not the serious, quiet soul that Nick was when he started school.

Did Daniel have attention deficit disorder? If he were in kindergarten today, would he be one of the many boys who are diagnosed with a disorder and treated for it? I am often asked about "hyperactive" kindergarten boys by both parents and teachers, and my answer is that I am extremely reluctant to diagnose hyperactivity in a five-year-old boy, precisely because he is not yet seven, and especially if he is surrounded by a "posse" of boys as active as he is. He is stimulated by the boy group every day, he has not yet experienced the socializing effect of kindergarten or the maturing effects of that daily dance with the teacher, and, most important, he has not completed the five-to-seven shift. I am not prepared to see a boy diagnosed until he has enjoyed the fruits of this all-important developmental period.

At the end of *Notes from Kindergarten* we learn that Daniel, now twenty-four years old, is "kind, caring, focused, independent and, as one might expect, imaginative." He became a musician, a percussionist, and now makes his living producing music, just like his father. His mother reports, "He's so happy now."

The theme of boys struggling with problems of self-control when faced with the structure and expectations of school is a recurring one. High activity levels and impulsiveness are issues for lots of boys in preschool; they will be an issue for many of the same boys in middle school and high school. But kindergarten is special, as are first and second grades to some extent. Developmentally, it is a time when seemingly "immature" behavior or uneven development is probably within the range of normal, something that a boy would naturally outgrow. The range of "normal" and the range of "fit" between a particular boy and the particular composition of his peer group, or between him and the personality or expectations of his teacher, his school, or his parents, make early diagnosis of hyperactivity or other disorders a gamble, even for the professional experts. And the stakes can be high.

A MOTHER'S NIGHTMARE: A RUSH TO JUDGMENT, DIAGNOSIS, AND UNNECESSARY MEDICATION

The mother is a gifted educator, a leader in the field of elementary education, and the memory of her own teenage son's early struggle in kindergarten still makes her heart ache. Chuck was (and still is) "very much a boy—150 percent boy. He loves contact sports," Katherine said, explaining that "as soon as he got his feet on him—fifteen months—he was running around and had a propensity to be strong-willed, singularly focused." As an educator, she knew that singular task focus isn't uncommon in boys whose verbal skills are lacking, as her son's were at that time. But like so many younger, not-yet-verbal boys, she says, "he got into hitting, and if he got really frustrated he might take a bite out of you, so there was a lot of trying to get him to use his words instead of his body."

But Chuck was all about body, from his toddler days on, and that hadn't changed by the time he was ready to start kindergarten. He was "always very active, out there kicking and throwing the ball," Katherine said. He was an eager learner in the outside world: the zoo, parks, and playgrounds. "He didn't show a great deal of interest in sedentary interests."

The challenge and concern over his abilities began when he started kindergarten and it became necessary for him to engage in reading activities at school and, at home, sit and do homework, Katherine said. Chuck was slow to pick up reading and needed Katherine's help with his homework. They would sit at the kitchen table and work on it together.

"He was up and over and under—he did everything with a chair except sit in it," she recalled, "and I was still learning the hard way. That can be a real strain

on a relationship. I couldn't understand why he couldn't just sit down—
the work would take five minutes if
he'd just sit down and do it."

At the same time, Chuck's sister,
who was three years old, was "blos-
soming in true girl form," Katherine
said. "She'd be asking for homework
while I was chasing and holding and

> My male coworkers help put my son's antics into perspective. Often they tell me similar stories from their own childhoods. Since these are professional people who have turned out just fine, it gives me hope! —Mother of two sons, ages five and seven

dragging and fighting with her brother at the other end of the table. That's
when it really struck me: I wondered whether he had attention deficit hyperactivity disorder [ADHD]."

Although she was an educator, gender differences in development weren't
getting the attention then that they are now, and she didn't understand the developmental nuances. "I was a girl, so I didn't know what it was like to be a boy,"
she said. She knew only that the struggle had become too much for her son and
herself. Her husband didn't feel Chuck's activity level was "a big deal," but eventually they had him evaluated for ADHD.

Following a thirty-minute evaluation, the doctor told Katherine and her
husband that there were two possible reasons for this pattern of behavior: one
was ADHD and the other was a mood disorder. The doctor diagnosed a mood
disorder—bipolar disorder—and instructed Katherine and her husband to get a
blood test done on Chuck so he could get started on lithium.

Stunned, they left the doctor's office without making the appointment for
the blood test. At home, Katherine said, "I cried for a month and my husband
just flat-out didn't believe it. But here was a professional, a medical doctor, saying one thing, and my husband, who is vested in not believing the worst of our
son, refusing to consider it, and I'm thinking maybe my husband is in denial.
He said, 'No, we would have seen it, or there would be other family members.' "
She read books on bipolar disorder. Yes, he had temper tantrums and was
strong-willed, "but it just didn't add up," she says. "So we didn't do anything
other than keep watching it."

Then she decided she had to "switch gears," Katherine said. "I was stressing
out, and it was so hard on the relationship. Every time I sat down to do a work-
sheet with him and he couldn't do it, I was thinking, *He's bipolar.*"

Finally, she said, she was able to think beyond her fears and ask herself: " 'Is

HELP YOUR SON DEVELOP FOCUS BY
GIVING HIM SOLITUDE

If you are raising your son in the modern world, you cannot avoid hearing constantly about "focus" and "attention"—the modern buzzwords in our anxious discussions of boys and school. What these words often mean are, "Why can't we get boys to focus on things we think are important, things such as paying attention to the teacher, seat work, and phonics?" The answer is that boys have always had trouble paying attention in school. Yet they have never had a problem paying attention for long, long periods of time to things they love. Indeed, that's exactly where boys naturally develop the ability to focus.

If you want your son to go to school with good attentional abilities, the best thing you can do is to give him some quiet time alone to engage in fantasy play with his favorite toys. And that means deliberately designing a home to provide the possibility of solitude. That means:

- Turning off the television

- Providing a quiet play space where you are nearby

- Playing games with your son (regularly but not constantly)

- Protecting that precious time by not scheduling him into too many after-school activities

Perhaps the idea of playtime for children was once common sense, or part of the natural evening rhythm of a home, but in a "crazy-busy" world, as author Edward Hallowell describes it, the elements of solitude are hard to come by. We now live in a country where the average home has more television sets than people. It is hard to find any space in a home that is not dominated by media.

I have conducted many interviews with boys and their families in their homes. The typical play space for a boy is not his bedroom; it is in the family room, adjoining the kitchen. It contains a couch and chairs, a desk with a computer, a CD player and speakers, shelves and bins for toys, and a huge plasma television. When the television is on, it makes solitude impossible and it profoundly distracts a boy from his play. Play, however, is his natural sanctuary, his natural default setting.

When I interviewed a seven-year-old boy named Matt in his family's den, he was at first enthusiastic about being interviewed, but after thirty minutes of my incessant questions he tired of adult conversation. I found myself talking with his mother while he sat on the floor and began playing with his *Star Wars* battleship, the *Millennium Falcon*. At first he described things to me—for example, "This is the TIE fighter"—and he demonstrated the sounds that the electronic R2D2 and Chewbacca figures made, but as soon as that quick tour was over, he withdrew from the conversation and simply began to play. His mother and I were sitting not six feet from him, but Matt was in a world of his own, absolutely absorbed in the flow of his own imagination.

That kind of imaginative play is a pearl of great price for a child, and it needs to be protected. However, it takes a philosophical commitment to create the context in which it can thrive. Too much television is the biggest threat to it; family busyness is the second greatest threat, and the computer is rapidly becoming the third. If the television had been on in the den, Matt could not have focused on his *Star Wars* play; at the very least, he would have divided his attention between the toys and the screen. There have been a number of research studies suggesting that television may reduce attention span (see page 221).

Research confirms that reading to children, taking them to museums, and telling stories were associated with increased attention. In my experience, the two most focusing and calming parts of a child's day are solo play and reading with parents.

In our worry about our children's academic futures, too few parents today can hold on to what their intuition may be telling them—namely, that the best academic grounding for their son may be quiet, sustained play at home and a kindergarten that emphasizes socialization, play, and the out-of-doors.

there a different way to accomplish the same task? Maybe it's okay if my daughter does it the conventional way and he does it a different way.' And that's what we did."

She got creative with homework incentives by appealing to his active, competitive nature. He would do chin-ups while she gave him spelling words. She quizzed him on his math facts and used his favorite tickling-wrestling game as a reward. "He loved it—it was a competition," she says. "Suddenly it was sort of a fun game, and there was an emotional response. He had a real need to be able to spell his words quickly. He was doing his work, but he was doing it on his terms—we were making a physical game of it, which was what his universe revolved around."

He gained traction in his schoolwork and began to engage more successfully with school. Year by year, he grew more focused and better able to delay gratification. By sixth grade he was earning all A's and B's. "School isn't easy for him, so he has to work harder at it," Katherine said, "but he is doing that: turning in his work, organizing his work." Katherine no longer sits down with him to get his homework done.

At school he's very comfortable and confident but he has a meltdown when he gets home. Sometimes it's pretty ugly. Some kids need to talk and be around people to unwind, but he's an introvert and he needs downtime, alone time. It took us a few episodes to figure it out. Now after school I whisk him to his to his room and put him in his little bed, put on his favorite music or story CD, and hang out with him a little. He stays awhile and then comes out fine. —Mother of a five-year-old son

"He just needed time to develop those skills," Katherine said. "Obviously, it was wrong to say he was mentally ill. He has learned to self-regulate, resist impulses. He's still very much a boy and likes to push and shove and slam doors and throw water balloons; there were just some other things that needed to develop."

Katherine's experience as a mother transformed her perspective as an educator.

"Going through that hard period with him made me realize that I needed to look more deeply and I couldn't keep going on the same track. I needed to rethink what it means to be a boy and what's okay. And in my research on gender issues and school culture, we often do see boys' qualities as 'not good' because our classrooms aren't really set up to accommodate them.

"I think a lot of boys historically have had their whole perceptions of school affected in a bad way by this. Some boys just check out entirely and get those D's and F's. It's a make-or-break situation."

As research has begun to emerge about the potential adverse effects of some medications on children's cognitive development and other health considerations, the stakes go beyond matters of academics and gender politics, Katherine believes. If her son had been ill and needed medication, then the risks would have been necessary and acceptable, she says. But the idea that they might have rushed into that decision hastily and exposed him to that risk unnecessarily sends chills down her spine.

I cannot, as a psychologist, suggest that you ignore the recommendations of mental health professionals. There are, in fact, children with bipolar disorder and little boys who are so distractible and impulsive or anxious and angry that they are unmanageable in a conventional school setting. That's real, but the ease with which we diagnose boys with mental illness and our lack of imagination in creating settings in which they might thrive while we wait for the development of their brains and their self-control is striking.

For most boys, the wait isn't so long: development is constant, even when parents are momentarily mired in doubt. A year after my first conversation with four-and-a-half-year-old Asher-dasher-crasher-smasher's mother, Brenda, she was no longer stewing over whether her son's behavior was normal boy activity or aggression. Asher, now five and a half, had given her the answer, she said:

> He's awesome now—we've definitely moved into a positive space where I am far less worried regarding the aggression. Don't get me wrong, he's still "all boy all the time," but just today his kindergarten teacher pulled me aside to let me know how fabulous Asher was doing in class. She said she appreciates how tender and thoughtful and protective he is of other children, and how he consistently uses gentleness and words to communicate to his classmates. A year ago I would have told her she must have mistaken me for someone else's mother. Now I'm seeing glimpses of the same things in him and am able to relish that moment and gain a little hope for raising a gentle-man.

Some things don't change. Asher is still a very active, physical boy. "He has lots of energy and if it's not put somewhere in a positive way he'll use it to antagonize his sisters, poke them or pop them on the head to try to start a wrestling match," Brenda said. But he can ride his bike solo now, and does so—along with other outdoor play—until he's happily worn out and can settle into quieter activities.

EXCLUSION, CONFLICT, STATUS, AND HIERARCHY IN THE BOY WORLD OF KINDERGARTEN

Every boy and girl in kindergarten has to face the social challenges of being part of a large group of children and must bear the inevitable stress of threatened rejection. Any parent who has volunteered for classroom or playground duty has winced at the insensitive remarks and sometimes cruel teasing exchanged over scissors and paste.

Cross-cultural research has shown that all children, even those younger than five, test each other with teasing in order to find out if they have the resilience and sense of humor to make them a good friend. A child who feels insulted and excluded may cry, withdraw, complain to the teacher, or retaliate with insults; an angry, impulsive boy may hit. Over the course of the year, children make friends, lose friends, and discover their social place in the class. They

DO NOT PANIC ABOUT EARLY READING

Most parents of children who aren't early readers worry about their son's or daughter's reading development. Parents of sons, in particular, worry early and often. In the age of globalization, as the speedy educational train is leaving the station, it is almost impossible not to feel panicky about a boy "falling behind." Almost every parent has heard that "boys don't like to read" and that they don't voluntarily read much when they are older. The temptation to strike hard at reading early in their lives, when you still have influence, is very strong. I understand. I am the father of a boy and I worried about his reading when he was little; I continue to worry that even now—he's sixteen—because of the distractions of computer and video games, he's not reading enough.

When your child is five or six, you must trust that reading readiness will be part of a larger developmental process. Every child comes to reading on his own individual schedule and no parent, no matter how dedicated, can speed that process up in any significant way. In any case, early reading is not a predictor either of brilliance or of school success.

If you panic about your son's reading, he will pick up on your anxiety, and explicitly or implicitly he will receive three messages from you: (1) there is something wrong with him, (2) reading matters more than anything else he does, and (3) reading is a hugely scary task. And if you stay nervous, he will be nervous, too. Advertisers of some reading readiness programs are banking on your anxiety to sell their products. Children in school need some combination of phonics, maybe twenty minutes a day, and whole language to become accomplished readers. Phonics and whole-language activities are part of most schools' curriculum. If educators are taking care of that, I do not recommend that you drill your child on phonics at home or book your child for after-school reading programs.

What you can do at home is to provide an enriched language environment *without anxiety*. Read to your son when you put him to bed at night. Indeed, I hope you have been doing so since he was very little, because the sound of your voice is soothing to him and helps him sleep. I hope you have read him his favorite stories over and over until he knows them by heart (and you're ready to scream and fling the book across the room because you have heard it so many times). The repetition will give him confidence that he can master language because he holds the whole story in his own mind. My parents read me the poems and stories of A. A. Milne many times when I was young, and some of them are lodged in my brain forever, along with *Horton Hears a Who* and *Horton Hatches the Egg*, and I am happy to have them there. (Perhaps those two books are responsible for my being a psychotherapist!)

Mainly, I hope that you continue nighttime reading for years past his first day of school; keep up bedtime reading until he is ten or eleven. At some point, he'll put an end to it, saying, "I can read by myself." Don't stop the tradition before he does.

When your son is in the word-loving stage between ages three and five, you need to make up silly words with him; indulge him in the all of the dumb knock-knock jokes you can stand ("Knock, knock." "Who's there?" "Orange." "Orange who?" "Orange you glad to see me?"). In other words, *have fun* with words and language. Rudolf Ekstein and Rocco Motto, in their book called *From Learning for Love to Love of Learning*, proposed that our motivation to learn emerges out of our early, loving family relationships. They were not entirely right. The best-loved child in the world with a language-based learning disability still faces huge barriers and can become deeply discouraged while learning to read. However, if your son comes to associate words and books with the most loving and fun times with his mother and father, then he has a great start to his reading career.

At the Beehive (Beginning School) at Catlin Gabel School, a progressive coed pre-K–12 school in Portland, Oregon, the walls are filled with the art and interests of four- to six-year-olds, as walls are at most preschools and kindergartens. But nowhere on the walls in this lively classroom environment do you see the early versions of conventional instructional materials or activity-promoting academics. This, despite the Upper School's standing as one of the most rigorous academic programs in the nation.

Catlin describes its Beginner School curriculum as focused on cultivating children's imagination and ingenuity by "exploring, building, and creating," and that is what you see. Here (alongside girls), the boys, like boys everywhere, gravitate toward talk of superheroes ("Only bad guys have guns—my guy is so strong he doesn't need guns!"), get in stubborn arguments with one another ("You're not the boss of me!"), and in the heat of a playground scuffle forget to "use their words" ("There were so many words I can't even remember them."). At snack time they turn their straws into laser weapons ("We can't use guns, but this is a laser!"), and at recess they gravitate toward other boys for a game of chase. All the common challenges in boy behavior that show up in schools everywhere walk in the door here, as well. However, the focus of the day is creative and cooperative play, hands-on projects and activities, conversation, and deliberate attention to "pondering"—learning how to stick with an idea and explore it, rather than the hit-and-run style fostered by hurried lives and high-speed media.

One of the most eye-catching displays of children's work features colorful six-inch-square felt panels, each hand-embroidered with designs and embellished with buttons and other add-ons of the artist's choosing.

"The squirmy, antsy little boys *love* this project," said teacher Allen Schauffler, a woman who has taught hundreds of young boys in her thirty-five years at Catlin. "I don't know whether it's the running their hands through the buttons, or what it is. Sewing is very *soothing* to them." But it is more than that. She described one boy in this year's class who, like many through the years, wouldn't seem to have very well-developed small motor skills. "He still holds his pencil like this," she said, gripping a pencil in her fist. "But look at this," she added, pulling forward a pink felt square sporting about thirty buttons, with the boy's name embroidered around the edge. Then she drew three more items forward: two envelope-size purses, a needle bag the same size, and a work in progress, a self-portrait with the needle still hanging from the face. "He will work on these forever," Schauffler said, "easily an hour at the start of the day, then come back again later." The face is the shape of a heart, with intricately embroidered eyes, nose, and mouth. It is smiling.

all have to learn to cooperate, even with children they do not like. That is the social work of kindergarten.

Boys have a somewhat different social experience in kindergarten than do girls. Though boys cooperate on building projects—remember Nick's green dungeon—they also fight for status and create a hierarchy in the classroom, with the popular boys dominating. At moments, boys tend to be obsessed with status and power. Whether a boy gets teased depends on whether he is disruptive, annoying, and obnoxious—or whether the boy leadership in the class requires a scapegoat. The lack of empathy and social sensitivity in kindergarten is noteworthy, and social cruelty becomes only more systematic and focused as boys get older.

A teacher once consulted me about a boy in her class who was so charismatic that all of the boys fought to play with him. His two closest "lieutenants" proposed to this most popular boy that he should indicate with whom he did or did not want to play by giving the thumbs-up or thumbs-down sign, marking social life or social death. Based on his signal, they would either invite in or drive away the designated boy. This example is extreme and unusual for kindergarten, but research suggests that boys, more than girls, create a social hierarchy, and they start to work on it immediately, in the first play session together.

Katherine's observation about school culture underscores an important point: the distinction between developmental discrepancies in ability, which affect what a boy can accomplish in the classroom setting, and developmental differences in interests and expression, which have nothing to do with ability but may produce behaviors that are treated as immature and inappropriate, something to be discouraged and trained out of a boy.

> *I used to spank but I stopped after I found myself too angry once and realized I needed to use another method of discipline. I remind myself that even during discipline, a son should feel safe about his father.*
>
> —Father of a six-year-old son

Verbal and physical jousting and jockeying among boys continues throughout their school careers. The hierarchies established in kindergarten are more fluid and less stable than they will be by third grade, but they are present and unmistakable. A father described the guy talk typical between his first-grade son and his peers: "They talk about who's best, first, biggest, fastest, whatever. They talk about science fiction shows they like, about favorite toys, about fantasy battles between good and evil."

Boys talk about who's boss and who's not, who's best and what matters most, relentlessly and competitively, whether the topic is athletes, action figures, video games, or the members of their own boy pack. At times the rapid-fire verbal contest goes so fast it seems as if they aren't really listening; they hardly pause before trying to top one another. But they are listening, because each speaker builds on the assertions of the boy just before him.

This competitive talk by boys is often upsetting to women in general, and mothers particularly. It seems so rude and aggressive, and no mother wants her son pegged as low-status by the other boys. Mothers often perceive this conversational style as "bad" or immature and reflexively attempt to interrupt it, stop it, or steer the conversation in a different direction. By contrast, fathers (and male teachers) tend to take it in stride, since they've heard it a million times in school and they understand intuitively what researchers have discovered: the purpose of the verbal and physical competition among boys in school is to establish a hierarchy that, once it is recognized and honored by the boys, naturally results in a diminution of aggression between them.

This is not to deny the reality that sometimes there is a true bully who has targeted a vulnerable boy in the class. When this happens, the victimized boy needs adult intervention and protection (and the bully needs supervision, limits, and perhaps therapy), but it is a mistake to perceive the vast majority of boy

SEX ABUSE: BOYS NEED OUR PROTECTION AND AWARENESS

For many decades, many people believed that sexual abuse was something that happened only or mostly to girls—that girls were targets of incestuous fathers and early adolescent girls might be abused by older boys or men, but boys were not similarly vulnerable. The shocking revelations about pedophile priests in the Catholic Church who systematically sexually abused boys over many decades and the increasingly familiar news stories about other incidents of sexual abuse of boys have awakened the general public to the reality that boys are targets of sexual predators. Parents are especially alert to the danger, and anxious. In their online survey responses, many parents of even the youngest boys listed sexual predators—along with war and violent video and computer games—among their top concerns about raising boys in today's world.

Approximately one in six boys is subjected to some form of sexual abuse when he is young. This figure is at best approximate and controversial, as are all child abuse statistics, because of differences in the way that people define abuse. Does abuse just mean physical contact between an adult and a child? Has a boy been abused if he has been flashed one time by an exhibitionist? What if an adult has shown him pornographic movies but not touched him, or he was persuaded to participate in a "circle jerk" (mutual masturbation) with older boys? Researchers differ in the way they define abuse of boys, which is why there is no single agreed-upon figure.

Nevertheless, various studies have revealed that somewhere between 3 percent and 24 percent of boys have had some "unwanted" or "abusive" sexual experience before the age of sixteen or eighteen. When I use the word *abuse*, I am talking about something that involves a power differential, usually a gap of more than five years in age between the victim and the perpetrator, and has some aspect of coercion, seduction, and secrecy. Researcher David Finkelhor, in his poll of college students, found that 8.3 percent of young men reported being abused as boys; Christopher Bagley and his colleagues in Calgary, Canada, found that 15.5 percent of boys had some coercive sexual experience as children, and 6.9 percent of their subjects had experienced multiple episodes of sexual abuse, the same figure as reported by girls. Researchers suspect that these statistics may be lower than the actual incidence of sex abuse because abuse tends to be underreported.

Contrary to popular belief, most sexual abuse of children is committed by relatives or family acquaintances; only the tiniest fraction is committed by total strangers. The idea that our son might not be safe with his uncle or cousin or grandfather is so upsetting that most people would rather not think about it at all, and many do not connect the dots when their boys manifest the symptoms of abuse: depression, sudden unexplained anger, outbreaks of anxiety, changes in behavior, or precocious and coercive sexual behavior with other children. Parental fears focus mainly on seductions by teachers, scoutmasters, and other authority figures, and the highly publicized kidnappings of boys by strangers that dominate the news periodically.

Preventative conversations aimed at bolstering our boys' awareness and self-protecting responses cannot stop all abuse of boys, but they may help. Robie Harris's engaging books (with illustrations by Michael Emberly) can help you talk to your boys about sex starting when they're little. Start with *It's Not the Stork!*, move on to *It's So Amazing!*, and by the time your son is ten or eleven, put *It's Perfectly Normal* in his hands. That may help both of you prepare for the tougher conversations about pedophiles. But in any case, if talking about these matters with your son makes you squeamish, or you don't feel you know exactly what to say, remember this: one in six boys is sexually abused before the age of sixteen, and his parents probably never had a meaningful conversation with him about the subject.

competition as dangerous and hurtful. It is not. Respect for this kind of boy banter is a crucial point, and one that is easily lost when adults attempt to impose "more mature"—more courteous and less competitive—standards for boys' conversation.

BOY STORIES, BOY TALK: FEROCIOUS, FANTASTIC, AND FUN

Dungeons, bad guys, stick fighting, and who is the boss of whom in *Star Wars*— these are the classic themes of healthy boy play and boy stories. Studies show that by age four, boys' pretend aggression occurred at twice the rate of girls', and by the ages of five and six, it is far greater than girls'—by a rate of six to one! Also by kindergarten and first and second grades, we see a divergence of themes that will characterize the reading interests of boys and girls throughout elementary school. How we react to these gender themes will tell both boys and girls a lot about whether we trust their interests—and whether we trust *them*.

The stories girls tell tend to focus on social relationships and often end with a cooperative scene. Consider Erica's story, dictated to Jane Katch, her kindergarten teacher: "Once there was a panda, and then an elephant came along, and they all had a sleep-over."

That's certainly not a boy-style story. Seth, a kindergarten boy in the same class, told a classic boy tale: "There was a horse, and he got killed by an old man, and then a unicorn killed the old man. And the unicorn lived happily ever after."

Now, your idea of a happily-ever-after story might not be a brief tale that involves two quick murders, but it was Seth's, and it is for many boys. When the girls in the kindergarten objected to it—Erica declared, "I live on a farm. I like horses." We were in the classroom filming the PBS documentary *Raising Cain* the day this conceptual conflict arose around Seth's story. How the teacher negotiated her way out of the dilemma is an interesting lesson in gender. What she did *not* do was ban so-called violent stories; she understands how central fantasies of fantastic power (and that includes murder) are to boy life, and how comforting they are for boys who may be feeling vulnerable or inadequate. She allowed them to tell their stories in the way they wanted, and created a forum for the rest of the children to discuss their honest reactions to these sometimes upsetting tales.

Whether they write the stories, tell them, or enact them with loud, excited dialogue or commentary, boys have a penchant for heroic adventure and a vivid repertoire of imaginary villains, and wherever you have good fighting evil, it's bound to get messy. Many grown-ups feel an urge to get boys to write or talk about something else, for fear of where it is leading. But where is it leading? And why are adults afraid of the fantasies of five-year-old boys? I think there are three reasons why boy fantasies upset us. First, most of the adults who overhear these stories are women—mothers and elementary school teachers—and boys' fantasies contravene almost all of the basic rules of feminine discussion: they are thick with conflict and combat and thin on emotional depth or relationship themes. Second, we live in a very violent society, and we're not sure why some boys grow up to be violent men, so we overreact to anything that we think could lead to violence without ever examining our assumptions about cause and effect. Third, and this applies to teachers as well as parents, we are worried that other adults will hear us "allowing" children to be aggressive, and thus colluding in some process that could lead to real violence.

If you are going to be the parent of a boy, you have to learn to trust his childhood fantasies and stories and those of his friends, even if they are not to your taste.

Of course it is important to distinguish between play violence and real aggression, but I think most adults and children are capable of distinguishing between the two. I do not even like the term "play violence" because it is inevitably judgmental to pair the two words. Play is play, violence is violence. When children in the dress-up corner of kindergarten pretend to get married or have babies, we do not call it "play sex" and worry that it is going to lead to precocious sexual experimentation, do we? That's because we understand it to be play, pure and simple.

> *I love that my sons have taught me to accept a level of chaos that I never would have thought possible.*
> —Mother of two sons, seven and eleven years old

If the difference is not intuitive to them, then both teachers and parents have to train themselves to see it. The problem is that if we do not appreciate boy play, which is the central form of expression of five-, six-, and seven-year-olds, boys are going to feel that we do not appreciate them. And that is indeed what they think. When I ask little boys about teachers' objections to their play, they always slump, grow sad, and say, "We're not allowed to do that," in a tone that suggests that school is an attack on their boy-ness.

When we look at such boy play through the adult lens of violence, we miss the opportunity to use it as a window into a boy's hidden emotions. Play therapist Lawrence Cohen describes a therapy session in which he took J.J., a toy-gun-loving seven-year-old boy, for a walk in the woods during one therapy session. (Therapists often take walks, shoot hoops, or engage in some other kind of active play alongside a boy as they talk, because boys are so uncomfortable sitting face-to-face for a talk about feelings.) Cohen says that as they walked,

> J.J. picked up a giant branch he could barely hold, put it on his shoulder, and said, "Hey, look, I have a bazooka!" I said, "Hey, J.J., I wonder why some kids are really into guns. What do you think?" He mentioned a few boys in his class who are even more into guns than he is (I found that hard to believe—he was *way* into weapons and shooting). I knew that J.J. was worried about his father, who had been very ill since he was a toddler. As he continued to aim his bazooka, I said, "Sometimes I think boys are into guns because it helps them feel less afraid when there are things going on that are scary." J.J. whipped around to face me (I had to jump out of the way of the branch) and shouted, *"That's not it! And don't tell my mom!"*

DECIDING ABOUT KINDERGARTEN:
AN INFORMAL GUIDE

If you are having difficulty with the "kindergarten or not" dilemma, it may help to consider the following factors and check your score against the key that follows. This helpful readiness checklist is from Kathleen Fraser, early childhood coordinator for the Town of Arlington, Massachusetts.

• *Age.* Is your son likely to be the youngest in his/her class? Was your child born in late August and you live in a town with a September 1 cutoff date?

• *Preschool opinion.* Do your son's preschool teachers recommend "another year to grow," or are they saying that he is fully ready for kindergarten?

• *Screening/school report.* Was your son screened to see whether he needs special help? Does his conference report reflect mostly "skill mastered," or are there a lot of "not yet" checkmarks? Information from these sources may tell you something about his current overall maturity and preacademic skills. (Remember that children develop skills and interests at their own pace. Questions on either measure do not indicate long-term problems.)

• *Pre- and perinatal history.* Was your son premature and/or very sick as a newborn? Do you suspect or know of such problems with your adopted son?

• *Health.* Has your son had serious or frequent health problems that took time away from typical routines? Consider respiratory, digestive, orthopedic, and ear, nose, and throat problems, allergies, and hospital visits.

• *Personal history.* Was your son adopted after his sixth month of life? Did he have multiple caregivers during the first two or three years? Have you or your son moved, experienced losses, separation, family disruptions or trauma (e.g., ill parent, parent discord, accident, fire, sibling illness)?

• *Parental perspective.* Do you have a strong feeling or personal reason for sending your son or keeping him at home? Were you sent to school too young? Are you determined to have an athlete with optimal size and strength in middle school? Do you question readiness but know that your son is eager to learn, well prepared, and pretty competent? Are you leaning toward sending him but hearing others advise otherwise?

Scoring key: After considering each of the seven factors, mark each one with a plus (this factor is not an issue) or a minus (this point raises questions, issues, or concerns). If you have more than four negative marks, you might want to check your list in a month or two and see whether you would change any of them, or talk again with your son's preschool teacher or pediatrician for their view. If you are doing this review more than six months before your son would enter kindergarten, you might be doing it too early. Many boys seem immature in March but ready to go by May of the year they turn five.

Remember that your wisdom about your son is trustworthy. There will be a "good-enough" time for him to enter kindergarten, and if you make the decision based on what's right for *him,* then it will be the right decision.

Some will argue that boys shooting each other with guns formed with their fingers leads to overexcitement and hurt feelings. I agree that it can; I've seen it happen. But lots of things in kindergarten lead to overexcitement and tears: exclusion, boys outshouting each other, boasting about Yu-Gi-Oh cards, and disagreements about popular athletes, superheroes, and the size and type of family car. Girls take their gendered version of teasing and relational sparring to hurtful extremes, too, to which adults tend to respond with correcting conversation, not fear and harsh predictions and punishments. All children must be taught self-control and empathy; you do not do that by banning a particular form of gender-specific play.

THE CRUCIBLE OF READING: BOYS STRUGGLE ALONG THE DEVELOPMENTAL CURVE

Brandon and I were sitting facing each other on a big beige couch in the den of his comfortable home in suburban Boston. It was the fall of his second-grade year; he was two days short of his eighth birthday, and he was talking to me about what he liked and disliked about school. Math best of all, he said. Art was good. And gym, of course. When pressed, he added social studies to his list because it was about "facts." What he had not mentioned was reading. I knew from his mother that he had not been able to read in kindergarten and that it had come very slowly in first grade. Indeed, he was becoming a fluid reader only now, in the fall of second grade. That was a source of embarrassment to him.

But he did have favorite books at home. He showed me the collection he and his sister shared, called "the Ologies"—an imaginative, highly visual, and information-packed series including *Dragonology, Wizardology, Pirateology,* and *Egyptology.* The books are a fun combination of fact and fiction. Brandon opened *Egyptology* to show me a "grandmother's journal" that was "kind of like a story," he said. "She either got eaten by an alligator or she was kidnapped," he said; he couldn't remember which. *Dragonology* came with another book inside: *Tracking and Taming Dragons.* "See?" Brandon said cheerfully. "And I also like *Pirateology*. It comes with a treasure map and you have to get the two pieces on it. I'll show you," he said, and jumped up to get the book.

Turning to his favorite spot in the book, Brandon opened up a treasure map, or half of a map with half a skull on the back. To complete it, you have to get the second half from a secret compartment in another part of the book. He showed me where that was hidden. "When you put it together it makes one big map," he said, then turned it over. "And when you do it like this you get to see the skull." And then he showed me a "really gross" picture of a cyclops.

For Brandon, books hold treasures: they link him to pirates and exciting monsters as well as to the interests his sister had when they were younger. However, he is not yet comfortable with the act of reading itself. That is not unusual. A significant minority of children do not learn to read fluently until late second grade or early third grade, and a majority of them are boys. When the average boy starts school, he is almost a year behind the average girl in language development—girls use more words than boys—and particularly in reading.

Reading is one of the toughest learning tasks in all of life. Once a person learns to read, he or she generally forgets how hard it really was to master. Reading involves bringing together a set of arbitrary written symbols, the alphabet, with a set of arbitrary sounds, the ABC's. Learning to blend and separate the sounds in words, learning all the rules and all the exceptions to the rules is a complex task. After many years of debate, we have never come up with a foolproof method for teaching reading successfully to all students. What we do know is that nearly twice as many boys as girls have trouble reading, are diagnosed with language disabilities, and are referred to special education classes. Many of those boys are referred to special education because they are behind in reading. Others are sent because they have emotional problems that stem from the frustration and shame of not being able to read.

WHAT FIRST-GRADE AND SECOND-GRADE TEACHERS SAY

Whenever I ask K–2 teachers to name the biggest challenge they see for the students in their grade, and those that are particularly challenging for boys, reading and writing top the list. Anna, who works in a public school and has eighteen years of experience as a first-grade teacher, wrote that the biggest challenges are "the expectation that all students will be reading on grade level by the end of first grade," "the expectation that all students will be proficient writers by the end of first grade according to our district rubric," and that "students will read at thirty-eight to forty words per minute by the end of first grade."

It was clear to Anna, as it is to so many first-grade teachers, that a large minority of boys in her class will not fulfill these expectations. Many boys arrive in first grade struggling with phonemic skills, so they are already considered significantly behind. My question is: behind what? Are they lagging behind the girls, the best boy readers, or the standards set by politicians and educators? And if they are behind the standards set by state departments of education, could it be that we are creating standards for boys that do not take into account their developmental trajectory? As another teacher noted, "Many of the boys who struggle are prime examples of not being ready developmentally."

There is no question that the boys who are considered significantly behind when they get to first grade are going to struggle with feelings of inadequacy from the beginning of their school careers. I could tell that Brandon felt defensive about his reading three months into second grade. He was obviously afraid there was something wrong with him because he couldn't read fluently.

What do boys do about such feelings? At best they are only temporarily sad or upset; what is worrisome is if they start to develop a hatred of school and become disruptive, or withdraw and become apathetic. The best possible scenario is that boys with problems in reading look for something else they can be good at. "Most of the boys prefer math," Anna told me. "They ask me frequently during the day if it is time for math yet."

For many it may be math, but for others math can be as intolerable as reading or writing or science. A boy's heart may belong to the arts—he may be a talented artist who fills his math worksheets with doodles and drawings, or a boy who would prefer the hands-on work of carpentry or sculpting. When a boy says

Q&A

Q: *I'm a divorced dad with very limited access to my five-year-old son because of a high-conflict divorce from his mother. He and I are close—I ache when I am away from him and beam when I am with him. He is always happy to see me and we have fun doing simple stuff together like riding the subway, visiting the fire stations, telling jokes, or cooking. When we're together we play a lot—at the playground, swimming, roughhousing—and we talk. But it hurts to feel like a visitor in his life, to have to live without him, and not have the opportunity to really raise him. I want to be a consistent positive presence in his life. Do you have any suggestions?*

A: Before I answer your painful question about the effects of high-conflict divorces and their impact on boys, I want to point out something that you may not be able to focus on given your situation: your son is a lucky boy. He has a father who loves him and who enjoys doing simple things with him, such as rough-housing and cooking. He has a dad who takes pleasure in his son's very existence. That is real love, and it is precious. There are many boys in the world who don't feel that from a father who is living at home with them. That's the sad truth.

You feel the sense of loss that comes from having a life that doesn't live up to your idea of fathering, and from missing out on the day-to-day contact with your son. That's an ache for both of you, but it is much harder for you than it is for him. This is all he knows; this is his life. You, apparently, had some-thing better in mind and you are always measuring the current situation against the dream of full-time par-enting that you envision. He doesn't. All you have to do is to say from time to time, "Son, I'm sure you know how much I wish I could live with you every day, don't you?" And sometimes you can say, "I wish your mother and I could have worked things out better for your sake." He'll hear your pain, he'll appre-ciate the message, he'll look at you and squeeze your hand, and he'll be thinking, *I'm sorry you feel ter-rible, Dad, but I'm okay. I'm glad I have you.*

he lives for recess and gym and finds every other class torturous, we assume he's joking, and he may be. Or he may be telling the truth about his experience of hopelessness in school.

THE WAY OUT OF "JAIL FOR BOYS"

"I think that jail starts in first grade for boys," says Gillian McNamee, the pro-fessor in charge of teacher training at the Erikson Institute in Chicago, and con-sultant to the Chicago public schools. "No boy would ever have invented school, not in a hundred years, and yet I think what school does involve is interesting to boys."

Gender differences matter, she says, and she believes the issue needs to be made a priority for discussion by parents and educators. She elaborates on the ways she sees that girls and boys differ in their reaction to school: The rhythm of school is a better fit for girls' fantasies; girls can be social, they can sit around the table together. When the teachers ask them to do "seat work" girls simply adapt better. Not boys. "They want to talk; they want to move." And from a disciplinary standpoint, boys get more than their fair share. "When they're anxious, they misbehave," she says, and they are "like a magnet for a teacher's need for a sense of control. The punishments they receive are the undoing of their sense of loving school."

Does that mean that boys will never be interested in the academic content of their first three years of school? Professor McNamee believes that they can be.

"Reading and writing are just ways of speaking and listening," she says. "Boys have no fundamental objection to reading and writing; we just have to hook them. There are tons of things that boys are interested in."

In the United States today there is a significant problem with boy underachievement in school. Boys make up two-thirds of special education classes, they account for two-thirds of the D's and F's in middle school, and they drop out of high school at higher rates than girls. Only about 43 percent of college graduates are young men. Our boys are either standing still relative to the performance of girls or are slipping backward academically. I believe the problems start in kindergarten and first and second grades because there is something of a mismatch between the developmental needs of boys and the way the early grades are taught.

What is frustrating to me is that educators have not been able to talk about these discrepancies between genders for many years, or they have been far down the priority list after racial and socioeconomic differences. Until we can do so, we cannot address problems in the way we teach boys in the early grades. Are performance gaps between the genders inevitable? Though academic underachievement by boys is seen in nineteen out of twenty-two industrialized countries, they are not seen in all parts of the world.

It is my belief that we are driving boys crazy in early elementary school with our need for early achievement and the relentless pressure for early reading. Many boys become demoralized and start to fight back against school early in their education.

What alternatives do we have to diagnosing boys and sending them into special education or putting them on medication? The answer is to create an environment in the first three years of school that recognizes the slower arc of boy development and provides them with the all-important social interaction and play opportunities.

Amy Vorenberg, for many years a kindergarten teacher and elementary school principal and now the head of a small private school in Philadelphia, declares, "You need classrooms where being 'smart' is not defined by reading and language skills. Early reading does not predict anything but early reading." She then sketches out a classroom where boys (and girls) might thrive.

> Good first-grade and even second-grade classrooms should have block corners and drama corners where kids can do all of these important thinking tasks—planning, strategizing, cooperating—but where it isn't so narrowly focused on one avenue. We need to go back to focusing on understanding community and strengthening group dynamics.

Weren't these precisely the skills that Nick was so proud of when he showed me the dungeon that he and his kindergarten buddies had built together at the beginning of this chapter? Aren't these the cooperative and strategic building skills that experience shows us come so easily to boys and will serve them—and girls, too—so well later in life? We should encourage these skills.

EMBRACING BOY ENERGY AND INTELLECT: A CLASSROOM AT WORK

Linda Dahl's second-grade classroom is packed—with workstations, clustered desks, the teacher's desk in a cramped corner, and, off by the windows, a long, deep, old brown leather couch where, during reading time, as many as "five little bottoms" park themselves and sink into silent reading.

Dahl, a twenty-year veteran of teaching and mother of two grown sons who as boys were "different as night and day," has a boy-heavy class this year: fourteen boys and nine girls. Nine of the boys are flagged as having behavior issues. Development is on parade here, as it is in any classroom, but the large number of boys, and boys "with issues," makes it even easier to see how diverse development can be, even just among boys.

Being the mother of boys "made me a whole lot better teacher," Dahl believes. Her classroom doesn't favor boys, but it does respect them and what she sees as their particular need for both space and permission to be active, along with the responsibility for academic learning and basic courtesy in community life, she says.

Reading remains a hurdle for many boys in second grade, and Dahl has broken down the required ninety-minute instructional time for reading into shorter blocks, with some freedom of movement and choices about where and with whom they read. They can choose between floor, seats, and the sofa. Some of them (most often non-squirmy girls) like to fill the couch. The boys almost always choose to sit or sprawl on the floor. Some days reading time is camp-out style and children can bring their favorite blanket, pillow, and stuffed toy to make curling up with a book more inviting. Some boys bring a soft toy, but for others it is an action figure that keeps them company, hopping from page to page as they read.

In this relaxed setting, the boys often cluster in twos or threes, leaning against each other or with legs draped across one another. Some position themselves like capital *L*'s, lying with back flat on the floor and legs propped up against the wall. Some read silently; a few read to each other in quiet voices. They tire of one position and shift to another, sometimes scooping up their things and moving to a different part of the room. But for the most part, they stay on task with their books. They know the reward is coming: shortly they'll be turned free to race out the door for recess. When asked what the favorite part of his day is, a boy replies: "Lunch, recess, the other recess, and PE."

In and out of the classroom, Dahl believes in hard work and free play. "We're afraid to let these kids play," she says, critical of prevailing attitudes that lead to cutbacks in recess and ever-growing expectations of organized sports for children. "They need unstructured play. There's a lot of value in unstructured play. It's a big mistake to cut back recess. They need to get that energy out."

At another school, Douglass Elementary School in Denver, Colorado, principal Kelley King took the bold step of making boy underachievement at her school a top issue after data showed what she considered an appalling gap between boys' and girls' achievement. "We could throw up our hands because apparently nobody had been able to do anything about it, or we could choose to try to do something," she says. "We chose to do something."

She and her staff set about studying all facets of the issue and had "an open conversation about our expectations of boys," she says. "If it was to look and act like girls, then that attitude and expectation wouldn't get us anywhere."

Instead they asked: "What is it about boys that is both a challenge and a blessing in the classroom, and how do we see their strengths as opportunities to be harnessed for their learning instead of obstacles?" King added, "I mean, little boys are little boys. They've been kicking a ball for the first five years of their lives when the girls were at the kitchen table drawing with markers."

Ultimately, the changes within her school produced significant results. Girls' scores stayed high, and boys made dramatic improvement in just a single year. "We had to make sure this was about effective strategies for all kids, including girls," she says. "These changes were to improve the instruction for all students and to close that gap for boys. It's working."

CHAPTER SIX

BOYS ON A MISSION

Your Son from Eight to Ten

*It was in 1868, when nine years old or thereabouts, that while looking at a map of Africa
of the time and putting my finger on the blank space then representing the unsolved mystery
of that continent, I said to myself, with absolute assurance and an amazing audacity
which are no longer in my character now: "When I grow up, I shall go there."*
—Joseph Conrad, A Personal Record: Some Reminiscences, 1912

A FOURTH-GRADE TEACHER TOLD ME THAT HER CLASS WAS DOING A UNIT ON Native American peoples and she had asked each of her students to give themselves a name reminiscent of Indian names, such as He Who Runs Like a Deer or Quiet River. The girls had come up with names she found beautiful and poetic, she said, while the boys had almost universally chosen sports-oriented names: He Who Is Good at Baseball and He Who Likes Ice Hockey. She found them uninspired. Any parent of a fourth-grade boy knows otherwise. In fact, if you live with a boy who is eight, nine, or ten years old, you

> *He is not as fluent a reader as some in his class, and feels angry that faster readers who are less thought-ful as they read and who evidence lesser comprehension have surpassed him in speed. He has cried at feeling misunderstood, underestimated by his teacher when it comes to reading.*
> —Mother of an eight-year-old son

know there is nothing richer or more meaningful to him than to master some-thing that matters to him and to be recognized and celebrated for it, as this Na-tive American naming tradition invites him to do.

The truth is that boys of this age define themselves by the things they love, the things they do in an active way, and the things that will inspire respect in other boys. Their sense of identity is intertwined with conventional notions of masculinity, so these boys were being developmentally appropriate when they chose sports, video or computer games, or other interests that clearly marked them as celebrated members of the mainstream boy tribe.

Erik Erikson described children between the ages of eight and ten as "pur-poseful, proud, and persevering." I have never heard a better capsule description of the age. For a boy, specifically, it captures the energy so characteristic of his passage from the little boy of early elementary school to the self-assured older boy.

If you are the parent of a boy this age, you are likely to hear proud bulletins from your son about his accomplishments. At seven he may have been full of complaints about school, its rules and requirements, and his own suffering in it, perhaps with wishful thinking that you, the parent, could intervene and change things for him. But between eight and ten he is trying to become the master of his world and he wants you to know it. He no longer looks to you to solve his problems in quite the same way he used to. And if he tried, for exam-ple, to get you to help him with social problems at school, he would pay a huge price for that with his peers. Third graders are all proud of keeping certain so-cial matters from their parents and teachers. "It's private," they say, and indeed, many things in a boy's life are his exclusive domain.

Your son is becoming the master of many small, complex universes filled with a seemingly infinite number of characters, most of whose names you will never know—for example, Pokémon and Yu-Gi-Oh monsters. Boys of this age are

TRY NOT TO PATHOLOGIZE BOYS

I work in schools and in the past I worked in hospitals. I know for a fact that they are filled with caring people who want to help boys, and there is no doubt that there are many boys who suffer from mental illnesses and benefit from diagnosis and treatment for ADHD, Oppositional Defiant Disorder, anxiety disorders, Obsessive Compulsive Disorder, and depression. At the same time it is undeniable that we have developed a culture of diagnosing and pathologizing boys in the United States. There are times when the push for peak performance—in school, sports, music, mood, motivation, and family dynamics—pushes boys into a corner where the vagaries of normal developmental are viewed and quickly labeled as ills.

Beyond concerns about the effects of unnecessary medication, overaggressive diagnosis of boys becomes destructive in the way it shapes our view of boys and their view of themselves. When I meet with boys over school or other personal matters, often they introduce themselves with their diagnosis, as if it were part of their last name or the first moments of an AA meeting: "Hello, my name is Tom and I'm ADHD." They resent the labeling, as if it explains them, sums them up; and yet they are resigned to the idea that this is how the world sees and understands them. Labeling we use to define a boy only obscures him. It is of no help to boys and no help to us, either.

If everybody has a diagnosis what is normal boyhood? Tom Sawyer could have had three or four diagnoses: his short attention span, an inability to pay attention to school, his willingness to fight other boys, his sneaking about out of the house at night, and his willingness to lie at the drop of a hat. What Mark Twain wants to tell us is that some of this is necessary for a boy to construct himself as a brave and independent person. Once we start pathologizing every little thing, we're not allowing a boy to build himself. At some point overdiagnosis of boys threatens to keep us from seeing the benefits to boys of risk taking, creativity, and adventure. I worry about the effects of that culture on our boys, because if we label so much of boy life as mental illness, how can they see themselves as healthy?

proud of being able to remember lists. Brandon told me: "Well, I could name some legendary Pokémons. They're still around, but now there are only one of each of them in the world. Two of them are Articuno and Zapdos, and another one is called is Latias." Later it may be baseball cards or Magic cards that fascinate him. While not every boy loves the idea of collecting cards, all are keenly aware that the card collectors have status at school. I know teachers who have banned cards from classrooms because they lead to such intense competition.

When a boy of this age plays team sports, competition kicks in there as well. He now measures his performances and the contributions of everyone

> *My son is being raised to accept and express his feelings, but I know full well that by a certain age he will need to suppress his emotionality outwardly to fit in with his peers.* —Mother of a son, eight years old

else on the team. One eight-year-old ice hockey player told me, "This kid named Brendan is better than me, he's faster than anyone except me. In soccer, Nikko is better than anyone, and then it is Mustafa and Matt and Mike and then me."

Your son may be learning an instrument and have his first experience of playing at a recital. His perfectionism and his frustration may begin to emerge when he does not play as well as he would like to. "He gets so angry when he can't do it right" is a very common worry of parents. Whatever he is doing, he is out in the world, practicing to be competent—someday as a worker and a potential provider. It may have been difficult at times to see the potential man in your distracted, tempestuous little boy of five or six, but you are certainly going to get glimpses of the future pilot or stockbroker in your eight- or nine-year-old. The skills required to collect baseball cards and memorize all the characteristics of Pokémon monsters lead quite naturally to the skills required of businessmen, financial analysts, and researchers. In many nonindustrial cultures boys of this age are already farming, hunting, or learning a trade alongside men to sustain the family economy. In the industrialized world, where entry into the adult workplace comes so much later, boys are driven to create their own domains for competition, mastery, and recognition.

A fourth-grade boy explained during class one day that the reason he never got around to his homework worksheets was that he was busy drawing. Then from the back of his notebook he pulled out pages filled with elaborate illustrations of young adventurers (boys and girls) dressed for battle. He explained that his Japanese anime style was the hot trend in screen games and graphic (cartoon-style) novels and had become a popular artistic pastime among some of the kids at school. He went on to describe the drawing he and his friends were doing as "a kind of game" in itself, and explained: "It's pretty much called the Japanese anime game, but when you're good you're called a sensei and you teach."

Whether it is a drawing game or any other game, hobby, or interest, these passions take effort and focus, and boys feel very strongly about them.

At this age, a boy's inner life may be obscured by his activity and devotion to external interests, but psychologically his identity is based not only on this out-wardly emerging self but also very much on his love for and loyalty to his fam-ily. When things are good at school and at home, his confidence in himself and life run high. If he is struggling in school, his parents are fighting or about to get divorced, or he has a disturbed sibling, it can be deeply distressing to him and can make him feel "inferior." He will combat those feelings by becoming a stoic. He may act as if he doesn't care about things he can't do well at school or about his fighting parents or struggling sibling; he may not let on to anyone that he has worries, because he feels that if he were to admit any of it, his world and identity would unravel.

The characteristic stoicism of boys is often misunderstood by adults, who may wish boys were more forthcoming, perhaps more introspective or emotion-ally open and expressive. It is essential to remember that stoicism isn't always something that's imposed on boys; it is something they invent for themselves to feel proud and grown-up. Stoicism is always part of independence. Your will-ingness to get through something on your own always involves a little bit of sto-icism, and you can hear boys saying to themselves, "I can do it." *The Little Engine That Could* is not just about perseverance, it's about stoicism, too. Boys this age are proud and persevering.

PARENTS WATCHING (AND WORRYING) FROM THE SIDELINES

This full engagement of the eight-to-ten-year-old boy with his world has its risks. Each stage of life contains a central psychological tension, as Erikson pointed out, and for children of this age, the dark side of all this industry is a sense of inferiority. Because he is constantly trying to prove himself by produc-ing things, memorizing things, or competing with others, sooner or later a boy is likely meet his limits and encounter defeat. Depending on his level of skill, he may encounter either a little or a lot of frustration in school, on teams, with friends, or in mastering the technological demands of his age, such as computer and video games. If a boy experiences too much frustration at any age, his sense of himself may be damaged. Frustration can lead to anger, and chronic frustration can make an angry boy. When your son was younger, it was easier to protect him from his po-

> *Acceptance, tolerance, and understand-ing sprinkled with love is a successful recipe.* —Mother of a ten-year-old boy

The Eight Lines of Development

The Developmental Story Advances

There are very few developmental surprises between eight and ten. From a biological point of view this is not really a "stage" because there are no major biological shifts. The big shift occurred between five and seven; eight to ten is a period of consolidation. The major changes in this period are social and cultural: your son's growing competence in the world and his relationship with his friends.

Physical Development

Boys do not make any major leaps in physical development during the years from eight to ten. These three years lie inside a period of steady growth for boys which really runs from age six until the beginning of puberty at around age twelve. The average six-year-old in the United States is forty-five inches tall and weighs forty-five pounds; the average twelve-year-old, just before puberty, is close to sixty inches tall and weighs ninety pounds. Your son will obviously add inches and pounds annually and he will become more coordinated, but growth is steady and he will be very recognizable to you—and to himself—from year to year during this period.

Boys this age will test their physical strength and ability almost any chance they get, climbing, jumping, running, and chasing each other. Sometimes they test themselves by challenging bigger boys. I have watched third-grade boys jump into a soccer goal and invite eighth-grade boys to kick at them (the eighth-grade boys did, with restraint). I routinely hear from fifth-grade boys that a big third- or fourth-grade boy has attempted to take them on; sometimes a smaller boy succeeds in intimidating an older one.

Perhaps the most pressing physical issue for boys this age in the United States is obesity. Since 1970, the number of obese children has quadrupled. Close to 16 percent of boys between the ages of eight and ten are obese, and the percentages are rising to match those in other industrialized countries such as Australia, where a quarter of boys this age are seriously overweight. This is a challenge for every parent because the physical development of our boys has lifelong consequences for their health, work, and quality of life. Too many boys are being afflicted early with serious weight-related illnesses such as type II diabetes and cardiovascular illnesses. Too many of our boys are fat and unhealthy.

Attachment

Sometime in her son's elementary school years a mother may become aware that her son is "in love" with his teacher. The powerful feelings of trust, admiration, and affection that a boy used to reserve for his mom he is now exporting into the world and bestowing on another woman. The excited admiration he has had for his father since he was a little boy he may start to lavish on his baseball coach. This is perfectly normal—indeed, it is very healthy. You would worry if your son never felt like loving a teacher or if he never had an inspiring coach. Nevertheless, it can be hard to see a boy transfer these strong feelings to another adult. To a parent, it can feel like a hurtful rejection. It is not. Your son has simply widened the circle of his attachments.

It is important to remember that a child with a secure attachment is going to be more exploratory and have better social relationships than a child who had an insecure attachment at the beginning of his life. When your son forms these bonds with teachers and coaches, it is evidence that you gave him a good start in life. The more difficult thing may be that he is clearly becoming more loyal to his group of friends than he is to his family and does not hesitate to imply that his friends are still more important to him than some family activity you are proposing. Even though he sometimes seems dismissive of his family, you mean everything to him and are the center of his world. A child with a secure attachment takes you for granted. I had a psychiatrist teacher once who said, "Good parents are like the floor. Children stand on them and never think about the support they're getting."

Social Development

Whenever I ask fifth graders what makes a boy popular, the girls say, "Whether the girls like him" or "Whether the girls think he is cute." The girls are already preparing lists of who should "go out" with whom, and most of the boys are oblivious to it.

As they are saying this, I glance at the boys, and they are shaking their heads, as if to say, *Sorry, ladies, we're not there yet. This is boy society.* And it is. Boys live for each other's company. Boys' preference for gender-exclusive play is strong in kindergarten and grows steadily right through fifth grade. By age eleven, in public play situations most boys choose to play only with boys—never with girls. Occasionally, parents and educators interested in gender equity have objected to the idea that teachers refer to "the boys" and "the girls" because it groups children arbitrarily. I disagree. Boy groups and girl groups are not arbitrary or created by adults; they are natural and self-selected.

Play is what binds the boys' group together, whether it is sports, video games, or running conversation about a movie or a television show. Even conversations between boys about movies and television have a competitive feel to them, with every boy talking as fast as he can to have his voice heard. Boy groups tend to be inclusive and will generally be open to any boy who wants to play the game, even if the core group is not all that excited about the presence of one unpopular boy. Slowly and gradually, this pattern of inclusivity will change as the good athletes distinguish themselves from the nonathletes and 80 percent of the boys separate themselves from the 20 percent of neglected, controversial, and rejected boys who occupy the social cellar of the class.

You may wish for your son to have a best friend, and some do, but the single close friend, a pattern common to girls, is seen less among boys, who tend to play in larger groups. Not all boys crave a best friend; it seems to be a stylistic choice or a geographic accident. When boys do have a friend nearby who is a close match intellectually and athletically, and they can play together *a lot,* the friendships they have are reciprocal and affectionate. Though boys do not use the word *love* to describe their feelings about another boy in the way that girls might, there is no word but *love* to describe the intense loyalty they display for each other.

Many adults experience boys' groups as somewhat raucous and raunchy. Dirty words and "swears" are common. The boys may seem antisocial, meaning that they play away from adults, take risks, and apparently do not care what adults think. That is all true, but do not take it personally. It is not meant that way. Boys are very proud of being able to run their own games without adult supervision; they cherish the excitement of being on their own, and they get very annoyed when you are constantly disapproving about what they are doing. If you observe successful teachers and coaches work with boys, you will notice that they watch closely but smile and laugh a lot.

Cognitive Development

One of the most striking aspects of boys ages eight to ten is their expanded knowledge base and their ability to remember things. They know so much about the world that it gives them reference points on which they can draw when they encounter new information. They can group information in meaningful clusters, and they have prodigious memories that allow them to master games. Michelene Chi compared the memories of ten-year-olds and college students by asking them to remember back to the arrangement of pieces on a chess board at several points in a chess game that was over. The ten-year-olds did better on the task than the college students (though college students did better with random numbers). Children of eight are also better able to accurately predict how much they can remember than a five-year-old is. You may find your son remembering things for you, even while he continues to forget his homework!

Boys of this age are also now a great deal more logical and strategic than ever before. They are also quicker and more consistent in using strategies. If you have been playing tic-tac-toe with your son, you will experience the change. When he was younger you had to let him win because he would make impulsive, illogical choices in how he filled in his X's and 0's. By age nine he understands the logic of the game as well as an adult, and should your attention waver, he will beat you or play you to a draw. He will want to play games with you and you will find it challenging to play with him.

The ability to keep a card collection requires the ability to sort and discriminate cards according to different criteria. Your son will be proud both of his collection, beautifully organized in ring binders, and of his memory. He is able to instantly produce facts about basketball or football players. This is, of course, a time when many American men make a lifelong bond with their sons over shared memories of baseball games they have watched together and the memorized batting averages of favorite players.

Academic Development

Educators and parents hope that by third grade the vast majority of children have moved past learning how to read and are now reading to learn. For the majority of boys this is the case, despite the general gap in reading skills when compared to girls. With their ability to read proficiently, they can read chapter books, master social studies textbooks, and solve words problems in math. Although they may not be as sophisticated readers as the girls, most boys are becoming proficient readers—they aren't failing. They may not enjoy reading. They may have to work hard at it—harder than their female classmates to meet a teacher's expectations. But they are doing the work and progressing.

Unfortunately, 41 percent of children in the United States are not reading at a basic level by third grade, and a majority of them are boys. Many of them are diagnosed with learning disabilities because they are behind in grade level or a specific subject even though they are of average or above-average intelligence. If that has happened to your son, you are worried and you are spending a lot of time with educators trying to figure out what his learning disability is and what you should do to address it.

The best-known of the learning disabilities is dyslexia, diagnosed when educators discover that a child has serious problems in reading even though he is bright. By nine years of age, children who read well have developed the phonological processing skills to allow them to read pseudo-words, words that are not real but can be read using all the rules for converting written letters into pronounceable words. Learning-disabled children are unable to do this because they cannot internalize the rules of reading and decode language. Research has shown that there are observable brain differences between average readers and learning-disabled children when the two groups are working on a rhyming task. With special remedial work learning-disabled boys and girls are able to develop compensatory strategies that enable them to read, but not all become fluent readers. If your son continues to struggle, his sense of self-confidence is at risk and you will have to support him for many years to keep him from becoming bitter about school.

All parents want their children to learn, and they worry about their child's education. If your son has made it through the crucial first three years of school with enthusiasm for learning and school, if your son is willing to do his homework most of the time and is not developing stomachaches or headaches, if he likes his teacher and has friends at school, things are going well. He may still say, "I hate school," and that is hard to hear, but most boys say it. In part, boys say it because other boys do; in part, they say it because their days in school are long.

Emotional Self-Regulation

With maturity comes self-control. The tantrums of preschool and the occasional meltdowns of the early elementary years are gone. Boys are accustomed to school: they no longer miss their moms, they are no longer afraid that they are going to wet their pants, and they are not as scared of the learning process and its frustrations. More than anything else, though, they have started to depend on their friends for emotional support. Small children need adults to regulate their feelings for them. If they are too excited or too anxious, they are compelled to go to an adult. By the time children are in third grade, however, if you go to an adult too much you earn a label: "baby," "tattletale," "suck-up."

After the age of eight, your son will try very hard not to run to an adult when he is upset; a boy hates to look like a baby in the eyes of other boys. Only the most anxious boys regularly run to grown-ups, and they pay a price for it in social disapproval. When a boy is anxious, other boys help him by pretending not to notice, in order to give him time to recover, or they coach him with admonitions such as "Aw, don't worry. It won't be that bad" or "Don't pay any attention, the teacher's stupid." These attempts to minimize what one boy perceives as a threat often rely on humor. When boys see that another boy is anxious and they want to calm him, they tease him lightly and find some way to make him laugh. Earnest adults can misunderstand these efforts, imagining that the group is mocking a vulnerable boy. I don't mean to deny that that can happen sometimes, but far more often, the group is trying to help a boy find his courage.

Moral and Spiritual Development

All children are moral philosophers. From a very early age they grapple with the big questions of right and wrong, good and bad, life and death. We do not always hear the philosophical dimensions of boys' thinking because they may throw us off with their concreteness or their boy preoccupations. On Martin Luther King Jr. Day, children in schools all over the United States discuss the life and death of the great civil rights leader. When a four-year-old boy hears that King was assassinated—information his teachers may have tried to keep from him—he may ask, "Did it hurt?" because he is focused on his own occasional pain and helplessness. A six-year-old boy may ask, "Did they catch the guy who shot him?" because his morality is based on the power of authority. It will not be until eight or nine that a boy asks, "Why would someone shoot Martin Luther King Jr.?" You can tell he is grappling with the goodness of the man and the evil of the deed because his morality is based on an equal exchange: good for good, an eye for an eye, you scratch my back and I'll scratch yours.

Even though boys are moral philosophers, in the sense that they engage with moral dilemmas, they do not think like adults until late adolescence. That is what Jean Piaget and Lawrence Kohlberg revealed in their stage theories of moral development. Boys and girls try to be "good" at every age; very few children are dedicated to being bad. Because they love their parents, they want to be good. However, "good" when you are in kindergarten means not making your mother or the teacher mad. "Being good" in second through fifth grade—Stage 2 in Kohlberg's scheme of the development of moral thinking—might mean behaving well for a teacher you like and behaving badly for a "mean" teacher. It is only by eighth grade that fully half of the class behaves not just to avoid trouble, but because they are measuring themselves against an internal standard of what a "good boy" or "good girl" owes to his or her community. We'll look more closely at the later stages in the chapters ahead. For now, it is important to remember that a boy may not be hearing what you think you are communicating, because he is not developmentally ready to do so. Indeed, when we speak to them about rules, referring to the social contract in the classroom, the boys may be thinking, *Whoa, the teacher's mad. She's going to keep us in for recess.*

Younger boys reason on the basis of self-interest; boys of eight and nine base their morality on a theory of exchange. It is only by age ten that a boy begins to base his morality on living up to what is expected of him, mutual respect and loyalty, and having good motives. Perhaps the biggest change in a boy's moral thinking is that he is able to understand an event in light of a person's intentions, not the objective outcome. For example, children of three or four will say that somebody who broke a plate accidentally should be punished, just because the plate is broken. An older child can appreciate the difference between an intentional, destructive act and an accident.

It is likely that during his first ten years of life a boy may experience the death of a pet or a grandparent. He will grapple with the reality and permanence of death as his cognitive development allows him to. At five years of age, he can grasp that death is permanent, but he has not yet come to grips with the idea of his own death. He still believes that he is invulnerable and that his parents can keep him alive. The psychiatrist E. J. Anthony wrote that an eight-year-old faces an "existential crisis" when he realizes that not only can his parents not save themselves from death, they cannot protect him, either. Boys can become quite anxious when they move from the protected thinking of young boyhood to the more realistic thinking of middle childhood and early adolescence. You can comfort him, but there is no protecting him from the emotional impact of these discoveries.

Identity

Boys crave membership in the pack of boys at this age, and define themselves by their shared interests, passions, activities, and attitudes. Of course, some boys are "different," but it may make them feel defensive to know they are. It is tough for a ten-year-old boy to say that he loves to read if his friends do not. Thank goodness for the Harry Potter books—they gave every boy reader a chance to celebrate his reading in public, and even compete with others over who read the latest book first or in the shortest time. The greatest gift to a boy's identity is a boy like himself, who confirms that he is all right.

tential failures. However, your ability to shield him declines dramatically as he enters the period from eight to ten years of age, because he is choosing the arenas in which he wants to compete. Every parent is left to stand and watch the struggle of his or her son from the sidelines, either unable to intervene and make a significant difference or rightly wary of intervening and robbing a boy of the important experience of resolving things for himself. That can be painful indeed for a parent whose son is frustrated and angry, especially if he begins playing out his anger and competitiveness in school.

ANGRY YOUNG BOYS: OVER THE TOP WITH FRUSTRATION

The most common psychological issue among boys in elementary school is anger. Boys struggling with difficult personal or family issues may be angry before they set foot in the school building. For many others, their frustration in school lights the match, and it's a short fuse to angry, belligerent, or hypercompetitive behavior at school and at home. Parents feel the heat and don't know what to do:

> He has school smarts but his physical and athletic ability are affected by cerebral palsy. My biggest concern is helping him have a wonderful childhood filled with friends, adventures, and love.
> —Mother of a nine-year-old boy

> My son will generally shut down when he is angry or upset. I have a concern that he internalizes his feelings.

> I think he is having feelings of incompetence at school that are troubling for him, and he seems to cope by doing a lot of negative attention seeking, verbal disrespect to others, noncompliance, and other disruptive behaviors in class. The anger has thrown me for a loop.

A boy's anger can come out as resentment of others, arguing with adults, touchiness, low frustration tolerance, and a loss of friends. At its worst, when a boy argues constantly with adults, or lies, becomes explosive or vindictive, and refuses to take responsibility for his actions, he may get diagnosed as having oppositional defiant disorder (ODD). This disorder is diagnosed far more in boys than in girls; various studies reveal that 9 to 20 percent of boys have ODD, but it is thought that changing cultural standards for boy behavior may be causing an increased diagnosis of this problem. Noted child psychiatrist Edward M. Hallowell, M.D., author of *Driven to Distraction,* says that ODD is a grab-bag diagnosis, vague and almost impossible to define. He sees it as a prime example of the "pathologizing" of boyhood by mental health professionals. Whether it is 9 percent or 20 percent of boys who are angry to the point of being out of control, these percentages represent a very large number, perhaps two and a half million boys. What makes them so mad? Is something missing in their families? Is school driving them crazy? How do we understand their fury, and how can we address it productively?

"PEOPLE DON'T LIKE ME WHEN I'M MAD"

Researchers have found that in a typical elementary school class, 15 percent of children are very popular, 45 percent are accepted, 20 percent are "ambiguous" or unclassifiable—ranked neither as popular or unpopular by their classmates—and 20 percent are socially at risk because their classmates overlook them, find them controversial, or reject them outright.

Boys with impulse control problems, boys with ADHD, and especially boys who have experienced a lot of family conflict are likely to find themselves rejected in this way because their aggression spills out in their social relationships. One mother, Bette, described the plight of her son, Wyeth, who was labeled as a troublemaker as early as kindergarten by teachers and other children alike, and was never able to shed the reputation. He appeared to be what we call a "rejected-aggressive child" who either intimidated or irritated his classmates in kindergarten and could not escape from his role as a provocateur and scapegoat. She reported that in school, "he always lives with a presumption of guilt," and as a result has been excluded by his peers. It has been extremely hurtful to both him and his mother.

Wyeth is a skilled athlete, and boys who are coordinated are often forgiven a lot of sins by other boys because everyone wants to play on a team with someone who is talented. Unfortunately, Wyeth had burned too many social bridges by third grade and his athletic skill cannot overcome his turbulent history with his peers.

Elsewhere, in a fourth-grade classroom nearing the end of the school year, a teacher's aide described her boy-heavy class, in which eight of the boys have been formally identified as behavior problems:

> We have a lot of very smart boys in here. Too bad their behaviors got in the way. They could have really been challenged. They could have fed off each other, you know, challenging each other in a good way. Instead, there's a lot of talking with other students, and even when the teacher tries to get the class's attention they often just ignore her and keep on going. Like with James—outright defiance. And then Eddie, he's probably one of the biggest challenges. He's had a lot of trouble at home. He's witnessed violence—some horrible, horrible stuff—and did not get help. And of course you see it in his behavior. He's very angry. Just defiant, angry, and rude.

My family was a mess—so I am just doing my best to make life different for my boys. —Mother of two sons, ten and seven years old

She went on to describe the issues that plague each boy and cause trouble for the class, though they often suggest a mixed bag of behaviors, not all negative.

Cody is an upbeat, articulate fourth grader, a short, wiry action figure of a boy in the class. He knows he's considered one of the "bad kids," and explained how they get labeled that way:

> Well, kids say I'm bad because I get in trouble a lot. But that's mainly just for talking, so I don't really think that's *bad*. Not like Patrick. I mean, he *kicked* Mr. Benning [a teacher] or something, but Mr. Benning was trying to put Patrick in a headlock because, like, Patrick was doing something wrong . . .

As for himself, Cody continued:

> It's a little bit for other stuff, like I don't really follow the rules, like at kick-ball I run on the blacktop and we're not supposed to do that, which I think is really stupid. They say it's so we won't hurt ourselves, but it's like 99 percent of the time it would be okay, or like 1 percent of the time we're gonna trip and fall. So you can run in a kickball game—that's okay—but you can't run just to play. You have to walk. You can only run on the grass and if you're playing basketball, but they still say to be careful, slow down. I usually do run, but I usually get in trouble for it. They're like, "I'm writing you down," and I say, "What'd I do?" and they say, "No talking back! Now I'm writing you down for something else." And I just said, "What'd I do?" They always think I'm talking back. But the rule is kinda dumb.

So Cody breaks the rules in class and recess and gets in trouble for that, but there is more. He is indeed the ringleader who directs other boys' mischief, and he acknowledged this has added to his reputation as a troublemaker:

> I went to the principal's office a couple times. I've never got suspended. I dared my friend to, like, trip somebody, but I didn't think he'd actually do it. But he did, so I got in trouble. Sometimes I just give them ideas, but I don't think they're actually gonna do it.

And finally, he conceded, he suspects he has become known for his angry outbursts, and not in a good way:

SUNSET LAKE: THE CENTERPIECE OF A FAMILY AND BOYHOOD ADVENTURE

As a boy of eight or so, most of my memories come from summers spent at my family's place in Foxboro, Massachusetts, where my great-grandfather, William E. Barton, had purchased an old farm and a lake in 1910 or so. By the time I was born, there were nine family houses up and down the road, and we had something of a family compound there.

My memories of that age are attached to the various challenges and goals presented to me by Sunset Lake, the centerpiece of the family property, and the rocks, and the boats on the lake. All of these were markers of my progress and growth. You could not use a boat alone unless you passed the swim test. I remember watching my brother pass the test and wanting my day to come, which would, in the normal course of events, have been two years later. At some point, perhaps when I was seven or eight, I successfully swam from the cove to the dam, a distance of about 400 yards—or was it only 150?—accompanied by my aunt. (It was the family's belief that you shouldn't do the swim test with your own parent; you had to do it with an aunt or uncle. They were almost certainly right.)

To this day, I can walk around Foxboro and see the granite rocks—to me at the time they seemed to be enormous outcroppings—with ledges that I conquered, including the huge Picnic Rock (but that was probably by age five) and other lesser rocks that had tricky shelves and cracks in which to put your feet. I can recall the sense of achievement I had as a result of conquering all these little Matterhorns of my youth.

But most of all, I remember fishing by myself, and I am sure this would have been around age nine or ten. I always wanted to catch pickerel, which were the wildest-looking fish in the lake—like miniature muskellunge—and much harder to catch than the omnipresent sunfish, perch, and catfish, which could be easily reeled in from the dam.

To catch pickerel you had to row or canoe up to the end of the lake. I spent hours in the rowboat, coordinating my strokes, rowing fast, covering what seemed to me the vast expanses of the lake. In fact, it was only a pond of about fifteen acres, shaped somewhere between a Y and a T, and when you went up one of the arms of the lake you were completely out of sight of adults.

I well remember standing at a certain rocky place on the shore of the upper right arm of the lake where I caught pickerel. And I remember feeling alone, and adventuresome, and a little scared of being out of sight of anybody sometimes, though of course I had done it before. And if I caught a pickerel, I felt big and successful. And maybe after fishing I would row all the way to the end of the T, where it got swampy, and I knew there were snapping turtles, but there were also many painted turtles on logs. I would try to catch them, with moderate success. It is hard to sneak up using a boat with oars. My aunt Joan, who was raised on nearby Cocasset Lake, boasted about having sneaked up on turtles by lying over the bow of a canoe, catching as many as fifteen or seventeen that way. I remember thinking about that over and over, wondering if I would ever catch as many as my aunt Joan had. Later, when I was thirteen and fourteen, I would use a canoe; indeed, you are more successful in a canoe, but I still never caught as many turtles as my aunt Joan.

Psychologically speaking, the whole deal during these years was, "I can do that!" Whatever someone else—your bigger brother or bigger cousin—had done, you wanted to do.

Well, kids think I'm mean. I get mad. Like really mad. People don't like me when I'm mad because I'm sort of mean when I'm mad.

What makes him mad?

I get mad when people call me "small" and stuff. Once I cried and stuff 'cause everybody was calling me "small" and they just kept saying it and they called me "super small" because I lost at this little race thing. And I started crying, because I get called "small" every single day by the same people and nobody ever stops and the teachers don't do anything about it.

Cody asked his dad and grandparents how to handle the teasing.

My family says fight back, but you can't just totally beat somebody up if they didn't do anything to you. I usually try to fight back, but I don't try to hurt them. And I'm the one who usually gets in trouble. I just, like, push them off and stuff. I try to get away, and if they don't like leave me alone I'll even tell a teacher, but if they, like, kick me or something I'll kick them back. And then I get in trouble.

> *I love my son! I am truly blessed—and scared to death that he will one day drive a car.*
> —Mother of a nine-year-old boy

If a boy is very proud, as Wyeth and Cody certainly are, rejection may make them angrier or more confrontational or competitive in reaction, confirming their classmates' (and teachers') worst judgments. Unfortunately, because boys are so hierarchical, once the status ladder has been established, it is difficult for a boy to change his social position. Wyeth's mother is right to worry that he may never be able to recover socially with his classmates in his current school. Unless he gets some treatment for his anger and resentment—and he is presently seeing an educational therapist—he might move to a new school with a chip on his shoulder and alienate teachers and peers there as well.

Bette recognizes that Wyeth needs a teacher who can see his strengths and teach him with patience and love. She admits that her son does not now trust adults. If that is true, it will be difficult for him to establish a relationship with a teacher who can show him the acceptance, tolerance, and understanding that he will need to feel for a prolonged period of time before he drops his angry, resentful stance toward school. He is a B student and, with reminders from his mother, does his homework pretty regularly; that academic ability will likely eventually bring him to the attention of a teacher, who may get Wyeth to lower his emotional guard. In the meantime, he may have to find his friends outside of school, with his winning flag football team. Bette comforts herself with the idea that even if he is not "part of the herd," one day he will be a leader.

The teacher and aide in Cody's class recognize the good in these boys and note they respond to patience, guidance, and encouragement. "If you find that little nugget and you can praise him about it, oh my gosh, you've made his day," the aide says. "It's awesome when you can find those things."

READING AND WRITING: THE STRUGGLE CONTINUES FOR MANY BOYS

For many boys, problems with learning to read in kindergarten, first grade, and second grade continue into the third, fourth, and fifth grades. Many boys struggle with school in general and with reading and writing in particular. Because the curriculum in the elementary school classroom is four-fifths language-based, reading is the centerpiece of learning; many boys avoid reading and say they "hate it." Parents want to know why this happening and what they should do about it. It is a national problem, at all levels. In Illinois, after state tests were revamped, girls' scores in 2007 showed an even greater than usual spike over boys'. In news articles, some experts suggested that the content and structure of the tests may somehow favor girls. Last year a mother in Massachusetts e-mailed me about a disturbing gender gap in that state's achievement test scores: "Is the test gender-biased, or are we failing to teach our boys to read?"

The answer is that we have more trouble teaching boys to read than we do teaching girls. By fourth grade, girls score better in reading on the National Assessment of Educational Progress (NAEP), the definitive test of reading and math achievement given to public school children in the United States. Indeed, fourth grade is just the beginning. Girls also outperform boys on the reading section of the NAEP in eighth and twelfth grades. The gap between girls and boys is most pronounced in eighth grade, with the average eighth-grade girl writing at the level of the average eleventh-grade boy. Is this gender discrepancy in language counterbalanced by the fact that boys do better in math than girls? Many adults believe that boys are "naturally better" at math because when they were in school thirty years ago, boys scored higher than girls in math. That is no longer the case; boys and girls are now essentially tied in math and science achievement.

The idea that school is not a good fit for boys or that teachers don't understand boys was one of the issues most frequently mentioned by parents who filled out my online questionnaire. This concern is heartening. As a psychologist who has worked with schools for thirty years, I have always found it painfully obvious that more boys than girls struggle in school, and especially in reading and writing. We all need to focus on what aspects of the classroom are difficult for boys, try to understand why, and do what we can to make them work better for boys. But first, I hasten to remind parents that the results discussed above on tests such as the NAEP reflect aggregate scores. They don't necessarily apply to any particular child: we are discussing the average boy and the average girl. There always have been and always will be strong boy readers for whom school is an arena of success and weak girl readers who struggle with language and need our support; the populations of both boys and girls are mostly in the great middle of the class. It is not the case across the board that the girls

PROTECT AND CHERISH A BOY'S CHANCE TO PLAY

Free play has a special place in development of boys. There is no replacement, no substitute, absolutely nothing quite as sweet for a boy as getting some distance away from adults, finding a friend or friends, and creating a good time for himself. I worry that modern life in America is a conspiracy against free play. We have come close to turning everything into work, including play.

Boys instinctively know the true nature of play. Play is what you do when you stand work on its ear. Play is something your parents have not thought up and of which they probably would not approve. Tom Sawyer showed us all when he outwitted his aunt Polly, who was determined to make him turn out to be well-behaved like her son, Sid, whom we all hate because he is such a proper little prig. She makes Tom whitewash the fence, and he turns it into a creative evasion of her instructions, persuading other boys that it really is fun and taking their trinkets in exchange for a chance to paint the fence. We smile broadly at Mark Twain's conclusion that if Tom were wise he would comprehend that

> Work consists of whatever a body is *obliged* to do, and that Play consists of whatever a body is not obliged to do.

Twain has explained beautifully why organized sports, as good as they are for fitness and for health, are not the same thing as true play: because the moment you sign up for a team and make a commitment to play through the season, you have incurred an obligation. Once you are obliged to do it, it isn't play anymore. Oh, yes, of course there are playful, exciting moments, but nothing organized by adults is true play. Can adults be nearby? Yes. Should adults be available? Yes. Can adults organize true play for boys? No, never.

A friend and veteran parent offers this mantra for resisting micromanaging or overorganizing your son's play: "When in doubt, just butt out." For a more thorough explanation, a recent report by the American Academy of Pediatrics (AAP) stressing the importance of play for healthy development concludes:

- Play allows children to create and explore a world they can master, conquering their fears while practicing adult roles.

- As they master their world, play helps children develop new competencies that lead to enhanced confidence and the resiliency they will need to face future challenges.

- Undirected play allows children to learn how to work in groups, to share, to negotiate, to resolve conflicts, and to learn self-advocacy skills.

- When play is allowed to be child-driven, children practice decision-making skills, move at their own pace, discover areas of interest, and ultimately engage fully in the passions they wish to pursue.

In 1989 a survey of elementary school principals found that 96 percent of schools had at least one recess period; ten years later, only 70 percent of schools had a recess period. The AAP suggests that reduced time for physical activity may be contributing to the discrepancy in the academic performance between boys and girls. As life and schools become more sedentary and academic, boys are suffering and their academic performance is dropping. Boys today are less competent because they cannot create their own play, not at recess and not after school.

Do everything in your power to allow boys to play with other boys in as free and unstructured a way as you possibly can. Help to create a safe neighborhood, talk to other parents about the need of boys to play, and give your support to any activities that will give boys time to just be together. It may not be easy, but the overscheduled, overtutored, overcompetitive life does not nourish the souls of boys.

get A's and the boys get C's. That said, it is important to figure out why boys, on average, do not do as well in reading as girls.

WHY SOME BOYS LAG BEHIND GIRLS AS READERS: FOUR THEORIES

There are four main theories that might explain why many boys do not do as well in reading and writing as girls do. The first one focuses on neurological-biological differences; the second on social learning differences; the third examines cultural forces, especially the culture of school and its impact on boys, and the final one focuses on the curriculum and pedagogy of reading. Briefly:

The neurological-biological difference explanation relies on a growing number of studies (which are still preliminary and not yet definitive) to suggest that the boy brain is not wired to process language as effectively as the girl brain is, or that elementary school boys are at a learning disadvantage because, for example, they have less serotonin available than girls and are therefore more fidgety in school.

Social learning theory suggests that because girls converse more with peers, they get more practice with words, and that because more women are teachers, girls have more powerful models for language and reading. Girls support each other's efforts to get good grades. The peer group experience for

> *I like to jump around and especially like to run and jump around. I can sit but sometimes it bothers me.*
> —Fourth-grade boy

boys is, by contrast, anti-intellectual and anti-academic. A boy is more likely to get teased by his friends for spending too much time with books or getting good grades.

Critics of school culture say that there is a poor fit between the expectations of school and the arc of boy development and/or that women teachers cannot accept boys as they are. These critics conclude that school is a hostile environment for boys, who too often are punished, diagnosed, labeled, or otherwise "pathologized" and sent off to special education classes, where they become demoralized and are poorly educated.

The final theory addresses the classroom experience of boys, suggesting that over the past thirty years, schools have stopped using reading materials and writing assignments that would appeal to boys, and that as a result boys look for their exciting narrative experiences outside of school.

Parents cannot wait for researchers to figure out which theory correctly explains boy reading problems. What I hear from parents is that they spontaneously arrive at all these theories on their own by the time their sons have been in school for three or four years.

"They're wired differently," a mother told me with conviction. Her husband chimed in, "Of course they are!" Parents see that many of their sons struggle against the rules of school and the demands of reading, and they conclude school is a bad fit for boys; they also see that when their son hangs out with other boys it undermines his academic ambition. Mothers also get a bit upset with their sons' teachers if they do not seem to understand boys' tastes in literature. As James was starting third grade, his mother told me: "I suppose I'm worried that in school things don't spark him. They take books away from him. He likes to read about things that are real, but even the easy reader books, they are all fake characters. He's always liked dinosaurs, Balto, gorillas, tigers. And the teachers really haven't figured that out."

Thomas Newkirk, a professor of English at the University of New Hampshire who has studied literacy at all levels, from preschool to college, concludes that if we are to successfully teach boys, we must first understand the boy experience of reading and writing. "Literacy too often seems unappealing and inactive to boys," Newkirk writes. "It gets in the way of the need to move, to talk, to play, to live in and with one's body."

In his insightful book *Misreading Masculinity*, Newkirk writes that for adult readers, and especially educators, the value of reading is self-evident. Furthermore, for educators (who are all fluent, dedicated readers), the greatest good is sustained silent reading. Not so for boys; for many, silent reading is an agony. Reading is something that cuts a boy off from interaction with the real world: he gets no feedback from it, he cannot interact with his friends, and there is no product! If a boy were building something out of wood, he could tell how well or how badly he was doing immediately, and he could share the experience with a friend. As far as a boy can see, to be a good reader means you have to be a bit of a loner. What boy wants to choose that fate? In addition, to be a good silent reader you have to sit still, control your body, and be quiet. If that were not enough to give reading a bad name with boys, the fact that girls seem to do it more easily than they do makes it a "girl" thing. Finally, as Newkirk points out, educators use seat work—work that has to be done sitting at their desks—to control unruly students. Reading and writing are often seen by boys as a punishment.

In every classroom the teachers are, like, "You guys are worse than the girls." I think it is something biological.
—Boy, age eight

How can a boy in elementary school who is struggling with reading and writing fail to draw the conclusion that he is trapped in an anti-boy plot, something that is not part of his real world? You can be sure that by the time he is in third or fourth grade, a boy has heard many other boys say, "Reading is stupid!" or "I hate reading." Unless your son is a boy who reads fluently and who finds sitting still easy—and such boys are a small minority in the classroom—it is likely that your elementary-school-age son has reached just that conclusion many times during his years at school.

Newkirk insists that we need to learn what it is that boys hate about school in general and silent reading in particular. He thinks that the two boy heroes of the *Captain Underpants* books show us clearly what boys hate about school: the power imbalance. Adults control the time, space, speaking rights, and choice of activities in schools. Boys often are not allowed to read what they want, nor write about what interests them. Are teachers aware of what boys object to about school in general and reading in particular? You bet they are! They hear it constantly and are keenly aware of the difficulties they face in getting boys excited about reading and writing. In my online survey, I asked teachers: "What classroom activity is the least successful with boys; what makes them slump and groan?" A sampling of their answers:

Writing and note taking

Silent reading

Asking them to write their ideas down on paper

Read quietly to yourself, then write a summary

Sit and listen

Sustained reading activity

Anything where they have to sit still for too long, especially if they're writing

Me lecturing at them (but I don't do that too much)

Sitting with their feet on the floor in neat little rows, writing longhand—you might as well shoot them

When I asked teachers to write what activities were the most successful with boys, almost no one responded with the mention of a specific subject such as math or science; rather, the teachers addressed the techniques they used for engaging boys' interest in any subject.

Start with a question that gets them questioning (wind them up), give them materials, and let them go. The fewer words the better.

Experiments that involve movement, self-deprecating humor, and friendly teasing draw boys in.

Choice and frequent movement.

Letting them do it on their own—not having to follow too strict a plan or a teacher's model.

I try to create opportunities for boys to move and be active in the classroom.

Boys excel from hands-on and visual techniques. I believe that they remember more and are more engaged when a concept is accompanied by a visual cue or a story.

Active games to assist memory. Competitions with a clear winner (as long as the results have a dab of luck so as to protect the ego).

You can see once again that the central issues for boys, no matter what subject is being taught, are movement, control of choice, variety, and interaction with the group. When boys are asked to do silent reading and summarize a book, usually there is no movement involved, the teacher controls the choice of book, and there is no experience of competition or any shared group outcome. Every teacher in the United States who is preparing children for state tests faces this quandary: the very thing you think you must do to prepare boys for the language tests makes them hate reading and writing.

Are there solutions to this dilemma?

Thomas Newkirk suggests that educators stop imposing our tastes on boys and give boys more choice about what they read in school—for example, allowing them to read comic books and sports pages. He believes many boys could write a heartfelt story based on the NBA standings printed in the sports section of the paper. We need to invite boys to write the kind of stories they love: science fiction, adventure, humor, and some gross stuff (the two boys in the *Captain Underpants* series get in trouble after changing the school sign to read "Please Don't Fart in a Diaper"—a surefire and engaging beginning to a story for third-grade boys!). And yes, we need to let boys write stories that contain violence because it is part of the culture, language, and fantasy life of boys—and that is what they are talking to each other about. In short, we need to let boys read and write anything that leads them to like reading and writing.

ADVENTURING: TELEVISION AND VIDEO GAMES

If boys are not reading, what are they doing? Everyone knows the answer to that. They are watching television or playing computer or video games.

According to Dimitri Christakis and Frederick Zimmerman, authors of *The Elephant in the Living Room: Make Television Work for Your Kids,* the average American child watches three hours—and sometimes more than eight hours—of tele-

DON'T GET OVERINVESTED IN YOUR SON'S SPORTS CAREER

I believe in organized sports. Indeed, I work at a boys' school that requires boys to play after-school sports, either interscholastic or recreational, three seasons a year. The school requires athletics in order to help a boy become fit, stay healthy, develop lifelong habits of exercise, and learn how to work as a team with other boys—and that is a short list. There are many more pluses than minuses, especially in an age of increasing obesity.

However, it is a problem when parents become overinvolved in a boy's athletic career, because gradually their level of involvement starts to overshadow or complicate his commitment. When you send your son into organized sports, you have to remember that the average American boy stops playing at age eleven, saying it is no fun anymore. That is the most common story. Stories of gifted football players such as Peyton Manning, son of Archie Manning, who grew up in an athletic family and shared his father's love of football are thrilling—and statistically rare.

It is perhaps fathers more than mothers who become wrapped up in their son's athletic careers. I understand why. Watching sports is part of most men's lives, both as a hobby and as part of their identity. Also, I am the psychologist for a boys' school and I have watched a lot of boys' games. The games are exciting and dramatic, and it is obvious that boys are enjoying themselves most of the time. It is fun watching them have fun. For many busy parents, watching their sons out on the court or the playing field is one of the most diverting pastimes in their lives.

As a therapist, however, I have heard a number of boys say, "The only thing my father cares about is my hockey," or lacrosse or football or baseball. I have sat with parents who have fallen into serious depressions when their son has suffered a knee ligament injury that might be career-ending. I have sat with a sobbing mother who was devastated by her son's failure to make a varsity team. He had told me that very morning that the hardest thing about being cut was the way his parents had reacted. Because of that, he felt like a failure.

It is important to remember that most boys will never play on a select team. According to Bob Bigelow, the former Celtics player who coauthored a passionate book about organized sports for children called *Just Let the Kids Play*, select teams are made up of the "least worst" children in a town. "The parents don't like it when I say that," he told me, but went on to point out that there are just not that many talented players in any given town. (Statistically, it is easier to be a National Merit Semifinalist than a Division I athlete.) Most boys will never play on a varsity team in high school, and only a small percentage of the boys who do will go on to play sports in college. That's a fact. Furthermore, according to sports psychologist Richard Ginsburg, it is almost impossible to predict the career of an athlete before the age of ten or twelve, because the entire deck gets reshuffled by puberty. Some boys become less coordinated and quick for their size; others become much more coordinated.

So enjoy your son's organized sports to the maximum. Yell and cheer for him and his teammates; do not criticize his play. But do not become too emotionally wound up in it. I have a cartoon on my wall, clipped from the *New Yorker*. It shows parents sitting in the stands at a high school game. In front of them are four cheerleaders shouting in unison: "Hang your fading hopes and dreams on your children's high school teams." I kept it up there to help me keep perspective when I was tempted to become too worked up about my child's teams. If you want a rule of thumb, you might try this: be sure that your son's love for his sport is always a bit greater than yours.

vision per day, more hours over the course of a year than he or she spends in the classroom. Children spend more time watching television than anything else they do except sleep. Of course, they do not differ from adults in their viewing habits; adults watch an average of twenty-eight hours of television per week, for a total of two complete months of TV watching per year (or nine years out of a life span of sixty-five years).

Any thoughtful parent worries about the impact of television on his or her child because TV has changed the life of the American family profoundly and continues to change it. Ninety-nine percent of homes in the United States have television sets; the average home contains more TVs than people (2.4 sets per home), and 66 percent of families regularly eat dinner while watching television. When researchers asked four-to-six-year-old children whether they would like to watch TV or spend time with their fathers, 54 percent said they would prefer television.

If they aren't watching television, boys are playing video games, and if they aren't playing video games, they are on the computer, surfing the Net or IM-ing their friends. Boys today are being raised in the middle of a digital revolution with an almost infinite number of choices of entertainment. The National Institute on Media and the Family reports that 79 percent of children ages seven to twelve play video games and the average child plays them eight hours a week.

> *One of my favorite subjects is running around. Like jogging and running. And also football. Especially running.*
> —Third-grade boy

This is a cultural tide of tremendous power. Can you stand up against it? Can you limit the amount of time your son watches television and plays video games?

The mother of a fourth-grade boy named Paul told me she was trying to limit TV. His elementary school's principal had strongly suggested that parents limit television viewing to weekends. Paul was not allowed to watch television during the week at all and was restricted to just three hours of television or video games per weekend day. She said that they fought about the issue every afternoon. When he got home from school, he would invariably asked her whether he could watch television or play on his Game Boy; her answer was always no. Paul would first complain, then argue with her, plead with her, reproach her, and finally announce that he had nothing to do and was bored. She felt his anger and could see that he was unable to entertain himself.

Though they lived in a well-to-do suburb (or *because* they lived in a well-to-do suburb), there was considerable distance between homes; there were no families with boys anywhere close to them. She didn't feel safe letting him out to play on his own or roam the neighborhood. It wouldn't have mattered; Paul didn't feel like going out into the yard without a friend with whom to play. When he was younger his older sisters would spend time with him, but as they moved into middle school and high school, they were now unwilling to play with him. He had friends at school, but had made no close friends with whom he could get together after school. And after the daily fighting over the television issue with his mother, he was not willing to do something with her. This had become their routine on the days when he was home; only after-school sports twice a week disrupted the negative pattern. This mother said, "I can see that he is bored. He doesn't know what to do with himself. My daughters do seem to know how to spend an hour."

Why is Paul's mother willing to do battle with him every afternoon? Why is she holding the line and why is he pushing so desperately hard? Paul's mother, like many parents, is worried about the effect of both television and video games on her son. She is aware that research has shown that excessive television watching can affect a child's academic performance, as well as his health.

It is only common sense to imagine that there is a relationship between TV watching and grades, and there is: the more hours of television, the lower the grades, because children who watch television a lot are obviously not spending the time reading, nor are they engaging in board games that involve reading. Children who have a television in their own bedroom, and who watch an average of two and a half additional hours of TV per week, are particularly at risk academically.

Perhaps most worrisome is that there is evidence that television watching can affect a child's ability to sustain attention. Since the most common teacher complaints about boys are that they "lack focus" or have problems "paying attention," and since there seems to be something like an epidemic of ADHD among boys in the United States, it is important that we know whether television is the villain. In an experiment conducted at Ohio State University, researchers split children into three groups: one group simply played, the second group watched *Mr. Rogers' Neighborhood,* and the third group watched *Power Rangers,* the most globally successful children's program of all time (and one that contains about 211 acts of "violence" per hour). After thirty minutes of viewing the programs, the children who watched *Power Rangers* could only sustain their attention spans for three minutes compared to six minutes for the other two groups.

When Christakis and Zimmerman followed up on the Ohio State finding, they discovered that for every hour of additional television per day that a child watched at three years old, he would be more than 20 percent more likely to show attentional problems, impulsiveness, and recklessness at seven years old. In the Ohio State experiment, children only watched *Power Rangers* for thirty minutes; in the real world, of course, boys watch *Power Rangers* much more than girls do, and they do it week after week. If watching such shows has an impact on attention, it is more likely to be seen in boys.

Researchers also have shown a strong connection between prolonged television viewing and childhood obesity. Because children who watch more than four hours of television per day are significantly heavier than those who watch less, and because research has showed some causal connection between television viewing and the propensity for violence (though there is still professional disagreement about what makes a child vulnerable to media violence), it only makes sense to limit a boy's exposure to television. Once again, parents cannot wait for the definitive study that proves television is harmful to children. Pediatricians have taken the position that children under two years of age should

GIRLS' AND BOYS' LEARNING STYLE "WORLDS APART"

Every April for the past ten years at the Chestnut Hill School in Chestnut Hill, Massachusetts, the fifth-grade class of girls and boys is divided into two same-sex groups for academic instruction. The school does this to give students a taste of what it is like to study in a same-sex environment as they near the time they'll be making a choice between a same-sex or coed middle school for their secondary experience, says Lindsay Garre, Spanish teacher at the school.

Teachers get an earful from boys regarding their preferences, says Garre. Their reactions range from being all for it to giving it a thumbs-down. One boy said he liked the all-boys class because boys could "act differently" without worrying that "the girls might think it's gross." Other boys liked it because "we can talk about guy stuff" and "socialize more," or "it's easier to learn because we don't have girls distracting us from boy stuff." One preferred the all-boys class, he said, since without girls "it is smoother because they are not here to argue with us."

Not all boys agree. One boy said that although he liked the all-boys environment because he could concentrate better on work, "I would never go to a single-gender school because in the real world boys and girls will be together. I still like being around both genders."

Another boy felt a coed classroom was the best: "I think that you have a lot of fun and you are with your friends. I think that I learn just as much with girls and boys than with just boys. I think I get a little bit more distracted when there are only boys."

Teachers also find the boys- and girls-only sessions illuminating, Garre says. It offers them an opportunity to learn more about how to teach both sexes effectively. "I am once again reminded just how differently they learn," she says, "and how differently my teaching approach needs to be for boys and girls. When teaching girls it is quieter, more focused, with more written activities and a more cooperative learning environment. Then when the boys come in, I find my voice gets louder, my energy gets higher, my activities have to be more hands-on, we play more games, and, boy, am I on the move! I have to *show* everything. I am exhausted after teaching the boys. At the end of each class, the two groups have learned the same material, but the journey of how we got to that place is worlds apart!"

not watch any television at all and agree with Christakis and Zimmerman, who say that "subsequent viewing should be both carefully selected and minimized."

If only life were that easy! Paul's mother limits his television watching, but she still has to deal with the question of whether to let him play video and computer games, and if so, which ones.

Many video and computer games are imaginative and creative; the Sims series of games is, essentially, the cyber version of playing house and building blocks combined onscreen. My son played it in many variations for years, and I admire the ingenuity of it. However, as boys get older, the games many are attracted to are violent and gory, games that put the player in the position of being the "first-person shooter." That is, in many video games the boy—and it usually is a boy who is playing—chooses his weapon(s), hunts bad guys or zombies, and kills them.

> *I do have violent games, but my dad says E-rated games are not fun.*
> —Fourth-grade boy

According to David Walsh, the director of the National Institute on Media and the Family, researchers are finding that third graders who spend more time playing video games were rated less positively by their classmates than were children who spent less time playing video games. There is some evidence that violent video games depress a boy's mood and make it more likely that he will get into a fight with another boy.

Much of this research focuses on older boys, but it's important to address the issue here because boys start pressuring their parents to allow them to play video games early in elementary school, and once your son starts playing these games in earnest, he is going to want to continue. One day I was discussing with my sixteen-year-old son whether these games are addictive. I said that the research findings were equivocal. In a tolerant but patronizing voice, he said, "Dad, of course they're addictive."

Why are boys so drawn to video games? First, they are visually exciting. If, as the research suggests, boys' brains give them an advantage in the visual-spatial realm and they are better than girls at rotating objects in space, then video games feed right into that natural ability. We all enjoy activities that feed into our cognitive strengths.

Second, video games make boys feel strong and capable. The games have a story line and a controller that makes a boy into the superhero he has been imagining himself to be since he was three or four. He gets to act out his magical powers. An adult may argue that game power isn't real power, but it clearly makes boys feel competent in a way that school doesn't and that just being a kid at home does not.

Third, we have seen that boys in groups separate themselves physically from adults early on in their play at recess. Video games accomplish the same end;

> *I'm not a tiny little boy anymore.*
> —Boy, age eight

they separate boys from adults because most adults do not play them, do not understand them, and generally dislike them.

Fourth, the social pressure to try these games and to like them is extremely strong. A boy's friends are all talking about them and they are saying, either implicitly or explicitly, that these are the games that real boys should be interested in. Playing video games is one of the informal tests of masculinity that are presented to boys.

Fifth, families today generally have two working parents and relatively few children, and their schedules are packed. With less parental time available for the children in the family, it is important for a child to be able to entertain himself. Because there are fewer siblings, there are fewer playmates in the house. Television and video games are filling a real vacuum in the modern family.

Finally, video games have replaced many of the outside explorations and adventures that boys this age used to have. At the risk of being nostalgic, American boys used to be able to play on their own outdoors, to play with friends in the neighborhood, to bicycle long distances from home. If a boy lived in a rural area, he could explore the woods; if he lived in a city, he could explore the streets with his buddies. The suburbanization of America, the increased reliance on the automobile, the decline of rural populations, and the dramatic increases in urban crime between 1975 and 1995, as well as increased parental awareness of sexual abuse and kidnappings, has dramatically changed the freedom that boys this age enjoy in the after-school hours. It's just not as common anymore for parents to say to their children, "Go outside and play and don't come back until dinnertime." Parents do not trust their neighborhoods and they do not trust their children's judgment.

The reason that Paul fights with his mother every afternoon, besieging her in hopes that he'll wear her down and get her to change her TV and video game rules, is that he is desperate. Paul's mother is not comfortable letting him play anywhere except their backyard; he feels he has outgrown it and he does not want to play alone. He has neither siblings nor neighborhood friends with whom to play after school. Furthermore, he doesn't play by himself or know how to entertain himself. His experience of boredom is very real. He will, over time, be able to develop a set of interests and activities that will occupy him, but

A BOY IS MORE THAN HIS SCHOOL PERFORMANCE

There is no question that in the globalized economy, education is important. That is indisputable. While it is important to monitor your son's school career, to get him support if he runs into difficulties in a certain subject, and to help him get a diagnosis and support if he has a learning disability, there is always more to him than his school performance.

There are very few boys who absolutely love school. Some do, the ones with what I call "school brains" (and that is not just IQ), but the majority struggle with some aspect of school: the adult control, the sitting still, the listening, the need to be organized and do homework. A boy can try very hard and not get the result he wanted. Mark Twain reminds us, "The harder Tom tried to fasten his mind on his books, the more his ideas wandered."

I have seen too many parents get so wrapped up in their son's school problems that they seem to forget all other aspects of his life. It is important for parents to remember that school is not the be-all and end-all in life. There are a lot of successful men who were not gifted students, and some who absolutely despised school but who find their passion in the workplace, at church, or on the athletic field. Keep the whole boy in mind, even when he is struggling in school.

right now he does not believe that he will. His mother is also worried about his "boredom" and afraid that she cannot find a solution to it.

The answer to Paul's need for activity is, I believe, outdoor recreation and a neighborhood full of boys with whom to play. Realistically, even if Paul had other boys to play with on his street, it is likely that if one of them had an Xbox 360 or the newest Nintendo, all the boys would be gathering at his house to play or watch each other play while they waited their turn. Concerns about social development, sedentary lifestyles, and safety have added impetus to the proliferation of organized sports.

BOYS AND ORGANIZED SPORTS

The solution for so many of the dilemmas of modern suburban child life has been organized sports. It has become almost a rite of passage for American middle-class children. Nine out of ten children participate in organized sports in their towns at some point in their childhoods. If you cannot let your son play unsupervised in the neighborhood, if your child is not within easy walking distance of friends, if you are worried about your child sitting in front of the television and

> *About 50 percent of the boys need more time to develop. They have sharp minds but the fine motor skills of a flatworm.*
> —Teacher (male)

gaining weight, then he will obviously be better off in a community sports program, surrounded by his friends and coached by caring adults. That is the conclusion that most American parents have come to: get your son in organized sports as soon as possible and keep him involved as long as possible.

By seven or eight years old, a boy is often motivated to join town sports for a multitude of reasons: his friends are playing baseball or basketball and the conversation in school is often about the ranking and success of various teams. Town teams have replaced the neighborhood as the central social hub of peers as well as parents, who show up to cheer, to provide transportation, and, of course, to supply snacks. The sidelines of a game are where a boy is likely to see his father. Dads often take a more active interest in a boy's sports career than in his schoolwork.

Furthermore, many boys from five to ten years old adopt sports figures as heroes and then want to emulate their idols. They have seen their heroes in ads on television, they have seen them play games, they wear jerseys with their names and numbers, and they identify with them. It has always been that way for boys.

Jeff, a father whose five-year-old started playing instructional hockey to be with his friends, remembered playing baseball with his neighborhood buddies when he was growing up. "We had wiffle ball leagues. I remember we all said, 'I'm up first, I'm Rusty Staub. . . . I'm up first, I'm Johnny Bench.' " (The names of the athletes with whom he identified as a boy forever date a man.) Now, of course, the names are different, but the feelings are the same. Sports allow little boys to dream that they are growing closer to being just like their heroes.

More than anything, boys at this age feel that succeeding in sports is central to their identities as future men. Most boys, whether they like it or not, are defined in the peer culture by physical strength and athletics and believe that success in sports will lead to achieving a masculine identity. That fact can lead to feelings of tremendous self-confidence and happiness in a highly coordinated boy athlete, intense frustration in a moderately talented boy filled with ambition, and poor self-esteem in a boy who is just plain lousy at sports or isn't drawn to them at all. Indeed, boys who do not find themselves interested in athletics or who are afraid of public competition may feel ashamed and question their own masculinity unless they have other areas of prowess that are recognized and celebrated by their peers.

According to researchers, children "reap profound benefits" from their participation in sports. They have healthier lifestyles and eat more fruits and vegetables than other children. Adolescents who engage in high levels of exercise are less depressed, have better relationships with their parents, use drugs less frequently, and have higher grade point averages. Girls who play sports in high school are less likely to engage in sexual activity, though that same effect is not seen in boy athletes. Perhaps most important, children who take part in sports are taking a giant step toward fitness and avoiding obesity.

In light of these facts, a parent would understandably wish to keep his or her child playing sports as long as possible, certainly into adolescence. However, this presents parents with a dilemma. If the majority of children playing sports drop out by age thirteen and if the psychological "playing life" of a child is about six years, then if you want him to enjoy those adolescent benefits, perhaps you should wait and enroll your child later, at age ten or eleven. But if you do not sign your son up early, when all of his friends are playing, you may miss the moment of great enthusiasm and he'll become accustomed to sitting on the couch playing video games and will not want to play a team sport later. Perhaps he will be so far behind in his skills that he will not be willing to take the risk to join a team when all the other boys are so far ahead. Better to start him early.

How does a parent decide? On one hand, organized sports appear to offer so many benefits: a boost for a boy's health, an outlet for his high activity level, a place to be with his friends, physically safe surroundings supervised by adults, and a common interest that parents and children can share. On the other hand, there are risks of organized sports: humiliation of boys who are not very coordinated (and it is important to remember that half of boys are below average in athletic ability), a boy coming away from team participation with a sense of inferiority, a boy being burned out prematurely because of excessive emphasis on winning, overspecialization, and overuse injuries, and depression or anxiety as a result of an overambitious coach or an overinvolved parent.

There is no single answer to any of this. The only right answer for your son is the best answer *for your son*. That is, you need to watch your son's reaction to organized sports. You need to decide whether to encourage him or back off, whether to keep him out for a year even though his friends are all playing, whether to allow him to move up to the select team with the hard-driving coach

Q: *I don't understand my nine-year-old son. He's not very communicative with me, but he is with others, such as child care providers. I tell him that I am not only his mom but also his friend. His dad is absent from our lives, and that gets him upset—he doesn't understand why he left. Sometimes the tantrums come out, and he is extremely emotional. He often cries at the silliest things. It's okay to show emotions, but sometimes I can't comprehend my son.*

A: Most nine-year-old boys do not communicate a lot with their moms, especially not in words and long sentences. Here's why: they think you know pretty much everything about them already, and if you don't know it immediately, they imagine you'll figure it out by this evening. You see, your son imagines that you can read his mind, because you nursed him, diapered him, anticipated his moods, knew when he had to go to the bathroom, and figured out when he was about to get frustrated. He thinks you have a sixth sense about him, so he doesn't need to tell you everything.

That's not true of child care providers and teachers. Your son cannot take for granted that they will understand him, and so he fills them in. I understand why you might be a bit jealous of that fact, but it won't do any good to tell him that you are his friend. He won't believe you: friends are friends, and moms are moms. As parents, we can enjoy very friendly moments with our children, but at the end of the day a kid's mom is someone who tells him when to go to bed, who makes him take a bath, who forces him to turn off the TV and do his homework, et cetera, et cetera. She's not his friend, she's his mother, and so he hides some things from her (all children do) so he won't worry her or make her mad.

It is also the case that boys pretend that they don't need their mothers because it makes them feel more grown-up and strong. That doesn't fool anyone, and it shouldn't fool you. He needs you more than he can ever say. He needs you to hold him when he collapses and cries, even if he can't tell you why he is so frustrated and mad. Just sit with him and say, "Honey, I know this hurts you. I don't understand what you are so angry about, but I'll sit here until you feel better." Ask him if he is upset about his dad—just a quick sentence—or if it's because he's not good at something he wants to be able to do. Tell him that if he is upset about his father's absence, well, then he's not wrong to be angry.

Don't indulge a tantrum, but don't punish it, either; try to be calm and relaxed until he recovers his self-control. If you tell anyone that what he is distressed about is no big thing, he will often get madder because he feels misunderstood. It is better to say to your son, "I know you're upset; I know that anger has got a hold on you. I'm sure you'll be able to get free in a couple of minutes."

because you think that he is resilient enough to handle it. And you need to watch your own reaction to organized sports. (See the sidebar "Don't Get Overinvested in Your Son's Sports Career" on page 218.) If you (or your spouse) feel you're getting too intense about it, give yourself a time-out and let your son call the shots.

Or, although sports can be such a positive thing for most boys, you may want to help your son avoid sports altogether if he gives you cues that he's not interested. There are other ways to get physical activity and a feeling of physical competence so important to this age group—for example, he can take up bike riding, hiking, swimming, or other noncompetitive activities.

ADD AND ADHD

We cannot leave the middle elementary years without a discussion of ADD and ADHD. In elementary school, the word most often connected to boys who are having trouble in school is *hyperactivity:* restlessness, fidgeting, recklessness, low frustration tolerance, inability to stay with projects and finish them. These are the years when most boys who are going to be called ADHD get the official diagnosis. The formal term used in diagnosis is now *ADHD* (attention deficit hyperactivity disorder with or without inattention), but many people continue to use the term *ADD* (attention deficit disorder) as shorthand for both. The most extreme cases of hyperactivity—I call them boys who walk across the ceiling—are identified in the early grades, and those boys are often in special education classes by third grade.

However, as academic demands increase, boys who are not so obviously hyperactive but are intensely distractible are going to start to fail classes or their teachers are going to find them hard to handle in the classroom. According to Edward Hallowell and John Ratey, the hallmarks of ADD are distractibility, impulsivity, and restlessness. According to experts, 5 to 8 percent of children suffer from ADHD, but the diagnosis is controversial. In some places it is seriously overdiagnosed and every active boy seems to get the label; in other places, it is underdiagnosed because doctors say they "don't believe in ADHD." Researchers who study the brains of boys who suffer from ADHD have shown that some of them have real and significant brain differences from other boys.

Despite advances in diagnostic technology, history remains the most important "test" in diagnosing ADD. The best diagnostic workup focuses on the history, and then can supplement that with selected neuropsychological tests, according to Hallowell and Ratey. Since at any given time a boy of eight to ten years old may be restless and inattentive at school, whether his high level of activity actually qualifies as hyperactivity is a consensus judgment that his teacher, the school administration, his parents, his pediatrician, and perhaps a psychologist or child psychiatrist must make. The official diagnosis in the *Diagnostical and Statistical Manual* of the American Psychiatric Association requires that there be "clear evidence of clinically significant impairment in social, academic, or occupational functioning." There is still a lot of judgment involved in deciding what is a "significant impairment," so the diagnosis of ADHD depends a great deal on the context.

In my work as a consultant to private schools, I have seen many boys diagnosed with ADHD because they cannot sit still enough of the time to meet the rigorous standards of a highly academic program. Is that really ADHD? I have seen other boys diagnosed because they had a boring or inflexible teacher. I suspect that some of these boys could move to a less demanding or more engaging program and find that their level of attention and activity is perfectly adequate. I suspect that if some of the boys got more sleep and watched less television they would have better attention spans, too!

ADHD is a topic that could fill a hundred books, and has already. I cannot cover it all in this brief summary. The caution I want to issue is this: 80 percent of the stimulant medication prescribed in the world for ADHD is prescribed to American boys. Either we have an excess of wild, restless boys in this country, or we do not know how to raise them, or our schools are driving them crazy, or we have no tolerance for their natural physical restlessness. In my experience, a small percentage of boys, perhaps 3 to 5 percent of a regular class, can benefit from the diagnosis because they will get more understanding from educators and some of them will receive the treatment and medication they need. Some people argue that the ADHD diagnosis is not real or can be used as a psychological crutch to excuse bad behavior, procrastination, and lack of discipline. My answer is that there is a huge range of boys, from the highly focused to those who are out on the tail of the bell-shaped curve in their inability to pay attention. Such boys suffer in school; we need to call them something. As Hallowell points out, we've always diagnosed such boys with labels such as "stupid," "lazy," and "bad." It is kinder to call them "ADHD" and try to understand that there is a range of brain differences in boys that makes it more or less easy for them to sit still.

SPORTS, SCHOOL, SIBLINGS, ADHD, AND TELEVISION: IS THAT ALL?

The externals of a boy's life at this age claim so much of our attention and concern, but isn't there more to a boy of eight, nine, or ten than fighting with his brother or sister, collecting cards, playing on a team, and mastering video games? Yes, of course. Your son is as deep and sensitive as he has ever been. It is just that at this moment he is totally committed to mastering the outside world. He is expansive in spirit and relentless, even obsessive in his approach to the world. Remember Erikson's three P's: purposeful, proud, and persevering. Your son wants to bring it all—whatever it is—under his control, and he wants to look good out there. He wants to have his "game face" on every day. He does not want to feel weak at any time, but when he does feel scared or inadequate he is certainly going to do everything in his power not to cry in public.

Because a boy of eight, nine, or ten is so focused on external mastery and so proud to be a young man, only his teacher, his mother and father, and his babysitter are regularly going to see his private sadness, his fears, and the healthy regressions—those sudden returns to little-boyhood—that are so necessary for human growth. It is important not to be fooled by all his activity and forget his psychology. He still needs his time with you, and it can be incredibly sweet. One mother wrote, echoing the sentiments of many:

> I love cuddling him. For me the satisfaction in being his mother comes in
> being there for him, connecting in a genuine way, being his champion, making him laugh, seeing him grow up even as he lets me know that he is still a
> baby inside in certain ways. I love comforting him and having him as a little
> (and wise) friend.

But what if your son isn't cuddly? As a boy turns his attention to other interests, it may seem that he isn't interested in connecting with you anymore, but that is often just an invitation for you to adapt your communication style to help bridge the gap. Play therapist Lawrence Cohen described a home visit with a mother, Vicky, and her son, Stan. Vicky, a single mother, told him that she was worried because Stan, eight years old and an only child, was "not able to connect" with her. Cohen was surprised to hear

> *I love that my son just keeps going, like the Energizer Bunny. I appreciate and admire his tenacity and ability to continue on in the face of adversity.*
> —Mother of a ten-year-old boy

this, since he had spent some time with Stan, and though he was an anxious boy, he did seem well able to connect.

"I thought maybe that the problem was that Vicky wasn't sure how to connect with Stan his way, on his terms," Cohen says. "So I asked Stan if he and I could make a connection.

"He looked at me, puzzled, so I explained a little about what I meant and suggested that we could shake hands, give each other a high five, talk about something, share a joke. He picked up a Lego guy—he was really into Legos—and handed a Lego guy to me. He made his guy stick one hand out. So I made my Lego guy stick one hand out. He stuck his Lego guy toward me, and I met him halfway and our Lego guys shook hands."

This was fabulous, Cohen thought, because Stan was showing his mom how he liked to connect—with a little bit of distance, not too intensely, and with a bit of uniqueness and creativity. When Cohen looked back at Stan's mom, "she had a look on her face that said, *You see what I mean? He can't connect.*"

Cohen explained to Vicky the meaning behind the Lego handshake, then suggested that the two of them connect. Stan jumped off his bed, stepped toward his mom, then turned his back on her. Could Vicky be right after all?

Then Stan walked backward across the room to where his mom sat, clearly disheartened. As the two adults remained silent, Stan started making beeping noises, like a truck backing up. He backed up slowly until he was in his mother's lap.

Cohen, as a therapist, thought this was absolutely brilliant, creative, and deep. But Stan's mom still looked discouraged, he said, "as if to say, *Please fix my broken child.*"

"At last I understood," Cohen said, "and I said to Mom, 'Your eight-year-old son is *never* going to sit and have a meaningful emotional conversation—with words—with you, like you do with your girlfriends. Give up that dream, because otherwise you'll never appreciate the very real, very powerful connection that you can have with him, and that he clearly wants as much as you do.' "

SIBLING RIVALRY: COMPETITION, AGGRESSION, AND RELATIONSHIP

When parents ask me about younger boys, two topics predominate: boy "aggression" and sibling rivalry. The issue of normal boy activity, aggression, and male violence weaves throughout this book because it arises in different ways at different ages. But for the moment I want to discuss sibling rivalry, which is, in fact, really just another question about aggression. How much conflict between siblings—especially between brothers—is normal and how much is too much?

> I'm delighted but with a bit of trepidation about how to raise a son who stays connected to his heart in a society that encourages males to ignore their heart's leadings.
>
> —Father of a ten-year-old son

I was speaking at a school when a teacher raised her hand and said, "My sons are ten and six and they fight all the time. How can I stop them?"

I immediately asked her, "What do you mean by fighting?"

She responded, "Wrestling and always competing with each other about everything."

"Does their fighting often end in tears?" I asked.

"Well, sometimes."

"How about blood? Have you had to take one or the other of your boys to the emergency room?" I inquired.

"No!" she said, shocked by the idea. Her reaction prompted me to ask another question: "Did you have brothers growing up?" The answer, as I expected, was no.

When I discussed sibling rivalry with Lisa, a mother who had grown up with three brothers, her response was quite different. Asked whether the fighting between her sons had ever resulted in bloodshed, she laughed and said, "Oh, I don't intervene unless there is blood." Short of that, she reported, she stays out of it, unless, of course, she cannot stand listening to the conflict, in which case she separates them and sends them both to their rooms. They cannot wait to get back together, to play and fight again. "Being the mother of boys," she declared, "is not for the faint-hearted."

Why is one mother so distressed by her sons' wrestling and competitiveness while the other waits for bleeding before she gets worried? Two things influence how a mother views the sibling rivalry between her sons: whether she had a brother or brothers growing up, and whether or not those brothers have maintained good relationships with her and with each other as adults. It is always going to be tough for women to appreciate—and I use that word deliberately and provocatively—the intensity of both the love and the fury that brothers can inspire in each other (more about that below) because a rowdy sibling rivalry between two boys breaks most of the rules involving the balance of competitiveness and cooperativeness in girls' relationships. Boys are often unrestrained in, even obsessed by, their competitive feelings toward one another.

I once attended a fiftieth-birthday party for a successful leader of a foundation. He was toasted by his brother, younger by three years, who was a film producer just as successful in his field as was his older brother (and a lot wealthier). What he said went something like this: "I competed with Jerry every day in every possible way. We competed about the most trivial things, like who could take the last bite of breakfast. I was younger and hungrier, but I would strive to save that last bite of my breakfast and wait patiently for Jerry to finish his food, whereupon I would slowly lift up my fork and triumphantly deliver the last bite of my meal to my mouth. For a moment, Jerry would allow me to think I had won, and then he would lift up his plate and remove from underneath it the piece of bacon he had surreptitiously secreted there at the very beginning of the breakfast. He always won in those competitions." Competing about the last bite of breakfast—boy behavior indeed.

Fathers: Fighting as "An Expression of Affection"

Because they have experienced boy and brotherly competition of this kind, men tend to be more relaxed about sibling rivalry. Men often have a feel for the excitement of the competition and see a benefit in it, but ultimately a dad, like a mom, is going to judge his son's competitiveness in light of his memories of his own relationship with his brother and how it worked out later in life. One father said, "We were ultracompetitive until a few years ago, but now we are each other's go-to guy and cheerleader." He was obviously not afraid of the competitive interactions between his sons because he did not see it leading to a bad outcome.

Nor was the father who reported that though he had been "distant" with one of his brothers until his teens and fought verbally with the other when they were younger, he is "best friends with both brothers now and

> *I think every minute with my son is a blessing. He is witty and funny, and he keeps me laughing. I can't wait to see how every year he is going to change, and I love every stage of development.*
> —Mother of a boy, nine years old

very fortunate for their relationships. We have a close family and I wouldn't trade that for the world."

Some men have difficulty recalling sibling competitiveness at all, because it was more than compensated for by the love and closeness they felt, and in any case they *expect* competitiveness between boys. One dad wrote, "I don't think there was ever any significant sibling competition, and we were all very supportive of each other. I am sure there was fighting among us, but nothing out of the ordinary for four boys that stands out in my mind."

A father who is currently alienated from his own siblings or who remembers the conflicts he experienced while growing up as cruel and distressing will naturally try to protect his sons from it. Harris used to fight with his older brother all the time, "probably acting out frustrations from my own dysfunctional youth." As a result, he tried to make sure that his own sons, who were three years apart, did not fight, and he identified with the one who was being "abused." However, he learned something new from the experience of watching his own boys' relationship. "I have come to believe that fighting among boys is, in a way, an expression of—I'm not going to say love, but affection (in some convoluted way)."

Mothers Worry About Adult Relationships

Most mothers actively hope that their children will grow up to be close and loving as adults. They do everything they can to promote that. Therefore, the short-term fear most commonly expressed by mothers is that wrestling and competition will lead to someone getting hurt; much more important, however, moms fear the long-term damage to relationships that could come from sibling conflict.

Traditionally, parents try to protect girls with brothers from the same kind of roughhousing that characterizes brother-brother relationships. Nevertheless, some girls, a minority, are right in the mix. Jan wrote: "My brothers and I fought like dogs—much to the chagrin of my parents. We were very competitive and we truly wrestled! However, my brothers were always punished for fighting with me. They were told no matter what I did, they could never hit me. I, in turn, purposely tried to egg them on. As adults we are very close and laugh about our fighting."

The problem is that no parent can guarantee that kind of happy adult outcome for siblings, and sometimes the stories are sadder. Donna describes a very unhappy relationship with her older brother: "My brother and I had a terrible relationship. He was always mean and tormented me until I 'broke.' I never wanted to be around him and we didn't respect each other. I'm surprised I even wanted a boy!" The relationship she had with her brother improved once they both had families, and they grew much closer when they cared for their dying mother, but it took years for things to get better. It is understandable why she recoils when she sees her son fight with his younger sister; she re-created the same family configuration that she grew up in, and the sibling conflict worries her.

One thing you learn by speaking to many different parents is that there is no one recipe for healthy sibling relationships, whether brother-sister or brother-brother. When parents emotionally deprive their children, when there isn't enough to go around, when they play favorites or for some disturbed reason set children against one another, the outcome is going to be bad. But for the most part it is difficult to predict whether siblings will be close when they are older.

When mothers bring me their anxieties about their son's relationship with their sisters or their brothers, I always ask a number of questions. First, does the same sibling always take the worst of it—for example, does the older one always dominate the younger one? Second, does the younger one have skills that the older one does not? Third, and most important, if you took a stopwatch and clocked the time they spend together, what percentage of their time together would be spent fighting and what percentage would be spent engaged in collaborative activities such as playing outside, doing sports, watching television, or playing with each other's friends?

When parents stop to think about the actual quantity of cooperative time versus fighting time, they often realize that the positive outweighs the negative by a ratio of perhaps ten to one. The problem is that the fighting is unpleasant, or it comes at the time of day when their mother is tired, or the boys are always trying to get their mother to adjudicate a fight whose origins are so obscure—and this can be true of a fight that is only ten minutes old, because it already has so much history, so many chapters—that there is no way to figure out who did what.

I advise parents to try to ignore most of their son's fighting, to avoid being the judge of guilt and innocence, and to simply separate the siblings if they insist on plaguing the household with their conflicts. When I advised one mother to give up her role as judge, she protested, "But what about justice?"

When a mother tries to come to a decision about what is just, she can never collect enough facts and is likely to end up with two dissatisfied plaintiffs, one smug and guilty, and one vengeful. Typically, when boys are separated from the conflict, they quickly recover their individual sense of equilibrium and soon are happy to be with each other. Better than maternal justice is to have two children who have learned, once again, that you have to resolve or modulate your own conflicts or you'll each end up in your own bedroom.

Linda's Boys: Ben and Joel

Linda e-mailed me a picture of herself and her two sons, Ben, age eight, and Joel, age twelve, standing by the ocean in Florida. The boys are in front of her, two handsome, round-faced boys in blue shirts, one blond and the other brown-haired. The older brother, Joel, has his arm around the neck of his younger brother and, as Linda pointed out to me, you cannot really tell whether it is a hug or a choke. There is clearly both love and power contained in the gesture. Linda believes that power rather than competition is at the heart of the psychological dynamic between them. "The rivalry is less a competitive rivalry than it is a power rivalry. Who's in charge is the question." But with a three-and-a-half-year age difference between the boys, "there has never been any question of Ben challenging Joel's position, his wisdom, that he should be in charge."

The boys are close for many reasons. The fact that they have lived through a divorce together and make the transition from their mother's house to their father's house together has bonded them. The fact that their stepbrother, who at age ten falls right between them in age, has wanted Ben to choose him over Joel as a playmate has pushed them together as well. They play different sports and different instruments, so they are not stepping on each other's toes in that regard.

Perhaps more important than anything else is that the brothers have developed a powerful tradition of play. At their mother's home there is no TV and thus no video games, so, as their mother says, "they really *have* to play with each other." She reports that for years, when Ben was younger, he would play whatever Joel wanted to play, but as he has gotten older he realizes that he has power.

If he doesn't want to play what his older brother chooses, he will just disengage. At that point it becomes completely clear how much the company of his younger brother means to Joel.

"If Ben goes away, Joel gets desperate. He knows he has to start his homework in an hour. Sometimes Joel has been sobbing outside Ben's door." Joel and Ben have separate rooms that are next door to each other, and their mother reports that sometimes they love having the power to say to the other, "Get out of my room," but when Ben was younger and he had a bad dream, he would not go to his mother's room; instead he would get into bed with his brother. It reminds me of a younger brother, a ninth grader, whom I once heard give a eulogy for his older brother, age eighteen, who had been killed in a car crash. The younger brother admitted that throughout his childhood and into his adolescence he had moved from his own bed to his brother's for closeness and support, and then he said what we all understood to be the absolute truth: that in losing his brother he had lost his best friend. I have known many boys for whom their best friend was their brother, even though they competed every day over who was disciplined enough to take the last bite of breakfast.

CHAPTER SEVEN

STARTLING CHANGES

A Time of Extraordinary Physical Change:
Ages Eleven to Thirteen

To me, puberty is going through a stage that makes you more mature.
You're not that kid-ish and you take life serious.
—Josh, age twelve

MY FIRST YEAR AFTER COLLEGE, I WORKED AS A SEVENTH-GRADE TEACHER IN a public school in a poor, rural town in New Hampshire. The building had eight classrooms, one each for grades one through eight. The eighth-grade teacher doubled as the principal, and I cannot remember that we ever canceled recess due to cold, even when it was ten below zero. We needed them to go outside! Every morning I faced thirty-five twelve- and thirteen-year-olds in a classroom designed for twenty-five students. My classroom was often chaotic; I was completely overwhelmed. I could not get the girls to stop talking and pay attention, and I had three really big boys—some who had been held back—who could not sit still for a second of the day. They fidgeted and made trouble from 8:30 A.M. to 2:15 P.M., waiting for the blessed hour when they could go home, get their guns, and go out squirrel hunting.

The veteran fifth-grade teacher, whose classroom was right across the hall from mine, required her students to take their shoes off and wear slippers. Her classroom was almost always quiet. She was able to get her children to line up to go out to recess. Her students were unbearably sweet to watch and nothing at all like the barely controlled mob in my class. One day she said to me, "I teach fifth grade because that's the last year they are nice." I did not like her use of the word *nice* because my kids were nice people, too, but I pondered what she had said. Was it really true that my students had changed so much developmentally from her fifth graders, or could I just not maintain control of my class? The answer: both.

For almost forty years I have listened to adults characterize middle-schoolers with shock and awe. They invent names for them, such as *preteens* or *tweens,* in an effort to capture the essence of them. Adults worry endlessly. "My son doesn't like to read." My son is "underachieving" or "disorganized" or "doesn't like school." Recently I was conducting a workshop for middle school administrators and one remarked, "It is around midway through sixth grade that the hormones hit and things start to unravel." Well, yes . . . every year, year after year.

It's impossible to tackle the entire subject of middle schools in these pages. And over the years, a series of Carnegie Foundation reports has done just that, thoroughly and admirably. Let me just say that I think the invention of the junior high was one of the biggest mistakes ever made in American education. The idea of putting hundreds of hormonally supercharged children together in one large building has never seemed wise. I support the return to schools with a K-8 configuration, because it helps middle school students to be able to see where they have come from, developmentally speaking. It is good for them to run into their first- and fourth-grade teachers in the hall and be recognized. In an elementary school they have the opportunity to be the leaders of younger children, which they surely can be, if we give them the chance.

But let's turn to the particular developmental tasks and challenges that boys face in sixth, seventh, and eighth grades. These are the inner drives and circumstances that define their school life and inevitably color their home life in the content of conversations and relationships with parents.

THE FIVE TASKS OF ADOLESCENCE

Let's step back for a moment and consider adolescence as a whole. For a boy in American society the entire span of the major physical, emotional, social, and cultural changes that we call adolescence goes on for many years. The years covered in this chapter—ages eleven, twelve, and thirteen—are just the beginning of a period that lasts for a minimum of seven years—to age eighteen—and may last as long as twelve or fourteen years. Most people in the United States say that they do not feel really "adult" until the age of twenty-five, and students who remain in school into their late twenties may continue to live very much like adolescents for that long.

While biologists tell us there *is* a formal ending to puberty, signaled by a deceleration in growth—usually around the age of fourteen for girls and seventeen for boys—there is no official biological end to adolescence, because it is a social and cultural phenomenon that differs dramatically from culture to culture. In societies where children have to go to work before the age of ten to help support their families or where girls marry at thirteen, there may be no period of adolescence or a very condensed one. In American culture, as in most industrialized countries where young people stay in school all the way through college, the prolonged financial dependence of young adults and their separation from the world of adult work can keep them psychologically adolescent until their mid-twenties. Adolescence is psychologically challenging for every boy, and for a minority of them it can be extremely tough.

Over the course of adolescence, a boy has to complete five psychological tasks. First, he has to adapt to the physical and emotional changes of puberty. Second, he has to transform his relationship with his parents. Third, he has to move out into a wider social world. Fourth, he has to begin to integrate his feelings of lust and his need for relationship and intimacy. And fifth, he has to create a new identity for himself, one that can take him into adulthood. These tasks are exciting and anxiety-producing by turns.

When we talk about developmental tasks, it's important to remember that a boy doesn't experience them as identifiable projects or objectives. From a teenager's point of view, it is just the living of life. We talk about them as tasks as a way to distinguish between the general developmental flow of the age and the especially strenuous and sometimes difficult challenges inherent in particular aspects of that development. Once puberty comes, a boy has to deal with it, even if he didn't ask for it. And there are kids for whom puberty is an unwelcome surprise. The physical changes can be unsettling or even embarrassing for some. It can be painful for a boy to reorganize his identity when it involves questioning his family's values, religion, and way of life. There are painful moments when he is transforming his relationship with his parents and knows he is hurting them and wishes he didn't have to, but he does.

Although the beginning of puberty kicks off all five of these tasks, we'll address the first three in this chapter and the latter two in the chapters ahead. For now, let's consider puberty's role in the full scope of male adolescence by looking at these bodily changes and their impact on a boy's identity in his family, with his friends, and in the wider world.

SEX AND SEXUALITY: GET USED TO IT

The principal of a suburban middle school had a meeting one night for the mothers and fathers of the sixth-, seventh-, and eighth-graders who filled her school every day. Familiar with the academic concerns of affluent suburban parents, and anticipating the usual questions about homework and honors math, she tried to focus the parents on the real drama of middle school: the astonishing physical growth of their children.

"When you send your children to us," she reminded them, "they *are* babies. When they graduate from here three years later, they can *have* babies."

Some parents in the audience gasped a little; even though they had lived through these changes themselves, they were not quite ready to think about their children becoming sexual so quickly.

What the principal was talking about was, of course, the powerful transformations of puberty. Puberty is, after infancy, the period of the most rapid growth in the human life cycle. It begins, at the very earliest, at around age eight for girls and as early as nine in some boys, and it is normally under way in all children by the age of fourteen. Before puberty, differences in the bodies of little boys and little girls are mainly restricted to the genitalia. After puberty, the bodies of girls and boys are different in the size, shape, composition, and function of many body structures and systems.

Puberty is the seminal before-and-after moment in a boy's life, a singular developmental turning point psychologically as well as physically. Understandably, the most profound physical aspects of it unfold largely out of view from parents. Fathers have the gender edge in understanding the experience but typically aren't inclined to speak of it. Mothers, who have been focused on every detail of their son's physical growth for nearly a decade, suddenly find themselves on the other side of a closed door, figuratively and literally. What's going on in there?

What is the physical story for boys? Typically, around eleven and a half a boy's testicles begin to enlarge. Since he has hardly experienced any growth in his penis and testes since the age of four, this represents a real change for him. His scrotum begins to redden and his penis gets longer. One year into the process, though he is not producing adult numbers of sperm, there will be sperm in his urine when he goes to the bathroom in the morning. He almost certainly has had erections as a little boy and may have had what are called dry orgasms as well, but now he is having erections at least once or several times a day. Though some boys experience nocturnal emissions—"wet dreams"—and are startled by them, many other boys have not waited for such a passive experience; they have started to masturbate regularly. Zella Luria, a professor of psychology at Tufts University, used to say that parents choose to talk to their boys about masturbation when their sons are thirteen, which she said is "about two years too late."

From six months to a year after the beginning of puberty, which is signaled by the enlargement of the testicles, a boy will develop a sparse growth of slightly pigmented pubic hair at the base of his penis; this hair will grow thicker and curlier over the next two years. This development is not lost on boys, who are watching and checking on themselves constantly. The first outward signs of their focus on their own bodies may not appear to be related to their secondary sexual characteristics. Instead, what parents may see is that their sons take to combing their hair for long periods of time, showering constantly, putting gel in their hair, or spending more time with their clothes, all of which mothers see as the sweet beginnings of adult self-care. But the underlying drama is sexual.

One mother shared this story about her son, who was a month short of his twelfth birthday. He had been an uninhibited little nudist before the age of five or six, but like many boys he had become quite modest during his elementary school years. (Elementary-school-age boys will often wear their underwear beneath their swimsuits, and many will not change in front of other boys in a day camp situation.) She had heard from his older brother that her eleven-year-old was starting to grow pubic hair, but he had not allowed her to see him naked in a couple of years. One day when he was taking a bath she had to get something out of the bathroom, so she tapped on the bathroom door, explained her dilemma, opened the door, threw him a washcloth, and said, "Cover your manhood," which he did as she walked in.

While she was going through the medicine cabinet with her back turned to him, he startled her by announcing, "I've got pubic hair now." "Oh," she replied, not sure what else to say. When, however, she turned around, he was standing up in the bathtub and pointing to his new growth of hair, barely more than shadow. More startling, he began dancing, literally shaking his booty in an MTV sort of way and waggling his now-longer penis very proudly. She laughed happily at his exhibitionistic display. "I had two brothers," she told me. "Sometimes you just have to laugh."

When a boy's body is changing, he is acutely self-conscious: totally focused on the new sensations of sexuality that affect him daily, embarrassed by his unpredictable and uncontrollable erections and his increasingly powerful urge to masturbate. At the same time, he is excited to be getting the beginning of a man's body, and he'd like to show it to someone or talk to someone about it, which is why the eleven-year-old impulsively took the opportunity to dance for his mother and show her his new equipment. The two nonverbal questions he was asking were *Aren't I fabulous and sexy now?* and *Can you accept and still love the new me?* He was also implicitly asking her whether he was normal. A boy unconsciously—or sometimes openly—looks to his mother for that affirmation.

One twelve-year-old boy became really anxious after reading a book on the bodily changes of puberty that his mother had purchased to educate and reassure him. He had read about ejaculating and became seriously worried that he might unexpectedly ejaculate in his pants at school, without any provocation or warning. She reassured him that that could not happen.

By the end of his thirteenth year, the average eighth-grade boy has experienced a significant growth in the length of his penis, he has thicker and curlier pubic hair, and his vocal cords have begun to thicken, so his voice has started to change. He is only a year away from having fully adult male genitalia. His major growth spurt is beginning or already well under way, and because his rising level of androgens has begun to change the composition of his perspiration, he smells more like an adult. As one teacher said to me, "Middle school boys smell funky!"

I have described the growth of the average boy; some are ahead of the curve and others are well behind it. There are always boys in an eighth-grade class who have not yet begun puberty, who still look eleven years old. As the psychologist at an all-boys school that begins in seventh grade, I am accustomed to looking down at thirteen-year-olds who are not yet even five feet tall and looking up at thirteen-year-olds who have passed my six-foot height. The variation is enormous, and it has emotional and social consequences. I remember that when I was in middle school I was acutely aware of the boys who had started to grow first and that those boys talked cruelly about the ones who had not developed by the first year of high school. Growth matters to boys.

It also matters to their parents, because the physical changes kick off a series of psychological changes that are unstoppable. Everyone in a boy's life knows that something is coming, but they're not sure exactly what. Neither is the boy.

A BOY ADAPTS TO THE PHYSICAL AND EMOTIONAL CHANGES OF PUBERTY

A mother once told me that she, her husband, and her twelve-year-old son had gone on a beach vacation and were staying in a motel and sharing a room. Her husband and son were sitting in boxer shorts playing chess. While his father was taking a long time to decide where to move his chess pieces, her son pulled the elastic of his boxers out and was staring down at his crotch. Suddenly he announced, "I have fifteen pubic hairs." Unlike the calmly bemused mother of the eleven-year-old boy in the shower, this mother told me that upon hearing her son's announcement, she felt dizzy. She instantly felt disoriented and at a loss to respond to her son, and she hoped her husband knew what to say. He did. He looked up from the chess board and casually remarked, "So, you're getting some action in your pants." The boy laughed, the father laughed, and the mother, though she felt relieved, experienced a profound gulf between herself and these two men.

The first sign that a boy is becoming a person with sexual interests may be his insistence on privacy. I remember that when I was around ten or eleven my older brother took the trouble to mount a lock on his door, which previously had had none. Parents may often feel literally closed out of a boy's life at this point. One mother complained to me about her son's retreat into his room at age twelve, and when I suggested that he might have a masturbatory life, she appeared shocked and said, "Isn't he a bit young for masturbation?" I turned to her husband for confirmation, and he shrugged, saying, "That's about right."

EVERY BOY STRIVES TO GROW UP

I have been speaking throughout this book of parents' need to trust in their son's development. Overwhelmingly that is the case, but there will be boys for whom trauma, mental illness, academic failure, or a terrible divorce interrupts or arrests their development. When that happens you will need to focus intensely on your son and get the help of school professionals or mental health professionals to help you puzzle through why his development has stalled. But the point of bringing professionals into your son's life is to get his development restarted. Just because your son has a bad learning disability or severe depression doesn't mean there isn't a healthy boy inside trying to develop normally. There is. It's a mistake in the long run to allow your son to be defined by a diagnosis or an academic problem.

A great South African AIDS activist who has spoken to more than a million South African children about HIV told me the story of a day he spoke to a school group in the front row of which were children in wheelchairs. When he was finished, someone told him a boy wanted to speak to him, and he went over to the chair of a fifteen-year-old boy suffering from cerebral palsy. The boy was sitting in a complicated wheelchair but spoke quite clearly to the activist. "Thank you," he said, "you're the first person to ever talk to me about the possibility of a sex life."

This is an extreme example, but it makes the point that it is essential for parents—and everyone—to think of the developmental imperatives, the sequence of normal development, because that's what's in the mind of every boy.

A boy's emerging sexuality does separate him from his parents, not only because he is developing a masturbatory life, which he wants to keep private, but also because his identity is changing. He no longer sees himself as little. He may soon be looking down into his mother's eyes. That's not likely to happen at eleven or twelve, unless his mother is very petite, but it may well occur at thirteen or fourteen. It shifts the relationships because there is a moment when she will be scolding him or instructing him and he'll suddenly think, *Why is this person giving me instructions? She's shorter than me!* In a boy's mind, power and authority have been connected with size, so his new height has changed the balance of power and may result in challenges to his mother's or teacher's authority. For some mothers, especially single mothers who do not have a man at home to back them up, it may mean that they cannot physically stop a boy from doing what he wants to do. That can lead to confrontations between mothers and sons. But this is not always the case.

A BOY TRANSFORMS HIS RELATIONSHIP WITH HIS PARENTS

I received a Christmas letter from an American mother who is married to a German man and is raising her son in Germany. The card read:

> Terry is in eighth grade and turns fourteen in February. He is taller than I am and has developed a deep voice that only occasionally squeaks. Next year he'll start gymnasium—the academic high school—in our neighborhood, majoring in math and physics. Most of his free time is divided between skateboarding, hanging out with his friend Luke, playing *World of Warcraft* on the computer, and downloading songs onto his iPod by bands with names like Disturbed and Mayhem. As ominous as that sounds, he remains his generally sweet self and manages to do his homework and practice saxophone without my having to nag too much. My husband and I enjoy his company as much as ever.

When she uses the word *ominous,* you can hear her bracing herself for the changes of adolescence, as if tumultuous behavior will follow inevitably as a boy becomes older. Because of what they see in movies and the media and overhear in the language of angry, alienated rock and rap music, parents often worry that their sons may turn rebellious and hard to manage. Boys, too, assume that their teen years are going to be wild, or at least challenging. That is not necessarily the case. At the end of the sixties, when popular culture indeed saw adolescence as rebellious, Daniel Offer, a psychiatrist, published a longitudinal study of adolescent boys that rebutted those cultural assumptions. He found that the vast majority of normal—that is, not clinically mentally ill—teenage boys are not, in fact, rebellious. One-third experience "continuous" growth, which is characterized by a boy gracefully assuming greater rights and responsibilities. One-third of teenage boys follow a pattern of "surgent" growth, characterized by long plateaus and sudden spikes of growth. Only one-third experience "tumultuous" growth. In fact, he found that social radicalism among teenagers was almost nonexistent and that self-satisfaction and parental satisfaction were the norm for the majority.

Your son may not be entering a tumultuous phase, but nevertheless, he must transform his relationship with you in order to accommodate his new body and his emerging adolescent identity. According to Terry's mother, for many years he and she had a daily, just-before-school routine. About ten minutes before he would leave for school, he would ask for "lap time." To her astonishment, he did not give it up as he became ten and eleven and twelve; however, as he began to grow, the only way she could hold him in her lap was to sit in a straight-backed chair. He would sit on her lap, facing her in a hugging position, with his feet almost touching the floor, his head on her shoulder, his arms around the top of her shoulders and her arms around him. This private, ten-minute ritual was conducted in complete silence. Though she cherished this time more than she could say, she would always allow him to initiate it by saying, "lap." Then one day, when he was close to thirteen, it disappeared, and he never asked for "lap" again. Nor did he explain his reasons. Did it just not fit with his self-image anymore? Was he self-conscious about his sexuality and the prolonged frontal physical contact with his mother? Was he uncomfortable having his father know that he still needed this little-boy time? All of the above? He did not say.

Many mothers, and some fathers, experience their sons of eleven or twelve beginning to talk less and less than they used to do. "I find it annoying when I ask him what he said, because I didn't hear him, and he says, 'Nothing,' " one mother told me. "I find it rude and have shared that with him, but he still does it often." Why do early-adolescent boys seemingly stop talking to their parents? Why do they respond to questions with the one-word answers and grunts about which so many parents complain? Girls, after all, tend to change their conversational style with parents somewhat at this age, too, but typically they become more verbally assertive or aggressive—not taciturn.

One veteran administrator at a boys' school told me that he thought boys fell so silent around this age because so much of their psychological energy was going into their masturbatory lives, and they were not going to talk to anyone about this, so they do not have much to say! Psychologist Ron Taffel would disagree that boys are verbally unreachable. He argues that they do not stop talking to their parents, that they are not just " 'junior' versions of 'withholding men.' " Boys continue to talk, Taffel says, but "at all the 'wrong' times—when they want something, when they're scared, when they're negotiating, and when parents are distracted."

A boy's failure to talk as much as his mother wants, or in the way that his mother remembers he did when he was younger, is the result of four related phenomena. First, a boy is declaring that he is developing a new identity: different body, gel in his hair, and new patterns of speech. *I'm different. Get used to it,* he is

The Eight Lines of Development

The Developmental Story Advances

Many mothers tell me they have felt that bittersweet shift, appreciating the older boy in front of them, while feeling acutely the little boy unceremoniously—and how eagerly!—taking his leave. One of the things you must do now is embrace the rate of change in your son's life and remember that he will be eleven one moment, thirteen the next moment, and a fifteen-year-old-wannabe the following moment: the hallmark of the age is the rapid fluctuations.

Physical Development

The early changes of puberty are the central story of boys ages eleven to thirteen, as discussed at the opening of this chapter. The rapid increase in a boy's height and weight, the increase in musculature, and the development of secondary sexual characteristics are the paramount physical and psychological aspects of a boy's life at this age. These changes are initiated by a signal from the hypothalamus to the pituitary gland to increase the production of various hormones. In boys, the testes are stimulated to produce testosterone, which results in the production of sperm. Boys in adolescence have more than ten times as much testosterone in their blood as they did when they were in elementary school.

Some parts of a boy's body begin to grow more rapidly than others. A boy's feet, hands, penis, nose, chin, and legs may start to grow before the rest of his body catches up and fills out. This can result in an awkward, gangly-looking boy—especially since boys also lose fat during adolescence. The increase in testosterone results in more defined muscles. Boys are intensely interested in these changes and track them closely, hoping to be "buff." Twenty years ago, only older boys playing on varsity teams lifted weights; now, many boys in early high school and even middle school are interested in developing a chiseled physique. Psychiatrists today are seeing more boys who have body obsessions that mirror those of anorexic girls.

Puberty hits talented young athletes in different ways. Some boys remain much the same as they had been in balance and coordination, even as they become larger. A few may become strikingly more coordinated and have significant muscle development as a result of puberty; others become somewhat less coordinated than they were as younger boys. This is not fair and it is not predictable. It can be a shock to the talented young athlete who expected to always be one of the best on the team but was left in the dust as other boys got bigger and developed more strength, but even if he grows, he may be left behind because his body is not as coordinated as it used to be. In my clinical experience, boys and their parents, particularly their fathers, never anticipate a decline in athletic ability and the understandable decline in motivation that accompanies it. Puberty is a genetic crap shoot.

Research suggests that early-developing boys enjoy some advantage in confidence and late-developing boys may suffer problems with self-esteem. It helps if a father who had the same genetics, or mother whose brother had a late puberty, can reassure a boy he will get his growth in time and he will be a man, just like his dad and his uncle. It is just the fear that you're never going to get there that consumes a late-developing boy. A boy like that may think about it ten, fifteen, twenty times a day, the fear that it will never happen for him.

Attachment

One of the most confusing, funny, and hurtful things about parents and their adolescent children is how embarrassed many kids so abruptly become about their parents. Young adolescents look up one day and suddenly the parents that they have loved are painfully uncool, clumsy, and sometimes so dense that the young teen can hardly bear it. This embarrassment does not usually happen immediately when the child turns eleven; however, it is there in moments and it gradually develops strength until, in some adolescents, the reaction is extreme: "I cannot stand being with my parents," one boy said. "I can't stand the way they talk, or stand, or think, or joke, or chew."

From the very beginning of boyhood, the tension between a boy's striving for autonomy and his dependence on his mother and father have affected the attachment relationship. That was the nature of the attachment drama at eighteen months and at three years, and so it is at twelve and thirteen. Girls may be more obvious in their wild fluctuations, but boys often feel the same thing and express it via a repressed or sullen manner.

Author Willa Cather perfectly described this fundamental ambivalence and the tensions in every family's life when she wrote:

> [E]very individual in that household (even the children) is clinging passionately to his individual soul, in terror of losing it in the general family flavor . . . the mere struggle to have anything of one's own, to be oneself at all, creates an element of strain which keeps everybody almost at a breaking point. . . . One realizes that human relationships are the tragic necessity of human life . . . that every ego is half the time greedily seeking them, and half the time pulling away from them.

I needed to quote a writer here, because psychologists don't usually use the words *terror* and *strain* and *breaking point* unless they are discussing mental illness. Willa Cather understood very well that these tensions are part of the everyday life of everyone in every family. They certainly are for some adolescent boys, who occasionally react with terror because they are afraid that they cannot hold on to their own souls when their parents are around. Some boys are so insecure in their identities that they keep the family at a breaking point by their need to pull away.

Your son may need you terribly one moment, be hurtful the next moment, and reject you the next. This rapid fluctuation between dependence and independence and between love and hate, and most especially the confusing experience of having a boy express his need for you in counterdependent ways, saying "I don't need you!" when he obviously does need you, is the single hardest thing about adolescent behavior for adults to handle. It is why so many parents lose their tempers with young adolescents. They are saying, "Make up your mind. Are you a kid or an adult? Do you need me or not?" Of course, your son cannot answer the question, because he is both a child and an adult, and he will be caught in that in-between state for five or six more years.

Social Development

Boys can be hard on each other at all ages, but they are most cruel to one another during the years from eleven to fifteen. In *Raising Cain* we referred to this as "the culture of cruelty" and outlined the ways in which boys attack one another's masculinity, usually through teasing, irony, sarcasm, and sometimes outright bullying. (See "The Culture of Cruelty" on pages 261–63.) Though there has always been competition and status seeking among boys, from the age of two up, it gets particularly intense as boys enter puberty and remains that way until midway through tenth grade, by which time the issues of size and dominance have been largely resolved. Every boy in this age group becomes accustomed to hearing the labels "gay," "fag," "wuss," and "wimp" thrown around and just hopes that he is not the target too often or that his tormentors are his friends "and don't really mean it."

If hanging out with a crowd of boys can be difficult for the individual, large groups of boys are also tricky for society, because they tend to engage in antisocial behaviors such as vandalism, drinking, smoking, and sexual behavior. Parents fear the effect of peer pressure on their sons, and they are right to do so. The level of conformity among kids increases from third grade to ninth grade, and adolescents have a higher tolerance of antisocial behaviors such as stealing from a store than third-graders do. It would be naive to expect your son, no matter how good a kid he is, to always stand up to or turn away from the behavior of a crowd.

Boys are more likely to act responsibly when they are in the company of one friend or with a close group of friends who share values and know each other's families. It is, however, always the case that as adolescent boys transform their relationships, questioning their family's values and spending less time with them, they use their friends as a "second family" to which they turn for support, affirmation, and (not always good) advice.

Cognitive Development

As your son grows into adolescence, he is going to begin challenging the conventional limits of society, because he is beginning to develop a keen interest in abstract ideas. This step, described by Piaget as the transition from concrete operational thinking to formal operational thought, is a huge one in the life of a boy. Over the next few years he is going to think more logically and systematically, and finally he is going to take a huge step by being able to think about thinking, his own and others'. Suddenly, he is going to think outside the box of family rules. Sometimes a boy discovers that he thinks more logically than one of his teachers does, and he questions the teacher in front of the class.

Many parents, and some teachers, experience this change in a boy's thinking as disrespectful or rude, and sometimes your son can express himself in blunt ways with a lot of attitude. However, you should know that the underlying energy comes from cognitive development. Your son's brain is changing and his capacity to think is expanding enormously. Class discussions in middle school and early high school change dramatically as early adolescents are able to think hypothetically and can take the point of view of others. For bright boys who have been finding the rote learning and elementary nature of class discussions boring, moving into abstract conversation is exciting.

Even though adolescent boys are more capable of logical thinking, future planning, and organization, they do not show those abilities all the time, especially in areas where they are not motivated. Perhaps the number one complaint that I hear from parents of seventh-grade boys is that they are still "so disorganized." Schools can help by emphasizing organizational skills and planning. That is one reason why I proposed that even eighth-graders start and end the school day in a homeroom with a teacher who knows the organizational weaknesses and strengths of his or her students.

Academic Development

The major shift in middle school is that the courses are now conceptually so sophisticated that all content areas are taught by specialists. The homeroom teacher is no longer able to teach multiple subjects because she cannot master and make interesting all that the children need to know. For that reason, middle school students move from class to class, a change that gives students more independence and requires more autonomy of them but which can be disorienting for some boys.

A second major shift is that homework demands increase in most middle schools. This is a shock to boys who have been coasting on their native intelligence for years. As in the athletic realm, where practice and effort may now be as important as native ability, in academics harder-working boys may now be overtaking boys who have been relying on their verbal ability and quickness but do not know how to study. Handling the increased demands for organization and quantity of production can be a shock. Some boys dig in against the increased demands of school, becoming resentful and even oppositional. Some boys who are part of deviant groups may begin to skip school and are starting to make plans to drop out as soon as they can. What makes a difference for boys (and girls as well) is having inspiring teachers who like middle-schoolers, understand their development, do not get into too many power struggles with them (though some are inevitable), and—most important from a boy's point of view—have a sense of humor.

Although researchers have not found any significant differences in the fundamental cognitive ability of boys and girls, the gap between boys and girls, who outperform them in reading and writing, is an academic fact in middle schools. Girls and boys also begin to favor courses on a sex-stereotyped basis, with girls saying that they prefer English and social studies and boys saying they prefer math and scientific subjects. When you combine these sex-stereotyped academic preferences with the physical and emotional immaturity of boys in comparison to girls, it can sometimes seem as if there are two different populations in middle school, defined by gender. That will not be the case in high school, where social class, interests, and intelligence will define the groups as much as gender will.

Emotional Self-Regulation

You may notice that around age eleven, twelve, or thirteen your son is more touchy than he used to be; perhaps he is occasionally explosive in his relationship with you. His mood may change more quickly than you remember; his sense of proportion may bewilder you. Events that do not seem so important to you may seem huge to him. The standard parental explanation for all of this is that your son is under the influence of hormones. How closely are adolescent moods and hormones connected? And if hormones are not responsible for adolescent mood shifts, what is?

Research has shown that there are some connections between mood lability, mood intensity, irritability, and conflict with parents and the primary hormones of puberty such as adrenal androgens, gonadotropins, and sex steroids. David Walsh argues that because the amygdala, the region of the brain that is the seat of fear and anger, has so many receptors for testosterone, it is stimulated by that hormone to produce an aggressive response in boys. There may be times when your son is going to have difficulty controlling his emotions because of internal pressure from hormones.

However, the scientific problem is this: while all boys have testosterone, not all boys fight or punch a wall in anger when they are teenagers. It is clear that personality variables matter a great deal. Some boys have been explosive since early childhood. Others have been even-tempered pacifists since boyhood and still are. But the most important variable affecting a boy's mood is probably context. Adolescent researcher Anne Petersen writes: "Research is now creating a more realistic view of adolescence . . . there is wider recognition that biology is only one factor that affects young people's development, adjustment, and behavior." She goes on to say that there is a "mountain" of evidence that what is important in the lives of teenagers is the context in which they are functioning. Context, of course, means the family, but it also means their school, neighborhood, community, and service providers.

We must not accept teenage boys' mood swings as the inevitable product of hormones. We have to look at the context. Do they feel respected? Do they feel useful and listened to? Research has shown the happiest moments for teens are when they feel in control of their situation, and the unhappiest moments are when they experience themselves as having the least control. That's why they can be so explosive with their parents, whom they view as having too much power over them, and so happy with their friends, in whose presence they feel equal and respected.

Moral and Spiritual Development

The change in cognitive ability with its development of the capacity for abstract thought, has a profound effect on a boy's moral thinking and may affect his spiritual understanding as well.

When he is in elementary school, a boy makes moral decisions based either on what we call "pre-conventional moral thinking" regarding the likelihood that he's going to get into trouble ("The teacher won't like that!") or on the basis of pure self-interest ("I'll borrow his glove"), but he does not mentally consult any higher principle involving rules, laws, and the rights of others in the community. Little boys may know about God and certainly know about rules (they have heard the teacher talk about them endlessly), but they do not have the cognitive ability to take the point of view of other people or understand the social contract that underlies those rules. All of that changes in adolescence. As boys grow, their egocentric approach to rules ("Can I get away with it?") changes into a "good child" morality in which a boy chooses voluntarily to live up to the expectations of others.

When a father yells, "Do it because I say so," imagining that he still has the power over his son that he did when the boy was littler, his son is thinking, *No, I do this because I choose to do it in order to maintain harmony in this family.* That represents a profound shift in his moral thinking, and it enables him to operate in a moral way when he is away from adults. But I have already said that boys are influenced by peer pressure and that other boys can influence them to do antisocial things. Of course, but they do not do them all the time; most normal boys are moral and prosocial in their behavior most of the time, unless they are part of a criminal gang. But none of us operates at our highest moral level at every moment (I have been known to exceed the speed limit on the Massachusetts Turnpike), and that is the case with boys, too.

By eighth grade, fully 50 percent of boys have internalized Kohlberg's "good child" morality and will act in accordance with those moral principles most of the time. When they have achieved the stage of "good boy" orientation, it means they have an internalized image of what a good friend, a good member of the community, should do when faced with a moral dilemma. It is not, however, a fully developed form of moral thinking, because they might protect a friend who is shoplifting ("He's my friend, and besides, the store has tons of money.") and believe that they have made a moral choice. They do not yet fully understand the necessity for laws, nor do they understand the social contract that underpins them. Those nuances in understanding emerge in Stages 4 and 5.

As for the 50 percent of boys who have not yet achieved Stage 3 moral thinking: most of them will in time. They haven't signed on to be "bad boys"; they just don't think about their behavior in terms of being a good citizen; they are still thinking about avoiding punishment. Boys may come to a fuller moral understanding by sixteen or eighteen, but not at thirteen. Most parents think that thirteen-year-olds have the capacity to understand adult rules in an adult way but choose not to do so. That is incorrect; they do not yet have the ability.

Identity

Every boy is the product of his temperament, his family, his education, his community, the influence of his brothers and sisters, his likes and dislikes, and his friends. It seems obvious that we are all the sum of our accumulated biological and social parts, but it also seems clear that human beings are much more than that, too. At some point a boy is going to have to take control of himself and formulate an answer to the question "Who am I?" Erik Erikson believed that the fundamental task of adolescence was to find an answer to the identity question, that is, to create a sense of identity.

He believed that every conversation, every conflict, every experience in adolescence contributes to an idea of oneself—an identity—that will eventually be coherent, continuous, and reliable. At thirty you can wake up in the morning and pretty much know who you are. That's not the case at twelve, because you don't yet know what you are going to look like, how tall you'll be, and where or whether you'll go to college, much less what kind of work you'll do as an adult and whether you'll be a good lover (whatever your sexual orientation) or a good husband and father. There is so much identity formation that a boy of eleven or twelve has to do before he finally feels adult and has a strong sense of identity.

Some boys, like Andy, the tennis player in this chapter, are trying to nail down an identity through the development of skills, and they become angry if anyone says it might turn out differently. As a parent, you worry when your son puts all his eggs in one basket like that. Other boys seem to drift and not define themselves by anything other than the whims of their friends. As a parent, you may worry about that because your son appears to be a conventional thinker, a follower, and does not seem to stand up for himself. The problem is that at eleven, twelve, and thirteen, most boys do not really know themselves well because their identity, their self, is as yet largely undefined and unarticulated. The task of boys between thirteen and eighteen is to try to define and refine their identities. Some are taking their time, while others are in a rush to claim identities, as we will see in the next chapter.

saying, and so he opens up on *his* schedule, not in response to his mother's queries.

Second, emotionally speaking, most parents do lag behind their son's growth. They often still speak to him the same way they did when he was ten years old, and he can hear that in their voices. Parents do not yet recognize how grown-up he is becoming, and he does not feel that they are acknowledging his new stature. This is one of the prime complaints of all young adolescents, girls and boys: "You treat me like a baby!"

Third, he is afraid that if he tells his parents too much, they will interfere with his autonomy. I have spoken to middle school children about their social lives for more than a decade, in individual sessions and as a speaker at assemblies. I take a microphone and wade into the crowd of students, asking them why they do not talk more to their parents about their social lives. This is what girls and boys say: "It's private." "It's embarrassing." "If I tell my mom too much, she'll try to do something." There is also this classic boy answer: "If I answer one of her questions, she'll, like, interrogate me for two hours!"

Finally, the society of boys requires that he swear silent allegiance to the group by putting some distance between himself and his mother. How does he accomplish this? By retreating from conversation and disclosure with her, certainly. And by openly declaring his independence from her to the group. That is accomplished in the insults that they hurl at each other about their mothers: "Your mother wears combat boots." "Your mother has a mustache." "Your mother's so fat she has to iron her pants in the driveway." These date back to World War I and yet are as current as MTV's *Yo Momma,* a show so popular and offensive that it has given "yo mama" jokes new life on Web sites and sparked at least one Internet petition to have the show yanked off the air.

When I was an undergraduate in college I worked briefly for a professor who was collecting these insults—called "toasts"—from inner cities all over America. They were memorably obscene and graphic. But is this game of competitive insults targeting mothers just an inner-city game? Not at all. I once asked a middle school assembly of almost exclusively white, wealthy private school students what insult was the one most commonly used, expecting to hear "gay," because that's the typical answer. Instead, a boy shouted out, "Your mother!" and the assembly hall exploded in laughter, mostly from boys.

VERBAL AND OTHER POSTURING: THE AUDIENCE IS OTHER BOYS

Why do boys of this age feel compelled to make such a sharp break with their mothers and all that mothers stand for? While the breakaway and insulting banter continues into later adolescence and adulthood, the phenomenon begins in earnest when boys are eleven, twelve, and thirteen. There are two theories that offer an explanation. First, boys who are beginning to amass their own psychological power suddenly see how powerful their mothers are, and they are afraid of them. Freud called this the fear of the "phallic mother." Instead of seeing their mother's power used in a loving way on their behalf, boys see it as obstructing their own march to manhood.

More compelling to me is the notion that boys are resisting their mothers because of how attached they are to them. Boys are embarrassed by their dependence on their mother, and they attack that bond in one another. The message to boys from the other boys is this: *You cannot be as dependent on your family, and as loving and loyal to your mother, as you used to be. You have to give up your babyish love for her. Oh, you can get angry and defend her when we insult her, but in the end you have to laugh with us.* As a result, mothers are sacrificed to boy society, and an individual boy has to learn to laugh about—and at—his most profound emotional attachment in the world. That's a price he has to pay in order to command the respect of other adolescent boys.

Why does a boy of twelve not want to be hugged in public by his mother? Why does a boy sometimes act as if his family and relationships with his parents are not as important as they used to be? One mother reported to me that as she was talking to her thirteen-year-old he was being dismissive and contemptuous of her. She upbraided him, saying, "If you treat me that way, you'll hurt our relationship." His reply was, "What relationship?" and she was devastated. How could he deny the depth of his relationship to her? The answer is that he disavows this most powerful relationship in his life to cultivate an image of independence that he can then take out in the world and display in front of other boys. The audience for his emerging sense of manhood is other boys.

He is rightly concerned that they are going to judge him by a new, adolescent peer standard, one that would disapprove of a too-close relationship with his mother. No boy of this age wants to be labeled a "baby," "wimp," or "wuss," and he will conform to whatever expectations the group sets for him in order to avoid the label, even though it requires him to hide his love for his mother. Not all cultures require this kind of disavowal of the family. In Latin America, boys of this age boast about their great love for and devotion to their mothers. In India, a boy is thinking about how his academic performance will allow him to support his parents in their old age. In these cultures, such declarations enhance a boy's standing with his peers as someone masculine and strong. Not in America, the most individualistic of societies. The psychological lesson from the public roasting of mothers is that boys will do—or appear to do—whatever is required in order to cultivate the respect of the peer group.

While all boys want to appear "independent" and "separate" during these years, only a few boys actually do cut themselves off emotionally from their mothers in these years. *The vast majority do not cut themselves off from their families.* They remain closely connected to their mothers even though, as a psychological matter, they fight their dependency feelings by being sulky, acting exasperated, or putting their iPod earphones in their ears when they get into the car with you so that conversation is impossible. Even as they proclaim their independence,

THE CULTURE OF CRUELTY

The "culture of cruelty" that engulfs boys in their middle school years is generally viewed as the invention of boys. It is boys, after all, who show up as the perpetrators, victims, and witnesses of the teasing, sarcasm, bullying, and cruel jokes at the expense of other boys' sense of masculinity that characterize this painful passage. But in truth, it is disingenuous to imagine that adults have no role in it, no influence over a culture of children and a ritual of cruelty that emerges as predictably as it does and as boldly as it does, often right before our eyes.

In the stories that men and boys tell me about their experiences of this particular period in their lives, adults play a significant role in three ways: by their absence or ignorance of the situation, by their subtle participation or complicity in the cruelty, or by their presence in ways that made a positive, even life-changing difference.

Indeed, parents and teachers often are unaware of the incidents of cruelty, or the pattern of such, that their sons are enduring—or imposing on others. A few boys will tell adults that they have been called "gay" or "fag" at school, or teased about their size or looks; most will not, because to do so would brand them as "wimps" or worse, prove their tormenters right. Some adults who know or suspect their son is struggling this way assume there is nothing they can say or do that can help; they keep their silence and their distance, "respecting" his need to work things out on his own and hoping for the best. The message to boys, however, is that the culture of cruelty rules supreme; it is clever and more powerful than adult society, and operates beyond the reach of those social rules of conduct. Its standards for masculinity—physical dominance, emotional suppression, and social aggression and cruelty—remain unchallenged. Its rules are the only rules: a boy must be cruel to be cool, or accept his lot if he is not. Adults who remain ignorant or absent fail boys and strengthen the culture of cruelty.

Adults also fail boys and actively expand and perpetuate the culture of cruelty when they ignore wrongdoing by boys against boys, or when they themselves use physical force or are hostile, shaming, or abusive toward boys. Sadly, this is the experience of many boys. One father shared his own memories of those years:

> It was a harrowing time. However, most of my problems came from cruelty at the hands of adults. Being an intelligent person, I learned quickly to avoid the aggressive boys during this period. But I couldn't avoid the teachers' and my parents' coercive and violent punishments. I lost all self-confidence during these years. The most chilling thing about what I went through in those years is that I accepted my role and internalized it so easily. Being a child, I just assumed something was wrong with me and that this was just the way the world worked. My self-confidence never returned.

Instead, I learned to substitute courage and persistence for self-confidence. But boys who go through what I went through carry a weight with them for the rest of their lives.

Often in these instances, a boy is singled out for "toughening up" or harsh judgment by parents or teachers who believe it is in his best interest if he is to grow up to be a self-respecting man—or stereotype of a man. But every boy wants to be a self-respecting man; social isolation, shaming, betrayal, and emotional silence work against that.

A boy's desire to "be a man" at all costs heightens his vulnerability around that point through puberty, but it also offers an opportunity for caring adults to have a dramatic impact. Parents, teachers, coaches, and other adults—especially men—who live or work with boys can make a critical difference in the life of a boy and within the boy culture. Their active engagement with boys this age in ways that appeal to boys' natural strengths can provide respect, empathy, encouragement, and a model of masculinity that includes a full range of healthy emotional expression. A boy who feels comfortable in his own emotional skin is less likely to inflict hurt on others and more resilient under the pressures of this age and all ages. This is the psychological foundation of a healthy masculine identity. This is what boys need. And this is the role open to the adults in a boy's life.

An innovative curriculum called BAM! (Boys Advocacy and Mentoring), created by Peter Mortola, Ph.D., and his colleagues, all counseling professionals in Oregon, uses physical challenge and strategic storytelling (but no lecturing by adults) in small-group settings to draw boys into activities that blend action, reflection, and emotional expression. These group experiences help boys cultivate a sense of connection, trust, empathy, and openness, enabling them to drop their defenses and engage with one another without the threat of humiliation. The curriculum is carefully designed to put adults in a mentoring role, lightly guiding but not directing boys as they work together to solve the challenge du jour. In this culture of camaraderie the rules are: no put-downs, no interrupting a boy when he's speaking in discussion time, the right to pass on a turn to speak, confidentiality, honesty, and openness to learning. BAM!'s goal is to help boys become more emotionally literate and relationally competent, and it works because it starts out by making them feel safe. When adults complain that boys do not "talk enough," they fail to understand that boys do want to speak about their inner lives but will do so only when it is safe. Mortola and others say that in group activities, boys are most emotionally open and expressive after a strenuous physical workout, such as a hike, ropes course, or simple game of chase or playground football.

The father of a thirteen-year-old boy suggests men could do a lot more to welcome boys this age into the world of men, supporting them through the developmental transition instead of leaving them to struggle alone and vulnerable: "Let's incorporate them into men's world sooner. They are tweeners for too long.

'I'm a boy and I'm a man. I don't know what I am.' Men remember that stage. We can tolerate that. Let's let them be both for a while."

Another father who works with boys says he sees the "boys whose inner lives are hidden in fear of being destroyed by the cruelty of others." He worries about his own younger sons:

> I know that the tenderness and vibrance my sons show now will necessarily become well-defended behind walls of tougher masculinity. As boys are given false "product masculinity" to emulate, they—and we—become confused about our worth as persons, about whether our vulnerabilities are shameful, about whether it's okay to need adult men to love us. And we feel terrified that others will discover that we *do* need adult men to love us.

In his novel *Lord of the Flies*, author William Golding tells the story of a group of schoolboys stranded on a jungle island during World War II. Isolated from civilization and adult supervision, the boys improvise a social order in which the strong, charismatic, shrewd, and even sadistic boys eventually and tragically prevail. The boys' descent into savagery is the central story of the book. But in the end, when the boys are rescued, it is an adult, a man, who steps in and leads them out.

Any man who has ever spent time in an eighth- or ninth-grade boys' locker room, any man who has heard boy-on-boy teasing, understands the culture of cruelty and has a wish to protect his own son or someone else's son from it. He understands boys' vulnerability to cruel, distorted views of masculinity; he wants to be that man who shows boys a way out. At the same time, many men wonder whether it was, in fact, all that teasing that made them tough in life, and so they are ambivalent about completely closing down the culture of cruelty. All I can offer is that after listening to boys in therapy for years, I can testify that what they remember are the men who had the emotional courage to reach out to them and make them feel safe in the middle school years. They have no use for men who employed sarcasm, ignored bullying, or acted like big bullies themselves. The choice belongs to every man—and to every parent, teacher, counselor, or coach. We may not be able to dismantle the culture of cruelty, but we can give our boys the tools to build something better.

however, they are accepting the care and organizing support of their mothers. It is vital that moms understand that the fundamental relationship is still in place.

However, this is a difficult time for mothers, because it often feels to them as if they are losing touch with their sons—which they are, in some ways—and they often get their feelings hurt. That's what happened to the mother whose son apparently rejected her by asking, "What relationship?" I don't believe for a second that he did not know that he had a relationship with his mom. He did. He was accepting her love on a daily basis and returning it silently, but he didn't want to deal with it verbally just then; he wanted to be "separate."

The question in my mind after an incident like that is whether the boy was able to join the family for dinner that evening and talk about some emotionally neutral stuff, such as politics or sports. Was he good-natured the next morning? Did he do his homework? You can assess the health of your connection with your son by watching how he "votes with his feet." Even if he doesn't want to talk, even if he doesn't say the right things, does he do the right things? If so, he continues to respect your values, continues to want your love, and is actually working to earn it.

In an earlier era, parents did not consider conversation between parent and child to be the ultimate test of the goodness of the relationship; rather, respect and obedience were what parents looked for from a child. When your son is no longer talking to you much, if he is no longer answering your questions, take stock of whether he is respecting your values and obeying the rules. If he is, you are probably okay; if he is not, it is possible he is becoming disconnected from you and the family.

If a boy becomes truly disrespectful and disconnected, he is at risk for depression and destructive behavior. If he is no longer trying to maintain the connection with his family, he will turn to his peers as his only source of emotional support. That's what opens a boy up to the siren call of peer groups and gangs: *We love you better than your parents; we can get you to manhood, they can't.*

From the beginning of adolescence, it is vital that parents ask for respect from their son . . . and choose their battles. You do not need constant verbal communication with your son if he is respecting your curfews and showing up at his appointments. You do not need to have constant control of him, so let go of how messy his room is (and you shouldn't be picking up his clothes and doing his laundry. He's old enough to operate a washing machine). What you do need is respect for the family and its rules. If you ask

> *Boys get in more trouble because they are trying to impress people.*
> —Boy, age thirteen

for that and receive it, you likely will still have short conversations with your son about the meaningful things in his life.

The mother of an eleven-year-old, who also has two older sons, told me that with all three of her sons she found it helpful to keep her sense of humor and perspective when they were in what she described as an "I-need-to-separate-from-my-mother mood" or were moody or angry "in a hormonal way." "I tell myself that it's his job as an eleven-year-old to be angry at me right now," she said. "Sometimes I say it to him in a respectful way—and it usually gets a laugh and breaks the tension."

I used to give a talk to parents of adolescent boys called "Parenting in the Transition Moments." That's what it is like at this age, because a parent has only short windows between waking and school, school and homework, homework and the all-important friends. You don't have to lose him at this age, but you are sharing him now with his peer group.

Though the peer group is extremely important, boys develop close friendships during these years, characterized by mutual respect, affection, and self-disclosure. The great American psychiatrist Harry Stack Sullivan called this the "chumship" stage. Though the word *chum* sounds quaint today, it is the case that for many boys a friend seems to become as important as family. Friends have the same interests, play the same games, seek out each other's company, and know the truth of each other's lives. Though boys do not obviously engage in the same regular personal self-disclosure as girls, they almost always know the facts of another boy's life. Unlike girl friendships, however, the code of male stoicism requires that a boy's problems, such as an unemployed father or alcoholic mother, *not* be discussed. Rather, boys try to protect each other by not discussing the thing they know. In the movie *Stand by Me,* the four thirteen-year-old boys who lie to their parents and go on a hiking trip to find the body of a man hit by a train know that one of their friends has been physically abused by his father, but they never mention it directly. They only allude to it, to protect his feelings.

DEEPENING FRIENDSHIPS AND A WIDENING SENSE OF ADVENTURE

At this age, the heart of most boy friendships is shared adventure. Though Mark Twain never assigns that archetypal American boy Tom Sawyer a specific age (Twain admitted that he was a composite of many boys), it is clear to me that Tom is between eleven and thirteen. He does not appear to be physically grown yet—his aunt Polly is bigger than he is—and he is engaged in a good-natured and continuous psychological war with her, with his teacher, and with Sunday school. Sounds like a middle school boy to me. What is his aim in life? It is to find a friend, even a disreputable friend such as Huck Finn, and have an adventure in which they can test their courage and independence. Sometimes, of course, they get more than they bargained for, the way Tom and Huck did when they ended up witnessing a murder in the graveyard, but as adventures go, that's what every boy hopes for: the bonus track.

If you ask any man what he remembers from his boyhood, you are likely to get memories from the ages of twelve and thirteen. At that age, he has enough independence to create opportunities on his own, he has a friend who has time on his hands and similar inclinations, and they do not need constant adult support.

Before you dismiss Tom Sawyer as purely fantastical fiction, let me share the story that a friend of mine, Arch McIntosh, gave me from the privately published memoir by his father, a general practitioner in the town of Old Fort, North Carolina. His father was himself the son of a town doctor, giving him the nickname "Little Doc." Foreshadowing the scientist he is going to become, Little Doc, at about age twelve, earns money by raising rats and catching poisonous snakes to sell to research labs: "The university pays $1.10 for each of the poisonous ones and fifty cents for six of the non-poisonous." During the summer of 1932, his parents let him and his friends go by themselves on a camping trip to a lake in the mountains—who would do that now?—where the boys smoke cigarettes (no warnings), have a frightening encounter with a bear and her cub (no counselors or park rangers), attempt unsuccessfully to bake a pie on their own (no instructions), swim naked in the muddy lake (no lifeguard), and take out a boat at night (no lifejackets) to gig frogs, only to have one boy stab another right through the hand with the ice pick they are using as a gig (no cell phone and no way to hike out that same night).

He describes a game called "fox 'n' dogs," a hunt-and-chase competition occupying many hours, for which Little Doc and his friends, "the Dirty Five," use the entire town as their field of play. Absolutely determined to get away from his friends, who have spotted him hiding in the church, Little Doc takes the stairs up to the top of the steeple, climbs the bell rope, and, as his friend begins to ascend the rope, leaps off the roof into a nearby tree. Without an accurate understanding of the physics of this maneuver, he fails to grab a branch and drops toward the ground, hitting branch after branch, until he lands on the ground, knocking himself out cold. Upon waking up, his only concern is to keep this information from his parents, which, despite his pain, he is successful in concealing. It is only during an X-ray for neck pain twenty-seven years later that he discovers that he fractured his second, third, and fourth cervical vertebrae in his fall.

POWER, IMPULSE, AND POOR JUDGMENT ON A COLLISION COURSE

These are terrifying stories to modern suburban parents, who become anxious when they have not seen their children for a period of two or three hours. I understand that terror because, as a parent, I have shared it. And I am keenly aware that boys of this age have terrible judgment; even very smart boys who are going to grow up to be doctors might impulsively jump off church roofs. In 1932, the leading cause of death in adolescence was disease. Sadly, in recent years the top three causes of death for adolescent boys have been accidents (mostly car accidents), homicide, and suicide. And I cannot tell you how many stories I have heard about boys walking on roofs and jumping from roofs—boys who should have known better. Shouldn't parents do everything in their power to protect their sons from these potential dangers? Yes and no.

We know that the brain of the middle school child is growing rapidly in keeping with the overall changes of puberty. The dendrites, branches of the cells that make up the brain (neurons), are increasing rapidly; the brain increases dramatically in size from eleven to fourteen. But as with the blooming of the brain in infancy, not all these new dendrites are connected to experience or to each other. It is through learning that neurons become connected together in ways that create memory, knowledge, and wisdom. After this period of tremendous growth, the early adolescent brain actually loses cells; it is winnowed down as the neurons that are connected to one another through learning survive and the disconnected ones die off. The end result is an efficient brain. However, the all-important frontal lobes, the seat of judgment, are not finished at fourteen, eighteen, or even twenty-one, not in boys or girls. Because girls are less impulsive on a biological basis and socialized to be more attuned to the reactions of adults, they tend not to make quite as many obvious, egregious errors as boys do.

"Why did you do that? What were you thinking?" we ask a sixth-grade or seventh-grade boy who has just done something so dumb we can hardly believe

THE DISTRACTIONS OF MIDDLE SCHOOL LIFE FOR BOYS

Boys in middle school are particularly challenged in seven ways: First, differential rates of pubertal growth among boys creates inside every individual boy's mind some worry about his identity: *Am I going to grow into the man I want to be?* Second, there is a distinct upsurge in the status-seeking behavior of boys and their cruelty to one another: *If I am not strong, will other boys step on me?* Third, every boy, either obviously or subtly, is trying to transform his relationship with the adult world through some kind of challenge to parents or teachers: *Do adults see the new, more powerful me?* Fourth, every boy wonders whether he is competent: *Am I going to be useful to anyone?* Fifth, boy culture tends to be anti-intellectual: *Girls like reading; we don't.* Sixth, the average boy is strikingly disorganized in comparison to the average girl of the same age. His notebook is such a mess: *There's too much to keep track of! Why do we need all those stupid worksheets anyway?* Seventh, on a daily basis, boys are both attracted to girls and see how far they are behind girls: *They're beautiful and sexy, but they look and think like women; we're just boys!*

These seven challenges dominate the mental life of boys from eleven to thirteen, and it is difficult for boys to put them aside long enough to pay attention to social studies or math or English. Many boys who were pretty good students in elementary school start to openly disparage school when they are in seventh grade. They mock adult values and declare everything to be "stupid" or "boring." Many do this even though they continue to work; the weaker students are the ones who are sucked out to sea by the undertow of disinterest that pulls at middle school boys. Naturally, the very best boy students continue to work hard at school, because academic success clearly is going to provide them with a route to competence and adulthood, even if they cannot absolutely picture how it is going to work out.

"Some people think school is a waste of time, but I want to finish school and go to college, to go to MIT and study technology," Josh, twelve, told me. "Since MIT has technology in it, I could work on a computer, fix computers, or work on car wires."

Meanwhile, other boys are letting their studies go while they dream about playing in the NFL or the NBA or in a band that makes the cover of *Rolling Stone,* no matter how unlikely their dream is to come true. I once interviewed a skinny seventh-grade boy whose mother and father had emigrated to the United States from Bangladesh to give their son and daughter a chance for a better life. Though his father stood five feet nine inches high, this boy assured me that he was going to play in the NBA if he practiced his dribbling enough. I admired his grit, but I have no doubt that his athletic ambitions were driving his parents crazy. Lots of middle school boys seem to have no idea of the connection between schoolwork and their future.

our eyes or ears. Some explanation is required; none is forthcoming. "I don't know," says the boy. *You must know!* we want to scream. Instead, we say, "There must have been some reason." Sometimes the boy has a lame answer; many times he just shrugs. He knows it would sound stupid or rude for him to say "I don't know" a second time. But in many instances, he really does not seem to know; it just seemed like a good idea at the time. We can punish him, sometimes we need to shame him, but he may not have an answer for us other than that his judgment was terrible.

By shaming, I do not mean ridicule or scolding intended to belittle or demean. Sometimes when a boy has done something immoral, ugly, and offensive, you have to call him on it on moral grounds. That sometimes means shaming a boy in the sense of saying to him, "You should be ashamed of yourself."

Let me give you an example. I consulted for a boarding school where two fifteen-year-old boys found a dead, rotting squirrel on the campus. They brought it into the dorm, put it in the microwave, and set the timer for fifteen minutes. The ensuing smell was so bad—unbelievably terrible—that the dorm was uninhabitable for three days, and everything in the building had to be cleaned or dry-cleaned. The boys had had a very good idea of what would happen when they put the squirrel carcass in the microwave, and they thought of it as a big joke.

The boys were instantly suspended, but they also were informed that their return wasn't guaranteed—and that was the truth. The dorm parents were so disturbed by the incident that they no longer wanted to have these boys in their "home." They wanted the boys expelled or transferred. The intensity of the response reflected the degree to which they had felt the prank was offensive, not only in a practical sense but in a moral one as well. The boys realized the gravity of their error, were indeed ashamed of themselves, and only with sincere apology and humility earned a second chance to stay at the school.

Tales of poor judgment, bad choices, shame, and regret cover a world of boy activity, often the result of an unfortunate confluence of emerging physical strength, a desire for power, uneven emotional self-regulation, and an underdeveloped sensitivity to the social and emotional cues of others. As a result, boys misread risks, misread their own strengths and vulnerabilities, misread others, and make mistakes.

RICK: "I NEVER REALLY THOUGHT I'D GET SUSPENDED . . ."

Rick was thirteen, in eighth grade, when his mother called me to say that her son was in big trouble at his middle school. He had been suspended for two weeks after putting his hands on a girl's buttocks during lunch period. His parents were, of course, angry at their son and worried by what he had done. They were also upset by what they regarded as an overreaction to the incident by the school administrators and the labeling of their son as a "sexual harasser." Nevertheless, they supported the punishment and required that he get some psychotherapy to help him understand his behavior.

When I talked with Rick two years later, he had gone on to become a strong student and varsity athlete, a bright and able fellow. He had matured as one might expect of a normal boy his age. He was not a sexually aggressive boy and was not perceived as a threat to girls. He had grown in his capacity to be introspective and think into the future. He genuinely regretted and was ashamed of having deliberately touched the girl inappropriately in eighth grade. However, although he accepted that the punishment was fair, he remained confused by the intensity of the adult reaction, despite the many conversations he had had with adults at the time and in the time since. He said, "I touched a girl's ass. I just touched a girl in one of my classes. I never really thought I'd get suspended from school. This was not a sexual act. It was just, 'Well, why not just do this?' " For most adults, the explanation, "Well, why not just do this?" is going to be highly unsatisfactory, and the assertion that it was not a sexual act is going to drive them wild. *Of course it was sexual*, the adult mind screams. *How could you not see that?*

If he was confused by his behavior, so were the adults around him. I am reminded of the title of one of David Walsh's books: *Why Do They Act That Way?* This engaging book explains to parents the role that brain development plays in the sometimes clueless and thoughtless actions of teenagers. For Walsh, the culprit in these incidents is the prefrontal cortex (PFC), a center of decision making in the brain, which is still incomplete at twelve. This means that "the adolescent PFC can't always distinguish between a good decision and a bad one, no matter how intelligent the kid is."

Even if we accept that Rick's brain was undeveloped, we have to hold him responsible, and, of course, there are other boys in his class with undeveloped brains who weren't touching girls' bodies in school. That means Rick's actions

SUPPORTING YOUR SON'S TRANSITION

What can parents do to support a son's successful growth and transition through the middle school years?

Limit screen time. Whether it is television or video games, limit screen time to an absolute maximum of two hours per night on school nights. For most boys, homework should probably be done in a quiet atmosphere in the kitchen, dining room, or similar place.

Know the cast of characters in his life. Know the names of his teachers and how he feels about them. He judges how seriously you take his educational career by how much specific, concrete information you have about his day, but you cannot get the information by asking him an open-ended question such as "How was school?" You have to gather information on your own, usually by attending school functions or, more important, by really paying attention to the characters and dramas at school when he is in the mood to talk about them.

Give him useful work to do at home. I do not mean just assigning him chores on his own. I am talking about useful work side by side with his mother or father in which he learns important skills. He has to show you his competence in some other way than just school.

Let him own his own success and failure. Finally, remember that his schoolwork is his own. Allow him to think for himself, write for himself, make his own science projects and history dioramas. Allow him to take responsibility for his choices. Allow him to fail, to get into trouble in school, and to suffer the consequences. How else is he going to learn?

weren't just a matter of his neurological development. They were motivated by something. What, in his psychological development, might explain it?

In Rick's case, a thorough review of his history and behavior suggested that he had been a hotheaded boy from an early age. The youngest of four children, he had always competed ferociously with his two brothers, who were six and four years older than he and superbly athletic. It was often tough for Rick when he was little; he would become intensely frustrated by not being able to keep up with his brothers and his friends. In our conversation, and after the process of self-examination that therapy had provided, Rick said he felt the act was a "power grab"—one of a pattern of unthinking, immature actions around that time, which also included nonsexual but nonetheless brash affronts to teachers and others.

Maybe it was a power grab. Maybe he was under a lot of pressure from

SEX ABUSE: AWARENESS, ATTENTION, AND
ACTION CAN REDUCE ABUSE

Boys from ages eleven to thirteen are particularly attractive to sexual predators for a variety of reasons. Why? They are becoming sexually more expressive or curious as a result of the changes of puberty, and yet their bodies may still lack the secondary sexual characteristics of adults, so they still look like children and are therefore attractive to pedophiles. Boys of this age are independent enough to spend time away from their parents, giving an abuser time to win their trust. Because young adolescent boys are still relatively small, young, innocent, and more easily coerced, a pedophile has a better chance with boys this age.

Other than checking police data to see if a registered sex offender lives in the neighborhood (and, if so, taking added precautions) and hoping our schools, churches, and youth organizations are alert in their hiring, parents often feel there is nothing they can do. But experts in the field say otherwise.

Counselors, doctors, and researchers who work directly with sexually abused boys, sex abusers, and sex abuse statistics say that breaking the silence and debunking the myths around sex abuse of boys can make a difference. It is something every parent can do and every community can support with a philosophy of prevention and attention.

How should a parent of a boy this age guard against his or her son being sexually abused by an adult? The temptation, of course, is to monitor and protect him at all times, but that both is impractical and will ultimately stunt his growth. We cannot protect our boys like that. It would contradict everything I have said in this book so far about a boy's need for undirected play with friends, away from his parents. It would contradict everything I have said about boys needing role models, such as coaches and teachers, in their lives.

The only way to prepare your son for that possibility is to talk to him about the fact that there are adults, mostly men but some women, who are sexually interested in boys, so he cannot be taken completely by surprise. Actually, prevention starts years earlier. You have to have talked to your son about sex, the facts of life, his body, puberty, and masturbation long before he arrives at puberty. At almost every age, such conversations will embarrass your son. Keep going. And when he is ten and you want to discuss pedophiles, he may try to dismiss the subject by saying, "Mom, I know about weirdos. Nothing's going to happen to me." Keep talking—not about generalized parental fears, but about the facts, so that he's well informed and you've made it clear you're not afraid to talk about the tough stuff. The idea is to create a conversational comfort zone around issues of sex and sexuality. (See the earlier discussion and book recommendations on pages 180–81.) But in any case, if talking about these matters with your son makes you squeamish, or you don't feel you know exactly what to say, remember this: one in six boys is sexually abused before the age of sixteen, and his parents probably never had a meaningful conversation with him about the subject.

Jan Chozen Bays, M.D., cofounder of CARES Northwest, a collaborative, community-based medical clinic for the assessment, treatment, and prevention of child abuse in Portland, Oregon, offers these pointers for parents:

• Boys need good male role models. They need healthy father figures. They will find who they can. Pedophiles know this. They can recognize these vulnerable, lonely, searching boys and are waiting to take them in. If there is not a father figure in your boy's life, make every effort to find one, and monitor to make sure it is a healthy relationship.

• The very worst wounding of boys and the very worst consequences (such as later drug abuse and violent and criminal behavior) come from a combination of sexual abuse and domestic violence. For the sake of your son's future, if you want him to be physically and mentally healthy and to stay out of jail, get out of such a situation as quickly as possible.

• "Stranger danger" is overstated. Boys are more at risk of sexual abuse from people they know and trust in their families and in their communities than from strangers. Fathers, stepfathers, and male relatives or trusted others are the most common offenders. But women do molest boys. Female sex abusers are a hidden problem. Even when people see it, they tend to dismiss it as "he's getting an education" rather than recognizing it as abuse. We are finding that some boys are sexually abused by their girlfriends, who make them have sex when they don't want to.

• Make sure your son knows what is and is not okay in terms of discipline and touching. Make sure he knows he can come to you if someone bullies or hurts him, if someone touches him in ways that make him uncomfortable, or if someone touches him and then bribes or threatens him. Make sure he knows that you will be grateful he told you and he will not get into trouble.

• If you want your son to be strong and be able to "take care of himself," enroll him in a well-respected martial arts program that includes families, and you attend classes, too.

• Be alert to signs that something is wrong. The new onset of bed-wetting, stool soiling, depression, angry outbursts, declining grades, and loss of interest in friends are clear signs that he's trying to cope with stress. They should prompt you to have a gentle talk. If he won't talk about what's wrong the first time, try again.

• Do things together. It doesn't have to be expensive—you can wash the car, clean out the garage, or take the dog for a walk, as long as you do it together. Talk with your son. Listen to your son. Tell him what he's doing right and what you admire about him. Love your son and let him know that you do.

testosterone; by the end of adolescence, boys have ten times more testosterone than they did before puberty. Perhaps he was just a boy with a middle-schooler's brain that had bloomed on the cellular level and had not yet been pruned by experience, and his prefrontal cortex could not stand up against the tide of testosterone. This incident occurred because he did not read the girl well and he did not understand his own motivations well enough to stop his hands.

It was, of course, a combination of all of those things: neurology, hormones, psychology, history, and social context. Those same volatile factors are present and different for every boy as he moves into the widening realm of the middle school milieu.

It is important to address overly aggressive sexual behavior by young adolescent boys, so that they have to think about the moral issues of sex, what is right and what is wrong, what it means when a girl says "no" (and what it means when she says "yes," for that matter!). It is vital that we not underreact to the sexual aggressiveness of boys. At the same time, I am appalled when adults overreact and label boys as "harassers" and potential pedophiles when they are simply acting impulsively, or because they are flooded with sexual feeling, or because they are experimenting. Zero Tolerance policies are, in my mind, problematic, because they fall so heavily on boys—there is a fairness issue here because girls can be both harassing and provocative in different ways than boys—and the rigid policies don't allow adults to make distinctions between young adolescent experimentation and real harassment.

THE DANCE OF SOCIAL AND SEXUAL DEVELOPMENT

Walk into any middle school dance in America or the teen party following a bar or bat mitzvah, and if you're there when it starts, this is what you'll see: a gaily decorated room, a band or DJ cranking up the music, a cluster of girls on one side whispering about the boys, a cluster of boys on the other side eyeing the girls, and an empty dance floor. Within a few minutes, the more socially confident girls and boys will be dancing, others will be commingling for conversation, and a few will be holding themselves at a distance still, in the company of a few good friends. By the end of the evening, the dance floor is full, a good time is under way, and all manner of social and sexually charged behavior is on display. Boys and girls who were socially tentative at the start of the evening have advanced a bit to a new comfort zone with each other. Some will have paired off and found their way to more intimate corners. Others will have paired off and broken up before the night is done, and the "dating" drama is already flooding the gossip channel between cell phones, text messaging, and instant messaging on home computers (some kids go home early).

Now imagine that scene lasting three or four years. And imagine your son living his life in the middle (or on the edges) of it: waking up to it, going to school in it, dreaming about it, worrying about it, sometimes trying to ignore it, all the while trying to figure out who he is and who he wants to be inside it. Add to that a new twist: his discovery that the girls he left behind in first grade are back—and seem primed to play in a new way.

He may first notice it when the girls start to talk about which boys and which girls would make a good couple. There has occasionally been romanticized or even sexualized talk between boys and girls since third grade, and he has laughed at it because it was funny, but it didn't mean anything to him personally.

Now, however, he does feel that it means something, because the girls he has gone to school with for years look different to him. They are cute. And one in particular is, well, really pretty. He finds that he notices her smile, and how good she is at school, and her breasts. He feels different when she talks to him. Most surprising to him, when other boys talk about her he gets a little angry and wants them to talk about another girl. He wants them to leave his girl

THE ARTS SAVE BOYS' LIVES

A middle school principal once said to me: "The arts save boys' lives." That thought kept echoing in my mind, and I went back to talk to him about it. "What do you mean 'saves boys' lives'?" I asked.

"Well, it allows them to express themselves and get outside themselves," he said.

"Get outside of themselves?" I asked. Yes, he said and went on to explain that it is through the arts—music, drawing, clay, and woodworking—that a boy can proclaim his true self. He described watching a boy build an abstract sculpture using pieces of wood. This young man was intensely focused on the placement of the pieces of wood in relation to one another, and he labored at it till he got it just right. When it was finished he was clearly pleased with the way it looked.

What else in a boy's life allows him to create something that produces that feeling of satisfaction? *This is mine. I made it. It represents me.* Very few things in school do. And it's a different feeling from succeeding in athletics. It is an act of creativity. Furthermore, most art has the advantage of involving movement. A middle school orchestra conductor told me that a mother had written to him, "My sixth-grade son loves two things: playing ice hockey and playing the violin." I was surprised and wasn't sure I saw the connection, and asked him to explain. He said that both in hockey and in playing the violin you're expressing yourself while moving. That makes sense.

If we see in the arts a chance for boys to move and create and take risks and reach a satisfying conclusion then we no longer think of the arts as something antithetical to sports or as frills in the world of school. We see the arts as a unique opportunity for boys to express their feelings, their hopes, and their fears in nonverbal ways.

In more than thirty years of being in schools, I have seen a lot of art—a lot of pictures drawn by children and a lot of student performances on stage. I can say with confidence that experience in the arts allows a boy to feel a sense of satisfaction that he cannot experience in any other realm of his life. And it allows him insight into himself that he cannot obtain in any other way.

I remember one high school boy who wrote about his experience singing in a chorus, feeling his voice joining with the voices of others in a community of sound. His description of it was beautiful. But just as important, the self-knowledge that he had gained from singing—the knowledge about his need for interdependence, his place in community, and his realization of his best self in cooperation with other people—was powerful indeed.

One last thought about the arts. An art teacher whose practice it had been to ban boys from "drawing anything violent" in her art classes heard me speak about freeing boys to draw what they wanted to draw and write what they wanted to write, even if it wasn't to the taste of teachers. This felt like a risk to her, and she took my advice with deep misgivings. For several months the boys kept checking with her, asking, "Are you sure we can draw whatever we want? Really?" She had to persuade them that she meant what she said. After a year of allowing boys to express themselves without prohibitions in place, she wrote to me saying that she realized that much of the art she had been getting for years was formulaic and compliant, flowers and houses and such, drawn for the teacher's benefit. This new art was different. Some of it pushed the boundaries of good taste. Some of it scared her. But when she allowed boys to express what was inside them, the drawings she got were deeper, richer, and more powerful than she had ever seen in her career.

There is art inside every boy. Our job is to provide them the opportunity to discover it and the vehicle through which they can express it.

alone. Why is that? He is a little annoyed with himself; she isn't really his girl. But he cannot stop hoping that she'll pay attention to him.

When the teacher is assigning working groups, he tries to get into her group, and he feels happy when he's with her, even if he isn't with his usual buddies. And they have talked and sat together at lunch; well, actually he asked her to sit with his group of boys and she agreed, sitting down, luckily, with three of her friends. They're not a couple, of course, but in his mind they have a special relationship that's not like the other dumb couples in the classroom that people talk about. He and his girl are smarter, not show-offs like them.

And then one day when the girls are laughing and talking about couples they mention him and her, and though he wants them to stop, he smiles and feels proud. Now he wants people to know; he wants the other boys to stay away from her. They're the talk of the school; when some of the boys ask him, "Have you kissed her?" he gets angry. "You're stupid," he says, but the thought lodges in his mind: might there be a chance for him to kiss her?

The idea is pretty exciting to him, and he thinks about it that night in bed, and the idea gives him an erection. Yes, he'd like to kiss her; he really would. It would be embarrassing and weird, but it would be pretty cool. And now he is thinking about her all the time; well, not all the time, but in a special way, and

"JUST THE RIGHT CAMP FOR MY CHILD"

When I was thirteen and a city boy, my mother declared that I was both lazy and obnoxious—she said I was in the back-talk stage—and that I should be sent away to camp. So I was sent to an all-boys canoeing camp, which I absolutely loved. It was one of the great experiences of my life. I returned home physically stronger and more confident than I had been two months earlier (and probably still as obnoxious).

Some years ago, when my son, Will, was twelve, I felt it was time for him to go to a sleep-over camp. Looking at my gentle and rather soft son on the edge of adolescence, I had a classic father's reaction. I thought he ought to be more independent, that he needed to get away from his mother's overprotective hovering, and that he could benefit from the physical rigor of more outdoor activities. Also, he needed to get away from his video games and his laptop computer for a month. (Well, he didn't think he did, but I sure thought so.)

Naturally, I wanted to pick a camp that would give my son the same incredible experience that camp had been for me. I recognized that he was not quite as athletic and outgoing as I had been at his age (and not nearly as contrary), so I chose a camp for him that had many of the same elements mine had had (boys only, campfires, canoeing and kayaking, waterfront activities, etc.) but that also had the things my son adored and which I was never good at (arts, woodworking, drama). We visited the camp at the end of the summer a year before he was to attend. He had a great time playing ultimate Frisbee with a bunch of boys and counselors. He said he liked it. So off he went.

He attended the all-boys camp for two summers, and I was very proud of him for doing it. He took risks and attempted things he had never done before, including kayaking and performing in skits in front of the entire camp. He received an art prize at the end of the second season. However, it was unmistakably clear that he wasn't really comfortable there. He didn't love it. As kind as the camp staff were, as friendly as the other boys had been, the camp wasn't really a fit for him. When I picked him up on the last day of the second year of camp, my son was stronger, more confident, and more challenging than he had ever been before. He looked me in the eye and delivered the news: "Dad, I don't want to come back here. This is your kind of camp, not mine. I'm not like you."

Ouch—that hurt. My intentions had been so good! Because his mother and I wanted him to have a camp experience that he loved, we renewed the search. The next summer we sent him to an arts camp that had ceramics, theater, woodworking, glassblowing, and theatrical lighting, set and sound design, among other offerings. He called us at the end of the first week to report happily that he had gotten a part in *The Rocky Horror Show* and that he was taking a stand-up comedy seminar. On the wood lathe he produced a beautiful martial arts fighting stick, with which he still practices daily. He wanted to go back next year for the full eight weeks. (Did I mention that he also had a girlfriend at camp?)

The other day I asked Will: "I know you loved your arts camp much better than the canoe camp, but do you feel you got something out of the canoe camp experience?" "No, Dad," Will said. "I wish I'd had those two years to go to the arts camp." Still casting about, I asked him whether they had had campfires at his arts camp. In an exasperated "duh" tone of voice, he proclaimed, "Da-aad, it's not that kind of camp!"

There is a parenting lesson in here somewhere, and I'm searching for it. Was it wrong to send him to the kind of camp I loved? Is it essential that a child love every camp experience? Can you predict what a thirteen-year-old will love? (I think not.) Is there some value in a son attempting to do the things his dad wants him to try, and thereby discharge some unconscious obligation to his father and better define his own identity? I hope so, because that's what happened in this family.

he just feels different when he is around her—happier, prouder, embarrassed, but stronger. He feels more grown-up when she's nearby.

What does that look like from the outside? As one mother of two sons, twelve and thirteen, wrote to me:

> Not much. The thirteen-year-old had a "girlfriend" last year for a couple of months, but nothing since then. As far as I know it involved some phone calls, instant messaging, one kiss, and saying hello in the hall at school. At the time, he had shared the fact with his brother before I learned of it. I was glad the boys had that together. I ask both sons every so often if they (or friends) are "going out" with anyone, and they answer me (without much detail, but they willingly answer anything I ask).

Her concerns about her sons' early forays into the world of sex, love, and intimacy are, she says, "that they will be pressured into sexual experiences too soon, that someone will break their hearts, or, even worse, that they won't experience romantic love."

The mother of another thirteen-year-old voices the hope of most parents: "That he be in happy and fulfilling relationships. That he not hurt girls on purpose. That he act tenderly toward those he cares about."

Many men can remember the girls they fell in love with in the fifth, sixth, and seventh grades. It doesn't happen for all boys, and the majority certainly reject the idea; nevertheless, they are touched by romantic feeling and have a giddy, confused, and ultimately sexual response to it. The father of a thirteen-year-old boy says he has tried to talk with his son about this part of life, but "he does not share with me." His concerns? "I don't want him to get hurt." And what would he like his son to know? "I want to tell him it's okay to have those feelings. It's okay to feel bad when things don't all go well. To be careful about disease and conception. To be respectful of girls and women."

WHERE'S DAD?

Years ago someone told me that Mark Twain remarked that around age twelve, a boy chooses a man to imitate and that he continues to imitate him for the rest of his life. Even though I cannot track down the exact quotation from Twain, I want to share it with the reader as I remember it, because it is true at several levels. First off, Twain is making the sly joke that a grown man is really still a boy imitating a man. I think many men, myself included, feel like that—and many women in their lives concur. At a deeper level Twain articulates the truth that the early-adolescent boy must have a man to copy if he is to become a man himself. Most important, he correctly perceives that the energy for connection comes from the boy. This might surprise some fathers who have difficulty coaxing their sons away from video games to do something with them, but they must not be deceived by superficial appearances. My advice to fathers: do not give up doing things with your son, because he needs you.

As a psychologist, I have heard so many boys talk about what they wish for from their dads that I believe there is an almost universal yearning in boys eleven to thirteen for a closer relationship with their fathers. This yearning arises in boys who have emotionally involved fathers right at home, in boys who have emotionally or geographically distant fathers, and in boys who have never known their fathers at all. Sadly, 35 percent of boys in the United States are living in homes without their biological fathers. Our forty-year epidemic of divorce has taken a huge toll on the intact family, the stresses of poverty

> *His eyes betray him most. I can tell if he is hurt, mad, happy, or sad by looking at them. He looks for physical contact when something is wrong.*
> —Mother of a twelve-year-old boy

and misguided government polices have contributed to the breakup of the family, and now many women are choosing to have babies without marriage or the possibility of a permanent father. Twenty-seven percent of children in the United States live in a home headed by a single parent, usually a mother. In 2006 nearly four in ten babies born in the United States were born out of wedlock.

Both genders suffer from the loss of fathering. From my work with women in psychotherapy who were abandoned by their dads, I know the loss is extremely painful for girls. After working with boys for thirty years, I have seen that having an absent father can damage some boys terribly and permanently, and that it leaves all fatherless boys with a hole—large or small—in their souls. Many will search throughout their adolescence and adulthood for some feeling, some something that they wish they had gotten from their fathers.

What are boys looking for in their dads or in a father substitute? We routinely say a "role model," and that is both correct and quite vague. What exactly is a role model for a boy?

> A man who can teach a boy both the skills that a man should know and the tools of the trade that a boy would like to know.

> A man who can show him how to manage the struggles that all men experience with their strength, their sexuality, and their vulnerability.

> Someone for whom the son can do something really useful.

> Someone who can say to a boy, "I recognize you as an emerging man." Without a father to witness his growth, how does a boy know that he is becoming the kind of man he should become?

Boys raised in homes without fathers are at higher risk for involvement in crime and for trouble in school, and they are more prone to have problems with their self-esteem. Youth-oriented programs such as Big Brothers, the Boy Scouts, the Boys and Girls Clubs of America, and mentoring programs recognize the yearnings of boys for men and attempt to meet those needs by providing attentive male leaders who are generous-hearted, patient, funny, emotionally balanced, and appealing to boys. Sadly, men working for nonprofit institutions have to be willing to work for lower salaries than they could make driving a limousine or tending bar. Good men willing to make that kind of economic sacrifice are tough to find, because working with early-adolescent boys is psychologically challenging.

Though boys desperately need their fathers, coaches, and other role models, guiding them through early adolescence is not easy, and there are moments of friction and confused emotion between even the most devoted father and son.

"My father is my hero," a teenage boy told me. His mother was dying of cancer, and "the way in which he has dealt with my mom's sickness is nothing short of heroic. If I grow up to be half the man he is I will be extremely proud," he said. Even so, he acknowledged that in a moment of anger "I told my dad to fuck off because he was a fuckin' asshole and that my parents were horrible parents. That was irrational."

In my online survey for this book, the fifty-year-old divorced father of a thirteen-year-old boy (and two daughters) described how important a role he believes a father has in the life of a son, and regretted that his communication with his son was not as effective as he wished. "Sometimes I can read his feelings, but only if he is upset," the father said. Otherwise, "I can't really tell what he is feeling." He went on to explain:

> I try to communicate with him and give him my life examples that seem to mimic his. I went through all the same things he did at the same age. But I have not developed the communication with him that I dearly wanted to make a difference in his childhood compared to mine. I have improved one thing: since their birth I have told them every chance I get that I love them. I try to be their cheerleader, motivator, and most positive influence. I try to teach the life lessons of how to go around, through, or over life's obstacles, rather than blame, complain, or justify.

This man adored his own father, a man who was home "every night and every weekend, and I mean every!" Asked to describe his father and their relationship, the love and admiration he felt for his dad was palpable in his 1,437-word response, the eulogy he wrote to lay his father to rest. Nonetheless, he unsentimentally noted that he felt the "need to improve on my dad's job." He explained, "My dad had a hands-off approach. I am not bitter, rather grateful, because he taught me to be self-sufficient and take responsibility." He himself struggles to find the balance: "I worry that I may interfere too much in my son's life and not let him stumble enough to teach him responsibility and to be self-sufficient. And I worry that I need to be more involved and communicating in my son's life."

Sons are always eager to impress their fathers, and terribly wounded when they fail to do so. At the same time they are pushy and competitive and want to be smarter, quicker, and faster than their dads. Fathers want their sons to do well and to have a better life than they have had, but they also are reluctant to give up their power and control. Friction and collisions are inevitable. In their research on adolescents and their families, described in the book *Divergent Realities,* Reed Larson and Maryse Richards wrote that a father's happiest moments are when he is teaching his son something that he knows. A son's happiest moments are when *he* is the expert, teaching his father something that the father does not know. How can they both be happy at the same time when each wants to be the teacher of the other?

MIDDLE SCHOOL: DISTRACTIBLE BOYS, MEANINGFUL MENTORS

Every middle school teacher struggles to create a classroom curriculum interesting enough to compete with this multitude of mental distractions. Every parent who cares about education is frightened that her or his middle-schooler will check out of the educational process, and tries hard to boost his motivation. Parents of learning-disabled (LD) boys are rightly concerned that the shame and humiliation of being in an LD class, or the social isolation that results from an LD placement, will turn their sons against school in a wholesale way, because those boys really do hate how hard school is for them.

What are the solutions to the academic ennui that is readily observable in middle school boys? There is no quick and easy solution. There are, I believe, four things that schools can do and four things that parents can do to keep middle school boys engaged.

It would be helpful if schools could give sixth-, seventh-, and eighth-grade boys homeroom teachers who know them well and could touch base with them every morning in a personal way. In my experience, boys who are not known personally by an adult become disruptive or alienated. It would be enormously helpful if those same teachers helped the boys organize themselves before heading home. A homework organization period at the end of the school day would do the trick. Schools should provide boys with some demanding physical exercise each and every school day. Finally, recent research and common sense suggest that we should make an attempt to hire more male teachers in middle

Andy: Father-Son Tension at the Intersection of Ambition

Andy, at twelve, was just about as intense and focused as a boy could be as we sat courtside waiting for his tennis lesson to begin. "Rafael Nadal is my favorite player," he said. "He has the same grip as me. I want to be like him when I grow up. The best in the world."

Andy was both proud of himself and hard on himself. "Sometimes I get down on myself if I'm not playing up to what I can. I know I should be playing a lot better," he said. His mother had originally suggested he give tennis a try when he was six, he said. He'd shown some talent for the game, and continued lessons with a series of coaches.

For the last two years, his father had been managing his tennis career. This he said with a big smile. "I have a good relationship with my dad. He drives me along to all the places and then he watches my matches and then he pays for the lessons." Indeed, Andy's father has rearranged his job as a real estate agent to be as available to Andy as he can be, to support Andy's tennis ambitions.

On the court, Andy was all ambition and his coach, Brad, was all relaxation. Andy would hit the ball as hard as he could, and succeeded in firing some shots past Brad. But what Andy couldn't see was that his coach was holding back a bit, measuring his shots so as not to discourage the boy. Andy might have great potential talent, but he was a picture of emotional fragility on the court. Being good at tennis meant so much to him—his dreams were so big, and he was so invested in proving himself in a man's world—that the men in his life needed to handle him carefully.

Andy's father and I began to talk quietly about his own days as a tennis star at his high school, though he hadn't been good enough to play at the college level. Intensely focused on his son's play, Andy's dad very soon began to analyze his son's tennis temperament and his tennis future in a clearly audible voice. "Andy gets quite nervous. He's shy. Kids who are successful in sports get some confidence in other areas of life. . . . Andy gets quite nervous before tournaments." As his father continued talking, Andy began to hit some shots long and others into the net. Suddenly he stopped playing and stormed over to the side of the court. "Dad, I can hear you talking about me. It is ruining my game!" He was furious. He returned to the middle of the court and resumed playing, and the coach continued to teach with a light touch, humoring, supporting, and challenging Andy by turns.

Andy's father continued to talk to me about his son's career potential—which he envisioned in the business of tennis, not the playing of it—and again his son stopped his play, angry and tense about his dad's comments. He could not tune out his dad's words, and they were unraveling his game, unraveling him. Later, his father told me that Andy had scratched from a match he was supposed to play the previous day with a talented adult. Andy had developed a headache, which his dad believes was psychological in origin. The coach would later tell me that Andy's dad was sometimes "very critical of his son's tennis game." Apparently, there was a history of the father both coaching and critiquing his son, and the boy had developed a hair-trigger response to it.

Andy and his dad were spending just about as much time together as any twelve-year-old and his father do in modern American. Researchers tell us that fathers and sons from two-parent families spend about 4.2 hours per week together. The logistics of getting him to tennis courts and tournaments required it, and Andy clearly valued his father's time and support. But there were tensions between them, exemplified by the father's insistent critiquing and the son's blowup on the court.

Andy's eruptions and his father's observations underline how perilous the father-son relationship can be at this age, when a boy is so determined to prove himself to his father and everyone else. It is a generous boy who can allow himself to be coached by his father, even in a team situation, without feeling excessively pushed, criticized, or ignored. I am talking not just about sports but about everything that a father would like to teach a boy, from carpentry to cooking to the cello, and everything that the son would like to learn from the father. These inevitable tensions between father and son mean that sometimes (and here I am speaking metaphorically) a tennis coach is needed—a relief pitcher of sorts, to use a metaphor from another sport. Father and son may benefit from a third person who can teach the boy and provide an alternative model.

With or without that "relief pitcher" in the relationship, a father can make a practice of both sharing what he knows and making it clear that he also values his son's experience and insights. This relational reciprocity between father and son creates a shared experience of mentoring across the generational divide. How do fathers and sons develop the ease, trust, and reciprocity that will allow them to negotiate the tense moments around homework assignments and grades, times when a son is likely to feel judged by his father and withdraw from him, moments when they may explode at each other? It may seem obvious, but dads and sons have to spend time together and have fun together; that's how they can build up credit in a relationship bank account that they will draw on later.

One summer, following a painful divorce that had stressed his family terribly and had left him feeling miserable, a father went for a three-week cross-country driving trip with his son.

They traveled back roads and stopped at what seemed like every crummy fast-food restaurant in the United States; they visited ball parks and took photos of each other doing dumb and impossible things (photos like the classic tourist-holding-up-the-Leaning-Tower-of-Pisa variety). The father created a Web site for the trip and they would post photos and bulletins of their adventures daily so the boy's mother could follow their adventures, but also so they were creating a record together. Those kinds of experiences between father and son can create both goodwill and good memories that can pull them through some rough times.

schools. The presence of some large men is calming for boys intoxicated with their new physical size and power. Male teachers also feed the psychological hunger for adult male role models that resides in every boy. This is not intended as a slam at women teachers, most of whom do a great job with boys. I have heard many women teachers say, "It is so good for boys to have men on the faculty," and it is.

A friend told me the following story about his mother. In the fall of his eighth-grade year he got an F and a D on his report card from a private school. When it arrived in the mail his mother read it and came into his room holding it in her hand. He expected her to yell at him. She said to him, "I don't think they'll let you pass eighth grade with grades like that, and they may not allow you to stay in the school, but I'm not sure. You'd better check with them." She then dropped it on his desk. From her manner and gestures he understood that she was not going to rescue him. She was not going to go to the school to talk to his teachers about it. He said to me, "It was at that moment that my education became my own."

Many parents today believe that they can and should manage their child's education for years and years. By eighth grade, a boy is capable of managing quite a bit, even if his judgment is not great. Now is the safest time for him to meet his limits, experience the consequences, and learn the lessons of school and life.

SINGLE-SEX EDUCATION: LEARNING FROM WHAT WORKS FOR BOYS

Because I am the psychologist for an all-boys school, I am asked constantly about all-male education and whether it is "better" for boys. People also want to know whether the public schools should experiment with single-sex education.

Q&A

Q: *My eleven-year-old son's lack of self-confidence worries me. He is very compliant, which has put us into a pattern I think is unhealthy for him—I tell him what to do and he just does it. He will even wear whatever clothes I tell him to put on. This means that instead of thinking for himself and taking responsibility, he waits for me to tell him what to do. How can I help increase his confidence? I took him to a child psychiatrist, but she told me that because he is in the range of "normal" (gets good grades, is successful at sports, and has good friends), there was nothing that she could do for him.*

A: So many mothers want to increase their sons' confidence or their self-esteem. If they took a step back and thought, they would soon realize that you cannot ever increase someone's confidence of self-esteem for very long. Of course, it is wonderful to have your mother love you and think you are doing a good job at school or in general, but what gives you confidence is developing skills. In order to have real confidence, a boy has to develop a skill, do something well, do it well in comparison to other boys, and have his skill make a difference in the world.

So, what parents can do is put their sons into situations where they can develop skills, where they can practice their new abilities (those skills) and get really good at something, and then put them into a venue where being better makes a difference. Very often, school doesn't give boys that feeling; sports may do it. So does art, or playing an instrument. (Learn to read music and play the instrument, practice until you feel fluent, then play in a band and be applauded—that's the sequence.)

At the very least, this should start at home. Since you can see that pushing and praise don't work, look for ways to step back, stop pushing, and let go lovingly. Stop telling him what to do. Give him space to get to know himself—negotiate his fears, discover his own interests and preferences, feel ownership of his mistakes and his victories. You recognize the unhealthy pattern you have developed with each other. So change your part of it. Stop telling him what to wear, for instance, and don't critique his choices. Instead of praise or disappointment, express confidence in his ability to make good choices for himself—and mean it. Hearing your confidence in him instead of your doubt or disappointment will do more to nurture his self-confidence than any amount of pushing or "supporting."

My answer is invariably that it is much more important for a school to be a good school than for it to be single-sex school. Small class size, high teacher morale, inspired leadership, and a challenging, interesting curriculum ought to be the top priorities in education; without them all-boys education would just be a gimmick in a mediocre school.

However, at the end of 2006, the U.S. Department of Education, which had been allowing single-sex public schools for girls for many years, finally allowed school districts to experiment with single-sex classes and single-sex schools for boys. I am glad for the decision, not only because it is more equitable on the face of it, but because educators can now experiment with best teaching practices for boys which ultimately may come back to the coed classroom. Since girls outperform boys in elementary school, middle school, and high school, 57 percent of college graduates are young women, and women comprise about the same percentage of those in graduate school, I think it is important to understand why boys in the United States are either standing still or falling behind academically.

Typically, schools choose to experiment with single-sex classes in middle school because it gives boys and girls a break from the sexual tensions in the classroom and the huge developmental gap between the genders at these ages. Girls are, on average, both physically and mentally more mature than boys in sixth and seventh grades; they started puberty earlier, and many finished their growth before some of the boys have even begun. Anyone who has gone through middle school remembers the huge social gap between girls and boys. Most boys are unable to deal both with the attractiveness and the maturity of the girls. They are still laughing, farting, falling all over each other, and taking off their shoes and advertising their smelly feet when girls want to be taken seriously. Though there are, of course, thousands of moments of tolerance between the sexes, there are also many moments of sexual tension and gender misunderstanding.

After Carol Gilligan wrote that girls "lose their voices" in early adolescence as they enter the sexual milieu—she called it the sexual marketplace—educators embraced the idea that all-girls classes would allow girls to express their opinions, take risks in science and math, and remain focused on achievement rather than losing their self-confidence. This has been and continues to be a powerful argument on behalf of girls' schools. However, the fact remains that girls are outstripping boys in educational achievement in the United States (see more on page 315), whatever the level of their self-confidence. (Boys appear to express more self-confidence than girls, even when they are doing poorly.) And girls are outperforming boys whether they are in all-girls schools or coed schools.

Advocates for single-sex education for boys, such as Leonard Sax, base their argument on brain differences between the genders. To me, the brain research is neither complete enough nor conclusive enough to support this position. In any case, boys' and girls' brains are far more similar than they are different, far more human than gendered.

From my point of view, the most compelling reason for all-boys classes comes from systems theory. When you move boys from a coed class to an all-boys class, you dramatically change the dynamics of the system. If a class is composed of just boys, they cannot dismiss learning as a "girl thing"; they cannot outsource reading and good behavior to the girls. If the class is full of boys, then learning must necessarily be a boy thing. Some are better at it and some are worse, but it is a male pursuit, because in such a class a boy finds that his classmates, competitors, companions, and intellectual colleagues are all male. He has to measure himself by a male standard, and the natural male competitiveness drives them to try to do better than the others.

I interviewed a group of sixth-grade boys from a school that had split the entire sixth grade into single-sex classes for English. I asked the boys to tell me their theories about why the adults would have chosen to divide them by gender. Here are some of their answers:

Boys and girls tend to behave differently. They are more rowdy when they're together. They get along better when it is separate.

When boys and girls are together, boys are trying to impress each other.

The girls are always trying to find a way to get us to fall for them.

Boys don't care. Girls read every chapter, you know.

Most of the girls, and a couple of the boys, are like three chapters ahead. We just read what we're supposed to.

Public education is never going to convert to single-sex education, nor do I believe it should. There are too many economic, social, and cultural reasons for coed schools. Indeed, the fundamental rationale for coeducation is economic; no small town wants to build two schools when it can construct just one. What is fascinating to me, however, is that we are having a debate even though we lack conclusive evidence that either type of school, coeducational or single-sex, is superior to the other. So I believe we should experiment and discover the best practices for boys and girls. Perhaps some common practices in the modern classroom, such as the emphasis

> *Boys like history. They get that it's a story. They like the intrigue, fascinating facts, wars, heroic deeds. Boys enjoy grossness, so I try to include some grossness and goriness in social studies.* —Fifth-grade teacher

on collaborative groups, desks facing each other, and writing in journals, favor girls. Perhaps boys miss reading fact-based biographies and competitions such as spelling bees that have been dropped from the modern curriculum.

Experiments in single-sex education will move us beyond the talk stage to the discovery of good practices for both genders. I believe the right place to launch single-sex educational experiments is middle school, because of the inevitable stresses between the genders as a result of puberty. "The worst is not being able to read girls' minds. And then being shorter than a girl," one boy said. For a boy of this age in a coed school, the ABC's of girls are a complex and compelling course of study.

CHAPTER EIGHT

MYSTERY BOY

What Is He Thinking? Ages Fourteen and Fifteen

He's fourteen—damned if I know what's going on in his inner life right now.
—Father of a fourteen-year-old boy

I COULD WRITE A CHAPTER CELEBRATING ONLY THE ABILITIES AND MOST endearing qualities of fourteen- and fifteen-year-old boys, because they are delightful. Parents have described their sons this age to me as funny, warm, kind, relaxed, sensitive, slow to anger, quick to forgive, easygoing, good-humored, brave, shy, confident, profound, compassionate, funny, empathetic, persevering, solid, mature, funny, intelligent, confident, enthusiastic, caring, honest, fragile, cerebral, athletic, tender, and did I say funny?

"He is relaxed (my daughters are much less relaxed) and has the best sense of humor of anyone I know," said the mother of a fifteen-year-old boy. "I love his view of the world." When her son spent a study year away from home last year, when he was fourteen, "the household balance was way off-kilter," she said. "There was no one to add humor and perspective to things girls and women get stressed out about. Now he's back and all is right with the world, or at least family life."

The father of a fourteen-year-old boy said: "I love spending any time with him. I love to watch him grow. I love to hear his observations about anything. I love to see him learning new things."

So that's settled. Fourteen- and fifteen-year-old boys will warm, even melt your heart—between the palpitations they cause. Those very same parents, talking about those very same boys, go on to describe the qualities they find so baffling, frustrating, and sometimes deeply concerning about their sons. The boys are disorganized, inexpressive, messy, irreverent, behind the curve, sloth-like, stubborn, dishonest, careless, prideful, self-centered, unmotivated, unthinking, unconcerned, sluggish, crude, disorganized, argumentative, hot-tempered, secretive, irresponsible, immature, lazy, confused, self-serving, self-centered, self-involved—and did I say disorganized?

Some parents are delighted by middle-adolescent boys; they love their independence, their competence, their humor, and how irreverent they are. They love having mature discussions with these boys, who are now abstract thinkers, able to articulate opinions and critique the adult world—when they feel like talking to you. Others are put off, unnerved, or overwhelmed by the challenge of managing that kind of boy energy when parental authority just doesn't impress them as it once did.

But whether you love the age or not, every parent of a mid-adolescent boy swings from curiosity to confusion to consternation as their sons come of age—specifically *this* age. A father wrote to me saying that at younger ages much of the time it didn't matter whether your children were boys or girls, but starting at fourteen, "gender really matters" and must be taken into account by parents in everything they do. Of course, the rationale for this book is that gender matters all the way through a boy's life and that we must never underestimate its power, both as a biological phenomenon and as a psychological one. However, I agree with the father that gender *really* matters at this age, because boys are powerfully influenced both by their own testosterone and by the behavior of other boys who are similarly influenced by hormones, as well as the behavior of girls, who add another hormone-sensitive variable to the social and emotional equation. Equally important is the fact that boys are shaping their own identities as young men even though they do not yet feel they are men. The pursuit of maleness and the definition of self as masculine are paramount for boys at this age.

This is a real problem for parents as they feel their sons slipping out of their grasp and moving toward independence. Said the father of another fourteen-year-old, "When I was a kid, I remember my parents talking to me about the 'evils' of sex, drugs, and rock-and-roll music. Now I just worry about the sex and drugs. Getting lost in today's world, even for brief periods of time, can be so damaging to kids, and I worry that he may not be strong enough to pull himself out of something if he gets into trouble or runs with the wrong sort of kids."

This is the age when it's typical for the divergence between boys' views and those of their parents to start to be pronounced. Boys are thinking, *No problem!* Parents are thinking . . . well, often they don't know what to think. For now, let's turn to the parental view. Then we'll step behind the persona of your teenage son and see his world as he does.

Parents of middle-adolescent boys are very likely to focus on their concerns, and it drives their sons crazy. A boy of this age is likely to think: *Here I am, getting to school on time every day (pretty much), being a good friend to my friends, helping my parents around the house (when they ask me), trying to get to know some girls, and playing my video games, and all my parents can focus on is the C I'm getting in history and the fact that my room is a mess. What's with them? They're so unreasonable. I'm getting three B's, and if my room bothers my mom so much, all she has to do is close the door. I'm a pretty good kid and they don't mention it; they don't seem to notice it. Why don't they say they're proud of me?*

Instead, if I am that boy's parents, I am going to zoom in first on the C grades, the clothes all over the floor, and the fact that even the abstract thinkers seem to close the door on conversation with their parents. These are the things that parents worry about—often needlessly.

Please remember throughout this chapter that the majority of adolescent boys are not depressed, not rebellious, and not underachieving. They may be doing things to irritate you, such as putting highly erotic posters of women in skimpy bikinis up on their bedroom walls; they may have different priorities than you do. Nevertheless, the vast majority are healthy, happy boys growing toward productive adulthoods.

For as long as I have been working with boys and their parents, more than thirty years, the most common parental worries about boys have had a timeless predictability to them. In the teenage years, particularly at the ages of fourteen and fifteen, moms and dads worry about what is going on inside their son's head. What are they thinking about? And how do you get them to talk to you?

P.J.: A Mother's Love, Loss, and the "Things I Should Have Done"

P.J. had just about the toughest elementary school experience that you could imagine. Aggressive and impulsive as a little boy, he did not get control of his anger at four and five, when most boys do. At seven, he could not tolerate frustration of any kind and was still throwing occasional, out-of-control temper tantrums if he felt a teacher had been unfair or had humiliated him. When I interviewed him on camera for the PBS Raising Cain documentary, he recalled that his female teacher, unable to control him physically, would call for the janitors, the only men in his elementary school building, to help her. "It took two janitors to hold me down," he told me with a shrug that mixed embarrassment and pride. His anger had been so great that he had scared off other children, and years later—I met him when he was in eighth grade—he was still somewhat socially isolated because other children well remembered how unpredictable he could be.

P.J. was a boy seriously at risk in early elementary school. It was his mother who had fought for him, getting him to mental health professionals who diagnosed him with ADHD and put him on medication that helped him control himself in school. She was the one who got him a counselor and required him to keep going to therapy for eight years. She stuck by him, fighting to keep him in mainstream classes when the school wanted to put him in special ed. classes for kids with emotional problems. She supported him with everything she had, even though she was a very young and inexperienced mother. She had married P.J.'s father when she was seventeen and he was twenty-two; P.J. was born shortly thereafter.

P.J.'s mother died at the end of a Halloween evening of trick-or-treating and seeing family—"it was my mother's favorite time of year"—just after he had diapered his six-month-old half sister at her request. "Can you do me one more favor?" she had asked him, and requested that he find her asthma pump. He couldn't locate it right away; by the time he did find it in her purse she was in serious distress. "Something is hurting me. I'm scared," she said, and she abruptly walked downstairs only to sink suddenly to the floor. "Keep breathing," P.J. told her, and held her in his arms. He remembered: "At that point I started screaming, telling her to breathe. I tried to pump her heart. I called 911 and said, 'I need an ambulance right now!' " But by the time the ambulance arrived it was too late. She had had a heart attack, and P.J. had been the only one with her. She was thirty-one years old. P.J. looked at me and asked:

You know what it's like to have your mom die in front of you? To know if you could have been five seconds quicker that you could have saved her, you could have helped her. . . . And I can't do anything but sit there and scream. I couldn't do anything to help her. To this day I don't think I can forgive myself. The one last thing she said, she told me that she loved me and she loved the kids too. And I said, "Everything is going to be okay." And I should have been able to help her. My best wasn't enough.

P.J. told me the whole story during an hour-and-a-half-long interview during which he cried continuously, tearing paper towels off a roll to dry the tears that kept flowing. His life has changed totally since her death.

Life was one way when my mom was around. Everything was in motion. I just had to go out and reach for it. Now I have to do things on my own, way more than before.

He now lives with his dad; luckily, he had a good relationship with his father even after his parents divorced (there is a very tender scene between father and son in the documentary). His father insists that P.J. do his own laundry, do the dishes, and help out in many practical ways, "so when I'm on my own I won't be lost." But emotionally he is lost, totally bereft and full of regret. Everything reminds him of his mother and what they could have experienced together.

It's the worst feeling in the world. And now that I think about how I used to . . . she used to ask me to go places with her and I used to say, "Naw, get out of here. I'm not going nowhere." I should have gone everywhere with her. The things that I did, I wouldn't have done. The things that I should have done. . . .

His voice trailed off; there are so many things he should have done, he said. I asked him whether he watches the Raising Cain video to see her, and he told me that he does, especially to see the early-morning scene at home. "I've watched it many times, just to hear her voice. She used to wake me up, saying 'P.J., time to get up, I love you.' " He concluded:

To tell you the truth, the one thing I would still ask of God—if he could pull that off, I would believe in God—if I could have one more day with her, have a conversation, go for a drive, take a walk with her. To dance with her. If I can do one of those things, just one,

I'd be the happiest person on the planet. I'd be happier than the happiest bride on earth, who just got married to the man of her dreams.

When mothers complain about the disrespect or distance of fourteen- and fifteen-year-old boys, I always remind them of two things. First, if you had a close relationship with your son and he did talk to you when he was young, even if he is pushing you away now, he is likely to open up again when he feels that he has achieved his manhood. Perhaps his sense of manhood will come with driving, or having a sexual relationship with a girl, or with going away to college; it is hard to predict exactly why or when, but at a certain point he will feel secure enough not to have to fight the psychologically regressive pull that his mother exerts. He will just be able to accept you and your love and support. Second, I remind them that every war historian who has ever written about young soldiers seriously wounded in battle has described how, as they lie dying, they invariably call out for their mothers. It is not an exaggeration to say that a mother is the foundation of her son's psyche from the beginning to the end of his life.

This perennial concern swept the nation as a panic in 1999, when I was on an extended book tour for *Raising Cain*. The book had been published six days before two desperately angry, unhappy boys armed with guns murdered thirteen people at Columbine High School in Littleton, Colorado, and then killed themselves. The American people were distraught, worried about boys, and frightened of them, and the media wanted answers. Radio and television stations were anxious to have boy "experts" give advice about how future school shootings could be prevented. I went on the road to try to provide some explanations.

The interviews continued for weeks and months, and I became accustomed to fielding the same questions about boys from city to city. However, I was struck by the fact that right after the cameras and lights were turned off, an anchorwoman or cameraman would turn to me and ask in all sincerity, "Could my son turn violent? He's fifteen and he doesn't talk to me." How was it that so many educated, hardworking, dedicated parents were both baffled by their sons and potentially afraid of what was inside them? Why didn't they feel they knew their own sons better?

I would quickly ask some follow-up questions of the anchorwoman or cameraman and would hear that her or his son was doing pretty well in school, had good friends, was playing in the band or was on a sports team, and admired his teacher or coach. I would then try to reassure the parent that it sounded to me as if her or his son was on track developmentally. However, I could see that any relief my words brought was momentary. Though they were grateful for my efforts, what they really wanted was to feel reassured by their own sons. They wanted to hear their sons say something more than "I'm fine. Don't worry about me," because parents of boys this age cannot possibly accept that at face value. After all, so often when a boy does a shocking, unspeakable thing and makes headlines, the news coverage includes interviews with parents or other adults who say the boy seemed "normal," or even if he was withdrawn or depressed, there was no indication that he was about to do something so terrible. Although subsequently details typically emerge that suggest there were indeed earlier indications for serious concern, the initial cluelessness of parents haunts us. "I know my son would never do anything like that," a worried mother told me, "but what do I really know? The truth is he doesn't talk to me about anything anymore, so when some boy somewhere goes over the edge, I realize how little I really know about my own son anymore. That parent could be me."

What makes our sons such strangers to us, and what makes even the normal pulling away of this age so uncomfortable for us? First, our sons' insistence on privacy hurts our feelings. Second, we are aware that they lie to us, and that's worrisome. Third, they may have a hidden life, compounding our worry.

For developmental reasons, a boy of this age seizes control of the flow of information about his life, and he can be quite stingy about sharing facts or thoughts with his parents. Just sensing that they are no longer in control can make many parents feel helpless. This is a predictable developmental phenomenon on the boy's part; nevertheless, it often feels like a personal betrayal, particularly if you have enjoyed a close relationship with your son during his early years.

As for lying, everyone who was ever an adolescent him- or herself—and that means everyone who is reading this book—is aware that teenagers either lie outright to their parents or choose not to mention things. They also are spending more and more time away from their parents, in the company of other boys (and girls) in houses that may or may not be supervised. How can you stay current with your son's life when he is a reluctant reporter? One mother commented:

The most difficult and worrying aspect is that pretty early on my sons, particularly the eldest, discovered that the less I knew about his interests, friends, goings-on, the better off he thought he was. I worked very hard at not prying, not seeming too interested, but I knew that I needed to be informed about many things.

Every parent who wants to respect her son's developmental need for privacy also is aware that he may be facing serious social and psychological challenges that are part and parcel of adolescence in the United States. Nearly every parent who responded to my survey talked about the temptations of drugs, alcohol, and Internet porn, and the impact these things might have on their sons. Some discussed girls luring their sons into early sexuality and were worried about the risks of unwanted pregnancy or sexually transmitted diseases, as well as a future of shallow relationships instead of loving ones.

> *When I was young I used to view my parents as all-knowing and think that I could never be on a par with them at anything, but as I have matured I realize that though they may be older and have had way more time on earth to learn, I can sometimes be the one who is teaching them.* —Boy, fifteen

A mother's worst fear is that something dangerous is happening in her son's life and she won't see it, hear it, or know about it. That fear came true for Shane's mother when she saw that her fourteen-year-old son had been "cutting" on his arm. Cutting, a type of self-mutilation that involves making shallow cuts on the skin, is typically associated with depression or other serious emotional distress.

SHANE: OFF AND RUNNING—INTO TROUBLED TERRITORY

"I'm not goth," Shane told me. "I'm an emo—emotional hardcore music, or emotionally outraged punk." Right from the start of our interview it was clear that Shane wanted to be precise, so that I would understand him on his own terms. And I appreciated it, because, like most adults, I cannot distinguish between the different types of alternative adolescent music or clothing styles. His hair is dyed black, and I remembered that he'd been wearing black gloves with the fingers cut off the last time I saw him. I could easily (and erroneously) have concluded that he was goth.

Shane is fourteen and handsome, with delicate features and an almost painfully thin frame that is usually clothed in tight black pants and a long-sleeved shirt. He looks like he is starving. His mother told me, "He doesn't eat much." Shane was leaning against a wall, half in shadow, and remained there for much of our interview. I was reminded of the many music videos that begin with a young man standing in the dark, alone, perhaps alienated or in pain or angry. Shane is all three. Though he was unfailingly polite—even sweet at times—in his conversation with me, he wanted me to understand his predicament. "I don't feel unwanted. I feel overwanted. They're trying to help me. They need to give me a little bit of freedom. I'm under house arrest. They say I have to show responsibility, but I need responsibility to show responsibility."

What did he mean by "overwanted" and "house arrest"? He was referring to the fact that he has been grounded indefinitely by his parents. His mother and stepfather are watching his every move because two weeks before our interview, Shane and two pals had run away from home. The police tracked them down after just a few days, following a trail of cell phone and ATM card use, and their bold bid for independence had ended abruptly where you would expect to find three eighth-grade kids at the end of the day: at home.

I once heard a parent say that life with her teenage son felt like Mr. Toad's wild ride, referring to the careening, car-crazed capers of Mr. Toad in the classic novel *The Wind in the Willows*. She was laughing at the time, and indeed, the image is fitting for the wild ride of adolescence: the rate of growth, physical and psychological, accelerates dramatically at puberty, sometimes dragging both boy and parents behind it. But for many boys, including Shane, their story takes a hard turn into darker terrain.

As we talked, Shane discounted his parents' concerned responses as ineffectual, misguided, emotional reactions, often based on old information. An insider to the lives of his friends, he pointed out that parents routinely miss clues or misread them, always one step behind the boys and their risky behaviors. The parents react to curfew violations and miss the hidden drinking. They react to blatant drinking and miss the screwup that triggered the binge. They catch a screwup and treat it like it's some big deal.

In his own case, Shane explained, it was his mother's discovery some months back that he had been cutting that had prompted her to send him to a psychiatrist. At my request, he rolled up his left sleeve and displayed a forearm with about fifty thin, pale scars. He explained that he usually made about five cuts per session. "It never actually hurt that much. It gives you a sense of your own mortality and takes away the emotional pain. I was just depressed. It wouldn't have to be anything that would make me depressed. I'd just do it and it helped."

The Eight Lines of Development

The Developmental Story Advances

Your son may be taller than you by now, or soon will be, and whatever authority your size once earned you in his younger eyes is history now. The key for a parent of a boy this age is to retain your moral authority when this new big boy presents you with unexpected challenges. He needs you to recognize that he is both a rapidly changing new person and the very same boy you have always known. It is when their boys reach about fourteen or fifteen that parents begin to speak of them as if they were aliens. That's a mistake. You need to recognize your beloved little boy in this new body—but *never* let on that you do.

Physical Development

Though a few late-starting boys are just embarking on puberty at fourteen, most boys of fifteen have achieved enough growth that the full impact of puberty on their bodies is now evident. They may have young-looking faces, but they have adult male genitals, long legs, and big shoulders, and for the first time in several years, they are taller than the girls around them. For a boy like Zach, who grew seven inches in the twelve months before turning fifteen, his new height is the central fact of his life: it affects his athletic career and his standing in his family because he is a foot taller than his mother and within striking distance of his father's height of six feet four inches. His height also affects his social standing in school, because he is taller than many of the junior and senior boys in his school and will be forever. Some junior and senior boys may see him as an upstart competitor and make a special effort to put him in his place. Girls who saw him as immature in the eighth and ninth grades are now literally looking up at him. So are many teachers!

Because their athletic classmates are getting so much attention from high-status girls, the nonathletes start to define themselves aggressively as counterathletic. In early high school the boys start breaking up into "jocks" and "preps," "geeks," and "freaks." Though there are numerous criteria at work in the shaping of male social groups, such as race and class (we will discuss them below), one of the bedrock distinctions for all boys is "athletic" or "nonathletic."

The problem for nonathletic boys is that in their eagerness to embrace their own interests and identity—whether that is debate, band, art, drama, Scholastic Bowl, or video gaming at home—exercise can vanish from their life.

If you are a parent of a fourteen- or fifteen-year-old boy, you have almost no influence on whether your son is motivated to be an athlete or not. There simply are boys whose male identity is not connected to sports. Many simply prefer physically demanding recreational pursuits. Happily, there is much physical work that a fourteen-year-old boy can do around the house, and you should ask him to do it. There is exercise to be had—and allowance money to be made—mowing lawns, washing cars, taking out the trash, and raking leaves. Also, you need not and should not drive your son everywhere; he can walk or bicycle at least some of the time.

Attachment

At this age, attachments are not as much based on actual physical dependence as they were in the past. Fourteen- and fifteen-year-olds spend hours and whole days away from their parents, so these are ages when a boy experiences himself to be big enough and competent enough to come and go as he pleases. For the boy whose home life is abusive or who finds his attachments too complex and painful, the idea of running away becomes a daring but realistic option. As a practical matter, in modern society it is extraordinarily difficult for a boy of that age to support himself, and in most cases—sadly, not all—the police are likely to find him if his parents have reported his departure, as Shane's parents did. However, the idea that he could theoretically look after himself has a profound effect on a boy's psychology. His attachments suddenly have an elective quality at this age. He doesn't *have* to love you, he chooses to love you. He doesn't *have* to respect his dad, he chooses to do so, and he likely may say exactly that in a verbal fight.

A boy feels he must regulate both his distance from his parents and his response to them; there are times when he blocks you from being attuned to him as you have been all of his life. While this is intensely frustrating for mothers, fathers tend to be more relaxed about it, either because they have not been as closely attuned to their sons or because they remember doing the same thing to their parents. "Don't bug him," they say to their wives.

At the same time that he may be opting out of the mother-son bond, he needs profound attachments in life because every human being does. So a boy may turn to a favorite coach, a teacher, the leader of an extracurricular activity at school, or a camp counselor. Here is someone he can idealize and even love; though boys avoid the word, I am witness to the fact that boys really do love their mentors at this time of life, and that the mentor-mentee relationship in school has all of the same structural elements of adult mentor relationships in business, for example. These strong attachments are an evolution of the parental attachments to include an outside person that allows a boy to grow in new ways.

One of the greatest gifts that a parent can give her son during this period is the psychological permission to make a close relationship with another adult. Such relationships can be life-changing for a boy. One of the greatest fears of parents, however, even as they give permission for their son to make an outside-the-family relationship, is that their vulnerable, idealizing boy will fall into the hands of a pedophile. By now, your son should know (from talks with you over the years) and trust that he can tell you if ever he is subjected to inappropriate advances by an adult (or anyone, for that matter). What is left for you to do now is get to know the person who is mentoring your son well enough so that you trust him, and then back off and let the relationship develop without your presence. A confiding relationship with an adult can help a boy feel connected and respected, which can help him sidestep many of the serious risk factors of adolescence.

Social Development

Earlier in the chapter we discussed the changing shape of boys' social lives, most notably the male culture of cruelty, and the emerging interest in girls. Boys become deeply attached to their friends, their group, and, unfortunately for some, their gang. This happens to boys from the most loving, intact families as well as to boys from the most dysfunctional families. Psychologist Ron Taffel calls the relationship between teens "the second family" and worries that peers are displacing the family in the life of contemporary American adolescents. This may be more true than ever, but it has long been the fear of parents as they see their influence wane and the effects of peer pressure increase. In the normal course of a boy's development, peers replace parents as a source of companionship, excitement, and good feeling at this age—and also as a source of emotional support and advice.

Cognitive Development

"How do I get my son to think about the future?" the father of a ninth grader once asked me. "I want him to focus on college," the dad said. "He doesn't act as if it means anything to him." Though at fifteen he may be taller than his mother and just as tall as his father, his capacity for planning ahead is not as developed as that of his parents. Many aspects of his thinking are not yet adult.

Through adolescence, boys are developing many different cognitive skills at different rates. Most important from an academic point of view is that a boy's ability to engage in hypothetical-deductive reasoning is growing, and this allows him to test the logic of a proposition in his own mind. His short-term memory may be improving as well, and that allows him to hold several ideas in mind simultaneously and compare them with one another. However, not all boys become sophisticated abstract thinkers. In early high school a boy may run into either the limits of his innate capacity or his developmental timetable. This is the boy who settles in as a steady C student, doing his best for the time being.

Most of the content in elementary school can be mastered with the proper teaching and hard work on the student's part. As the material increases in complexity, hard work and good preparation are not sufficient for complete mastery. Students must possess a greater cognitive capacity to handle the more difficult, abstract material in high school, and they have to be exposed to formal operational problems that will stir them to become abstract thinkers. High school courses are typically tracked, with the brighter kids going into the "honors" and "college prep" tracks that require formal operational thinking and less academically inclined or less motivated students winding up in the "regular" or "remedial" tracks.

Tracking is controversial, because it deprives some students of the opportunity to be challenged by high-level material or to hear sophisticated, logical discussions, but it is not irrational. It is tougher for a teacher to cover sophisticated material when the class is made up of a mixture of concrete operational thinkers and formal operational thinkers, and some students are simply overwhelmed by the cognitive complexity of the material. In most of the rest of the developed world, there is a significant separation of students at age twelve, thirteen, or fourteen between the highly academic students and those who are not as academically capable. In Japan, for instance, students take an entrance exam for admission to an academic high school; those who fail the test go to a remedial high school in which they simply complete their elementary school skills and learn a trade. That was always the case in England, where twelve-year-olds took the O-level exams and were sorted out into more and less academic programs.

As a parent, you always want to support your son's potential, but until now it may not have been clear whether that potential lies in sophisticated academic work or some other field of endeavor. By ninth grade your son's teachers will know whether he possesses the powers of reasoning, metacognition (the ability to think about thinking), and the ability to think in unconventional and imaginative ways that will allow him to do sophisticated academic work. If he does, then he'll be equipped for coursework that requires it; whether he is motivated to do it remains to be seen. However, if your son is not developmentally equipped for that academic rigor, it can be a setup for chronic struggle and failure. You support your son's fullest potential by respecting the mind he has and supporting the most challenging and appropriate academic placement for him.

Academic Development

As a general rule, it is possible to differentiate between the more capable and less capable students by the beginning of high school, but that is not invariably the case with boys. Because they mature more slowly than girls in all ways, it is possible that you may have a late bloomer, cognitively, emotionally, or in terms of his ability to organize himself. I have certainly seen boys who seemed to wake up and focus in middle to late adolescence, suddenly becoming much stronger students. I have seen inspiring high school teachers energize and motivate boys who had disliked school previously. Many men have told me that they did not become sophisticated thinkers until they arrived in college and applied themselves to a problem that seemed relevant and related to an eventual occupation.

If you hope to help your son achieve in high school, whatever his level of innate academic ability, the best thing you can do is help him with time management and organization. More than anything, the average boy in high school struggles with being disorganized. Boys tend to carry everything with them in their backpacks because they are physically strong, but they do not know what they have in them. If it were up to me, the majority of boys would be enrolled in study-skills classes and would be taught how to use planners and how to manage their homework time. Such skills would be every bit as important to them in life as the content of advanced classes that they may or may not remember. In any case, because so few high school boys will show their work to their parents, and even if they did, many parents are not capable of helping their sons with the content of advanced courses, the one thing that parents can do to help ninth and tenth graders is to remind them to attend to their work, to limit screen time, and ask them whether it is done. If it isn't done, it may help to ask them where they are in it, how it's going, what's left to do, and what their strategy is for completing on time—though not all those questions at once. Sometimes they may stall out in the process of taking an assignment from start to finish, and attention to the process itself offers them a chance to step back and see where they're stuck, and a way to reason through how to get back on track. Some boys do not need this monitoring, some will accept it, and others will resent it and fight it. You will need to work out what role he will let you play in his academic life, but I believe you may still have a role in the first two years of high school; it will be less and less, if any, in the junior and senior years.

One thing over which you likely still have some control is television viewing. Remember the substantial research linking television time with academic woes. In just one of the most recent studies, researchers at Columbia University College of Physicians and Surgeons and New York University School of Medicine reported that frequent television viewing during adolescence was associated with higher risk for attention problems, learning difficulties, poor homework completion, and adverse long-term educational outcomes. Maybe your son is tuning in to TV because he is already turned off to school for other reasons. Whatever his reasons for turning it on, TV is unlikely to make matters anything but worse.

Emotional Self-Regulation

Adolescent self-control and judgment seem to go backward in late middle school and early high school. Boys appear to their parents to be more sullen and less joyful, more egocentric and less helpful than they may have seemed just a year or two earlier. They now avoid things in the family that they used to enjoy. They suddenly are embarrassed by their parents or younger siblings in public and can turn angry when family members inadvertently act in ways that make them feel acutely self-conscious or ashamed. My own mother's voice rings in my ears: when I turned fourteen she began to complain, "Where has my sunny boy gone?" When she asked it, it would infuriate me. It seemed to me a demand that I stay a little boy and not grow up.

Hormonal shifts are partially responsible for the mood changes of early adolescence, and there is nothing that a parent can do about hormones. A boy has to become accustomed to the new messages and impulses that are racing around his body. Perhaps you can require that your son get enough sleep, negotiating reasonable school night hours and allowing him to sleep late on weekends, because boys of this age need enormous amounts of sleep. They might naturally nap throughout the day, alternating moments of high energy with complete lassitude.

As we have discussed, much about a boy's mood depends on context. Is he with his friends or his family? Does he feel that he is in control of his destiny, or does he feel that he is being bossed around by adults? As a school consultant, I have watched teachers work with fourteen- and fifteen-year-olds, and if I were to characterize their successful techniques for working with this age student, it would be to maintain a sense of humor, don't get into power struggles, allow them to express themselves before you express yourself, and give them a physical outlet.

Boys will gradually gain more control over their emotional lability and their need for impulsive, exhibitionistic displays. Senior boys laugh at ninth-grade boys when they see such behaviors, both because they are so "immature" and because the senior boys well remember that they were like that two short years ago. If you want to be reassured that your ninth-grade son is going to get a grip on his emotions, go watch some senior boys. They will seem enormously mature by comparison with your emotionally raw son.

One of the ways that boys continue to control their emotions is to work at being stoic. While we usually refer to the *problems* of stoicism for boys, there is a reasonable, healthy role for stoicism in adult life; it enables us to keep our emotions in check as we work through challenging moments. The only thing you need to worry about as a parent is whether your son's apparent stoicism is depression and/or whether he has started to treat his emotional distress with drugs and alcohol.

But avoiding contact with adults who might provoke them—that is, their parents—and suppressing their feelings is a normal developmental phase at this age. Though this is frustrating for moms and dads, you have to learn to respect this rather rigid form of self-control. It helps a boy maintain his sense of masculinity and his dignity when he is full of feeling. He will gradually become more open once he is acclimated to his growth, once he develops a better vocabulary of feelings (girlfriends are a help with this), and once he has a more solid identity.

Moral and Spiritual Development

Perhaps the most prominent aspect of the early high school boy's approach to spirituality is skepticism and even cynicism. Why is that so? As they develop a greater ability to question the logic of adult propositions, boys become more critical of absolutes, and they can see the double standard at work in adult behavior. Being no longer as intimidated by authority, they feel freer to question it. Identifying adult hypocrisy is a major occupation of ninth- and tenth-grade boys; they can be both accurate in their perceptions and withering in their criticisms. Remember Mark Twain's much-quoted observation: "When I was a boy of fourteen, my father was so ignorant I could hardly stand to have the old man around. But when I got to be twenty-one, I was astonished by how much he'd learned in seven years."

This critical stance toward adults stands in stark contrast to the rather flexible, self-forgiving morality of middle adolescents. From an adult point of view, adolescent boys often break rules, can give no reason for doing so, and display little remorse. That is because they are playing a different game than the adults are; they are testing themselves, taking risks, and holding to a morality that makes their group of friends the most important moral touchstone in their lives. Being loyal to the group, not being a "rat," protecting his friends from being discovered drinking beer or smoking marijuana—these may be the highest form of morality for a fifteen-year-old boy, who is likely to be a Stage 3 moral thinker in Kohlberg's scheme describing progressive stages of moral development. The stage is characterized as the "good child" stage mentioned earlier, but at this age that also means being a good friend, which may put a boy into frequent moral conflict.

The group is so important to a boy that at times his strongest need is to be a good group member in his own eyes and in the eyes of his friends. There are other times when he will want to be a good person in the eyes of his family or his girlfriend, but without being grounded in a Stage 4 understanding of rules and laws, his morality is attached to the opinion and behavior of others around him. Asked by an adult why he committed some moral transgression, he will shrug and say, "I don't know," but what he means is: *I am a conventional thinker. I was going along with the group and trying to be a good friend. Now I see that while I was loyal to my buddies, I failed to be a good son or a good member of the community, but hey . . . I was with them at the time.* As a parent, you need to hold your son morally accountable while understanding that his new life outside the family will put him into frequent moral dilemmas: friends versus family, friends versus school.

Identity

In the years of childhood, a boy is dependent for his identity on his parents, his brothers and sisters, his church, his neighborhood, his personal interests, and the sports team he roots for. As he grows up, much of his identity is provided by his social groups, the "uniform" he chooses to wear (prep, hip-hop, goth, etc.) and the labels that are available to him, or affixed to him, in high school. Is he a "nerd" or a "prep" or a "freak"? If others call him that, must he accept it? In the next chapter I interview a young gay man in college who said he was labeled as "gay" from the beginning of middle school but who rejected the label. He knew he was homosexual, but he did not accept the label of "gay" in the way the boys in school used it against him. He denied it, fought back against it, and competed in many different ways in an effort to prove he was not "gay" in the way they meant it. He still does not accept the label fully. This tendency to react against a label—"that's not who I am"—is characteristic of this age.

Identity is not complete at this age. Critics of the concept of identity claim it is never an absolutely permanent or stable part of the personality. That may be so, but it is demonstrably more solid in early adulthood than it is at fourteen. When Zach tried to define himself for me, he said:

Yeah. I see myself as someone who is kind of content with being a little bit above average. I don't have to be the greatest soccer player, the smartest kid in the class. I'll never be left behind. . . . I don't want to sacrifice being a good student or a good friend just to be one thing. . . . In school I work hard and that's been working for me. . . . I try to be respectful to adults, I try to be nice to my friends, I try to be funny.

If identity is the part of the psyche that guides and directs the self, it relies on self-knowledge, self-control, a sense of continuity, and a sense of coherence to maintain direction. There are not many tenth graders who have a firm sense of all four. They are often surprised by their own actions, may lose self-control with some frequency, and may change identity as they move from school to home, from one social group to another, or from home to work. At this stage of adolescence, a boy's identity is not yet complete. It won't be until he achieves a measure of independence from his parents.

Not surprisingly, the doctor diagnosed depression and prescribed antidepressants. Shane questioned the point of all that drama and the drugs. "I was cutting myself. I forgot to put on a sweatshirt one day and my mom saw. I don't think about suicide. I've never actually thought about a plan to kill myself."

The cutting was what got his mom worked up, he said, "but I had not been cutting for months when they saw me." And as for depression, "I don't consider myself depressed now," he told me. "I have been on antidepressants for two months." He expressed doubts about whether the medication was helping him. I asked why he hadn't fought being put on medication. His answer: "It didn't matter to me. I wasn't cutting anymore."

If you wonder how someone so bright could acknowledge that he had been depressed, so much so that he engaged in cutting, and then argue that a diagnosis of depression and treatment with medication amounted to an overreaction by an intrusive mother, you are thinking like an adult. Even a boy with a keen intellect, as Shane has, can't will his brain, mind, and body to mature on command, quickly and evenly.

Earlier in our conversation Shane had wanted to talk about books, and he told me that he has an IQ of 144 and read *Romeo and Juliet* in fifth grade. He's been spending much of his eighth-grade year reading Faulkner and J. D. Salinger. I asked him about *Catcher in the Rye*. He loved it. He thinks it is a realistic portrayal of adolescence.

Shane described his intellectual isolation at school and how he feels different because of how much he reads. One of the boys on the runaway adventure is an exception. "He's one of only two people as literate as I am," he said. "He's really smart. He reads the same or more than I do.".

As we talked, Shane's tone remained casual. It was hard to tell whether he has the flat affect of a depressed person, or whether his casualness is an affectation, or whether he is really not worried about all of this. He talked about everything—suicidal feelings, psychiatric hospitals, drugs ("Pot was nothing special"), alcohol ("I've only been drunk seven or eight times"), Salinger, and assorted romantic interests—in the same matter-of-fact boy voice. He used the kind of don't-worry-about-me tone that makes adults want to scream, *What do you mean, it was 'no big deal'?* and rend their garments.

Here is a bright boy, just fourteen years old, from a loving family—albeit his parents divorced and his mother is now remarried—who has discarded academics, experimented with drugs and alcohol, engaged in self-mutilation, gotten suspended from school for drunkenness, and run away from home. He is failing several courses at school and will not get credit for his eighth-grade year. In spite of all this evidence, Shane acts as if his life is completely under his control. I use the word *act*, but it wasn't an act. He told me in all sincerity that he just needs to be given more responsibility again. He is not unaware of how adults see all of this; he simply does not share their view of him.

He has a life. He feels something special for his girlfriend, a kind of "caring" for her and from her that he has never experienced with anyone else. He has a good relationship with his dad, who was a seriously rebellious teen himself in high school, and he appreciates that his mother is going to leave him alone, by which he means she will stop bugging him when he turns eighteen, even though right now she will not. He doesn't think in the future tense. He cannot imagine that at eighteen he will feel any different than he does right now. He cannot foresee the day when he might want to go to college and perhaps depend on his parents for four additional years. In his mind, he is world-wise and ready to be independent. He wants to write music and to be a poet. He is already writing poetry.

I asked him whether I could print one of his poems in my book, and he said yes. He printed a poem out, then explained that he does not know why he wrote about being teased. Even though he is seen as nonconformist and a "total druggie" by his schoolmates, after eight years of karate no one will fight him, and he is so much smarter than other boys that "if someone calls me a fag because I wear tight pants, I have a better vocabulary and I'll tease them until they cry." Here is the poem he handed me:

Where have all the good times gone?
To be replaced by teenage angst and woe be gone!
Now they tease and they taunt, they irk and they nag
How I wish it would stop, how I wish they would die!
They call me stupid; they think I don't try,
They're coddled and rich,
They don't know what it's like
To be cold and unwanted
To have no one that cares, to have no one to talk to
How I wish it would stop, how I wish they would die!
How I wish it would stop, how I wish I could die!

As alarming as these lyrics sound, especially the closing lines, they do not foretell that Shane is going to go mad like the shooters at Columbine or Virginia Tech. He is experiencing the angst and isolation and anger that are often part of a boy's adolescent experience. It's all there in the lyrics of the heavy metal music and other music, media, and literature of the age. Many boys listen to the music and write the poetry, and 99.9 percent of them do not commit crimes or kill themselves. In fact, it is the rare one who does.

Having talked more extensively with Shane about his life view and struggles, it was the first two lines of his poem and the angst and isolation they express that I wanted to ask him about. Earlier he had dismissed the changes of puberty as routine, nothing stressful at all. He had read all about it and "wanted it to happen" because he thought it signaled new freedom from his parents. He also wanted to maintain the adolescent boy's stoicism. In a more candid reflection on that period of change and the impact on him, I asked if he thought the changes of puberty might have set off his depression. He answered with some surprise in his voice, but new self-awareness, too, that although he had never thought about it that way before, indeed, the depressive period had followed that period of dramatic change and tension in the family.

Six months after my initial interview with the family, I talked to Shane's stepfather, who said that he and his wife, and their son's psychiatrist, felt he was no longer depressed. That didn't, however, mean that things were smooth; Shane's parents were still trying to stay even with his "wild ride." He and his friends hadn't tried to run away again; that was good news. The bad news was that he was still smoking a lot of weed and was still occasionally skipping school. His father, mother, and stepfather were working hard to communicate with one another and were monitoring and supervising him as closely as they possibly could. Shane was sometimes cooperative and often not. Though he had agreed to go to a new school in the fall, one that specializes in helping "alternative" kids succeed academically, he would sometimes announce that he wasn't going to go to it. All he needed, from his point of view, was to be left alone, to be allowed to spend time with his friends, and to have people not get upset when he drank or smoked marijuana.

The problem with adolescence, for both parents and mental health professionals, has always been that it is difficult to differentiate between a challenging, somewhat rebellious but psychologically healthy adolescence and a clinical problem that needs professional help. Because adolescents experience their feelings so strongly, and fluctuate so dramatically in their reactions to events (and to their parents!) it can be tough to figure out whether a child is experiencing depression or a normal phase. For Shane, who clearly has been depressed in the past, issues of autonomy and identity formation are still central to his development. There is likely to be a lot conflict ahead, conflict that a pill cannot cure. Only steady parenting, including the wisdom to call upon professional and other outside support, offers the safest passage and best possible outcome.

DEPRESSION IN ADOLESCENT BOYS: A LONG WAIT FOR DIAGNOSIS

Did the biological changes of puberty set off Shane's depression? That seems unlikely, because there is no proven connection between the biological changes of puberty and depression in males. Indeed, boys under the age of ten are more likely to be diagnosed with depression than are adolescent boys, while depression is twice as common in teenage girls than in teen boys. After puberty, most boys feel bigger and more confident than they used to, and they enjoy the freedom their parents give them; they feel better than they did when they were younger.

However, the impact of the major physical, social, and intellectual changes that accompany puberty can sometimes hit a boy such as Shane very hard. He had many risk factors in his life that could have precipitated a depression: his mother suffered from depression, his parents divorced when he was six—a particularly vulnerable age for boys to suffer a disruption in the father-son connection—and there had been conflict between them over the years. Shane also possessed a sharp, unconventional mind that permitted him precocious insight into adult

RAISING EMOTIONALLY LITERATE BOYS

While little boys are often emotionally transparent, especially to their mothers, it can be difficult for adults to read the feelings of older boys. Boys lose facial expression from ages seven to fifteen because they are under constant pressure, both internal and external, to present themselves as strong and competent. That is why when you ask them, "How are you?" they typically answer, "Fine." When you ask again they say, "Really fine," which can mean "Don't bug me," "I really am great," "I really don't know much about my-self," or "I don't want to talk about it because I feel terrible inside." Which one is it? How can you tell if your son is okay? And beyond that, how can you tell if he is growing up to be an emotionally literate boy who has the ability to read and communicate about his and others' emotions?

A boy is obviously at risk if he is emotionally illiterate. How can he make a satisfying marriage if he cannot read his wife's feelings? How can he succeed in the workplace if he cannot empathize with others?

Fathers who talk to me about the issue are often concerned that their sons not grow up as locked up as they are. One dad considered emotionally damaged men to be his unfortunate family lineage, and he desperately wanted to change that for his son:

> I don't want my son to be emotionally aloof like my father, and I don't want him to hide from his pain with drugs and alcohol like my older brother and father have done. And I don't want my son to feel like he has to hide his feelings and suffer silently, much like I did as a boy.

Parents often ask how much hiding of feelings is too much. We do not, of course, all show our feelings in the same way; the average boy and girl typically differ on this dimension, and many boys struggle with revealing their feeling life. Why? An eighteen-year-old boy provides an answer:

> The emotion that best describes why I don't show my feelings would definitely be shame. I'm afraid of not being understood. I'm afraid of being laughed at. . . . The scariest thing a man can do is cry because you are throwing yourself on the mercy of others and people can be really cruel. What if people think you're stupid for crying? What do you do then? You have to deal with embarrassing isolation. . . . As a black male I'm not supposed to have fears.

This burden does not affect just young black men. A white high school student wrote:

> As a male, I have experienced many things with emotions, but mainly confusion. Feelings and how males are "supposed" to feel are two completely different things and can cause chaos inside the minds of many men. Personally, I have a few male friends I can talk to, but not too many. I find that I am able to share my thoughts with females with more freedom. I think it may be because the stereo-

type is always there with boys. Even in talking with each other, something seems a little off, as if each time someone might call us gay for talking to each other."

If you are going to communicate with a boy about his feelings, you must do six things. First, understand and acknowledge his pride in his masculinity and the pressure he is under to look strong. Only when he knows you understand his point of view can he feel safe. Second, realize that boys express a lot of feeling through humor. When they appear to be mocking feelings, they are, in fact, telling you what they are feeling. So, for instance, if you had a group of boys on a ropes course who were about to rappel down a cliff, they would all feel scared, but they would likely just tease one boy about his obvious fear. At that point you can say, "Gentlemen, everybody is scared here. Anyone who denies that backing off a cliff is at least a bit frightening is lying to himself. Everyone gets scared up here."

Third, realize that boys express many of their feelings through activity and body posture. You can read boys' body posture and say, "This is hard to talk about, isn't it?" or "Well, I can tell everyone is uncomfortable with this."

Fourth, put your emotional cards on the table first ("I am worried about you, and I don't know whether I should be"; "I can see your mood has changed, and I'm confused by what's happened"). This is especially important for dads. How can you expect your son to share his feelings with you when you insist on looking strong at all times yourself? If I had to give gender-stereotyped advice, I would say that men should model feelings for boys; women should stop expecting boys to express feelings in the way girls do, and stop being disappointed in them when they don't.

Fifth, challenge boys by telling them that emotional courage is real courage. When I am working with boys in groups, talking about family problems or divorce or whatever, I always say something like, "I know this is hard to talk about. It takes guts to do it," or "This isn't easy, so I don't expect everyone to be able to talk here." That gets them to talk, because they feel the challenge.

Sixth and finally, watch carefully and read your son's behavior with others (parents don't always get to see—or rarely see—the best of their sons). If you don't see any signs of empathy in your son, check on whether other adults do see his altruistic side. And then watch how your son treats his siblings and his friends.

Boys won't necessarily use a lot of words; they might never say, "I really love my younger brother," but if your younger son provokes your oldest son and the older one wrestles the younger to the ground using obvious restraint and without really hurting him, you can be pretty sure he loves him and feels fundamentally protective toward him. If a boy responds with empathy to someone who is grieving, if he supports a disappointed teammate with a pat on the back or the butt, if he mentions someone else's pain in passing, if he falls silent and broods in the face of tragedy, you can be sure that your son has feelings and is developing emotional literacy. It just may be too risky for him to talk about it right now.

Be patient. Be available. For as long as it takes.

failings and hypocrisy, only deepening the discouraging view for him. Whatever individual risk factors tipped Shane toward depression, he is one of a significant number of teens who struggle with depressive symptoms.

Fifteen to 20 percent of teens will suffer from symptoms of irritability, sadness, problems in concentrating, worthlessness, loss of energy and interest, and suicidal feelings for some period during the years thirteen to eighteen. Though girls experience more depression than boys, boys are at risk because a boy is likely to go for three years before his depression is diagnosed and treated. Why do boys suffer for so long without their parents or teachers seeing that they are in trouble? There are four reasons.

First, since early boyhood, boys have been socialized to hide "weakness" in order to live up to a masculine ideal of strength and competence. Therefore, when a boy feels anxious, is sad, or lacks energy, he may judge himself to be incompetent and feel deeply ashamed. As a result, he is going to try to hide this "weakness" from his peers and parents so that he does not look like a "wimp." Many boys deal with anxiety and depressive feelings by silently castigating themselves.

Second, because a boy this age is physically away from his parents more than when he was younger, and is also in the process of transforming his relationship with them, he may not be opening up to them as much as he did in the past, and they may not have the chance to read his moods. Indeed, he may be deliberately keeping things from his parents in order to feel more adult. Since he has not practiced talking about his feelings with his friends—that's not generally acceptable in a boy group—he may not have the language to express his internal state. In *Raising Cain*, we called the problem "emotional illiteracy" on the part of boys; they simply haven't had the practice in articulating their internal lives.

Third, he may have found expression for his feelings of depression in an alternative teen culture that parents find off-putting and hard to understand, as Shane did. Though they may not like the lyrics they hear or the black clothes their son wears, they cannot tell whether he is "just" goth or emo or instead is really depressed.

Boys tend to express their depressive feelings in ways that are annoying, infuriating, or antisocial. For a majority of depressed boys, the leading symptoms are irritability and anger. Some express depression by what is called "acting out": drinking, reckless driving, stealing, lying. Adults are often so busy reacting to these as disciplinary matters that they do not look to the underlying sadness or anxiety. Even clinicians can be mistaken about boys this age. One researcher found that one of the chief causes of the late diagnosis of depression in boys was that while clinicians asked girls about their sadness, they did not straightforwardly ask boys whether they felt sad. When I asked Shane, who has cuts all over his arm and is on antidepressants, whether he felt sad, he qualified his response: "I don't feel especially sad. Just kind of morose and really lazy. Not tired, but tired like I want to lie down in a dark room."

Sadness is not a manly or strong feeling. Neither is anxiety, and that is why boys try to hide their severe anxiety states. Whenever I hear of a boy who has stopped going to school in ninth or tenth grade, I don't immediately think that he has just dropped out. I imagine that he has become so anxious that he is afraid to go to school and risk having people see how frightened he has become. I am grateful to the television show *Monk*, whose main character suffers from obsessive-compulsive disorder, one of the most serious of the anxiety disorders. It is good to have people see that boys and men can suffer from terrible anxiety, because they do, but they almost always try to cover it up.

> Boys bounce back quickly. You can write them up one day for cutting your class, and the next day they want to be your best friend. They're often the same way with each other—fighting one day, best friends the next. Girls are not like that—they hold grudges! —High school teacher

Finally, I have spoken to many parents of boys who had rationalized their son's depression as part of the normal rebelliousness of adolescence. As a result of early psychoanalytic concepts permeating popular culture, and frequent media representations of alienated youngsters as representative of most adolescents, we assume that the teenage years will be rocky and rebellious. As Daniel Offer pointed out years ago, that is not the case for the vast majority of boys. Chronic irritability, a decline in academic performance, prolonged apathy, irresponsible behavior, feelings of futility, and excessive sleep or disturbed sleep patterns are *not* a normal part of a boy's adolescence. They are signs of depression. Is it the case that on any given day your adolescent boy can sometimes be irritable, apathetic, and lacking in motivation? You bet! The operative term when it comes to depression is *chronic*.

Sometimes a boy is caught in depressing events or circumstances and needs the time and emotional space to work through them. However, if your son seems sad and psychically paralyzed for weeks at a time, if he is angry all the time, or if he seems driven to do irrational, self-destructive things, you must consider that he may be suffering from clinical depression. When he is psychologically available for open conversation—and I believe that moms and dads know those moments—ask him whether he feels sad. Do not delay in seeking treatment for him. He is likely to fight you, because the thought of seeing a therapist makes him feel weak and defective, and it annoys him. Remember, he may be irritable because of depression; being depressed undermines his sense of strength and masculinity, and he hates that. The fact remains that if he is depressed, he needs help.

THE PROBLEM OF (RELATIVE) BOY ACADEMIC UNDERACHIEVEMENT

Parents who care about academics and grades often worry that their sons are "underachievers" or that they "don't seem to care about school." "He's not living up to his potential," a mother or a father says. "He could be getting A's instead of B's," or "He could be getting B's instead of C's." It is typically at the beginning of high school that parents start to worry and wonder how they might motivate their sons to be more ambitious about their studies. With the competitive college admissions fever spreading all the way back to nursery school now, the stakes for the freshman year of high school are higher than ever. Parents say their sons do not seem to understand that, or if they do, they don't seem to care.

Occasionally I hear from parents about a conscientious eleven-year-old boy who gets very anxious before tests, thinks his world is going to end if he does not do well, and is very tough on himself about homework and grades. There are, of course, fourteen- and fifteen-year-olds who have their eyes on the prize, know that they want to go to an elite college, and have a realistic understanding of what they will have to do in the next three or four years to get into one. However, the anxious, ambitious eleven-year-old and focused fourteen-year-old are exceptions in the boy world. Many more fourteen- and fifteen-year-old boys radiate a kind of indifference about school that drives caring parents crazy. "He doesn't think about the future," they complain. "Doesn't he realize . . . ?"

The problem of boy performance in school presents a daily challenge for parents hoping to get their son's butt in gear (this is the technical phrase), and we'll turn to those issues of individual motivation, performance, and potential among high school boys shortly. But first it's important to understand the national issue of boy underachievement, which is driving contentious debate among educators, academics, and public policy makers in virtually every community in America. That issue, which I also addressed in Chapter 5, is boys' relative underachievement in school when compared to girls.

In high school, as in elementary and middle school, boys do not do as well academically as girls, on average. Whatever edge men may have for now in the workplace, when it comes to education—grades, homework, and overall academic achievement—girls outperform boys all the way from elementary school to graduate school.

Over the past forty years, the United States has seen a remarkable change in the academic success of boys and girls. Forty years ago, 58 percent of college graduates were men; now, 57 percent of college graduates are women, and this gender gap is expected to grow soon to 60 percent on most college campuses. Fifty-five percent of all bachelor's and master's degrees in the United States go to women.

Two-thirds of the D's and F's given out in school go to boys. Boys are one-third more likely to drop out before finishing high school than are girls. Girls score eleven points higher in reading on the National Assessment of Educational Progress in eighth grade and twenty-five points higher in writing. Education reporter Richard Whitmire writes, "Between 1992 and 2002, the gap by which high school girls outperformed boys on tests in both reading and writing—especially writing—widened significantly."

In my state, Massachusetts, there is a clear gender gap on the mandatory state tests, the MCAs. There are thirty-eight districts where more than 50 percent of girls scored at the advanced level on the tenth-grade English exam and only four districts where boys did the same. High school girls take more advanced placement courses of all kinds than do boys, a significant shift from four decades ago, when boys predominated in the top academic classes.

There is controversy about how big the gap is between boys and girls and whether, in fact, there has been a significant change. Judith Warner, writing in the *New York Times,* says that the claims of a boy crisis in education are overblown and believes that we are in a period of "anti-girl 'backlash.' " Ann Hulbert, writing in the *Washington Post,* notes that girls have always outscored boys in reading and writing and that the scores have been pretty stable over time, though she does acknowledge that boys' reading scores have declined "somewhat" over the past decade. She suggests that "viewing school issues primarily through a gender lens" is a mistake that leads to wrongheaded one-size-fits-all prescriptions for each sex. Furthermore, it might blind us to the biggest obstacle to success for all children: socioeconomic inequality.

There are reasons to be cautious about reaching sweeping conclusions about the relative performance of boys and girls in school. There are many boys who do well in school, and there are many girls who do poorly. Sadly, inequalities associated with socioeconomic class, race, and the kind of community in which children live, as author Jonathan Kozol chronicled in his book *Savage Inequalities*, profoundly affect the educational outcomes of all children in the United States. That said, there is now enough strong evidence that academic achievement patterns are changing along gender lines, and we must try to understand the relationship between gender and school performance.

Thirty years ago, most educators I knew were upset about girl underperformance in math and science. They worried that girls weren't living up to their potential in math: they suffered from "math phobia" and resisted taking physics and calculus in high school. It was true. In 1971, girls lagged seriously behind boys in math and science on the NAEP. For thirty-five years teachers have focused on girl performance in the sciences, and that gap has been closed. Girls now perform almost as well in math and science as boys do; they are just a few points behind.

Today, the gap between girls and boys in writing is bigger than it was in 1971; in fact, it is *six times larger* than the gap in math concepts, where boys hold a very small and disappearing edge. In writing, the gap between the genders is statistically just as big as the shameful, historical gap between whites and blacks or between whites and Hispanics.

What should we make of this new gender gap, and what should we do—as we did when girls lagged behind—to help boys close the gap? No one knows. The phenomenon of boy underachievement relative to girls is seen in nineteen out of twenty-two industrialized countries. There are a lot of theories as to why it is happening. Honestly, I cannot choose among them, and I know that educators are not certain, either. I have been speaking to teachers and school administrators about the problem of boy underachievement for several years, and I always hand out the following list of the top ten reasons for (relative) boy underachievement and ask the audience to vote for their number one explanation for why boys are falling behind in school and why fewer and fewer young men are graduating from college. I invite you to speculate about which of these theories provides the most powerful explanation for why American boys are, on average, falling behind girls.

Top Ten Reasons for (Relative) Boy Underachievement in School

1. *The girl brain is better adapted than the boy brain for the modern school.* A growing number of studies demonstrate differences in the way boy and girl brains function. For example, girls are better at fine motor tasks, such as handwriting; boys have an edge in gross motor tasks, such as throwing. Boys' brains are more variable than girls'; there are more boy geniuses and far more mentally handicapped boys. Perhaps the girl brain is—or always has been—a better fit for the classroom. Before the feminist revolution, we discriminated against girls in school; perhaps we are only now seeing the true potential of the girl brain.

2. *Girls have been getting a more consistent, encouraging message from their parents and teachers for the last thirty years.* For the past three decades, schools have been recruiting female math and science teachers with the explicit mission of encouraging girls to stay in the sciences, moved physics to ninth grade so girls do not opt out of it, and in general supported the academic ambitions of girls. We have been saying, "You go, girl!" to America's girls. Perhaps we have neglected to give boys the same clear message in the academic realm or are giving them a confused message.

3. *Schools are hostile environments for boys.* With its demands for sitting still, sustained attention, and verbal production, schools have always been tough for boys. Boys have always represented the vast majority of disciplinary cases in school, as well as suspensions and expulsions. As schools are eliminating recess, focusing on rote learning for state tests, and punishing boys for their high activity levels, school is increasingly intolerable for them.

4. *Teachers are not teaching boys in the right way or with materials that appeal to their interests.* Boys and most teachers have very different tastes in writing and literature. Boys favor action, adventure, science fiction, fantasy, horror, comics, and television plots. Women tend to prefer novels and first-person narratives, family stories and journals. Boys tend to like writing about vio-

lence; women teachers, especially, are appalled by it. A number of critics suggest that the decline in boys' writing has to do with the clash of tastes between boys and teachers.

5. *Not only do boys not support each other's academic ambitions, but the anti-academic boy culture discourages individuals from achieving.* Status among girls may be helped by a girl's strong academic performance. In boy culture, risk taking, resistance to authority, and being "cool" are highly valued. If a boy is a hardworking student, he may be teased and labeled as a "suck-up," "wuss," or "nerd." As one high school boy described it: "Being intellectual and being smart are two different things. Being intellectual has the stigma." His friend added: "The girly one."

6. *Boys have a different strategy for doing school.* Teachers and parents complain constantly about boys trying to get their work done as fast as possible, without really caring about the quality of it. Boys may take a minimalist approach to school, trying to complete the work in the least possible time. Or they do a cost-benefit analysis of the situation, deciding it does not merit the effort.

7. *Boys lack male role models, both inside and outside of school.* In preschool through middle school, between 79 and 98 percent of teachers in the United States are women; the few male teachers are heavily concentrated in high schools. Because of divorce and births to single mothers, 35 percent of boys live in homes without fathers. Fathers do not attend parent information meetings or other school events nearly as often as they come to boys' sports events. Perhaps boys do not have the male role models they need for academic achievement.

8. *There are too many distractions in the lives of boys.* Schools have been sharing children's attention with television for decades. Now, schools have to compete with the vivid and exciting world of video, computer, and online games, which appeal strongly to boys' greater visual-spatial ability and their desire for competition. Boys experience themselves as feeling more powerful and effective in games than they do in school. Even high school girls tell me that boys do not do well in school because they spend so much time playing games.

9. *The roles of men and women have changed, and boys are in despair.* Perhaps advanced industrialized societies are undergoing such a fundamental change in the lives of men and women that boys are confused about what their place in adult society will be. Without heroes other than sports figures, and without an idea of their place in the family, boys no longer have a clear goal.

10. *The patriarchal attitudes of boys reduce their motivation.* We have not yet achieved equity in the workplace between the genders. Women still earn only 78 percent of what men earn, and they spend much more time with family than do men. Research on motivation shows that women are not willing to sacrifice family time for work in the way that men are. Boys are not unaware that traditional gender roles will favor them in the workplace. One tenth-grade boy said to me, "I don't need to get A's in school. The girls get A's but then they all leave their jobs to have babies."

Human beings are complex, and so are schools; no single explanation can account for the relative underachievement of boys because so many factors are involved. School is not easy for all girls and hard for all boys. Nevertheless, boy underachievement is a national problem, a social inequity that needs to be addressed. A ninth-grade girl once said to me, "If someone has to be ahead, why not girls?" I am fine with that, as long as someone *has* to be ahead. Perhaps we can never achieve equality in educational outcomes, but I would like to understand why boys are falling behind and be sure that we are offering them an equal playing field.

I want parents to know about boy underachievement because I want them talking about it in every town in America. Recently a woman in the Johnson City, Tennessee, public schools told me that when they began to focus on boys and writing, in one year the boys' scores went up thirteen points. Other districts where boys' underachievement has been addressed as a priority also have seen significant improvements. The only way we're going to help boys as a group to achieve more in school—to reach their full potential—is to think out loud about the problem, get discussions going in PTA groups, have teachers address the gaps, and try new techniques for engaging boys. Nothing will happen if we accept the idea that "boys just don't like writing." That's what we used to say about girls and math. There has got to be a generation of parents—moms and dads like you—who care enough to push for attention to this issue in the schools.

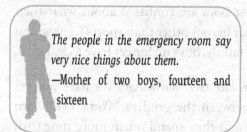

The people in the emergency room say very nice things about them.

—Mother of two boys, fourteen and sixteen

Can parents' attention on the big issues of boy underachievement nationally achieve a turnaround for one underachieving son? It can. When parents and teachers focus collaboratively on creating boy-friendly structure and instruction in schools, it can make a difference in the classroom where your son sits, and that may well be what changes everything for him personally.

UNDERSTANDING A BOY'S POOR PERFORMANCE

If the national issue of boy underachievement relative to girls compels us to study our schools and educational philosophy for answers, the individual issue of a boy's poor performance compels us to study the boy. Parents who are worried about a son's grades in eighth grade or in early high school have to understand what is happening for him in school if they want to figure out why he isn't living up to their hopes for him. Blaming the system is not going to help. Changing the system doesn't guarantee that all boys will flourish. And changing schools, if that is an option, may or may not solve the problem. A boy can fail in any environment, even the best, most boy-friendly school, for a variety of reasons. A boy may be underachieving in fact; that is, what he accomplishes is clearly below his capabilities. Or he may be underachieving only against the backdrop of his parents' higher hopes and wishes.

The relevant question about a boy's disappointing performance is why, and the meaningful answers will be found, first, in the developmental life of the boy, taking into account all eight lines of development, and then at the intersection where his development meets (or fails to meet) your expectations. For instance, is he a very bright boy struggling with subtle learning differences or the internal tension of uneven development? Is he a boy of average intellect, whose passion for other realms of endeavor is distracting him from the difficult academic demands of the day? Is he anxious about family or friends, about school, or in a more general way that makes it hard for him to focus on learning? Is he overwhelmed in some way? Underchallenged in others? Is he in trouble? Is he in love? Once you gain that perspective on your son's experience, the next step is to figure out whether you have the skills or resources to support him or the leverage to motivate him.

The label "underachiever" doesn't really tell us much about a boy. Instead of defining him by what he *isn't*, it's more helpful to look at what he *is* and then identify what he needs in order to do his best and get the most out of school. In my experience, high school boys who are not doing as well as their parents might hope fall into five groups: struggling, learning-disabled, cruising, otherwise engaged, and allergic to school.

Struggling boys. The vast majority of boys who get poor grades in school are not, in fact, "underachieving." They are making their best effort and are struggling academically because they aren't academically inclined and the work is extremely hard for them, or they are of average intelligence in a very hard-driving school district. A mother in one high-performing district in a high-performing state once said, "A boy with average intelligence is considered 'at risk' in this town." It is humiliating to know that you struggle with academics that other boys find easy. It makes you want to curse your books in frustration and run away. Struggling students crave teachers who can make learning fun, and they require the ongoing respect of teachers and their parents in order to stay motivated. This is the boy for whom the old-fashioned "As long as you're trying your hardest . . ." is the right thing to say.

Learning-disabled boys. We diagnose learning disabilities when adults—often teachers—find a puzzling discrepancy between innate ability and academic performance. Why would a bright boy who can talk up a storm resist reading or fail to get anything out of the material he just read? The explanation is likely to be a reading disability. Why can't a boy with high test scores pay attention and follow a class discussion? He may have ADHD. We used to call boys with learning disabilities "lazy" or "slow." Now we are able to focus on the areas of their brains that work differently than those of other students. The attention to learning disabilities—or learning differences, as some call them—in U.S. schools over the last thirty years has been a huge help to children, but it is no panacea. We do not have a cure for learning disabilities; they do not go away, and they are demoralizing for any boy. Parents struggle to support LD boys, who do not find a diagnosis to be the comforting explanation that their parents do. Boys often hear the diagnosis of learning disability as code words for "dumb" and "defective" and they fight the diagnosis ("Everybody says I'm ADHD, but I'm not") because they resent it.

Is it possible for a bright boy with a learning disability to get through elementary school and middle school without his disability coming to light? Yes, it happens all the time. A ninth- or tenth-grade diagnosis of a nonverbal learning disability in, for example, executive functioning or processing speed may not come to light until a boy hits the workload of high school and does not have the organizing help he had from his teachers in years past. If a boy who has done reasonably well in middle school is suddenly overwhelmed in high school, if he is making an effort and it isn't paying off, he could be drowning as the result of a hidden learning disability. Parents need to talk with his teachers and perhaps the school guidance counselor or principal (at a smaller high school) to solve the mystery.

The cruising (or good-enough) boy student. There are boys of varying levels of academic ability who are, in their parents' eyes, "underachieving," yet the boys themselves disagree. Interview three boys and one may believe that C's are good enough for him, another that his B's are just fine, and the third that B+'s and A−'s are a must. Even though their parents fervently believe they could get better grades, the boys are unmoved. This is how they are going to do school.

I have described such boys as "cruising," but that's from an adult point of view. The boys are likely to feel that school is hard, perhaps pretty boring, that they do enough homework, and that there are other things to be interested in in life: girls, friends, sports, a part-time job, their cars, and so on. It is not that a boy like this has a particular passion. It is just that he likes himself the way he is. In the Broadway musical *Li'l Abner,* the main character sings a love song to his lack of ambition describing how he does nothing for hours, improving "his powers," and finishes with: "If I had my druthers, to choose from all the others, / I'd druther be like I am." In other words, such a boy is saying, *I see that there are other ways to do it, but I like my way.* That male adolescent self-satisfaction, that "cool" attitude, the lack of what used to be called "get up and go," may drive parents crazy because they cannot get him excited about the admissions criteria for college. But this isn't easy to change in a boy, especially if he is working at the same level as his closest friends.

The only way to motivate a boy who thinks he is doing a good-enough job in school and cannot see the point of killing himself to get better grades is either to continue to hold high expectations for him and express your ideals and some sense of disappointment or to negotiate with him about what incentives you might put in place to induce him to change his priorities. Does he want driving privileges? Maybe he has to maintain a B average to keep the car on the road. Is there a special purchase he's been saving for? Maybe an A earns a contribution to his fund. Some parents balk at the idea of "bribes," but I call them incentives; they work in business, they work in economics, and they work for kids.

I knew a boy who was cruising with lackluster grades at a fine private high school where his parents had placed him hoping he would distinguish himself academically. All he wanted was to transfer back to the public high school, where he could rejoin his old friends. He promised his parents he would work to make good grades there. But his unhappy parents argued that, given his performance at the private school, they had no reason to believe that once he was back with his friends he would have the self-discipline to work hard and make good grades. They finally came to a compromise: if he could earn straight A's the next term at his private school, proving his willingness to work hard for what he wanted, they would let him make the transfer. He did it. They kept their promise. And he kept his.

In good humor, I can make another suggestion. You might give your son so much work to do around the house that homework looks like an attractive alternative to his chores. Or you might become philosophical, accept the son you have, and cheer him on in the endeavors he chooses to show his drive.

The otherwise-engaged boy. There are boys who develop interests outside of school that are so compelling that school can no longer hold their interest. The satisfaction, not to mention the applause, that talented athletic boys experience playing their sports or that superb chess players can get from winning tournaments, or the sense of usefulness that boys get from their paying jobs, editing the school newspaper, being part of a band, photography, music or—gulp—their computer games (or online businesses) is, to some, far greater than anything mere grades can offer them. Though it is exciting when a boy discovers a passion he wants to pursue, sometimes this can present challenges to his parents.

On one hand, if you have a son who is talented and doing something he loves, you are the luckiest of parents. What more could you ask for? On the other hand, what do you say if he begins to invest so much in volleyball, for instance, that he starts to seriously neglect his academics? What if you believe (or are told) that he is not a Division I or Division II talent, but he is pouring himself into the game with the belief that he is going to be a recruited college player? Who tells him the truth? And what if he does not believe it? What if he simply tries harder?

Even if he *is* a Division I recruited talent, one injury could end his career. As a psychologist consulting to schools, I have seen boys with rotator cuff problems or torn ACL ligaments drop into serious depressions after their injuries. They feel completely worthless when they cannot participate in their sport. The psychic risks of having all your eggs in one basket are real, and the observation "Well, you can devote yourself to your studies and get into a good college that way" may be cold comfort indeed.

Some boy pursuits are so hard for parents to fathom that they make the risks of athletics look rational and understandable. What if your son dreams about being in a rock band and plays a kind of music you hate? How can you evaluate whether he is any good and whether he has a future? The path to success for someone playing in an alternative rock band may be impossible for any adult to chart. There is no coach who can tell you, perhaps not even the music teacher can predict, and you cannot trust the word of your son's friends.

Even more problematic are video games and the Internet. The mind-meld between boys and screen games starts young, and by the time they reach high school many of them spend more time in front of a TV or computer screen playing than they do in any other single activity outside of school. Gaming is their default position. Parents worry about excessive gaming because it pushes bedtime later and later, claims time and attention their son could spend studying or engaging in physical or family activity, and may have detrimental effects on the brain or behavior that simply aren't known yet.

The problem of ninth- and tenth-grade boys staying up later and later at night is a common one, because they do not get a shot of the sleep-inducing hormone melatonin until 10:30 P.M. They don't feel sleepy before that. A boy might be staying up late even if he were not playing screen games. If, however, his grades are falling, he is becoming socially isolated, and he is behaving in a bad-tempered, churlish way to his family, then you should be concerned, primarily about depression and perhaps about the content of the games themselves. Later in this chapter we'll look more closely at the issue of recreational screen time, setting limits, and what boys have to say that may surprise you.

The traditional way of persuading a boy to keep up his academics even though his heart is really in a sport is to require him to have a minimum GPA in order to play on the team. Some schools make the same requirement of students in music, drama, and other extracurricular activities. Even better is a coach or school club advisor who insists on the connection between nonacademic interests and school performance. Some parents suspend cell phone or Internet service to "eliminate distractions" until their son shows he can success- fully manage his schoolwork first. However your son is otherwise occupied, it is possible to use his interests both as leverage for negotiating improvements in his schoolwork and as a conversational bridge across the silent expanse. If your son is not in actual crisis, you may find that the most productive approach is to be philosophical about your son's passion and his school performance.

The allergic-to-school boy. In my book *The Pressured Child,* I talked about chil- dren who seem to be allergic to the school environment. There are some boys for whom, from the earliest days of school, the physical experience of being in a class with other children all day, the psychological experience of having a teacher controlling *everything,* the frustrations of having to sit still and focus on paper-and-pencil tasks, the humiliation of grades—or any of a thousand annoy- ing things about the school environment—are simply intolerable. If you have a boy who is allergic to school, it is going to be a struggle to keep him going until he finishes. As he starts high school, the stakes rise as the temptation to drop out becomes less a fantasy and more a distinct possibility. Many dropouts leave for reasons of economic stress, family dysfunction, lack of support, mental ill- ness, or substance abuse problems. The cures for those problems are not within the purview of this book.

If, however, you have a boy whose overall life is okay but who struggles in school and hates it actively, you have to locate people or experiences that can give him hope. In elementary or middle school, you may have spent significant time at the school or on the phone, forging an alliance with a sympathetic school administrator who understood that your son was allergic to school and was willing to match him up with the most understanding teachers in the building. Perhaps you took a proactive role in encouraging his interests outside school so he would have sources of self-confidence to bolster his strength to "do his time" in school. You were most likely by his side and in his face, so to speak, on homework and time management issues. In those ways, you were an active participant in his school life, attending PTA meetings and the like, and he could see your commitment and be moved by it.

At the high school level, it is much harder for a parent to be a continuing presence, especially as a boy seeks to establish his autonomy, his own presence, in his school realm. However, it is never a mistake to talk with his guidance counselor at the beginning of the ninth-grade year and lay things on the table:

"My son hates school and he has struggled all the way." Explain that your son needs the most enthusiastic, boy-friendly teachers to help him get through, no matter what the courses. Then you have to negotiate with your son about maintaining a minimum grade point average in order to have the optional privileges and opportunities he hopes to acquire in high school.

MR. CONVIVIALITY: FRIENDS, COLLEAGUES, AND CONSENSUAL SEX

Boys will say that their friends are "everything," and they really mean it. At this age, a boy's parents are "boring" and they cannot make him feel "cool," but his friends can. From a boy's point of view, when he is around his parents, they make him feel little and immature, and it seems they are constantly reminding him of his unmet responsibilities. (Well, isn't that what we parents do?) When he is around his friends, he is usually having a great time, and even when he's not, he says he is, because it is better than being at home, where time stands still. When he is with his group, he is "in the flow." It is no wonder that friends are so precious to middle-adolescent boys.

All nonhuman primate males—whether chimpanzees, gorillas, baboons, or rhesus monkeys—start to spend more time in the company of agemates as they enter early adolescence, and they occupy themselves by hanging out, fighting each other, bluffing, hooting, flirting with the females, and provoking the older males in the troop. Human boys are no different. Every time I drive past a high school and have to wait for a group of adolescent boys to cross the street in front of me, strutting, showing off, and ignoring the drivers (me!), I feel annoyed and I bristle. Then I remember how I was at that age—hanging out with friends in New York and annoying adults on the bus with our raucous behavior and vulgar jokes.

If coalition building is a central activity of adolescent baboons, it certainly is for adolescent boys. I draw the conclusion that these social behaviors are biologically based. But whether or not the group behavior of early adolescent boys is biological or cultural, it is powerful and has an impact on the outside world. The vast majority of public vandalism is committed by fourteen- and fifteen-year-old boys in groups. Dan Offer, the adolescent psychiatrist and researcher under whom I studied at Michael Reese Hospital in Chicago, used to say that if he were walking down a dark street at night and saw a group of boys coming toward him, he would be more worried if they were fourteen than if they were eighteen. Fourteen-year-old boy gangs, he felt, were the most unpredictable, the most volatile.

As boys become more interested in girls and attracted to them, they want to begin to integrate girls into their social groupings. This is not easy to do because they are most comfortable hanging out with each other; that's what they have been doing since the age of three or four, and they are practiced at it. They have created established hierarchies through verbal and physical jousting; boys have elected their heroes and idols. However, the highest-status boys do not always enjoy the same standing with girls as they have with their peers; the homely, inarticulate wide receiver with an unbelievable ability to catch a forward pass may not have the same impact on girls as he has had on boys. It may be the smooth-talking, "cute" boy who commands more attention. Therefore, the entrance of girls into the picture shakes up the old order; it produces new challenges, victories, and defeats.

Girls do not immediately enter a boy group, nor do boys enter a girl group. They become connected in one of three ways. If a boy and girl are dating for a period of time—the relationship could be as brief as a week or two, or, rarely, it could have lasted for months—they bring their friends from the boy's group and the girl's group into contact with one another. Sometimes an established boy group sits with an established girl group at lunch, or a boy group may simply stop by and talk with a girl group. Gradually, some groups become more integrated, and in high school they will hang out with each other more of the time until some groups become permanently mixed.

This mixing of girls and boys is an old story, but it is a stressful one for boys because the types of teasing with which they have to deal multiply and become more complex. The boldest, most physically developed boys often tease girls in a crude, sexualized way, which strengthens their bonds with like-minded friends but makes other boys uncomfortable. Boys who enjoy the friendship and conversational company of girls are often teased by other boys for being less than masculine or socially unsuccessful because they seek out the company of girls. And in the unkindest cut of all, girls themselves will occasionally tease boys for being "gay" because they choose to sit with girls. Negotiating all this can be treacherous, and it all happens in public. Any boy or any girl who is starting to have sexual contact knows that there is some likelihood that his or her private moments may become a topic of public conversation.

Parents, of course, worry if their boys do not seem to have a group of friends, but parents whose sons do have a group of boys they hang out with worry about peer pressure and wonder if their sons are out drinking and trying

328 / **MYSTERY BOY**

drugs with their friends. Many of them certainly are; the trick is to know which ones. If a boy is "going with" someone or hanging out with a mixed group, parents worry that he is beginning sexual relationships with girls. There is a pretty good chance that he is. By the end of their fifteenth year, 43 percent of boys have had some sexual contact with a girl; 25 percent have had vaginal intercourse, 35 percent have had their penis touched by a girl, and 30 percent have received oral sex. And what about gay boys? It is estimated that 3.9 percent of boys this age have had oral or anal sex with another boy.

If parents remember their own adolescent experiences with drugs and alcohol, they are right to be vigilant about what their sons are doing with their friends. If parents remember honestly when they first kissed someone, "necked," "made out," or "hooked up" (depending on their generation), they should not be shocked that their own boys are beginning to be sexually active at these ages. Responsible parents try to prevent their sons from drinking or using drugs for a multitude of reasons (we will discuss alcohol and drug use in the next chapter), but at ages fourteen and fifteen the leading reason should be that alcohol has a much more powerful impact on the growing brain. The earlier a boy starts drinking, the more likely he is to become alcoholic later, so heavy experimentation at fourteen or fifteen may have a price. When it comes to sexual behavior, parents recognize the inevitability of sex but have the impulse to at least try to slow it down.

That healthy parental mistrust of what is going on when a boy is with his male friends sets up an inevitable family-versus-peers conflict. "Mom, you know them," your son argues. "You can trust me and my friends. We're not going to do anything bad." That is true . . . some of the time. If the argument turns into a debate about the quality of his friends or rumors about what they might be doing, it has headed down the wrong track because your son will feel that you are judging the character of his friends. You are also treating him like an "innocent" who can be corrupted by his "evil" friends; that is almost never the case. Both are insulting.

Some parents are lulled into thinking that because girls are present, their sons will behave more responsibly. That is naive. Girls this age are under internal hormonal pressures themselves, they are interested in sex, and they almost never restrain boy drinking behaviors, even if they do not join in at the same level. I recall a woman asking me whether she should allow her "very responsible" fifteen-year-old son to attend a coed sleepover at a girl's house. "Nothing's going to happen," he had assured her. "We're all friends, we're all in honors classes, we're all responsible kids." Come on! Sex happens. Last time I checked, responsible kids have sex, too, and their friends—male and female—do not try to stop them. Indeed, it becomes grist for group conversation because it is your son's social group, not you, that decides when it is appropriate to have sex.

As with nuclear arms control, the operant phrase for parents is "trust and verify." That means you should know where your son is, where he says he is going to be, and whether there are going to be responsible parents present at the house he is visiting.

SCREENS, SCREENS, SCREENS: INVASION OF THE BODY (AND BRAIN) SNATCHERS

All parents worry a bit—some more, some less—about their sons playing video games. Every adult who reads the newspaper knows that the boy killers at Columbine High School had played a lot of screen games and posted disturbing blog-style communications before they went into the school to shoot people. We also read that there are many violent and "criminal" video games, such as Grand Theft Auto, that boys have access to despite the games' M rating.

There are indications that boys can become addicted to Internet gaming. *The New York Times* reported that the Chinese are so worried about boys playing online games for hours and hours (instead of studying for hours and hours) that they lock them up in institutions and subject them to electroshock therapy. What do we know about video games and their impact on boys?

Numbers tell a love story. Video games play a huge part in the lives of American boys. More than thirty-three million Game Boys have been sold in the United States since the device was introduced in 1989. Sony has sold more than a hundred million PlayStation 2's worldwide, and the PlayStation continues to sell more than four hundred thousand units per month in the United States, according to the manufacturer. The same source says that 75 percent of children between the ages of twelve and seventeen play a video game at least once a week, though boys tell me that number sounds low for their peer groups. After age seventeen, the frequency of play declines, so between the ages of thirty-five and forty-four, only 24 percent play video games. Though girls are playing games such as The Sims, experts estimate that 80 percent of gamers are male.

That certainly is the case in my house, where my daughter, Joanna, began playing at age six as something to do while she waited her turn to swim at the YMCA. She soon abandoned her Game Boy, however, resurrecting it only for long plane flights. Will, now sixteen, has played these and other games steadily, and increasingly, since the age of six or seven.

What makes these games so compelling to boys? Will explains:

> Guys sometimes want to be someone else. That's why online games are played by so many now. You can become someone else to a whole new world. I mean, you can read a book. But in a video game you can interact with all the characters, and occasionally you can change the entire outcome. So the way I see it is that you get a great deal of satisfaction from playing a game.

Aaron, twenty-one, a graduate student who grew up gaming while balancing an academically demanding high school course load and extracurricular music commitments, says that in high school the games "were just fun and amusing, an extra draw to kids who are not particularly athletic."

The lure of screen games over physical activity—especially for boys who aren't involved in sports otherwise—is one of the key concerns of parents and anyone who cares about boys' health. Obesity is an epidemic among children in this country. The effects of so much gaming, most of it with violent or disturbing content, on mental and neurological health and development also pose serious concerns among parents.

There is a body of research on media effects to suggest a correlation between watching television and aggressive behavior, and preliminary research that suggests that video games activate sites and thought aggression in the brain. David Grossman, a retired U.S. Army colonel and psychologist, has written passionately that we are desensitizing our kids to violence and "teaching our children to kill" by exposing them to video games that are very similar to the ones that the U.S. Army uses to train recruits. Other experts argue that children have always been fascinated by violence. Bruno Bettelheim argued that "gory" and "frightening" fairy tales such as "Hansel and Gretel" have always been essential in helping children to resolve internal conflicts between their own loving impulses and their aggressive ones.

Harry Jenkins, the director of the Comparative Media Studies Program at MIT, writes that the lab-based experiments on media effects are artificial, the results contradictory and ultimately inconclusive. He also points out that "the rate of juvenile violence in the United States is at a 30-year low," and concludes that "no research has found that video games are a primary factor or that violent video game play could turn an otherwise normal person into a killer." That is precisely what the games allow a boy to do as fantasy, however, which is what is so unsettling to even the most accepting adults. Will's description of the Hitman single-player role-playing game that he currently enjoys offers a chilling plot line and an assassin character that the player inhabits:

> It's a game that puts you in the shoes of Agent 47, a genetically engineered assassin, the result of a cloning experiment designed to create the perfect hit man. In the first game, Agent 47, the main character, was just some kind of killing machine. But slowly over the course of the games you see him develop a conscience. You see little things that make him appear more human. At one point he even owns a small pet canary, which he seems to love. . . . Despite the fact that his conscience development is written into the script, the feeling of watching him "grow" was truly awe-inspiring. I think it's the fact that you see Agent 47 realize what he is doing is wrong that gets you. It's like seeing a child realize the difference between right and wrong.

When I asked Will to share more about the story, I learned that Agent 47's situation includes other threads of humanity and moral development. He is an assassin, true, but much of his activity, violent though it is, is on the side of "good"—an effort to rescue a good and kindly priest who has been kidnapped. The story has that complexity, and the graphics are not simply blasts of blood and gore. This animated assassin is drawn to show emotion—and yet be emotionless when on the job, a subtle psychological detail Will appreciates about the game story and design. For many boys, the games are appealing from this technical perspective, including high-end graphics, sound, and music, says Will, who is an artist himself.

> A lot of different aspects make the Hitman games great. One is the eerie dark setting that the music and scenery give. The music, which is done by Jesper Kyd, is fantastic. He does this great music which he himself conducts. It adds this dark theme which sets you into Agent 47's head. The scenery also can be dark in various levels. Those levels vary from questionable nightclubs to the old bayou. But it all adds to this overall eerie underworld feeling.

Will's willingness and ease in writing (he e-mailed his comments to me) about the game, as one might write about a film or novel, offer an interesting glimpse of the ready connection boys are prepared to make between academic skills and instructional materials when the materials interest them. But that doesn't eliminate parental concern over excessive use. A boy hunched over a screen isn't getting exercise, isn't getting outside, and isn't going over to friends' houses.

Indeed, the more sophisticated the games have become, especially the online multiple-player games, the more potentially addictive they can be, especially if a boy is struggling in school and feels the need to look elsewhere for success, Aaron explains.

> What's especially addictive is that they're formulated so you can't win. You exist in a world, killing bigger monsters and getting better gear, but you will never win. The credits will never roll. In that world, you're no longer measured by your age or physical characteristics, or voice or anything. It is a completely level playing field. And on top of that, the social aspect is key. The players literally create another world where physical inequalities completely disappear and they have complete control over how their character is regarded and who they become. If you invest sixteen hours in that game, you will succeed, you will be rewarded. It can overtake your life. It can be hard to draw the line.

No matter how articulate the explanation or argument, my worries are the same as those of most parents who watch their sons devote themselves to video games. I'm concerned about the amount of time my son spends on them, whether they are affecting his grades in school, and whether he is reading enough. I wonder if it will make his thinking more violent, whether it will contribute to a lack of exercise, and most especially whether gaming reduces his interest in the out-of-doors. The facts of his life undercut my worries: Will's grades have been going up in recent years, he is mostly self-directed about his homework (his mother still occasionally asks him whether it is done, but he beats her to the punch by telling her), he has an active social life with good friends, and he plays on an ultimate Frisbee team in the fall and spring and lifts weights in winter. The fact is that he's never been very much interested in the out-of-doors, not since he was a little boy. Video games didn't do it; he always preferred Legos to outside play.

Would it have been different if there had been more boys in the neighborhood for him or his best neighborhood friend hadn't moved away? Would he have been different had there been no video games? Probably, maybe—who knows? The point is this: he has grown up in the era of video games, and that's what his friends and classmates play. When we go on a family vacation, he takes his PlayStation 2 with him, and the moment he plugs it into the television in the vacation condo, his two older male cousins, one a college student and the other a marine, sit down beside him and start to play.

My son, like many boys, feels that playing video games puts him in a mas-

Q&A

Q: *My son lies about the littlest things, even when the truth is obvious or will be found out soon. Then the fact that he has lied becomes a bigger problem than the original issue. Why do boys choose to lie?*

A: All children lie, not just boys. For complex reason boys seem to like to lie right to your face. And in the most unlikely circumstances. Even when it's clear to you they're going to get caught. In younger children, lying is the result of magical thinking; they're trying to control the world through a lie. In older boys, lying is a way of carving out territory that they control and adults don't.

The healthiest part of lying is that it is risk taking. And the ability to take risks leads in many boys to courage, creativity, and entrepreneurial ability, to name a few valued qualities. If you see your son's lying as risk taking rather than intentional moral violation, it may help you respond more effectively.

For many boys who lie, the best approach is to say "Nice try, buddy, but you're busted." You can do it more gently with a young magical thinker, and with some force with an older boy who is gaming you. But in any case, excessive shaming of the boy for lying shouldn't be your initial approach. You should see if he's willing to revise his story once he sees that the first version has gone down in flames.

You should be worried only when a boy continues lying when he's been caught at it in the past. Then he's telling you that he's driven to lie for emotional reasons, that he feels aggrieved and helpless, and that he is trying to make the world into a better place for himself. In those cases it's important to understand his motivation for lying. You may think I'm not willing to take a moral stance on lying, but that's not the case. I believe moral guidelines underlie everything we do with children, and it is crucial that we confront boys with their lies. (Once they're past the magical thinking age, at least.) But you don't have to do it in an outraged, accusatory way that suggests you believe he is developing a bad character. Every child attempts to lie at some time or another in childhood. It may be situational, recreational, or more deeply emotional. You'll learn more about your son if you focus less on the lie and more on the "why."

culine tradition: this is what boys do when they are teenagers, these are the adventures they have together. He feels that who he is today is, in part, the result of having survived the battles he has fought online. My quiet, somewhat shy and anxious son has never had a serious physical fight in his life, nor has he ever gotten in trouble at school for aggression. He has, however, killed a lot of zombies in the last year.

Other parents face a harder struggle. The mother of a high school boy said her son was so addicted to World of Warcraft that she takes his laptop away from him at 10:30 P.M., when she heads for bed. "I sleep with his laptop," she said. "Actually, I stop by my fourteen-year-old daughter's room and take away her cell phone because I found on the bill that she was text messaging at 2:00 A.M., and then I collect my sixteen-year-old son's laptop and take them to my room." She added, "I think he's relieved."

The man I sat next to on the plane, a CEO from Silicon Valley, said that for a Christmas project he bought all the component parts for a highly sophisticated gaming computer for his son. They built it together, a real "father-son project," the father said, but by March he had to take it away because his son's grades had dropped so much. He bought him a simple replacement laptop and removed all the software except for a word-processing program and one highly restricted Internet access program. Every time he goes away on a business trip, however, when he returns his son has persuaded his wife to give him the gaming computer back, "because he tells her there is an important piece of homework on it that he has to access."

Where do I come down on the issue of video games as a citizen, a father, and a psychologist? As a citizen, I worry about the coarsening of our civil discourse and the images of violence to which our children are exposed. I am repelled by rap music and disgusted by the endlessly trivial and celebrity-obsessed news programs on cable TV. It bothers me that our children are exposed to so many violent images. However, I do try to remember that the truly awful violence we see comes not from video games but from television coverage of real wars, real genocide in the world. The images on the evening news are far more upsetting (and/or desensitizing) than the dead zombies piling up on my son's TV screen.

As a father, I want to supervise and monitor my son's life so that it is healthy and balanced. If my son were impulsive and had trouble controlling his aggression, if I observed that he became overstimulated by playing video games and was rude and out of control after he played them, I would restrict his access to them. That's common sense. If I thought he was becoming addicted, I would, of course, intervene.

But we have to ask: what constitutes an addiction? Is it playing two hours a day or four hours a day? Is playing nine hours on a weekend an addiction? There are many citizens in the United States who watch an average of twenty-eight hours of television per week. Is that an addiction?

Will says he knows when to quit: "My mind just tells me. It just seems to monitor what I do." Aaron, looking back, says there were times in high school when he would quit playing for a full month at a time. What signaled him to stop? Was it exams or term papers or pushing for the highest possible grade in math? No. It was early symptoms of carpal tunnel syndrome—aching hands and wrists—that would tell him it was time to stop, and he would. Later, in college, he made the choice to cut back on gaming to focus on his studies when earning top grades became his priority—and not because his parents pressured him about grades or gaming.

Are boys who love screen games doomed to academic failure, violent outbursts, or stunted lives? Clearly not. However, I think parents need to limit their sons' time with all screens—television, video game, and computer—to leave time for family dinners, conversation, exercise, and social interaction.

As a psychologist, I think that the scientific evidence for the connection between violence and video games is as yet inconclusive; we need to keep studying whether video images have a different impact on the brain than do other artistic representations of violence. But whatever we learn, as an advocate for boys, I am annoyed that the public assumes that boys have no judgment, that they absorb everything in the media as if they have no filter in their brains that allows them to differentiate between fantasy and reality. They do. Normal boys, just like normal girls, can tell the difference between a video game and real violence. Though they may have been watching screen murder and mayhem in movies and games for years, boys understand the tragic reality of the bloody conflicts we see in the news each day.

Our public debate about video games is, I think, something of a red herring. It distracts us from focusing on more painful and harder-to-change aspects of American culture that may be destructive to the lives of boys: divorce, the loss of fathers and family time, domestic violence, the decline of communities, and inadequate education for too many boys in poor neighborhoods. Let's be honest: violence is not on the rise among the children of stable middle-class families that value education, even though their sons are spending a lot of time playing video games.

BOY SOCIETY: RESHUFFLING THE CARDS IN THE CULTURE OF CRUELTY

In the movie, *Stand By Me*, four eighth-grade boys, on the cusp of turning fourteen, lie to their parents and go on a hiking adventure together. Without them being able to articulate it, this trip is the last celebration of their childhood friendships, which will end soon after they get to high school. As the four boys are sitting around in a junkyard, one boy looks at his friends and says, "This is really a great time," and they agree. The narrator, Richard Dreyfus, speaking as one of the boys looking back years later, says, "We knew exactly who we were and where we were going. It was grand."

After all I have said about the dramatic changes of puberty during the years from eleven to thirteen, it may sound contradictory to say that boys of that age know exactly who they are, but from a social standpoint, they probably do. They know who they are because they are surrounded by neighborhood friends, school friends, and teammates of many years who know their histories and affirm their identities. High school changes much of that.

When a boy moves to high school the social deck is radically reshuffled. He and his eighth-grade classmates will go from being the top of the heap in a K-8 neighborhood school or middle school to being at the bottom, surrounded by much more powerful boys. Because most high schools are academically tracked, his social group may be separated as they are assigned to different classes based on academic ability. The ninth-grade girls, his longtime classmates, will generally ignore him and his friends and start looking for attention from older boys. When I have asked eighth-grade girls what they are looking forward to in high school, they have said, "Some real boys."

But it isn't just the girls who are focused on the older boys; it is the boys themselves who are intimidated by the size and maturity of bigger high school boys. Heading for high school can make a boy feel very little. Zach was five foot five in January of his eighth-grade year. Now, in the spring of his ninth-grade year, he is six foot two, but he still remembers how impressed he was by the bigger boys, and he continues to wonder if he is making the grade physically.

I was worried because of my mom; my dad is six-four and my mom is five-two. I remember last year looking at the ninth graders and seeing how big they were and how strong they were. I still wonder if *last year's* ninth graders were bigger and strong than I am now.

Zach looks at his body in the mirror every day and is trying to persuade his mother to buy him a weight set to use at home. Whether the high school experience hits a boy in the physical or academic realm or whether he is overwhelmed by the size and anonymity of the institution, he is likely to feel insecure with the transition.

Perhaps the toughest part of high school is that there is a new social order, a new status hierarchy. As boys from different schools gather in the high school, there is going to be jousting for position. Older boys will be tempted to humiliate the younger boys in order to impress the girls, and many boys will make crude attempts to dominate girls in order to impress each other. The classic boy-on-boy attacks focus on a boy's size, his lack of cool, and his masculinity. The labels "gay" and "fag" and "wimp" continue to be used as much or more than they were in eighth grade. Unhappily, many girls will also enter verbally into this game of cruelly evaluating a boy's masculinity, thereby driving nails into his social coffin, at least temporarily. I think that eighth and ninth grades can be the toughest years in a boy's social life.

In *Raising Cain* we discussed the "culture of cruelty" that afflicts the social relationships of boys during the years from eleven to fifteen. This is a period of what researchers call "gender intensification," in which the definition of masculinity is narrowed and becomes more stereotyped than it was in elementary school, certainly, and even more demanding than it was in middle school. Boys test each other with constant teasing, requiring that the boy who is attacked control his feelings and not show too much "weakness." Those are the rules of the game and every boy knows them, prompting psychologist William Pollack to term them "the boy code."

If your son becomes reticent or withdrawn during these years, there is a reason. He may need home as a sanctuary from the rigors of social life in school; he may need to pull back from both the boys and the girls, because he finds them potentially treacherous in different ways. He is not, however, going to turn to his mother or father for reassurance, for three reasons: (1) for a boy it is humiliating to admit that he is (still) being teased—and that it hurts—when he is in high school; (2) he wants to look like a man in his father's eyes, and that means handling what is happening to him; and (3) he doesn't want to tell his mother

INSIDER TIPS FROM EDUCATORS:
WHAT TEACHERS WANT PARENTS TO KNOW

Parents often underestimate the influence they have as role models in their son's life, especially as he grows older and seems more distant. A thirty-nine-year veteran boarding school teacher told me: "Even in a boarding school, where we have the kids nine months a year, we have nowhere near the influence that the parents have on their children before they get here. Frequently, parents give us credit for the positive development or progress a child has made, but the truth is that if they have not laid the foundation by teaching the value of education and principles of moral thinking, our influence as teachers is limited." Teachers like this who work extensively with boys from kindergarten through high school offer these suggestions to parents who want to support a son's optimal development in the school setting:

• Listen to them. Ask questions. If their answer doesn't mean anything to you, find another way to ask the question. There is some meaning of value in most everything a boy will tell you.

• Don't look over your son's shoulder at every movement he makes and every vicissitude that comes his way.

• Draw the line between being an advocate and being an enabler. Don't be the voice in his ear telling him that the teacher is unreasonable, he can't do the work, or he needs more help. When problems come up at school, don't instantly reach for the phone to talk to the teacher, advisor, or dean. And don't be quick to blame others for your son's circumstances. Ask your son how he plans to approach the problem, and then accept his attempts at growing up.

• Be generous with honest praise. Be firm, but also be honest and vocal about your love for your son—especially dads!

• Focus on *his* gifts and talents, instead of trying to create a boy in the image you want him to be.

• Let your son grow. It's tempting to have the finished product in mind when your son starts school, but be patient with the process, the valuable steps of progress and failure that will shape him.

• Don't make excuses for your son. Children need to know that their decisions, educationally and morally, are, in fact, their own decisions. Boys desperately need to take ownership of their own lives.

- Create realistic expectations, but let your son fail and figure out how to succeed on his own. If you truly believe in him, he will, too.

- Model responsible communication for solving problems. If your son complains of a bad teacher or course, contact the teacher in a collaborative way to learn more, and show your son how to engage in that process of fact-finding and, if necessary, respectful conflict resolution.

- Set limits and stick to them.

- Never say "My son would never do that."

because it will upset her and make her feel helpless or, worse yet, drive her into some unwise attempt at an intervention. This unwillingness on the part of boys to share what is happening to them is intensely frustrating for mothers who can see their sons' emotional pain and want to help, and who are not satisfied with curt replies to searching questions.

There is another explanation for why boys may withdraw socially during the ninth- and tenth-grade years. They are too old for playdates, perhaps too young for a real date, and, above all, too young to drive. It makes a boy feel dependent and stupid to have to ask his mother to drive him everywhere, and yet his license is still so far away. During these two years many boys settle for the company of their brother, sister, or computer. Parents sometimes get anxious about this, worried their son is becoming a recluse. It's not likely. You might transform this lull into a bonus with something as simple as making your home an accommodating hub for his friends to gather. (If you took my advice in Chapter 2 and ignored pricey developmental toys in favor of saving the money for pizza, now is the time to raid the piggy bank.)

FATHERS: LONGING, TENSION, AND RITUALS

Fourteen and fifteen can be a tough age for fathers and sons; it can also be a pretty wonderful time for them. Mothers have told me in all sincerity that their fourteen-year-old son and their husband are "best friends." I was once speaking to a fifteen-year-old boy whose parents had grounded him for two months after they caught him smoking pot with a friend. When I asked him how upset he was about the punishment, he shrugged and said that it didn't really matter because he was still going to be able to hunt with his father on weekends during the upcoming hunting season. He was not being arrogant, nor was he suggesting that his parents were weak in their choice of punishment—it was clear the boy didn't welcome being grounded. He was just relieved to be able to do his favorite activity with his dad.

In contrast, boys have told me they have "nothing to say" to their dads or that their dads are "jerks." "There is no point talking to him" is a frequent complaint from sons, or "He doesn't know anything about me or what I like." I have known many boys who have taken a swing at their dads during an escalating verbal conflict, but almost always this occurred after the father attempted to hit the son first. It is hard for me to remember any case in which a boy has swung first. The child's respect for the father's power and size endures into adolescence, but once a boy is provoked, he may suddenly discover that he is bigger and more muscular than his dad; he may suddenly be ready to take the gloves off. "That's the last time he'll do that," one boy told me, with a tone of warning, after reporting that his father hit him on the back. Another tenth grader who punched a wall and broke his hand during an argument with his father proudly proclaimed, "He was lucky I didn't hit him."

What normal psychological tensions affect father-son relationships at this age? The health and happiness of any individual father-son pair depend on a number of factors. Naturally, what is most important is how close father and boy were during his childhood years. The more good memories and rituals they have to fall back on during adolescence, the better. But much depends on how both father and son react to the change in their relative sizes, how graceful a father is in ceding control to his son, how ferocious a son needs to be in declaring his independence, and whether the family is functioning well.

As boys develop bigger bodies and experience sexual sensations, they look around for male rivals against whom to test themselves, both with their friends and at home. Freud believed there was a fratricidal impulse deep in the unconscious of every boy. Perhaps, as a father, I don't want to believe that my son is harboring fratricidal yearnings, but I do believe that some of the challenging behavior of boys is biologically driven. I remember my son, Will, coming into the kitchen at fourteen and suddenly wanting to wrestle. These invitations had a different feeling to them than the fun wrestling when he was younger (when I was assured of a gracious victory). This had a challenging, I-want-to-push-you-across-the-room feel to it. I know a man suffering from multiple sclerosis whose son refused to accept that his father was as sick and frail as he truly was. The son wanted to box with his father, and after many requests by the son, the father reluctantly agreed. The son won easily and was depressed to find that it was no contest. He wanted to experience his father as a strong competitor against whom he could test himself.

How a father and son manage the complexities of the son's growing strength and the father's diminishing power is a psychological drama—indeed, the second act of the Oedipal drama we saw in the four-year-old boy. A healthy father wants his son to grow past him in psychological strength and success, but perhaps not quite as soon as the boy wants.

Men in general and fathers in particular want to feel like they are in control. Mothers tend to recognize that they are not always able to manage the outcome of a conversation with an adolescent, whereas fathers continue to insist to researchers that they are "in control" of conversations with adolescent girls and boys. The father's need for control may spark a son's need to prove that he is in command of his own destiny.

If there is a family crisis—separation, divorce, or disclosure of a father's infidelity—it may suddenly inflame the subtle competition between father and son. In such situations, boys tend to side with their mothers and may drive their fathers away, assuming the mantle of "man of the house." I know a seventh-grade boy who stepped into a nasty verbal fight between his mother and father and took a swing at his dad; two years later he still had very little contact with his father. One boy, whose father had run off with his secretary, refused to communicate with him in any way. "I would rather cut off my right arm than speak to my father," he told me.

Underneath, however, a boy always hopes that he can keep a connection. And many will work at trying to stay connected to a man. In a "letter to my father" assignment, one boy wrote:

> Do not forget that I am going to miss not seeing you every day, but we will
> get through it, okay? Everything will be fine eventually. I am going to visit
> you whenever I can. . . . I do not see you as a failure even though you think I
> do. . . . I know there is nothing you can do about your current situation. I

know that it is not really your fault. . . . Even if it were your fault, I would for-give you.

Boys do not always make that kind of effort to stay in touch with a man who, for one reason or another, has cycled out of their lives. Boys often let their relationship with a noncustodial fa-ther drift away. "He doesn't know much about my life," they say. Perhaps such a boy feels a divorce has forced him to make a choice and he chooses his mother; perhaps the unfamiliarity of the father's new home, dislike of a stepmother, or, most especially, a fa-ther's devotion to new half siblings can demoralize a boy, making him feel that there really isn't a place for him in his dad's new home. He bravely volunteers for—or perhaps resigns himself to—that role of "man of the house" in his mother's home. His devotion to her and his brothers and sisters can be intense, but as I saw in my work as therapist to boys whose parents were divorcing or di-vorced, the loss of a father leaves a hole that nothing quite fills. There remains a profound hunger for an active, loving father in their lives.

> *My problem is organization. Grades don't tell you how you are going to do in life. I don't do my homework. I'm too confi-dent and I think I can do the homework in five minutes. I read other books: Chekhov, Hemingway.* —Frank, age 15

The research evidence is clear that boys from father-absent homes are at risk, particularly academically and in their relationship to the law. As a psychologist, I am witness to the fact that the psychic wounds of father absence run deep. When a boy is not living with his real father, it leaves him feeling abandoned and ashamed. The feelings of abandonment are obvious, but why is he ashamed? At some level a boy always wonders why he wasn't lovable enough or appealing enough to keep his father's interest. Maybe he wasn't really "man enough" to command the loyalty of that most meaningful man in the world to him: his dad.

It means that for the rest of his life a boy has to invent himself as a man, be-cause he does not have nature's intended model at hand. He either has to create himself as a man from the two-dimensional images of men in the media or else he has to borrow a role model: a teacher, a coach, a "big brother," or a mentor.

"Boys are looking, sometimes *starving,* for positive male role models," a woman teacher told me. "Fathers, coaches, male teachers, guidance counselors—boys who don't have one or more of these in their lives will listen and respond to their female teachers, but they are still lost when it comes to whom to emulate."

Men know this. Many step forward in that capacity for boys—even simply through their casual relationship with their son's friends—and they have saved more lives than they know.

MOTHERS: TAKEN FOR GRANTED

And what about mothers, who have been largely absent from this description of boy life in the mid-teens? Aren't they still doing most of the work of cooking for and feeding these growing boys with their high metabolic rates and monstrous appetites? Aren't some of them *still* doing their sons' laundry? Aren't they driving the not-yet-licensed boy to school in the morning, reminding him to do his homework, fighting with him about his bedtime, and incurring his wrath by checking on where he is going on Friday nights? Isn't it mothers who sense when their sons are struggling academically? If boys are going to open up to anyone, isn't it mothers who listen to their anxieties about a first relationship with a girl? Yes, a boy has almost always turned to his mother, but at fourteen or fifteen a boy may stop talking and shut her out.

He's not totally shutting her out; he's just taking her for granted. In my experience, boys of this age are more likely to be respectful, even vigilant, around their dads because of the competitive tension that exists between males, but if a boy has had a close, attached relationship with his mother during the early years of his life, he just assumes that she will continue to monitor him and love him, even when he is dismissive of her.

Why is he dismissive of her? I outlined many of the reasons in the previous chapter: the boys around him require him to disavow his dependence on his mother, his own need for privacy causes him to pull away, his image of himself requires that he act independent. Because she was his confidante when he was younger, he fears the regressive pull of her presence: he knows that she knows all of his vulnerabilities, and he is afraid she will unexpectedly tap into them and make him cry. He doesn't want to look weak to anyone, not even to her. One senior boy, looking back, reflected on this dilemma in a school essay:

> Being with your mom was a little release of your feelings; whatever you felt or whatever you wanted to do that was looked upon as frail among other males, you could do around your mom. But even that got a little tricky. You didn't want your mom to see you as a girl, either, so half the mask would come back on.

Obviously, a fourteen- or fifteen-year-old boy is not truly independent, yet he tries to feel like an independent young man while always counting, unconsciously, on her love. He imagines that she is standing nearby, ready to support, to inquire, to intervene, to make him a sandwich or to do his laundry—although she should not. A fourteen-year-old boy is perfectly capable of doing his own laundry and, in my opinion, should be required to do so. As for sandwiches, I know a mother who asked her twelve-year-old daughter to make a sandwich for her fourteen-year-old brother because "he doesn't know where anything is in the kitchen." The daughter refused, saying, "Mom, that's your fault."

A son's attitude often hurts his mother's feelings; his anger can scare her; his physical size and masculine interests can sometimes intimidate her. Olga Silverstein, in her feminist take on raising boys, *The Courage to Raise Good Men*, sees this as a crucial period in the lives of mothers and sons. One day, she writes, a mother wakes up and instead of recognizing her beloved son, she sees a "large hairy stranger in his underwear." The mother may back off and act clueless about her son's life and boys in general. Silverstein believes that is a tremendous mistake: only mothers can access their son's emotional life, and no one else will do it, especially not fathers and other men, whom she regards as emotionally damaged by their own boyhoods.

I have mixed feelings about Silverstein's advice. I believe you have to give your son more psychological space than ever before; you cannot know everything about him, and you must not pester him constantly. He will rightly resent your constant intrusions and will drive you off. If you are struggling with his shutting you out, try to remember how much your mother knew about your social life when you were fourteen.

That said, it is crucial that you not fear him or disqualify yourself from understanding him. Yes, it is hard sometimes to know how to keep loving him when he acts so ungrateful or distant. The casual self-absorption of fourteen- and fifteen-year-olds can be infuriating and hurtful. I don't think there is a mother in the world who hasn't, at times, wanted to go on strike and stop working so hard to maintain the connection with a teenage boy who appears uninterested, uncooperative, or unappreciative.

"It's as if I don't exist as a person for him," a mother told me, half sad, half angry. "When he refuses to acknowledge that I exist in his life, it feels as if I really don't."

Having been the therapist to boys who have lost their mothers, all I can say is that you do exist for your son, despite outward appearances. This applies even to terrible mothers, whom sons spend a lifetime trying to banish from their psyches. And it applies to the vastly larger and diverse world of loving mothers, whose sons, caught up in their own internal and external concerns, simply aren't in a developmental place that allows them to acknowledge this.

Now is a good time to spend some quiet moments (especially if your son isn't taking up your time in conversation) remembering other developmental phases you have seen come and go in your son's life. He couldn't sleep without a night-light and then he could. He couldn't tie his shoes and then he could. In just that way, he'll move through this development moment as well.

When I asked what the most satisfying thing was about their relationship with their son, one mother was hard-pressed to think of anything: "I struggle daily with my teenage son," she said. "I'm trying to find a satisfying aspect right now." Another reported, "At this point in his life this is a very difficult question to answer as he views his parents in a negative light. Because we get very little in the way of 'warm fuzzies' from him, I am thrilled with any communication on his behalf. Last night he actually asked us our opinion on a subject. However small, this was viewed as a giant step by both my husband and myself."

Patience usually pays off, most mothers tell me. "I really like my son," one mother wrote. "He has turned into a wonderful young adult, though it was a little rough in the beginning, like up until he was fourteen."

Ultimately, you can trust in development, as this mother describes with some surprise and relief:

I think the most satisfying thing for me is that we survived high school and now we get along so well. A year ago I would not have thought it possible. High school was very difficult for my youngest son—he's very smart and capable, but he just hated the whole system. Now he see's himself as an adult who has choices that he can make for himself. That realization seems to have given him much more confidence. The most satisfying thing about my relationship with my older son is that he is growing up to be such a wonderful man. He's smart, kind, funny, creative, and very happy in his life.

CHAPTER NINE

ON HIS OWN

Ages Sixteen to Eighteen

It was no longer a question of "Can I do this?"
but rather "I am doing this, and I was just letting you know."
—Eighteen-year-old boy

THE IDEA OF INDEPENDENCE HAS A POWERFUL GRIP ON THE MINDS OF BOYS from sixteen to eighteen. They feel that their manhood is right around the corner, and they look for a chance to announce it. Perhaps it is the heritage of a revolutionary country and the heroic imagery that boys embrace from an early age, but for many boys, their sense of masculinity is connected to an idea of separateness, of being free of the bonds of family duty, and of overthrowing the authoritarian rule of the parents, or at least appearing to do so. A boy in America is driven to declare his independence from his family. He demands it of himself and his peer group demands it of him.

The independence he wants is psychological, not financial. He still expects to occupy his room and perhaps have his parents help pay for his car insurance and perhaps his college tuition. Nevertheless, he wants to transform the nature of his attachment to his parents one more time. That attachment bond, which was renegotiated at ages two

> I think selfishly quite often that it's my life and I should not be living it in accordance with the desires of others, to put it bluntly. —Eighteen-year-old boy

and five and fourteen, must now go through a process of separation and individuation which will allow him to launch himself from his family into young adulthood.

One sanguine sixteen-year-old boy observed that "as one gets older, mood, language, and overall communication change between a son and his parents." He went on to say that he speaks often and openly with his parents—"I can honestly say that I tell my parents everything"—though he immediately added that more lately he's felt inclined to "watch what I tell them." "Sometimes I just have to be alone, and be chill with no interactions." They seem to respect his autonomy, he said. "I can now talk to them whenever I want, and not talk to them without them being offended. It's cool like that."

The mother of an easygoing eighteen-year-old described his senior year of high school as "more poignant than anything problematic or painful," as he established his autonomy in ordinary, everyday ways. He became more focused in comments about his future, strategizing how best to launch himself into college and life. He showed more maturity in choices he made (even though his room stayed a mess and he had to be reminded to do household tasks), and often shared his reasoning in a casual way—as an adult might—tacitly informing them that he had thought things through and had made a well-reasoned choice. He did it all without the defensive tone or spotty considerations that were typical of an earlier age, even just a year before, his mother said. And yet his tone invited no comment from his parents.

For their part, they no longer routinely quizzed him about whether he had considered this point or that one. Either his comments made it clear he had thought things through sufficiently or his track record reassured them without a need for detail. On occasions when they did have a concern about his choice, the respectful style of communication already established between them made it easier for them to share their thoughts and raise questions without sounding judgmental. If the conversation turned up new information for him, he would acknowledge that. Sometimes it tipped the balance toward a different choice, sometimes not.

Only in retrospect, after he left for college, his mother said, did she realize the extent of the transformation that year for all of them. "We thought of him as the one growing up with our guidance, but really, we were all growing up, and it turned out he was guiding us, too, showing us what he needed from us and teaching us how to let go."

The degree to which boys feel compelled to push for their independence depends on the perceived or real constraints they feel in the context of their relationship with their parents and family.

Scott, a boy from suburban Connecticut who had enjoyed an extraordinarily close relationship with his mother during his boyhood, was closely supervised by her during his teenage years. That was his family's way. "If she hadn't done it, my father would have," he told me. "I didn't have the ability to go out with friends without explaining every little detail to my mom," he continued. Her authority could not be questioned; the policy was "If you don't tell me who you're going out with, there's no going out." By senior year, Scott found this level of reportage unacceptable; he took "extreme measures."

> I called my mother one night from a party and said, "Mom, I'm sorry, I'm not coming home and I can't tell you where I am." She was pretty devastated.

I could tell that Scott was sorry he had felt it necessary to hurt his mother and that he had been relieved by her subsequent reaction. "The next day she was so glad to see me. It was all like, 'I understand. We'll work things out.' " Apparently she understood the psychological imperative that he felt and found a way to loosen the control she had taken for granted.

Ryan, who was raised in the United States, joined his parents in London, where his father was working. His parents gave him the independence—and a credit card—to return to the United States for the summer, to attend a summer camp and stay with relatives. He took the opportunity to charge a hotel room to the credit card, providing a place where he could meet up

Parents? Be looser and more understanding. If you can, think like you did when you were a teenager, while still using your mature wisdom. With this, you will be more lenient and more understanding. —Boy, age eighteen

with a girl, a friend from camp, so they could sleep together (and lose their virginity together). When he returned home, his parents found a photo of them in the hotel room, a condom in his wallet, and the hotel charge on their credit card bill. These discoveries led to an extremely uncomfortable talk. When I asked if this had been his declaration of independence from his parents, he said it might have been, except being caught in that way had made him feel a little more dependent. Now, at eighteen, he believes his true independence comes from the fact that he is open with his parents, both about his drinking (legal in London) and his sexual life. Now he can say to them, "I'm hoping to get with this girl," and they take it in stride.

Jack, a boy from a small town in Ontario, received a scholarship from a local civic club to take a year overseas. His father, who wanted Jack to join the family business eventually, encouraged him to go to Spain and work on his Spanish, an important language in the business world. His mother hoped he would go to France. He ignored their wishes and chose the Czech Republic in the half hour before the interview with the scholarship committee. (More about Jack at the end of this chapter.) Was his choice impulsive? No, it was "rebellious," he said. "I came to Europe to be separate from my family's work. To find my own identity so that I didn't fulfill my father's set goals for me."

How, and under what circumstances does a boy declare his independence from his family, and is it necessary for a boy to make such a declaration? Most adolescent boys think it is essential to announce their separateness from their parents in some way. The story is a time-honored theme in literature and film. There is the earnest young cub reporter in *Almost Famous,* an autobiographical film version of the Hollywood director James Cameron's life as an underage reporter for *Rolling Stone.* The fifteen-year-old boy lies about his age to the magazine's editors and goes on tour to write about a rock band. His mother, a single parent, is so terrified that he will reject her outright, as her daughter has already done, that she goes along with his plan, doggedly attempting to supervise her son's safety (and virginity) by phone while he is traveling with a quartet of wild, drug-using rock musicians and their groupies. But isn't *Almost Famous* just a modern version of *The Adventures of Tom Sawyer* and *The Adventures of Huckleberry Finn?* Haven't young men always felt compelled—and been required by our culture—to go off into the wilderness, to take risks on their own, away from their parents, to prove their masculinity and adulthood?

One eighteen-year-old boy wanted to drive from New York to Chicago—

about thirteen hours away. His parents said they would let him do it only if he stopped overnight on the way. He agreed. He dutifully arranged to spend the night with friends in Buffalo, but drove through instead, calling his parents from Chicago at the end of a long driving day to announce that he had arrived there. He had driven 800 miles straight through on his own. They were astonished and not entirely happy, but it was a done deal and he had arrived safely. He needed to show them that he was strong enough and independent enough to do something like that on his own.

Many parents have told me of boys coming home and announcing that they befriended complete strangers and stayed at their house overnight, made the acquaintance of a homeless person and repeatedly taken him food, or stayed up all night seeing someone through a drug trip. Boys tell their parents stories of hitchhiking, snowboarding down virgin slopes and setting off small avalanches, or jumping off a granite cliff into a water-filled abandoned quarry. The one thing they all have in common is that their parents would have suggested that they *not do that*. Ultimately, parents of risk-taking boys or parents of multiple boys have gotten surprised so many times that they tell their sons, "Don't tell me. I don't want to know."

For some boys, the sense of independence isn't something declared through dramatic action or distance, but something that emerges nonetheless, developed over time. David, eighteen, described his experience, reminiscent of the more seamless metamorphosis described at the opening of this chapter:

> There was never a watershed moment when I earned a license or received an award and felt like I had achieved independence from my parents. I imagine that becoming an independent adult is a culmination of the thousands of moments where my parents might let me make my own decisions. Living with the consequences of my own decisions is a skill that I will be developing long after I leave home.

When I talk to a boy about his life, he takes pains to declare that although he respects and loves his family, he is his "own man." Seventeen-year-old Neal told me that a boy becomes a man when he's "totally self-reliant and independent." He repeated "independent" for emphasis. For Ben, a high school senior, becoming a man means "taking a more active role financially and making decisions related to my long-term success. I must strategize." He is referring to planning for college, working to support himself, and long-term career plans.

Peter sees it as an internal shift from an adolescent fantasy of freedom to a more mature reality of responsibility for self:

> I would say by eighteen it's important to remember that we are coming out of the years where we think we are independent, self-knowledgeable, and competent and getting into the years where we actually are those things. Therefore, we are starting to deserve the space and autonomy that we have probably been whining for for many years.

Becoming independent is your son's job at this age, and it can be gratifying—and challenging—to witness.

INDEPENDENCE, RISK, AND DRIVING

Many boys achieve the feelings of independence they want just by getting a driver's license. Getting a license may be the single biggest step in independence for most American boys, because in most states they are able to get one at fifteen or sixteen. Being able to drive away from home without being chauffeured satisfies their need to feel separate and avoid being supervised. For boys in big cities where subways and buses are the more common way to get

> *I think our boys are far more anxious than most realize because they manifest their anxiety by adopting aloofness, avoidance, sullenness, overinvolvement in escapist activities. . . .*
> —High school teacher

around, other privileges may take the place of the driver's license rite of passage. Whatever signals the official graduation to greater freedom of movement, it makes boys feel excited and free and grown up. Dennis told me that driving had changed his life. "It separated me from my peers who didn't drive and made me feel more mature. My parents trust me more," he said.

Ben, a high school senior, said he was pleasantly surprised but "utterly baffled by the almost overnight deference of power my mother has bestowed on me."

> Admittedly, I am now eighteen and have never been in trouble for breaches of conduct at school and have been getting good grades, but the freedom I am

now experiencing, particularly with my driver's license, makes me feel a heady euphoria and sense of possibility. The one thing for parents to realize is that the interaction their children have completely free from parental presence or interference is in many ways the most valuable and most bonding.

That is exactly what the quest for independence is for boys, individually and collectively, especially as they become independently mobile: a bonding experience rich with "heady euphoria and a sense of possibility." In that context, even the simplest excursion contains the defining qualities of a great bonding experience in adolescence: It's done with peers and feels safe in their company, it is away from parents, and it includes an exciting sense of adventure.

Some boys achieve a sense of independence by developing a crowded school, athletic, and social schedule. Combined with the ability to drive themselves, this means they are rarely around the house. "I never see him" is a common parental complaint about a busy suburban high school boy. Still others find a way to take some sanctioned time away from home, either in the summer or the winter. One boy who took a semester abroad to study said he had learned

> how to be more responsible for myself. My family did not come with me. I had to do my own laundry. I couldn't ask people for money, I had to budget my time, you have to get things done for yourself. Coming back was tough. It was like I had graduated.

And this is the central psychological dilemma that adults and boys of this age face: many boys feel grown-up and ready to be independent, even though they are still two years away from high school graduation. Their parents can see they are not yet ready to be on their own: they are still too impulsive and ready to take stupid risks because their judgment isn't all that great. Acknowledging and accommodating a boy's desire for autonomy and independence when he is still young is the most common struggle that parents face in these years. Most decisions that a parent makes when they have a seventeen-year-old revolve around the nexus of how much independence to give him. *How good is his judgment? How has he done when we have allowed him independence in the past? Are we giving him enough independence so he does not need to make a dramatic grab for it?*

Sometimes the temptations of a neighborhood gang, a compelling or strange friendship, or a love relationship take a boy out of the sphere of parental influence, and it is only extreme measures that can hold them. Whatever it takes, everyone recognizes that a boy's judgment is sketchy and it is helpful for him to know that there is a parent waiting up for him at home, ready to look into his eyes, smell his breath, and hold him accountable.

The single mother of Cedric, an academically talented African American boy who made it out of a failing school to an Ivy League college (his life story is told in Ron Suskind's *A Hope in the Unseen*) practically confined him to the house during nonschool hours to avoid the dangers of the neighborhood. Perhaps I should say he allowed her to confine him to the house, because there were other boys in his neighborhood who were joining gangs. A man in his thirties told me that the only thing that kept him from going completely off the rails in adolescence—he was drinking, taking drugs, and partying hard on both Friday and Saturday nights—was the absolute family requirement that he be in attendance and respectful at Sunday dinner with his grandparents. "They absolutely insisted on that," he said. "It was my anchor and it saved me."

As much as they may resist or protest, most boys need their parents to exercise some kind of restraining influence on them. They need some external check on their impulses because they are under such internal pressure to prove their independence and their masculinity that they are driven to take risks, especially in social situations with other boys. Lynn Ponton, M.D., in her book *The Romance of Risk*, argues that risk taking is a central part of identity formation in adolescence. It is worth noting, however, that not all boys like risk, or serious risk. There is a significant minority of boys who don't want to end up in the emergency room. There is a range of boy personalities: some boys are sensation seekers and are temperamentally more likely to take risks, while other boys are cautious, more attuned to the "risk-benefit analysis," as one put it. They may even say clearly that they don't feel that need to do "stupid things" to prove their independence or their masculinity. And they mean it. Some boys mature earlier and development better judgment sooner, while for other boys judgment is a long time in coming; however, you cannot ever absolutely trust the judgment of an under-eighteen boy when he is with his friends.

Most boys, even the very brightest of them, on occasion show terrible judgment in pursuit of their manhood, especially after they get their driver's licenses. It is always shocking to parents when their academically gifted son takes risks that everyone would have assumed he had better sense than to do. But IQ and judgment are not perfectly correlated, and boys who feel they are too good or compliant in one area of life may, paradoxically, feel required to make up for it with some display of bold, brash (high-risk) masculinity in another area.

Though girls take risks, they are not driven to take the physical risks that boys do with drugs, alcohol, and driving. That's why car insurance is so much more expensive for boys; their rates are pegged to their much higher rates of accidents. The leading cause of death in the teenage years is accidents, and boys are more than twice as likely as girls to die this way. Six thousand teenagers in the United States die in car accidents every year; two-thirds of them are boys. Interestingly, girls do not exercise much restraining influence on boys when they are doing daredevil acts. Indeed, when boys are involved in drinking contests, girls tend to become spectators, whether excited or passive, and boys play to them. The girls don't want to come across to risk-taking boys

> They have tender hearts, they can be very anxious, and they are more willing to not try at all than fail.
> —High school teacher

as uncool by sounding like parents; they also know how important risk taking is to boys in proving their masculinity.

Though we should try to limit the risks they take, it is essential to understand how strongly they feel about their freedom of action. It is at the core of their identity, and often finds its fullest expression in activities that involve risk. Those activities may be acceptable, even celebrated ones—snowboarding, surfing, or rock climbing—or they may just be whatever presents itself, such as daredevil driving or a dare of the moment, most of which parents never hear about until they go badly. Autonomy of action is what every boy of this age seeks. As a parent, you are going to have to negotiate with him about his potentially risky interests and behaviors.

In order to maintain your connection with a boy this age and to help him think things through, it can be helpful to hear from him exactly how he assesses the risks he is taking. That is how I would suggest you respond if he comes home determined to be a small-plane pilot or go hang gliding or scuba diving. Your first impulse may be to say, "You're too young," but his passionate insistence and examples of other boys his age who do so will demand another round. (I know this because I badgered my parents as a teen over precisely this passion—scuba diving—and ultimately was victorious.)

How do you talk to a late-adolescent boy about risk? How do you talk to him specifically about the risks he is taking—that is, if you find out about them? What can you say? *It would make me a lot less frantic if I could hear from you how you assess the risks of this activity* would be a good conversation starter.

Engaging in that conversation with genuine respect and interest in his thinking can be highly informative and productive. You may discover he is more aware of risks and ways to minimize them than you thought. Or not, in which case, in a calm conversation, you can model a way to think and talk about the ideas of acceptable or necessary risk and senseless or unacceptable risk. You can ask him which risks he feels are acceptable and necessary and where he would draw the line and step back.

In regard to senseless risks, such as drinking and drinking and driving, you can tell him that you're concerned about things you hear and would like to know how these issues are showing up in his peer group and what his personal philosophy or code of conduct is about them. You can state clearly your hopes and expectations of him and your reasons for feeling so strongly on the point. You can ask him how he'll handle a situation—for instance, if his only ride home is with a friend (or parent) who has been drinking—and come up with a contingency plan that's reasonable. Having you rescue him won't be attractive to him, but together you can think of a "cool" friend, teacher, or relative who would be pleased to be a backup. And of course make sure that he knows the consequences for illegal or ill-advised choices—both legal and in terms of school activities, college plans, and personal privileges. That's not a threat. It is important information that may sway him toward prudence in a moment when the peer impulse is otherwise.

When I interviewed him in the spring of his senior year, Peyton was a very hardworking student and captain of his baseball team, a responsible, clear-headed young man. No one would have described him that way a couple of years before. He had gotten drunk during the summer before sophomore year, and throughout sophomore year he had engaged in underage drinking at friends' houses. His grades were falling and he had been lying to his parents about his whereabouts. He had told his "cover story" too often, he said, describing how his parents eventually confronted him about the drinking and deception. "One of the best talks I ever had with my parents was when they sat me down and said, 'We know what you're doing. You can't be going to a movie every weekend. You can't see that many movies.' " After confronting him with his lying, he said they told him: "The important thing is that you're honest. We

The Eight Lines of Development

The Developmental Story Advances

The challenge for parents of boys sixteen through eighteen years old is that boys very often do not want their parents to understand them. They want to be in control of their own development and monitor it in their own way. However, the following eight points may reassure you that he's on track.

Physical Development

At sixteen or sixteen and a half, a boy usually has a good idea of how tall he is going to be as an adult. Even if he continues to grow in height until the age of twenty or twenty-one, as some boys do, the rate of growth begins to decelerate dramatically by seventeen. He will be filling out in the last year and a half of high school, adding the muscle and weight that make senior boys look a lot older than tenth graders, even if they are not all that much taller.

Having completed the bulk of his growth, a boy is faced with a psychological task: accepting the body he has gotten from his family and nature. He may be disappointed that he is not taller or bigger or faster. Such thoughts are quite common among boys; they worry. Many boys go to the gym or buy sets of weights and lift at home. They measure themselves against the strength of other boys by informal wrestling or pushing, or they actually make the challenge "I can take you," to which the other boy replies, "I'd like to see you try."

Some boys become obsessed with bulking up, constantly looking in the mirror, examining their muscles, and checking their weight. In the most extreme cases, some exercise obsessively, and these boys may need to see a psychotherapist or even be hospitalized to treat what may be a condition called body dysmorphic disorder, roughly the male equivalent of girls who become obsessed with thinness and develop anorexia nervosa. But for most boys, their preoccupation with their bodies is normal for this age.

The reality of varsity tryouts and the inevitable cuts forces boy athletes to face the truth of their situation. Boys who have been waiting for puberty to make them into better athletes may be disappointed. By junior year they are either big, strong, and coordinated enough to play their sport at the varsity level or they are not. Boys who were great at sports when they were little may be dismayed to have other boys move past them physically. The failure to make the varsity team in a sport that a boy has played all of his life can be psychologically devastating for some, especially since not being part of the team may mean that he loses touch with his social group. Boys can become depressed as a result.

For the majority of boys who never were all that good at or interested in sports but who were willing to play on recreational town teams up through eighth grade, high school can mean the end of regular physical exercise. There may not be enough intramural teams offered to them, and high school PE classes may not be sufficiently strenuous. Many boys who are developing an "alternative" identity also cultivate an attitude of disdain for physical exercise. This is worrisome. New research suggests that daily exercise improves not only fitness but mental health and academic performance as well. In light of the rapidly rising rates of obesity among U.S. adolescents as well as the incidence of anxiety and depression, all high school students need to engage in meaningful exercise every day.

Attachment

The end of high school and the departure for college, the military, or work and an apartment raise the most profound issues of attachment in parent and child, because what has been taken for granted for so many years—the ability to touch base, the ease and frequency of contact between parent and child, "I'll talk to him about that tonight"—suddenly is at risk. As a parent, you worry that you haven't really prepared your son for independence, either practically or emotionally. Boys start to worry that despite their size and experience outside the home, they might not really be able to manage their emotional lives when they're on their own. After all, they have been relying on their parents to listen to their complaints and triumphs for years (when and if they have chosen to talk).

This separation-individuation phase of late adolescence is fraught with tension, because the questions it raises in the minds of parents—*Will he be okay on his own? Did we prepare him properly? Will we be lonely without him?* and *How close can our relationship be if he doesn't live here?*—can only be answered with the passage of time. And the questions that arise in your son's mind—*Am I as independent as I want to be? Will I be lonely?* and *Are you going to be okay without me?* (sons are well aware of their parents' dependence on them)—are ones he may not want to articulate.

You will find a more or less graceful way to let your son go off to college or the military or work, because you understand that his growth requires it. Most boys find a way to tell their parents that they love them and will miss them. And once a boy has left the house, both son and parents will develop a way to stay in touch. Gradually, the panicky cell phone calls from him to you ("Mom, Dad, I have no money to eat") and you to him ("Have you seen a doctor for that?") will diminish, because you will see that he does okay on his own and you will trust that the powerful attachment that existed between you when he was little still lives in both your minds and can be refreshed with occasional contact and visits. It does not have to be maintained through checking. That said, a satisfactory resolution to this new phase of attachment is not achieved until his twenties. It is around twenty-five that most young men feel "adult." There will be a lot of going back and forth until then.

Social Development

Socially speaking, the last two years of high school are a relief for many boys, because the popularity wars and cliques of middle school gradually die away. The popular girls and "queen bees" of seventh and eighth grade may try to hold on to their position, but they no longer exercise much power and the deep-voiced, big athletic boys who dominated boy gatherings in eighth and ninth grade have either made the varsity teams they longed for and are now fully engaged with those sports or they did not and have gone on to other pursuits. In either case, the boy who previously may have felt bad about being shorter or nonathletic is able to live his own life, pursuing his own interests. Though many high school students spend the first two years of high school discussing who is a "prep" and who is a "jock," "stoner," or "freak," the truth is that people are not so easily classified by others as they once were in middle school.

Interest groups come to dominate the social life of the high school, and there is a place for everyone who wants to participate. At this point, any boy is likely to be able to find other boys who share his interests, and if they have their driver's licenses, they are able to create a social life that grows out of school life. Late high school is often a time when the class intellectuals, the "nerds" and "geeks" of middle school, begin to find steady girlfriends with whom they share honors-track classes. Through their respect for hardworking boy students, the girls begin to disrupt the boy social structure so carefully worked out by boys in elementary school. One man, after describing some painful middle school and early high school years when he was on the margins of the boy group, told me that midway through high school he discovered that "if you talk to girls about things that interest them, they will sleep with you." The boys most seriously at risk socially in late high school are the ones who struggle with mental illness and have become socially isolated or who, out of desperation for social contact or because of substance use, have joined a fringe group.

As boys begin to fine-tune their identities, they customarily narrow their friendships to just a few trusted male buddies, and this group of friends then hangs out with a like-minded group of girls. Boys of this age are as likely to call a girl who is a friend as they are to call a close male friend. What is different about friendships in late high school is that boys are eager to claim and celebrate their friendships, as if to say, *I am discriminating and hard to please, and my friend has earned my trust; therefore I'm not embarrassed to say how important he is to me.*

In senior year, most boys and girls want to make the effort to become a unified senior class, and many times they succeed in healing some of the historical differences between them and pulling together. On graduation day from an all-boys school, one expansive senior boy who was asked who his best friends were threw out his arms and said, "Everyone in this class is my friend."

Cognitive Development

Perhaps the most frustrating thing for parents of most adolescent boys is their lack of future orientation. They have adult bodies now, they are capable of thinking abstractly about a wide range of issues, and they can be extremely critical of adults. Yet they seem to lack that most vital adult trait: worrying about their academic futures.

There is significant growth in cognitive development during the years from sixteen to eighteen. Boys are moving continuously, if unevenly, from the thinking of children, which is focused on concrete realities, to adult cognition, which is characterized by the capacity to think about possibilities, to think about thinking (metacognition), to think beyond old limits, and to plan ahead. You will see signs of his capacity for metacognition when he starts using three-by-five cards to study for a test, uses mnemonic devices to help him remember formulas, and says, "I remember better when I study this way." He is telling you that he has the ability to observe his own thinking ability. There are other signs at home that a boy is operating at a higher level of awareness. A boy who has never had an interest in the political world suddenly becomes aware of politics; he starts to read the paper and registers the headlines. Your son may become passionate about an idealistic cause or organization because he gets the "big picture." Finally, he may begin to plan ahead for his own life.

These are cognitive developmental achievements, a result of the growth and refinement of his brain, which has been enriched by an education that has thrown his thinking processes into disequilibrium by presenting him with complex problems to solve. No matter how many times you ask your son to plan ahead, he may not actually experience the thought in his mind until his brain has developed the capacity. So often a boy will say something to me like, "My parents talked to me a thousand times about college or the exams, I don't know—I guess I didn't really believe them." It is premature to make boys choose a career path at seventeen or eighteen. However, too often we allow boys to to keep their options open almost endlessly and do not force them to develop precollegiate skills. That's why so many of them become overwhelmed by the combination of personal freedom and organizational skills required once they are in college and they drop out.

Even so, they can show equanimity and patience with their own unfocused thinking, as this sixteen-year-old boy did when I asked about his plans for the future: "Long-range? Who knows. Honestly, I know that whatever plans I make now are made so prematurely that they'll most likely be changed a hundred times over in the course of the next few years."

Academic Development

The most important feature of academic life in high school is tracking. Though the comprehensive American high school attempts to offer academic possibilities for all children—a democratic and developmental ideal I admire—as a practical matter it begins to sort students in much the same way that many other countries do—by ability, by motivation, by preparation, and, unintentionally, by social class—and for much the same reasons. We then offer a top-flight education to "honors"-track students, a respectable education to "college prep" students, an anemic academic program to "regular"-track students, and sometimes a throwaway education to "remedial" students.

If you are a parent who cares about education—and the vast majority of parents do—you will want your son to be in the highest possible track in high school that he can handle, because you will want him to encounter the challenging curriculum that will stimulate his thinking and cognitive development and give him college-level skills. The problem is, of course, that in order to stay afloat in demanding honors or college prep courses, your son will need to be organized, and he will have to plan ahead and manage his time. Many boys have not yet developed sufficient abilities to do this in the early and middle high school years.

The biggest problems for high school boys are organization, time management, and motivation. It is tough for parents to see their sons still scattered and disorganized at the beginning of high school. I have seen boys show up late for special review sessions to help them prepare for a retest on an important exam. They had done poorly on the first exam, knew very well that they hadn't mastered the material (they had failed, after all) and that they were being given a second and final chance, and yet they showed up without books, without paper, or looking like an unmade bed.

In fact, many high school boys appear to be almost as disorganized as middle school boys. Of course, they are not that disorganized, but the amount of work has increased enormously and their executive functioning may be below average. Executive functioning consists of eight elements: (1) being able to initiate work, (2) sustaining attention, (3) cognitive flexibility (shifting tempo from task to task), (4) good working memory, (5) organization, (6) planning, (7) self-monitoring, and (8) emotional control. In a discussion I conducted with high-school-age "underachieving" boys of five different nationalities in an international school in Europe, they described coming home and being unable to force themselves to sit down and work. They really want to do their homework and they are full of good intentions when they get to their house, but the lure of food, sleep, a nap, instant messaging, Facebook.com, or calling a girl on the phone is too powerful.

What boys need, more than anything, is regular help in organizing their day and week, planning their homework, and managing their time. At the most effective schools, the teachers are tracking every boy's performance and require the ones who are slipping to attend mandatory study halls. A study hall time in a quiet room with a (nonparental) adult presence can help a boy overcome many executive functioning problems, particularly initiation, distractibility, planning, self-monitoring, and emotional control. Some personal attention from a tutor can make a difference with the others. The problem is that because they are adolescents and proud of their independence, they may fight off all efforts by their mothers and fathers to help them. For boys of sixteen, seventeen, and eighteen, it is usually less humiliating and more effective to have teachers, tutors, and counselors help them with their academic work. I wish teachers had more time to help boys on a one-to-one basis. We say that girls care more about their relationships with teachers than boys do, but my experience tells me that some boys require the powerful, sustained attention of a teacher to do well, and it has to be a teacher who is willing to track down a boy and say, "You missed my extra-help session. I want you to come on Thursday."

Emotional Self-Regulation

Though it is cliché to say that adolescence is an emotional roller-coaster ride, it is true for many teenage boys. Normal adolescent boys (I'm not talking about clinically depressed teens) have higher highs than adults do, and they can have lower lows. They feel things more keenly than we older people because we are more experienced, considerably more jaded, and more accustomed to our hormones than they are. They are often impulsive and can be quite mercurial. A boy can go from being very happy one second to being extremely annoyed the next and totally enraged two minutes later, but he will calm down very quickly once the issue is resolved. As any parent knows, he is more likely to be highly reactive in this way when he is arguing with his parents.

There are five things that help a boy regulate his emotions. First, it helps him to become accustomed to his body and strength, because when he first gets his growth and musculature, he is likely to try to solve problems by "going after someone" or hitting a wall. Second, it helps him if he has developed the intellectual complexity to see things in shades of gray rather than black and white, so that he doesn't react in an outraged way to a perceived injustice. Third, if he has enough confidence in his own independence—for example, if he has become an experienced driver, or if he has a girlfriend—he is less likely to feel threatened in a negotiation with his parents. Fourth, it helps him if his *parents* can maintain their cool. An out-of-control father storming about the house or a mother weeping is likely to incite a boy to more exhibitionistic displays of temper. It is no surprise that research shows that a father who demonstrates self-control is more likely to have a son who maintains self-control. Fifth and finally, it is crucial that the adults in his world not fear him as a boy.

Moral and Spiritual Development

You may be seeing your son's moral and spiritual development emerge in the way you might have hoped at this age. On the other hand, even though you know he understands right and wrong, he may be lying to you occasionally about his whereabouts and about his drinking; he may be selective in following school rules. He may not want to go to church anymore, preferring to sleep in on Sunday mornings; he may express doubts about the existence of God, or skepticism about the intentions of the church. He might appear cynical in comparison to the more devoted and faithful boy that he was five years earlier. That cynicism is probably the result of three forces in him, one that is more superficial—the desire to appear "cool" to his peers—and two that are more profound.

The desire to appear strong, independent, and emotionally in control may conflict in a boy's mind with religious devotion. I watched the head teacher at a Christian boys' school in Scotland try to get four hundred boys to sing a hymn together at a morning assembly. There was considerable reluctance on the boys' part. Even after a brief practice session, the hymn started tentatively. It was only after each boy could hear the male voices around him that he was reassured on a social basis that it was okay to sing, and the hymn got stronger with each verse.

The superficial social reasons for a boy's reluctance to participate in anything spiritual can be overcome. There are more profound reasons for his apparent reluctance: psychological discomfort and development. First, moral dilemmas and moral conflict are actually uncomfortable and cause mental disequilibrium; second, a boy may find that a growing moral awareness conflicts with his desire to act in an independent way and "do his own thing." During middle school and early high school, boys are moving from a more utilitarian you-scratch-my-back stage of moral thinking to a "good boy" mentality, in which you honor relationships with your friends and a few select teachers whom you respect.

Identity

Educators often say about a seventeen- or eighteen-year-old boy that he "knows himself" or that he has "found himself." Parents can sometimes feel that their son has "come into his own," that he now possesses some adult quality that was never there as fully in the past as it is now. However, the quality we are describing is not just grades or artistic and/or athletic prizes; it is more than just the sum of a boy's school achievements. It is his own accomplishment. We also see boys who have not "found themselves" in some way and are floundering in their lives. What both educators and parents are noticing is, of course, the achievement of identity or the lack of it.

There is an ongoing debate in psychology about what identity really is, how stable it is, and whether a boy has the same identity in every social context. Is he the same boy when he is at home as he is with his friends or as he is with his girlfriend? The consensus is that a person's identity is not fixed and permanent, that it can change over the course of life—after all, a boy may have an identity crisis in his twenties, or a midlife crisis in his late forties—and that identity is not easily measured. Nevertheless, it is evident that some boys have created a stable idea of who they are in late adolescence, and they are better off for having achieved that sense of identity.

How does a boy find his sense of identity, and what does it consist of? Only he can say, but we do know that it involves some active mental searching, both internal and external, and a willingness to take risks. An identity is achieved only through experience, not through passive waiting, and you cannot be given it by your parents. Indeed, we say that boys who accept an identity from their parents, who agree to be exactly what their families say they should be in the future, have a "foreclosed" identity. They did not stay with the search long enough.

You have to create an identity on your own. Late adolescence is the first point in your life when you have enough independent life experiences, advanced cognitive ability, and support from society to have a continuous sense of who you are—past and futures—to be able to do that. A basic identity at this age is made up of three elements: sexual orientation, some philosophy of life, and the ability to make a commitment to a vocation in the future. It gives a boy confidence and psychological weight to have an identity.

Some boys have difficulty achieving it by the age of eighteen: Either they are still being formed—"he's young for his age," educators say—or they enter a period of identity instability that Erik Erikson called "diffusion" and in which they are psychologically all over the place: unhappy, lost, not self-confident, susceptible to fads and cults and drugs. Another group of adolescent boys enter a moratorium, a period of "time-out" when they simply cannot make a commitment to an idea or a vocation. I know a young man who, after doing brilliantly in college, took off a year to bicycle across the country. When a boy who has been a good student or an obedient boy suddenly steps off what he considers a "treadmill" leading him away from who he feels he should be, it can be unnerving for parents. However, parents should know that a moratorium can and should lead to a richer, more complex personality in the end.

Most boys do not achieve a fully formed identity by eighteen. Indeed, most young men are still working on their identities through college and into their middle twenties. However, even if it isn't the end of the journey, eighteen is an achievement. Celebrate!

know what you're doing, but we don't know the extent of it. But if you tell us we're going to let you do some of it, just not all of it."

I asked whether his parents then gave permission to engage in underage drinking, and he said no, but they did agree that he could go to houses when adults were not present as long as he was honest about where he was, and that he could drive in a car with older boys as long as they were sober. Could they be sure that he would keep his side of the bargain, in light of how he had been lying to them? Not really. But, as Peyton talked with me, it was clear how relieved he was that his parents had exercised some parental control over him. That conversation and a more honest communication with them afterward contributed to the turnaround he eventually chose to make.

Many men say that in addition to the stories of adventure their parents never knew about, there were other moments when the cautious one in their band of brothers dragged his feet just long enough for them to come to their senses, or the crazed or drunken one was reeled in by the others before he did something *really* stupid. Boys' loyalty, camaraderie, and sense of adventure can work both ways, at times rushing them headlong into harm's way, and sometimes saving them from it.

Every family is challenged by having a late-adolescent boy. He is old enough and smart enough to see your faults while still lacking the judgment to accurately assess his own. He is physically so large that you cannot block the door to prevent him from leaving if he wants to; he'll go out the back, or out the window, or right through you. All you have is your love, your moral authority, and your willingness to negotiate with him. You have to talk with him.

Essentially, your son wants to be treated like an adult and will be more inclined to cultivate those qualities if you treat him like one. In the end, you have to acknowledge that he is big, that he is becoming his "own man," and that you cannot protect him. You have to honor his love for his car, his snowboard, his surfboard, or his girlfriend. That's who he is.

TALKING TO YOUR SON ABOUT SEXUALITY

Boys generally try to avoid talking to their parents about sex. One mother reported that when her husband tried to talk to her son about sex at the dinner table, her son got up, said he was "going to vomit," and left the table. So much for that discussion! Spencer, a senior in high school, said that his parents had talked to him four or five times about sex, but that each of these was "more of a lecture than a talk." One such conversation ended when "my father threw a box of condoms my way."

Conversations about sexuality are not easy for parents or boys; because either boys or parents often bail out on them, they are also usually incomplete. When I ask high school seniors about whether they have had a serious or helpful talk with their parents about sexuality, the vast majority of them say no.

If you do not speak with your son about his sexual life on a number of occasions in early adolescence and middle adolescence, you will have almost certainly have missed the boat. By the age of seventeen, 46.9 percent of boys have had sexual intercourse with a girl and 6 percent have had oral or anal sex with another boy, so more than half of boys have embarked on a complete sexual life. Just over 62 percent of boys will have had intercourse with a girl by the age of eighteen, and almost 70 percent of boys will have either given or received oral sex from a girl by the age of eighteen, according to the Centers for Disease Control. If you want to have some influence on what your son does sexually, you cannot wait until the night before he leaves for college!

If you talk to him, what are you going to say? Are you going to ask him

> *He hates it when I talk too much about something that I think is important. I know, I know, he'll say. One sentence is enough. Let me figure out the rest on my own, seems to be the attitude.*
> —Mother of a sixteen-year-old son

to remain abstinent until marriage, are you going to ask him to treat girls with respect, are you going to wish for him that he be in love before he sleeps with someone, or are you going to throw him a box of condoms? Will you remind him that laws about "age of consent" mean that sex with an underage partner is illegal no matter how willing both parties may be? What are you going to say to your son about oral sex? In the last twenty years, kids have reversed what had been the traditional order of sexual experiences. Oral sex used to follow sexual intercourse; now it precedes it in many cases. Are you going to tell him that a boy should say no to a girl who has offered to give him a blow job?

Many parents are realistic about the high probability of their sons engaging in sex if it is offered to them; however, it always helps a boy to think through questions regarding sex: what the relationship with the girl should be to support that kind of intimacy, what her expectations might be after having done that, and whether he has empathy for a girl's situation. In truth, anything you can find the courage to say will be of help to him. Even though adolescents tend to rely on the peer group, not parents, for cues to begin a sexual life, it is never a mistake to share your values with your son. Many mothers have said to me that the thing that really irks them about the idea of boys receiving oral sex is that they hear boys don't reciprocate by doing the same for girls. There is truth in what they say. By age seventeen, 66 percent of boys have received oral sex from girls; only 52 percent have given it. If you have strong feelings about that imbalance, do you or your spouse actually have the courage to talk to your son about it?

Sometimes a boy may open the door for you. One mother reported that when they were in the supermarket, her son asked her to buy him some condoms. She asked him if he was planning to have sex, and he told her that "he wanted to practice putting them on so he could be good at it." This mom went on to say that her family is very open about sex, and that she emphasizes safe sex and that it is not just the girl's responsibility to make sure she doesn't get pregnant. The mother of another boy reported that her son had been having an intense relationship with a girl his age for three months. The teachers in his school told her that he was too distracted by her. Her daughter reported to her that one of his friends from out of state told her that he "gets head" from girls. When the mother confronted him with this comment, the boy claimed that he only "makes out." Where could she take the conversation from there? What would you do?

At the very least, you could then ask, "Well, if you make out, how far away are you from oral sex?" If he then says, "Oh, Mom, you don't have to worry about that," you could say, "I'm not worried, I'm just curious why boys would say that you 'get head' from girls. Are you telling stories to your friends that aren't true?"

Sexual questions are ultimately questions of moral and values. No psychologist can give you an answer to them because moral values cannot be proved or disproved by psychological research; they are matters of family belief and religious observation. You have to consult your feelings, your experiences (good and bad), your memories of your own actions, and those of boys who were sexually exploitative and boys who were generous and loving in order to offer your son a model of behavior. As a psychologist, all I can do to help is to report what boys tell me, what I observe about the impact of certain experiences on their behavior, and what the research confirms: If you are going to have successful conversations with your boy about sexuality, you have to know what you believe and you have to not be naive about what he sees in society and has experienced in his own life. You also have to respect that your son is going to be making his own decisions about his sex life, and his choices will very likely be something he keeps to himself. "I sometimes don't feel like it's necessary to involve them in my life," an eighteen-year-old boy wrote to me, "and I never discuss my romantic relationships with them."

PORNOGRAPHY: PASTIME OR PROBLEM?

Americans spend about $10 billion a year on "adult entertainment," which, according to CBS News, is as much as they spend attending professional sporting events or going out to the movies. According to the Family Education Web site, boys ages twelve to seventeen are among the leading consumers of pornography in the United States. One-third of thirteen-year-old boys have seen pornography, according to researchers. As the psychologist at a boys' school that runs from seventh grade through twelfth grade, I am told by the older students that every boy in the school has seen Internet porn except perhaps a few seventh-grade boys, who might—as one sixteen-year-old said to me—"still be willing to lie about it." Boys have been busted for viewing pornography on school computers or their own laptops in classrooms across America. One high school girl told me that it was no secret at her school why so many boys liked to go to the library for lunch. There they could use their laptops to access the Internet wirelessly, and scroll through the porn sites in peace.

Certainly every older boy I interviewed for this book had seen pornography. Jeremy saw naked images of women for the first time when he was in second grade. He found a copy of a "*Kama Sutra*–like" massage book in his grandfather's attic. He thought about it a lot and remembers fantasizing about "kissing girls in the movies" at the age of seven. By third grade he had seen porn on the Internet. His reaction: "It definitely made me horny. I don't know, it doesn't seem . . . It's not that surprising. All of my friends say, 'Look at this site.' "

Now eighteen years old, he continues to look at Internet porn, but he does not feel he is addicted to it (one of the concerns some adults express), nor does he feel that his pornography viewing has distorted his relationships with girls. "It is so raunchy, it's so disrespectful. It is sinful sex," he said. "Not to say you don't look at it, but you don't take it as an example of what real sex is like."

I asked him whether he feels guilty or weird about looking at porn. He said he does not. "That's my point: I don't value what I see. It's this stupid stuff, it's fake, but it turns you on." I gathered from this that he used porn, as most teenage boys do who use it, to accompany masturbation.

For Rick, who is eighteen, the experience of seeing pornography in early seventh grade or perhaps late sixth grade was extremely powerful. "A friend said, 'Isn't this funny?' and I remember looking at it. It was almost like a drug—you like it, and you become familiar with it." He has been a constant viewer of porn ever since, up until a few days before our interview, when he had been talking to a girl about pornography and was astonished to discover that "she's never seen it in her entire life, apparently, which I believe, but which I cannot comprehend." As a result of their discussion, he had decided to take a pledge and not look at porn or masturbate for two weeks. "I don't know whether I have ever gone two weeks without masturbating," he told me in a matter-of-fact way. Apparently he and his friend, a girl, had discussed male sexuality in some detail.

> This girl wanted to know about the life of boys, which I respect. I've talked to girls and asked them if they've masturbated and I cannot imagine that they haven't. It's depressing to me. Not looking at porn—that's such a large aspect of life. Not pornography, but sexual ideas and nudity are so important. The way I take it is that my friend, the girl, has never seen a guy naked.

In survey responses, boys acknowledged looking at Internet porn much as boys twenty years ago might have admitted to looking at *Playboy*. "I feel a little

Overcome a Fear of Boys

It is said that some animals can "smell fear"—a horse, for instance, knows when the rider is confident or terrified and acts accordingly. I don't know whether that is true about horses, but I am certain that boys can sense when adults are frightened of them. I have seen experienced teachers—mostly women, but some men—avoid walking down a school hallway because there is a large group of raucous boys there and the adult doesn't want to feel intimidated by the boys. If the boys should happen to see the adult avoid walking down the hall, they are probably absolutely aware of the adult's fear and the reason for it and will act in a more obnoxious way as a result. They will react with contempt if a teacher scolds them or attempts to discipline them out of fear of "what they could do." They will, however, calm down and break up quite quickly and in good humor if a teacher who is not in the slightest frightened of them walks up and talks to them. I have seen that enough times in a school that I am sure that boys require adults to help them contain their collective energy and reactivity. That is what effective school administrators do. If, as a parent, you become afraid of your teenage son, it is essential that you talk to someone or get support, so that you do not fear his feelings. If you fear him, you are useless to him. He does not really want to frighten you; he just wants to be strong and act scary, but if he does succeed in terrifying his parents, then he is all alone in the world.

weird" about viewing it, said one boy, eighteen, "but then I make up some excuse about it being okay if I've got nothing to do."

I cannot say that I am surprised by this, because as a psychologist who has worked with boys both in coed schools and all-boys schools, I have talked to a large number of boys about their relationship to pornography. Whatever the frequency of their use, most boys consider their interest in seeing sexual content quite normal. And indeed, curiosity about sex and an interest in sexual imagery is normal for boys.

I have received calls from shocked parents who have discovered their sons routinely look at pornographic Web sites, some whose sons appear to have become "addicted" to pornography, parents who have found S&M porn sites on the family computer, and those who discovered from the phone bill that their sons had spent hundreds of dollars on a "phone sex" 900 number.

Are these behaviors typical? Though learning that their son is viewing pornography may be upsetting to a mother, and perhaps of concern to a father, it is also considered a statistical norm, in that most boys do it at least occasionally. The other behaviors—phone sex or a fascination with deviant sex—are statistically rare but probably do not indicate a disturbance. The boy whose parents discovered he was looking at an "orgy" sex site admitted to them that he was a virgin but said that once he became sexually active he intended to try this stuff out. (Time will tell whether he finds a willing group or whether he falls in love with a girl who is not quite so taken with the images and ideas that excite boys.)

The discovery of a boy's interest in pornography usually prompts parents to confront a boy with what they have found. This is probably not the best way to have a first conversation about sexuality. The boy is so ashamed at being caught that he probably won't be able to hear anything his parents say about more wholesome sexual interests. It is always better to address these questions with boys in a normal way, year by year, advancing the conversation in a natural way over time. You're more likely to hear about his interests and his curiosity as they develop, and about his experiences as they begin to unfold. And if you'd like to know about something he hasn't mentioned, you can always ask him. It is never a mistake to use your son as a consultant.

How? In a tone of respectful inquiry—not inquisition—ask your son: "How does a boy your age think about sex? What do most boys think is normal? Does that include oral sex? Has anybody that you know of in your class had sex—sexual intercourse—with a girl? How did it work out for them? What do you think girls are looking for when they go out with a guy? Do you feel ahead or behind other boys? Does that worry you?"

NORMAL SEXUALITY

Not so long ago, in a section like this on boys and sexuality, "normal sexuality" would have come before the conversation on pornography because sex magazines like *Playboy* were more of a simple, secret, stimulating aside to boy life. Today, the prevalence of pornography in a highly sexualized popular culture has made it a defining feature in the sexual landscape of boyhood, and it's important for parents to understand the environment in which normal sexual development unfolds for boys.

There is a wide range of normal sexual behavior in boys. Some early-maturing boys start having sexual contact with girls very early, as early as twelve or thirteen; other boys will not have kissed a girl at sixteen. As a result, it is impossible for an expert to say when things should happen. They happen when they happen. There are just a few things to remember about your son's sexuality. A boy usually has an active sexual life with himself, involving fantasy and masturbation and pornography, for a long time before he ever actually touches a girl. He may also have an active romantic life in his mind, thinking about girls he admires and wondering whether the girl he likes so much in school is "just a friend" or could be something more. He is drawn to girls, has strong opinions about them, and talks about them with other boys, all the while pretending it doesn't mean that much to him.

The trigger for sexual activity in a social group comes when some of the more socially sophisticated kids, typically the boy athletes and the popular girls, become official couples and word starts to spread that they have done something together: perhaps kissing in sixth grade, and possibly oral sex in eighth grade (remember, boys are notorious for boasting about sex, and girls are no longer as demure in discussions with their peers as they used to be—the word gets out). Sexual activity then follows a sequence that most people remember, from kissing to intercourse. The only variation on the classic progression is that this generation of children has indicated that oral sex now is likely to precede intercourse and that many kids believe you can have oral sex and still be a virgin.

The problem with early sexuality for teenage boys is that it is difficult—almost impossible—to maintain an intimate relationship without a coherent identity of your own. Most teens, whether boys or girls, are too dependent for their identities on their peer group or their families or a role at school to be able to sustain it in relationship. For boys, whose identity in the group has been based on strength and athleticism, a long-term relationship requires a new kind of identity—openness, thoughtfulness, consideration—that has not been required of them by their male peers. That, in and of itself, can feel threatening to a boy. He may start to feel that the relationship is making him unrecognizable. Boys literally fear that they will lose their identities in a girl—be engulfed by her and her concerns. That is why they deny that they have felt love, and that is why they have such reluctance to say the word *love*, as if by saying it they become Samson falling into the hands of Delilah. Soon their hair will be cut off—a clear symbol of castration—and they will lose all their strength.

A girl, on the other hand, might feel that a relationship is central to her identity. Cultivating long-term one-on-one friendships is more a girl phenomenon; she is accustomed to talking with her friends about their relationships, about the intricacies of individual loyalty and group membership. This is more familiar territory for girls than for boys. And that's where the clash occurs. Her need to have a relationship may make her willing to go further in sexual exploration than she feels comfortable with in hopes of solidifying the relationship. That opens her up to exploitation by a boy who wants the sexual experience but is not ready for the intimacy. This is an old and painful script for boys and girls. Girls define themselves through relationships; boys define themselves through accomplishment.

I believe that the formation of an identity really prepares the way for true intimacy, and since boys do not have mature identities until late adolescence, most of them—there are notable exceptions—cannot sustain love relationships in the high school years.

Plenty of adults have cherished memories of high school sweethearts and their first love, and sometimes sexual relationships; some become lifelong friends. Others just remember them as first, often fumbling forays into emotional and physical intimacy. And many boys and girls (and some boys and boys) are engaged in meaningful romantic relationships that make their high school years more fun and fulfilling. But I have been the therapist to many young men and young women as they struggle to recover from relationships. It makes one want to recommend starting later. Here's the problem: sex happens, and being in a relationship with a girl may bring a boy important new experiences that help affirm his sexual orientation and his maturity. There are, without doubt, early, healthy sexual experiences between girls and boys that are mutual and reciprocal and lead to growth. There are also superficial and exploitative sexual relationships that leave scars. No one can predict which kind of relationship it is going to be before they embark on it.

I was once speaking to a high school audience in Florida and opened up the floor to questions. A girl asked, "Dr. Thompson, is it true that all boys care about is sex and that most boys will lie to girls to get it?" I can assure you that the assembly hall became very quiet as the students watched me search for an answer. This is what I said: "Yes, that's mostly true. Because boys experience their sexuality as more urgent than girls do—they get erections and are accustomed to having some relief in that department—they tend to push for sexual activity in a relationship sooner and with more intensity than girls. While girls certainly experience sexual desire and passion, it tends not to need to be *right now*. And so, in order to persuade girls to have sex with them, boys say things they don't mean. If a girl absolutely believes what a boy says in that moment, it could turn out to be a lie and break her heart." Hasn't this always been the case in human history that men push sex more than women do? Traditionally, haven't men been the predictable exploiters? Has it changed for this generation?

No and yes. I think things have changed a little bit. Since the invention of birth control, families do not protect the virginity and "honor" of their daughters as strongly as they used to. Since the feminist movement, girls consider themselves the equal of boys, and they compete with and against boys in all arenas now. That means that some girls are susceptible to challenges on the sexual front. Someone—either a boy or a girl—can dare her to give a boy a blow job, for instance. An eleventh-grade girl told me that the popular girls in her class announced just before summer vacation that every girl who was still a virgin ought to sleep with a boy before the start of eleventh grade. The girl's face told me she had taken the challenge. "Any regrets?" I asked her. She shrugged and said, "Not really."

Girls who hang back, girls who want to wait to have sex, may be mocked. What used to be honorable for girls or for boys may now be seen as timid.

INTEGRATING LUST, INTIMACY, AND INTEGRITY

No matter how much they think about sex—"Sex and sports. That's what boys think about," one eighteen-year-old boy told me—boys often have deep yearnings for intimacy. Many of them have romantic hearts as well. You may remember a father in an earlier chapter who said to his twelve-year-old son, "So, you're getting some action in your pants." The answer for an older boy is always yes. Sex is very compelling for boys; they think about it all the time and are getting erections frequently. That's the biology. But nothing about the biology of sex helps boys with the psychology of sexual intimacy with girls. They are hearing about that in conversations with other boys, and sometimes with girls. William Simon and John Gagnon called these social instructions "sexual scripts." The content of this self-made curriculum ranges from the philosophical to the practical, from fantasies to findings based on hands-on experience.

"Boys have more direct lust, while girls have more of a longing need," an eighteen-year-old boy said, describing his experience (or perhaps the prevailing script among his friends) of the difference between girls' and boys' sexuality.

"Boys' sexuality is more rough, or they just want it more," said another boy, sixteen, adding that boys' sexuality is often misunderstood. "The media portrays them as sex-hungry people," he said, but boys just as often keep their desire to themselves. "They don't show it. Guys are shy like anyone else."

What's love got to do with it? Each boy has powerful individual needs for love, for intimacy, for affection, and for support. How boys integrate these threads of need into their lives is the story of their relationships in late adolescence and into college. The great American psychiatrist Harry Stack Sullivan called this process the integration of lust and intimacy. Though *lust* is an old-fashioned word, I don't know a better one for describing what boys are experiencing at this age.

If you going to take the plunge and discuss sexuality with your son, you will need to understand what boys want out of relationships. Do they want sex or do they want love? Do they want to prove their masculinity by "getting with a girl" or do they want the conversation and companionship? The answer is, of course, that boys—like girls—imagine having it all, a fully loving and sexually satisfying relationship, but they do not know how to accomplish it. They have no experience in how to integrate their sexual yearnings with their romantic longings and weave them together into a successful relationship. Maintaining a successful relationship is, after all, one of the most complex things for adults to do; how can a boy master all the component parts when he wants four things, and the pieces don't seem to fit together? What are the four goals that boys pursue in relationships?

First, boys want to have sex. They want sex because their hormones, their bodies, their eyes, and their fantasies demand it. That's the way evolution designed males. Boys are turned on by the sight of girls; they are drawn to their bodies, their hair, the sound of their voices, the shape of their breasts, and the sight of their genitals. You don't need a psychologist to tell you this; just go to a museum and see what men have painted since the beginning of pictorial art: women's bodies. Any man who is honest can remember being almost overwhelmed with desire—no, that's too tame a word—with outright lust when he was a teenager after being in close proximity to girls. One frank educator, speaking with boys about sexual desire in a sex education class, described it as feeling like "electricity coursing throughout the body." It was hopeless to fight it, he said; you could only channel it appropriately.

Second, boys want to love and be loved. Boys, like girls, have been seeking love from the moment they were born. They have always sought affection from their moms and dads, the interest of their teachers, and the loyalty of their friends. As they separate from their parents, they look to girls (or boys, in the case of a gay boy) to provide the intense love that formerly they received from their parents, in a new form.

Third, boys want to feel masculine; they want to fulfill the "tests" of sexuality that will prove that they are truly men. In most cultures on earth part of becoming a man requires that a boy or young man sleep with a woman. Indeed, it is difficult for a boy to think of himself as a "real" man without having had intercourse. I have been the therapist to brilliant young men at a local university in Cambridge, Massachusetts, who had devoted themselves totally to their studies in order to be admitted to an elite college, but once there did not feel like real men because they were still virgins. In other words, being a Harvard man doesn't qualify you as a real man, not without some sexual experiences.

Fourth, a boy does not want to be hurt or rejected in his sexual and romantic pursuits. No boy wants to be told that someone else does not find him sexually attractive; it is hurtful. Boys dread having a girl say, "I think of you as a brother," because it means she doesn't find them attractive. At the same time, boys also fear being "dumped." Though boys may laugh and pretend that they are interested only in sex, any therapist knows that boys are sometimes less well equipped to handle rejection than are girls. They can be absolutely devastated by the loss of love on which they have become surprisingly and profoundly dependent. The obsessive, tormented ex-boyfriend is a figure in literature, but it is also a reality in a psychologist's office—and sadly, in the news when they turn violent or self-destructive. I have met many boys who, following the abrupt end of a romantic relationship, feel totally devastated.

It should be obvious that these four goals are sometimes going to be in conflict. Is a boy going to be satisfied with being loved by a girl who is not willing to have sex with him? Probably not, not indefinitely anyway. Is a boy willing to have sex with a girl whom he does not love, just to check off his conquests on his list of masculine achievements? Quite likely. Will a boy lie to himself and pretend he just wants sex—or tell his friends that's all he wanted—when he really hoped a girl would love him? Certainly. Does a teenage boy sometimes just want a girl as a friend, someone with whom he can share his thoughts and feelings, and not want the complexities of a sexual relationship? Absolutely.

How does a boy sort out all of these contradictions and complexities? He does it the way everyone does: through experimentation, his best loving effort, and making painful mistakes. Can he articulate for his parents what he is up to? Probably not, because much of it is embarrassing—you can't share the intensity of your sexual longing with your parents—and much of the time you cannot articulate what you really want and need because you don't know yourself that well.

Some boys will discuss their romantic interests with one parent or the other (it usually isn't both parents). However, a majority of boys clam up when asked about a girlfriend; it is almost unbearably embarrassing to have a parent ask them about a love interest because they feel transparent and incompetent, or because they simply *don't know what to say and don't want to be judged.*

The reticence of boys usually relegates parents to discussing sexual behavior and moral values, which is, I believe, a parental responsibility. Even if you don't know specifically what your son thinks about sexually and what he yearns for romantically, it is incumbent on parents to bring up the topic numerous times throughout his adolescence so that you can communicate your values and your hopes for him.

THE DARKER SIDE OF SEX AND POWER: CHOOSING TO RESPECT WOMEN

While every boy hopes to impress women and to "sweep them off their feet," there is a darker invitation open to boys: to dominate women. Images of men shouting at women, scaring women, and hitting women (and even hunting them in movies like *Scream*) are available to boys all the time. There is a substantial thread of masculinity that suggests that boys can be real men by dominating women, physically and sexually. Though the vast majority of men and boys are appalled by the idea of rape, it always exists as a possibility because men are physically larger than women. I don't think there is a man on earth who has not been tempted to use his physicality to impose his will on a woman.

When a boy enters the sexual marketplace, whether that is in high school or when he leaves for college, it is almost inevitable that he will find himself in an ambiguous situation with a girl, perhaps an emotionally needy girl, or one who is quite drunk, and he will be tempted to take her to bed, push her a bit to lower her inhibitions, and then have sex. The problem is that the situation a young man may rationalize as consensual may feel like rape to the young woman, whether in the moment or the next morning. An attorney for a university who has handled fifty of these cases says they are always messy—often a sequence of mixed signals or missed cues, and always undeniable poor judgment. Even if they do not land in the local district attorney's office, which some deserve to do, they always end up as a disciplinary matter, typically with the young man leaving the college, his reputation destroyed.

Because the possibility of boys physically dominating girls is real, as much as a boy wants to have a sex, as much as he believes that the girl (drunk or not), is an adult who "wanted sex as much as I did," and because the reality is that some men do, indeed, rape women and concern about rape is justified, this means that every young man has a special responsibility to avoid the appearance or occasion of any version of coercive sex. And how does he do that? By having an image of his own manhood that specifically forbids him to intimidate or exploit women.

A respected high school senior remarked with uncharacteristic disdain that he had a low opinion of another high school boy, an arrogant boy who was a little younger, "on the basis that he's disrespectful to women, and that's important because in the social world here you're supposed to be respectful. He is not respectful of anybody, especially girls, and he treats them like shit. You don't do that and still be accepted by me."

Upon hearing about a college freshman taking sexual advantage of intoxicated girls on weekends when so many drift from campus parties or bars, one upper classman said, "Only a jerk would do something like that." I understand him to be saying that the boy in question did not have enough self-respect, or a firm enough idea of his masculine identity, to avoid the situation or show restraint. Every boy is going to be tempted to exploit women at some point in his life; only his own image of himself as a responsible man can save him.

GAY BOYS

Every parent of a boy has wondered, even if just for a second, whether his or her son might be gay. When boys are young parents wonder because, in the course of play, a boy may dress up in his mother's shoes or wear her pearls, or he may put on a rhinestone tiara. His behavior momentarily raises the thought that he is effeminate, and that he might really wish to dress like a girl.

When I speak to parent audiences, fathers often ask halting, awkward questions about the possibility and what a father can do about it. "I play soccer with him a lot," one father said haltingly to me, "and I want to know from a psychologist . . . I mean, . . . if a father plays with a boy, he's not going to be, well, you know . . ." He didn't finish the sentence, but I knew what he meant.

Some parents worry because the idea of their son being gay makes them uncomfortable. Others worry because, as one mother told me, "life is difficult enough for boys without having to deal with hate and discrimination over your sexuality. Life is just that much harder on gays."

Since no one knows for certain why some boys grow up to be homosexual, we are all left to wonder. Scientists do not know what "causes" homosexuality, or even whether it is a fixed and permanent state. After all, there are men who have homosexual experiences in boyhood or adolescence that do not predict a lifetime of homosexual behavior, and there are men who, after being married for twenty years and fathering children, suddenly declare that they are gay and leave their marriages. How do we know a boy is homosexual, when do we know, and what is the role of a parent in any of it?

To the best of our knowledge, homosexuality is not a disease. Some people may consider it a sin, but more than thirty years ago, the American Psychological Association and the American Psychiatric Association both officially declared that the histories of homosexual men are not consistent with mental illness and said they would no longer diagnose homosexuality as a disorder. That was the end—or should have been the end—of the theory that held that an overbearing mother and a distant father could "make" a boy homosexual. This theory has filtered down to the public. The father who said he played soccer with his six-year-old son was trying not to be distant so that his son would not turn out gay. (I'm glad for him to enjoy time with his son; there is no evidence that playing sports prevents homosexuality.)

Brain research suggests that there are differences in a brain nucleus in gay men and straight men. One study found that gay men's brains reacted to a compound in male sweat very much like the brains of women do, lending support to the idea that there is a connection between a sense of smell and sexual orientation. Another recent study concluded that being a younger brother of many older brothers increases the statistical likelihood that a man will be gay. (However, only a small minority of men turn out to be gay in any case, whether they are younger brothers, older brothers, or only children.) This suggests that some change in a mother's antibodies and the uterine environment she provides for second and third boy children influences sexual orientation. In general, scientists think that the evidence is building that sexual orientation is not a choice; it is biologically predetermined.

I do not believe that boys who are gay voluntarily choose an alternative lifestyle for which they will suffer hate and teasing all of their lives. Most gay men report feeling that they were born that way and knew from early on that they were "different." In some boys there are signs very early on that their parents and teachers can see. A mother once said to me about her second son, who was very effeminate: "Well, I knew I was going to stop after two children and so I prayed for a girl. When I look at Robb, I think maybe God sent me a girl in disguise." Elementary school teachers routinely report to me that they have a boy in class who identifies with the girls and consistently plays with the girls. The teachers intuitively understand such boys to be gay; Richard Green's longitudinal study of "sissy boys"—those who are determined about cross-dressing or who choose feminine roles in play—found that the vast majority of them turn out to be gay. However, they constitute only a minority of boys who turn out, eventually, to be gay men. They are just the most obvious. Many gay boys are not noticeably effeminate. Many boys do not signal us that they are gay until they are well past puberty, have had some sexual experiences, have taken the time to struggle with their sexual identity, and are ready to announce their orientation. I know a mother who worried for years that her son, who was a Division I athlete at an Ivy League college, was a lonely, isolated kind of guy. When he finally came out to her in his final year of college, telling her that he had fallen in love with another man, he expected her to be upset. She was profoundly relieved to hear that he was capable of love and had connected to other people, because he had hidden his need for intimacy so effectively that she wondered if he was capable of such feeling. His father was profoundly distressed that he was gay; his mother was glad that he could have relationships.

If your son is gay, he is likely to feel "different" in elementary school. He will have a pretty good idea that he is gay by the age of nine or ten, and he will have his sexual interests definitively confirmed when he embarks on a masturbatory life at eleven or twelve because his sexual fantasies will reveal the object of his attractions. Because of a boy's awareness of his difference in elementary or middle school, I discussed gay boys briefly earlier in this book. But it is around seventeen or eighteen years old that a boy may feel confident enough to come out publicly as gay. That was the case for Brody, who, after years and years of being teased, responded to a highly public e-mail accusation that he was gay by re-

Brody: Gay in an All-Boys' School

"My parents have stories about me coming home in second grade saying, 'I have a crush on this boy,'" Brody told me as he sat in the campus dining hall at the Ivy League university he attends. He continued, "And they said, 'You have to have a crush on girls.'" Despite their attempts to correct him, he never did and never has; he loves girls as friends but has never been attracted to them physically. He thinks he felt "real love" for a boy in sixth grade. "He never knew it," Brody says. When he arrived as a new seventh-grade student at an all-boys school in southern Connecticut, he told his classmates on the first day that he was going to a Britney Spears concert. They immediately labeled him as "gay" and teased him about being homosexual continuously for five years.

His response was consistent; he absolutely denied he was gay every time a boy threw the word at him, and he competed on many fronts to counter their image of him. He is very proud of having attended an academically demanding all-boys school, and threw himself into the life of the school. "I did all the sports. It wasn't like I hated sports—I just didn't like the environment that sports fostered. I didn't mind doing the sports." But mainly, he was engaged in artistic extracurricular activities: music, photography, and theater.

Internally he accepted that he was gay by eighth grade. It was that year that he first kissed another boy during the summer, but he continued to hide his identity and avoided any situations that could compromise him: "I've never, ever showered in a group shower. I always went to the seventh and eighth grade showers [individual showers with curtains]. I was afraid that someone would say, 'What are you looking at me for?'"

He reported that going to the gym was a high-risk situation for him. Before going into the building, "I had to breathe deeply," and he always felt "unwanted in that gym." The saddest part of his life in high school, however, was that he couldn't hang out with other boys at the school whom he knew to be gay, for fear of being identified as "gay" by the majority. His fear of being teased kept him from having healthy relationships with boys like himself.

When I was interviewing Brody I remembered hearing Dan Savage, the gay sex advice columnist, being interviewed on National Public Radio. He told the interviewer that the bravest boy he'd ever known was someone who came out at an all-boys, blue-collar Catholic school. According to Savage, this boy was beaten up every day but returned the next day to face another beating. One cannot underestimate the courage of a gay boy in any school environment. In *The Pressured Child* I wrote about a gay boy who reported to me that a classmate tried to run him down with his car. He came out publicly so that the school authorities would be forced to protect him. Things are getting better for gay men and women in the United States, and particularly so in some states strong on equal rights, but day-to-day life in school is still pretty tough for gay boys because a majority of Americans acknowledge disliking homosexuals. As a nation, we no longer think that racial prejudice is moral; we disapprove of ethnic prejudice and teach our children not to jump to assumptions about Mexicans or Muslims, for example. But the majority of Americans still disapprove of—even hate—homosexuality; it is our last "legitimate" prejudice. As a child psychologist, I am concerned about our dislike of homosexuals because our hatred does not fall just on adult men and women, who may be strong enough to stand up to it; our hate is also felt by 3 to 5 percent of children—two and a half million schoolchildren.

Brody's parents learned he was gay when he was fifteen. They found an online chat conversation on the family's computer that he had minimized but forgotten to delete in which he described himself as gay. They talked to him about it. His father cried, and his mother has not completely accepted it to this day. "She is still upset about it," Brody says, four years after the conversation. They tried to argue that because he had not had much sexual experience, he didn't know if he was really gay. His counterargument was, "I have experience with masturbation. Doesn't that count?"

For a gay boy, the issue of his identity is inevitably wrapped up with the issue of sexual orientation, though at this point in his life Brody rejects this. He does not want to be called "gay" or "bi" or anything. He doesn't want his sexual orientation to define him. He thinks it pigeonholes him and diminishes him if he accepts the label "gay" as if that is all that defines him. He relies on the writings of the French historian and philosopher Michel Foucault, who wrote on the history of sexuality and rejects labels. "I don't believe in labels. I don't believe it is a tangible identity," he says.

Nevertheless, Brody absolutely accepted my referring to him as gay. He just didn't want me to think that gay was all he was. How reasonable. Does the term "straight" capture everything about a heterosexual person's life? Now a sophomore in college, Brody thinks that he was able to get into an Ivy League university because he was so socially isolated in high school that he worked incredibly hard on his academics. He has found a large and accepted gay student population at college, he says.

sponding, "Maybe I will come out when I get to college." That was his first public announcement of his sexual orientation.

LATE ADOLESCENCE AND MENTAL ILLNESS

As late-adolescent boys begin to separate from their parents and to spend more time on their own and with peers, some become more vulnerable to mental illness. Their lives are more complex, and they face disappointments in love—boys and girls who have been in love experience more depression than those who have not—as well as disappointments in athletics and failure in school, all of which may hurt them and from which their parents cannot protect them. Parents are constantly at the side of their younger sons; they provide emotional support, empathy, rules, and supervision for them in childhood and early adolescence. As they spend more time away from their families in the years from sixteen to eighteen, the majority of boys gain confidence and experience; however, a small number of boys suffer because they no longer are as protected and held by their parents' caretaking.

The increase in freedom and the decline in supervision make it possible for boys to hide their symptoms from their parents. As we have seen, even normal, healthy boys keep their sex lives secret and lie to their parents about their whereabouts; it is therefore likely that boys will try to hide symptoms of depression that make them feel bad, or rationalize them as normal. Many mothers have said to me, "He sleeps all the time. I'm worried that he's depressed. He keeps telling me he's fine." Maybe he is and maybe he is not. Increased sleeping certainly is a symptom of depression, but it is also typical for boys this age to sleep a lot when they are at home, spending most of their waking time outside of the house. How do you tell depressive sleep patterns from normal sleep patterns? It isn't always easy at this age.

Making an accurate psychiatric diagnosis in late adolescence has always been problematic for parents and professionals. Because adolescents sometimes express their feelings in angry, impulsive ways, because adolescents can sometimes be moody and hostile toward adult authority, and especially because they flaunt alternative identities, adults are often baffled and tempted to say that there is something "wrong with them." Does that make them psychiatrically ill? Don't teenagers outgrow most of these problems? Aren't boys more likely to be moody and disagreeable at fourteen than at twenty-one? Is every boy who dresses in black and listens to rock music depressed? The answer is that some are troubled, most are not.

The biggest problems in late adolescence are conduct disorders (6 percent are diagnosed with them), personality disorders (3 percent), depression (5 percent in all adolescents, more in girls than boys), bipolar illness (1 percent) and schizophrenia (1 percent). Each one of these disorders is worthy of a book, and it would be impossible to catalogue all of the symptoms of these illnesses here. Suffice it to say that if your son often bullies, threatens, or intimidates others, has been physically cruel, or has committed an armed robbery, he likely will be diagnosed with conduct disorder. If he seems to have a profound disregard for the feelings of others or constant contempt for people, he will be thought to have antisocial personality disorder. Depression comes in two forms, major depression and mild depression, and though it is seen twice as much in adolescent girls, it is dangerous to boys because most boys who commit suicide have been suffering from depression. If a boy starts to hallucinate, develops delusions, and cannot take care of himself, he is developing a psychotic illness or schizophrenia, either of which can put him at risk for suicide. Bipolar illness is characterized by marked changes in mood and energy, from the sadness of depression to the fast-talking restlessness and sleeplessness of a manic state. If your son develops any of these symptoms, even if they are only brief and he insists he's fine later, don't delay in having him professionally evaluated.

SUICIDE

The three leading causes of death of adolescent boys in the United States are car accidents (48 percent), homicide (14 percent), and suicide (12 percent.) Approximately 1,612 boys die every year from suicide, and most of them have been depressed before they take their own lives. The rate of suicide among teens increased steadily from 1950 to 1980 and leveled off in the 1980s. Suicides started to decline in the 1990s, when psychiatrists began to prescribe the SSRI antidepressants (Prozac, Zoloft, Paxil, Luvox, etc.) for adolescents. They have been a powerful tool in fighting teenage despair.

What parents need to know is that while girls make more suicide "gestures" and attempts, boys represent 84 percent of the completed suicides among teenagers. Why are boys so much more at risk than girls? They may be more reluctant to report how sad and desperate they feel to their friends because it is

384 / ON HIS OWN

FATHER FIGURES IN THE QUEST FOR MANHOOD

During the filming of the PBS documentary *Raising Cain*, I interviewed ten Hispanic and African American boys at the Boys and Girls Club of Chelsea, Massachusetts, on camera. Chelsea is the poorest city in the state, filled with African American and immigrant families from the Caribbean struggling to make a life. When I asked the boys how many of them had fathers, they all tightened up, shrugged, or looked around at one another ironically, ready to be surprised if anyone did. No one did, not really. Some of the boys had known their fathers early in their lives, but no boy there lived with his father or had a close, ongoing relationship with his dad.

I asked them, "Who is the man in your life?" and they all immediately understood what I was asking from a psychological point of view. One boy said, "My mom," and stuck to his answer despite the laughter and teasing that followed. Another boy said, "My coach," and explained that his lacrosse coach helped him with the important decisions in his life. Still another boy named Hugo pointed to himself and said, "Me." He was sixteen years old. Though he had never experienced fathering, he was trying to provide it for himself and for his two nieces who lived in his house. I admired and still admire his courage, but it is almost impossible for a boy to invent himself as a father when he has never had a model. And though Hugo's "mother" (who is really his grandmother because his drug-addicted mother abandoned him) is tremendously devoted to him, he is at risk.

Both common sense and research suggest that it helps a boy's journey toward manhood if he has a father. I have written earlier about how men differ from women in their parenting styles and I have described the almost universal yearning for a father in adolescent boys who don't have one and the longing for a closer relationship with a father in boys who do have a dad at home. But what is it exactly that boys are looking for from their fathers. Is it advice? Love? A role model? And if the father is supposed to model something, what exactly should he focus on in order to help his son?

There is no prescription that I can give a father here, because there are almost an infinite number of ways to be a dad. Many dads don't fulfill stereotypical expectations: they don't fish, they don't hunt, they don't like sports. It is not important whether a father does certain activities with his son. All I know is that a father, no matter what he is like, is a presence for his son; he embodies masculinity just by being there, and his boy measures himself against his father in thousands of ways. He wrestles with him to test his strength; he imitates his father because it makes him feel more grown-up to do so; he disobeys his father to proclaim his autonomy; he does a lousy job on his chores to find out whether his father really cares if he does a good job or not; and he looks at his father's face for love and approval. "How am I doing, Dad?" he always wants to know. Without a father present, a son has no easy way to measure his progress toward manhood.

In his remarkable one-man show, *600 Sundays*, the comedian Billy Crystal memorialized his father, a busy record store owner and producer of jazz music records who worked six days a week and died when Crystal was only fifteen. Because his father worked both days and nights, the young Crystal saw him only on Sundays—600 Sundays—but that, he makes clear, was enough to last him a lifetime. He knew who his father was and how he measured up as a son. If his father's death left Billy with the enduring wish that he'd had more time with him, he certainly used the image of his father as a guide and model.

That said, I have known many wonderful men who, as boys, lacked a father and have turned out to be responsible, masculine men. I reject the idea, promulgated by politically conservative child-rearing experts, that a boy absolutely must have a father in order to grow up to be a stable, responsible, masculine man. That is rubbish. It does not doom a boy if he lacks a dad at home; indeed, some boys are better off away from the alcoholic, abusive, belittling fathers that fate has given them. The lack of a father, however, does mean that a boy has to look farther afield to assess his progress toward manhood. He has to check that he is doing what other boys do; he will have to watch his teachers and other boys' fathers for some indication. And, of course, he will check with his mother to see if he is turning into the kind of man she admires.

What he cannot do very well is get a good idea of masculinity from what is offered on television and in commercials. The male role models offered on TV are hapless fathers, beer-drinking attenuated adolescents, coarse gangsters, or entitled professional athletes. (Thank God for the tormented detectives on *Law and Order*; at least they are struggling with ethics and self-control.)

It is not easy to grow to manhood in a culture that provides so many two-dimensional images of men in the media and so few meaningful male initiation rituals besides athletics that can make a boy feel he is part of the world of men. What helps every boy to see that he is on the right track is a close relationship with a man: his father, his grandfather, a teacher, a coach, a Big Brother. No matter how wonderful a mother he has—and I have met some sensational mothers for boys—it helps him to have that masculine presence in his life to reassure him.

not "masculine." They may take their lives while under the influence of drugs and alcohol; they may use more sudden, lethal methods, such as guns and hanging. Finally, a suicidal boy is much more likely than a girl to lie to adults about his true plans when he is asked. However, after a boy dies he may leave a trail of conversations that make it clear he had been contemplating suicide for some time and may have been giving clues, as more than one boy has done in e-mails and postings on the Internet.

If a boy indicates in any way that he has a suicidal plan, it must be assumed that he is working on two contradictory tracks: to live and to complete his plan. When psychologists interview boys who attempted unsuccessfully to commit suicide, they find the majority of boys are grateful to have lived; sadly, some try again until they "succeed." The determination of late-adolescent boys cannot be underestimated. They often hold themselves to an ideal of masculine courage in the face of their own deaths that adults find almost impossible to comprehend.

MANHOOD, RESPONSIBILITY, ALCOHOL, AND THE NEED FOR INITIATION

Boys of seventeen and eighteen think a lot about whether or not they are men and what they have to do to get there. In a group interview Justin said: "Guys worry a lot about being guys. That's just that basic issue: am I actually a guy, do I have what it takes to be a man?" And what do they think makes a boy into a man? Dan said, "You should be independent, operating completely independently." Another boy said, "It mainly revolves around guys respecting girls. That's a big thing for me." A fourth boy declared that a man was someone "who's always relaxed and is so confident of his own strength that he doesn't need to prove it to anybody." Finally, one boy suggested, "It means you take life seriously but you don't have to take it seriously all the time."

The truth is that late-adolescent boys just are not sure how they are going to become men. In individual interviews I almost always ask, "Do you consider yourself a man?" and boys almost uniformly say no. Sometimes they hesitate and say yes, though with little conviction. Many try to describe a state between boyhood and manhood. Alexander answered: "Probably more a man, but probably in between. I'm a boy in that I still depend on my parents. I'm not living on my own, doing my own thing. There's no control I can cause. There's still the control of school."

Though Alexander's sentence "There's no control I can cause" is awkward, we understand what he means. He cannot yet have an impact on the world. He feels pretty useless. He thinks—or should I say hopes—that going to college will provide the answer, or perhaps finishing it will. "When I get out of college I'll become an actual man," he speculated, but immediately went beyond that: "I guess I become more and more of a man when I take responsibility for my life."

Over and over, boys of this age convey a desire to be effective, to have an impact, to mean something to someone in the wider world. The two words they use most are "responsibility" and "respect." Boys believe manhood is taking responsibility for yourself and others, looking out for the "little guy" who can't protect himself. It also means respecting other people and earning the respect of others. However, it is very rarely that boys say they feel they can achieve manhood through success in school. "They don't respect me for my brain," one smart boy said, with an edge to his voice.

The problem of this age is the search for manhood, and while schools provide many tests of ability, they are unable to provide a conclusive test of manhood. Indeed, our culture is unable to provide any convincing rite of passage from boyhood to manhood. U.S. society has become so affluent that we don't need their work; in fact, we need to keep them out of the workforce so that they do not compete for adult jobs. Families have become so suburbanized and mechanized that boys cannot make a significant contribution to the family economy, and in the information age we need them to stay in school endlessly.

What happens when a boy of eighteen, who can see the end of high school coming near, still does not perceive any clear road to manhood? What happens when a boy is unemployed and does not feel responsible for anything outside of himself? I think we've known the answer to that since Shakespeare's Prince Hal. He hangs out with his buddies and drinks. He searches for role models such as Falstaff who claim they can show him how to be a man, and he drinks some more. It seems to me that the search for manhood and drinking are closely related.

Every sixteen-, seventeen-, and eighteen-year-old I have ever interviewed has had at least one drink, or many drinks. I have not interviewed many heavily religious boys and did not interview any boys in the Mormon church, which forbids alcohol, so my sample is biased. However, for many of the boys with whom I spoke, drinking was the primary focus of the weekend. They know it is against the law, they know they are not "supposed" to be drinking, they may have to lie to their parents about it, they know they may end up getting sick, but they go right ahead and guzzle down the beer—or hard liquor.

Why? It allows them to feel comfortable with girls, it allows them to express emotions that they ordinarily suppress, and for boys who are depressed, anxious, or angry, alcohol is a form of self-medication. When a woman asked the eighteenth-century literary figure Samuel Johnson why men drink to excess and make "beasts" of themselves, he said, "He who makes a beast of himself gets rid of the pain of being a man." Johnson was right, and it was the heart of our

> *There are more things to communicate about now, such as going out, drinking, girls, but I have kept my parents out of the loop for a lot of it.*
> —Eighteen-year-old boy

argument in *Raising Cain* that boys drink to fill the emotional void that they feel. However, at this moment I want to emphasize that boys drink in an effort to reach manhood because we do not offer them another satisfactory way to achieve it. Our high school boys are drinking more and more in an effort to act like men, because they feel useless so much of the time.

And what happens to a boy who goes off to college? He is joining the highest-drinking segment of the American population. Forty percent of two- and four-year college students have consumed more than five drinks on a single occasion in the previous two weeks. That 40 percent figure outpaces their non-college-going peers (35 percent) and high school students (31 percent). There is a lot of binge drinking going on among late-adolescent and young-adult college students, and the vast majority of it is done by boys. Heavy drinking is considered one of the routes to manhood in our society. Getting drunk is, of course, a dead end, and most boys discover that on their way to genuine manhood.

American culture does not provide a ceremony or a ritual that formally marks a boy's transition from boyhood to manhood, yet boys yearn for rituals, and if we don't create them, boys will continue to make them up on their own: hazing, athletic initiations, drinking contests, vandalism, and even criminal acts. Gang membership provides a form of initiation for boys. Perhaps the United States is too large and too diverse a country to be able to devise one single way to take boys to manhood. Jews ask their thirteen-year-old boys to participate in a bar mitzvah, a test of knowledge and studiousness that is celebrated in public. The Mormons send their eighteen-year-old sons out on a two-year missionary quest. That leaves the vast majority of boys in America with no prescribed manhood ritual at all. We don't take them out of their daily lives; we don't burn their childhood clothes and ask them to pass some difficult test. We don't give them structure and responsibility and something important to do. I repeat: for most boys, high school and college do not feel "important" in the way they need psychologically. Boys who go into the military, of course, find their manhood and their meaning in service to their country, but with the volunteer army, that is now a tiny minority of America's young men.

If it were up to me, the United States would require a year of service from every eighteen-year-old boy and girl, starting either at the end of high school or at age eighteen. It could be a year of military service, but there could also be many other kinds of service that young people could perform, including taking care of older people, children, or the natural environment—something along the lines of the Peace Corps, AmeriCorps, or Teach for America. I am recommending this for psychological reasons. Such an experience, if it contained some aspects of a rite of passage, would produce better citizens and a more cohesive society. Perhaps I am a dreamer, but I also think it might create a more dedicated, less rum-soaked group of college students. In any case, I absolutely believe that it would produce healthier young men. It would be helpful for boys if they had to give a year of their lives to society. It would make them feel responsible, and it would bring them the respect of the community and self-respect.

Until such time as we have universal service, parents and schools should strive to arrange the growth experiences that boys need in order to feel like men. A boy needs to be (1) away from his parents, (2) under the supervision of men whom he respects, (3) taking some social, emotional, or physical risks, (4) in a position of responsibility for himself and others, and (5) facing something larger than himself, whether it is God, nature, illness, poverty, or an entirely new culture and language. There are many situations that can provide a boy with these elements, from rebuilding ruined houses in New Orleans to strenuous camping, working with autistic children, or perhaps even touring with a band. Indeed, there are so many that I cannot catalogue them all. In the following section, we will meet two boys who have achieved a striking degree of independence through their experiences in a foreign country.

EMERGING INDEPENDENCE AT EIGHTEEN

What does a psychologically healthy eighteen-year-old boy look like? How do we recognize the end product of all this work by parents and son to produce a good boy, a good young man? It is difficult to say, because boys of this age are so close to adulthood it is like asking what a healthy adult looks like, and there are literally billions of answers to that question. From a psychologist's point of view, when a boy has mostly completed the five tasks of adolescence outlined in Chapter 7, he

I talk with my father the most, because our days overlap most frequently and he prods more often. —Boy, eighteen

PASSAGE TO MANHOOD

The boy sitting next to me on the prop plane from Toronto to North Bay was seventeen years old, a rising high school senior with a slight beard. He had the misfortune to be sitting next to a child psychologist, a so-called expert on boys, who would pester him with questions for the entire trip about how he was spending his summer and why. "This is kind of like a final exam," he observed, trying to get me to relent, but I wouldn't let go.

After he had gamely answered a number of my questions about the summer camp to which he was headed, I sprang the big one on him, the question I have asked many boys his age: "Do you consider yourself to be a man?"

"Yes," he replied immediately. Then he caught himself, hesitating momentarily before declaring with conviction: "Well, no . . . but I will be in August!"

What could a seventeen-year-old boy do between the last week of June and August that he could anticipate would make him a man? American culture doesn't have any universal ritual that sees a boy through that psychologically difficult passage from boyhood to manhood. Many boys—actually, almost every boy—struggle with what it means to become a man. Boys (or young men, if you prefer) in their late teens and into their early twenties wrestle with a riddle: *What test do I have to pass to become a man, and who will be able to recognize that I have reached that point?* My young companion thought he had found an answer.

It turned out that he was going to embark the next morning on a fifty-day canoeing trip that would take him and nine companions through lakes, rivers, rapids, mud, and ferocious mosquitoes, all the way up to Hudson's Bay, a distance of six hundred miles. He and his friends had been preparing for this by developing wilderness skills for the last four years at their camp. They would carry all of their own food; they would not shower for weeks; they would take risks and they would suffer. Toward the end of their journey they would see the northern lights and would visit an Inuit settlement. They might see moose and wolves, but, he told me, they were not going to be tourists. "This isn't about seeing wild animals," he asserted.

What was his definition of manhood? "It's taking responsibility," he said. "At the end of the day, it's taking responsibility and taking things you've learned from others and creating your own self. It's about finishing a grueling portage," he went on. "It's about doing work and getting a result."

Didn't he get that from school and varsity athletics? No. Though he did well in school and had bright college prospects, school didn't address his hunger to be a man. Not even playing sports could do that: "After sports you go home, take a shower, and watch TV." When he was on a canoe trip, he felt as if he made a sustained effort that connected him to all the boys who had canoed before him at that camp, for more than a hundred years.

What were his friends back in Ohio doing? "Hanging out. They're playing video games. Video games are the stupidest things," he declared. "I hate them. I mean, movies are interesting, but video games?" His contempt was obvious. Did his friends understand his choice? "No, it's frustrating. You try to explain to them how great it is. You tell them about paddling all day, and cooking your own food, about the mosquitoes and carrying a wood canoe, and they say, 'What, are you crazy?' "

This kind of trip, he acknowledged, "is not for everyone." It would be hard—but at the end, in August, he would feel as if he was a man.

This young about-to-be man described his father as a "good guy," his mother as a hardworking professional, and his stepfather as financially successful, but none of them seemed to hold the key to helping him become a man. American culture has no universal ritual for helping boys move from boyhood to manhood. Yet every boy yearns to be a man, and traditional societies always took boys away from their parents for an initiation rite. We no longer have such rituals, but boys still wonder: *What is the test, where do I find it, how do I pass it, and who will recognize that moment when I pass from boyhood to manhood?* We fail to provide a meaningful, challenging path that speaks to the souls of a majority of boys.

The key to his manhood lay with the counselors who would accompany him on the journey, and with his companions whose lives he would protect and who would, in turn, look out for him.

Being in the out-of-doors isn't the only way you can achieve the feeling of being a man, though. You can get it taking on a tough job, singing with your friends in a group before audiences, or doing community service. All of those take commitment and courage. The outdoor setting just sharpens the issues of risk and courage. There is something that happens in the outdoors, and that is that you strip down to the essential things: safety, companionship, and a shared sense of mission. You set aside all the busyness and crap of daily life, and that allows you to think about what it actually means to be a man.

is close to the manhood that he will achieve in the next few years. (1) He has become acclimated to his pubertal growth, he has made peace with the body his genetics have given him, and he takes care of himself. (2) He has transformed his relationship with his parents into something more of an honest, adult relationship. (3) He has developed reciprocal friendships that sustain him in his life outside of his family. (4) He has become capable of both sexual expression and true intimacy, even if he has not totally integrated them both into a fully realized love relationship. (5) He has developed an identity that acknowledges the contributions of family and school, but that is unique to him.

I met both Jack and Neal in the Czech Republic when I spoke at a conference there. Jack, a Canadian, was on a Rotary Club scholarship in a student exchange program. Neal had lived abroad with his family for almost his entire life. When I interviewed Jack, the study-abroad student, he was just a few weeks away from his eighteenth birthday. He did not yet consider himself a "man," because he still had to return to his small town in Canada for his final year of high school, but during his year abroad he had achieved a level of confidence and individuality that you could feel when you were in his presence. Neal did not think he had reached manhood yet, either, but he had played for a foreign soccer club, had recovered from a serious athletic injury, and was getting ready to graduate from high school and move to a different country for college. Neal was thoughtful, honest, and in possession of his own identity, even if he was not totally sure of what his adult life would look like. Both boys had achieved an impressive level of independence, productivity, and social responsibility. If they did not yet consider themselves men, they had tested themselves in the world and had, in their estimation, passed those tests.

Jack: Controlling Destiny

Jack is a handsome, six-foot-tall boy with close-cropped black hair who dresses in dark colors, much like a European adolescent. Economic independence from his parents is a paramount feature of his identity: "I worked three jobs last year so I didn't take money from my parents. If I'm not paying for my things, I feel useless." Jack took a year off from high school, allowing his classmates to graduate without him, to become an exchange student for three important reasons. He wanted to define himself as different from his family and escape, at least temporarily, from what he perceived as the family's wish to groom him, the oldest son, to take a lead role in the family business. Second, he wanted a break from a long relationship with a girl in his high school that had become burdensome. Third, he wanted to redefine his relationship with his father and his brothers by asserting his independence. He told me, "It makes me feel good to be in control" of his own life.

It was clear that high school had become claustrophobic for him. Though he was successful as captain of the debate team and had dated a popular girl for three years, the relationship had become a "high school drama." What no one except his mother knows is that he broke up with the girl when she pushed him

REMEMBER YOUR OWN RISKY BUSINESS

When we were making the PBS documentary *Raising Cain*, we gave teenage boys cameras and asked them to film things in the lives of boys that people do not ordinarily see. A group of boys from an affluent suburb of Boston, all seniors, all smart, all college-bound, came back with film they had made on the night of a heavy snowstorm. They had tied one end of a rope to the back of a pickup truck and the other to a child's plastic sled occupied by a large boy. While his companions drove down an unplowed road at thirty-five miles an hour, the boy in the sled swung wildly from side to side, like a water-skier behind a power boat, and he came terrifyingly close to lethal encounters with trees and telephone poles.

As a parent, you watch the film with your heart in your throat. You want to scream at the screen: *Stop, that's so dangerous!* But what you hear in the soundtrack is the boys whooping and shouting. One of them yells, "This is the best fucking idea we've ever had!"

No, no, it's not! It can't be! we think. And then we remember our own lives. We all had to take some risk, big or small, to feel grown-up. It was a risk to smoke, or steal something from a store; it was a risk to let someone else touch your body; it was a risk to dive into dangerous waters. Having a secret or private life was an essential part of becoming your own person, too.

At an evening parenting talk, a forty-two-year-old man, the father of two elementary-school-age children told us, "My mother thought I was really a responsible boy; she always trusted me," he reported. "She would have been shocked to know that I was on the roof of the school, prying off the skylights with friends so we could drop sixty-five feet into the school pool . . . in the dark." There was a sudden, collective gasp in the room. I spoke for the audience: "Don't you know that rehab hospitals are full of young men who have done things like that?" "Of course," he said. "But we were pretty sure we were dropping into the deep end. Besides, I let a friend go first."

Well, there it is, every parent's deepest fear: that our children will do something risky and we won't be able to stop them, we won't even know. We're terrified that even the most responsible boy could lie to his mother and drop from a rooftop skylight, sixty-five feet into a school pool in total darkness. I asked the man the classic psychologist's question: "How did you feel when you did that?" "Great!" he said, "Absolutely great, totally grown-up."

You could have the most loving, attentive, on-the-job parent in the world and you would still have to keep things from them. You may not have to drop from a skylight into a school pool, but you have to have something that they don't know about and didn't preapprove. Remember?

If you are in denial or trying to pretend that you didn't do what you did when you were a teenager, you cannot speak honestly with your son about the risk. If you pretend to yourself, as some parents do, that you never lied to your parents, not even by omission, then you cannot be realistic about your own kids. You are acting the part of an innocent and it will undermine your credibility.

If, however, you do remember the intensity of your feelings, about this or any aspect of adolescence, then it becomes possible to understand why kids are vulnerable and more likely that you'll muster your courage and talk with them. That's when you'll hear some of what you need to hear, and learn what you need to learn. If you really want to know about the secret lives of teenagers, start by remembering your own.

to have sex with her. They had never had intercourse in their long relationship and he felt as if sleeping with her might mean fulfilling her dream—no longer his, though he admits "we talked about it"—of getting married. He wasn't ready for that level of commitment, and he could not wait for graduation to start his own life. He was also tired of playing video games.

Since arriving in the Czech Republic he has found a new life for himself, giving up video games and falling in love with a twenty-year-old Australian woman. "I feel more for her than I did for the girl at home," he said. And to everyone's astonishment he has mastered conversational Czech, a notoriously difficult language, in a matter of six months. Like many Czechs, he drinks a beer with lunch and another with dinner, though he says that he avoids drinking a lot on weekends so he isn't tempted to sleep with another exchange student now that his new girlfriend has returned to Australia. They are trying to maintain their relationship. He continues to call his mother regularly and says she knows everything about his life. He does not talk to his father about the intimate matters he discusses with his mother.

He does not know what he is going to do in the future. He loved both his courses in school that focused on possible careers, but he has had so many ideas for his future that he is frustrated by his own inability to stay with any plan. He calls himself "spontaneous" and says he has that "leader thing" and that he takes care of his fellow exchange students the way he used to care for his younger brothers. Well, not exactly the same way—he used to cook for his brothers and help them with their homework, and now he picks up the bar tab for his fellow exchange students, but it is still caretaking. He thinks that he doesn't work as hard as he could in school, but he knows that when he finds the right thing for him, when it "clicks," he'll throw himself into it completely.

Neal: Serious About Sports

Neal is a small, thin boy with penetrating eyes and a cautious demeanor. He says that he has been emotionally "guarded" since the end of sixth grade. Because he is short and carries himself so casually, with a slight hunch to his shoulders, you might not guess that he is a gifted natural athlete. In his short life he has played on select boys' soccer teams in the United States and Europe, wherever his family moved to follow his father's postings. Indeed, Neal was such a talented striker for his highly ranked Czech club team that it seemed as if he might make the jump to the professional level in Europe—until he blew out his knee in a tournament in Croatia. It wasn't even a real game, just an exhibition match, and the unfairness of that fact left him bitter for a time.

He now plans to go to a university in England and study sports psychology (his mother is English, his father American). He also plans to play soccer at as high a level as he can for a university club team, but he says that he no longer has the "spring" that he used to and he cannot run long distances. His identity has long been shaped by living an international life with his family, by the loss of friends who moved away in sixth grade ("That's when I became guarded"), and most centrally by being an athlete playing with teammates whose language he did not speak. His soccer skills allowed him to bridge all international barriers throughout his boyhood. His dream of dreams is to move to Spain eventually and coach his beloved team, Real Madrid, but he is realistic about the chances of that. If that doesn't work out he'll coach at the university or school level, or practice sports psychology. He has started to coach kids' soccer teams, and though he is disappointed that he cannot teach them sophisticated plays, he says, "You have to build teamwork and motivate them."

After his two closest friends left the school, Neal floundered socially and then started drinking with the popular crowd in eighth grade. "It was an awkward time," he told me. "I was lying to my parents." He has had an on-again, off-again sexual relationship with a girl who is "really great, but she has a lot of emotional issues." He gave me the impression that he is trying to pull back from the relationship, but said, "I'm not sure I really want to let her go; I just want to make it simple."

Neal feels that his parents have given him an enormous amount of freedom as an adolescent. When he was younger, they never talked together about drinking or sex ("I assumed they knew"). He has wondered if he missed something by not having the sex talk with his parents and says that they aren't "that close" today. He said, "We get along," adding: "It is hard for me to say that I would like to have talked to my parents about it, because it has worked out good. I appreciate the kind of freedom that they gave me. It worked for me, but I understand why it wouldn't work out for somebody. I've always wanted to do things for myself. I've never wanted to be dependent."

I asked Neal if he considers himself a man. He answered, "Probably not," adding, "Right now I'm living at home. It is hard for me to consider myself a man if I'm living at home." What is his definition of manhood? "It is when I am completely independent of my family, financially. There must be some emotional aspect to it as well."

When I asked him who really knows him, he answered, "I know me." He elaborated, saying, "I haven't really seen the point of opening up. It's ironic. Opening up and talking has really helped the few times I've done it. You're always thinking in the back of your mind whether you want to sound cool. In high school you cannot really find someone who really accepts you or I haven't found that person yet." But he expects to find someone. It is just tough because he has been emotionally guarded for many years, since his two best friends moved away. "I probably have never gotten over that sixth grade experience," he told me, but he expects someday "to settle down and find someone, someone whom I think I can know forever."

Jack and Neal are two healthy eighteen-year-old boys. They are not finished products; they are works in progress—aren't we all—but they are psychically strong and growing. In their short lives they have both found love; they have both been able to work at something they cared about deeply. When Sigmund Freud was asked what made a person normal, he replied that it was the capacity for "love and work." Jack and Neal have shown that capacity. They love their

> *Although raising my sons was a horribly depressing time in my life and they put me through hell, they are my biggest joys now. Sometimes I feel that they had to get all of their aggression out when they were young so that they could be great men now.* —Mother of four sons, the youngest nineteen years old

parents; they have also shown an ability to take care of siblings, girlfriends, and friends. They have competed, succeeded, and been injured by life. They have experienced anger and bitterness at the way life has thrown them around, yet they have responded with resilience and creativity. While both boys look upon turning eighteen as a significant marker, they recognize that it is artificial and not the true beginning of anything. When I asked Neal about the closeness between him and his parents he said: "Would I have wanted to be closer to my parents?" Then he shrugged. "There is still time for that."

Many parents tell me that their sons shut down verbally and seem to pull away from them for long periods of time between early adolescence and late adolescence. That might mean between ages twelve and sixteen, or fourteen and eighteen. But at a certain point they come back. When your son feels he has accomplished what he needs to achieve on his own, when he has had the experiences away from you that allow him to trust himself, he can open up to you more fully. Mothers in particular always hope that they can maintain open communication with their sons through these years; it is rarely as open as they hope. Fathers who respect their son's autonomy and do not insist on controlling the conversations with their sons may hear more than they did when he was younger.

YOUR SON'S OWN SUCCESS STORY

It's easy to look at these two boys and see success—successful boys on the brink of manhood, and successful parenting because we tend to attribute children's success to good parenting. But it's important to remember two things:

First, these two boys are just two versions of success in a diverse world of boys (including yours), each with his own story of challenge and accomplishment. Some will find success in familiar terms that are easy for parents to recognize and celebrate, whether that is in college, the workplace, or perhaps community service. Some will find their purpose in realms a parent might never have imagined, but can—must—learn to appreciate. Many of the success stories I hear are most remarkable in how a boy has made his way, found a life he loves, and persisted to follow his own calling (finding it in his own time). This, despite pressures and pitfalls, and some challenges of his own making, which made it a hard go.

Sara, whose son Steven, now twenty-two, was mathematically gifted and fiercely independent, told me how she had tried desperately to keep him in school for years as she struggled as a single mother to find work that would enable them to live in a home, a school, a town, for any length of time. They moved twenty-four times. "I wanted him to go to college," she said. He skipped school and dipped into drugs. Over her protests, Steven chose to leave high school, graduating with a GED, and instead of going to college he chose mechanical engineering, in a manner of speaking. Today he builds lowriders—a kind of custom-designed, hydraulics-hyped stock car hybrid—with his friends. He also built a thriving portable welding business serving local businesses, often in an emergency moment when essential equipment has failed. He is well known and respected for the high quality of his work and his unfailing reliability. "He loves what he does," Sara said with pride. "He's a miracle."

> I cannot think of my son without smiling. I expect a lot from him, and I think he expects a lot as well. I hope we are both right.
> —Mother of an eighteen-year-old son

Her trust in his development dawned slowly over time, with his insistence on crafting a productive life of his own imagining. Disappointed as she was at the time he dropped out of high school, she adjusted her own imaginings and threw him a GED party when he completed his high school work. She continues to celebrate him as a young man, even at twenty-two. "I call him every day and tell him I love him. My job is to make sure the guy knows I love him and I believe he can make good choices for himself."

The second thing to remember is that, should you worry that you have been an imperfect parent, be assured that some boys grow into fine young men having had great parenting and some accomplish that despite deeply flawed parenting. If you are reading this book, you are a caring parent and your son has gained from that. All good parents second-guess themselves sometimes. All loving parents worry, and all parents doubt themselves (even child psychologists such as myself). There is no final exam in parenting, no certificate, no graduation. There is just no one out there who can give you a grade as a parent, except your son, and that will come later.

Being a parent is the most humbling job that any of us ever do in our lives. The best parents struggle at times, even with the easiest of children. As the great pediatrician and psychoanalyst D. W. Winnicott wrote, "You have sowed a baby and reaped a bomb. In fact, this is always true, but it does not always look like it." So your son is a kind of boy "bomb," full of energy and fury, passion and pain, love and happiness. Would you have wanted anything different in a son? Your joy in parenting is going to come from watching him engage fully with his life, overcome disappointments, find love, and, perhaps, become a wonderful father himself.

TRUSTING DEVELOPMENT: NATURE'S BEST PARENTING GUIDE

We have traveled a long journey in this book, from that sonogram image of a boy on the way and the imaginings of those early days to the complex lives and reflections of eighteen-year-olds a few short steps away from manhood. What worked for the boys in this book? What did they need from their parents? To return to the question raised in the opening pages of this book, what does your son need from you?

The answer is love, of course—the most intense, devoted love of which we are capable, attuned closely to their personalities, needs, and shifting developmental requirements. They need our support and guidance much of the time; they also need to be outdoors, far away from us, engaged in undirected play. They need us to ask about them, and they need us to respect their privacy. They need their sports, but they also need the arts to express themselves. And yes, they need us to keep our sense of humor, because being a boy is funny. Being as active, restless, and impulsive as many boys are is just plain funny; having a penis and thinking about sex all the time is funny; needing to win at every stupid little contest is funny. Having to be brave, self-sufficient, and masculine all the time can make a boy look quite ridiculous at times (men, too). We laugh and smile and trust that all of this boy stuff will turn into something good.

A Note to Mothers

Over the years, many, many women have come up to me and said, "My son has changed my life," or "I just love my boys. They're great!" and you can tell that they

> My oldest son, who was a terror when he was growing up, has become my most sensitive son of all.
> —Mother of four older sons

have fallen in love with their boys. They have fallen madly in love with their sons, with their son's friends, and with the idea of boys. Most important, they have come to trust in their son's development. These mothers have seen that there is a deep wisdom in the way boys grow, because it prepares them for their lives as men.

Mothers, you must trust boy development. Whether it is more nature or more nurture, boys have developed a way of growing up that makes them recognizable to other men and makes most of them—not all—good life partners for women. Please don't try to raise your son to be what we laughingly used to call a "sensitive New Age guy." Your son will figure out your scheme and he'll fight you. Instead, try to raise him to be the best father he can be, perhaps like your husband or father, or perhaps simply like the most loving, playful, emotionally strong man you know. Whenever you are frustrated, whenever you despair of your son, picture him playing with his children: the daughter he adores, the son who so resembles him. The mental picture of him with his children will pull you through the toughest times and guide you to the best decisions. And please, know that he will feel your love in his bones every day of his life. All boys and men carry their mothers with them in the foundations of their soul.

A Note to Fathers

Dads, you too have to trust in boy development. It seems odd that I should say it, because you were a boy once, but sometimes we forget—or we wish we could forget—how vulnerable and scared we were as boys. Sometimes we think that boys can be turned into men if we just control them and guide them to avoid all the mistakes we made. We cannot possibly do so; they will do some dumb things. Please don't try to raise a "successful" man, whatever that means. Your son probably won't want to be successful in exactly your terms.

Like his mother, you, too, should endeavor to raise him to be the best father he can be. When you are worried about his grades, college, or video games, look at him and try to picture him as a father, speaking to his son and daughter. Remember that your son will say the words to his children that you have said to him in much the same tone of voice; your image will be in his head as he speaks.

A son has his father inside him forever. He thinks about him, loves him, imitates him, and competes with him until his dying day.

Most men say that their relationship with their father was complex, often difficult, and sometimes disappointing. But despite their fathers' flaws, many boys and men tell me they love—or loved—their fathers and carry that "best man" with them into their own lives as men. The father of a ten-year-old boy summed it up simply: "I want to be as good a father as mine was." Whether you can say that about your own father or not, raise your son lovingly, and be assured, one day he will say it about you.

EPILOGUE

Leaving Home

IN APRIL OF THEIR SENIOR YEAR, I ONCE ASKED A LARGE GROUP OF TWELFTH graders, "What's going to be the toughest moment for you in the next six months?" I was, of course, trying to get at their fears of leaving home and going off to college. Boys typically let the girls answer that question and the girls usually oblige, talking about crying a lot on graduation day, or leaving their friends, or saying goodbye to their parents when they get dropped off at their college dorm. However, on this occasion a senior boy stood up to speak. At six feet five inches he was a big guy, in all ways a heroic-looking young man. And this is what he said:

> The toughest moment for me is going to be in the fall of freshman year, when I leave the library late, walk across a dark campus, walk up a dark stairway, and walk into a dark dorm room. Then I walk across the room, open the refrigerator, and find ... there's nothing there.

Everyone laughed. I laughed. As we know, boys have a way of going to the heart of feelings with humor. Essentially this imposing boy was saying, *I'm going to be afraid of being alone, I'm still a little scared of the dark, I'm going to miss my mommy, and who knows—maybe I'll starve to death.* Of course. Try as we might to deny it—and teenage boys sometimes do a great job of acting as if their parents mean nothing to them—we are all extraordinarily dependent on our parents, our family, our brothers and sisters, our friends, and the comforts of home. It is tough to launch yourself out into the world as a young man.

Because of his training as a boy, your son may feel that he is required to deny his dependence in order to make the transition from home to college, to the military, to his own apartment. "No big deal"—that is part of his male identity. He may look uncomfortable when you cry. He may not be able to say, "I'm really going to miss you, Mom and Dad." As nice as that might be for you to imagine, he may not be able to do more than mumble "Love ya" when you tell him how much you love him. It is possible that before he leaves home your son might become irritable and off-putting. I hope you won't get too hurt; I hope you will use some humor yourself. Perhaps you can threaten, "I'm going to be your worst nightmare of a sobbing, clinging mother." He'll smile and say, "Mom, don't go there," or "Not necessary."

One of the reasons we are all fascinated by the letters that men write to their families from the battlefield—and this has been true from the Civil War to Iraq—is that they are usually such honest, powerful expressions of men's true feelings. Gone is the diversionary humor, the misdirection, and the minimizing that usually characterize male communication. Facing the threat of possible death in battle, men put it on all the emotional line.

Please know that your son has just such feelings about his family, most likely very deep and even tender ones. It's just that, hey, this is college, or this is just moving to an apartment of his own, or whatever. No big deal. And he knows he's coming home again. His growing up is not finished yet. There is plenty of psychological work to be done between mother and boy and between father and boy, and your son may know that better than you do. Parents of high school seniors, preoccupied with the loss of a boy's daily presence in the house, mistakenly think that parenting is over. One father admitted that in his older son's last two years of high school,

> we had some friction over curfew rules. He was determined to stretch the rules, and I had been so accustomed to a boy who didn't often break the rules that we had some time of friction. I see it now as a fear I had of losing control over him, over his life as he was finding someone new to share it with. We can laugh about it now.

His son is now twenty, halfway through college, and they can laugh about it together. That is because their relationship is vital, ongoing, and mutually respectful. That is because this dad is grateful to have been the father of boys. He writes: "It has been great to see my sons emerging as young adults, with their own personalities, foibles, and dreams."

I know a mother and father who were really distressed when their youngest son, an easy, lovable boy, was in his senior year. "He's our last child and we're really going to miss him when he leaves," they told me. By March of his senior year, he was so irritating that they could not wait to see him leave for college. He was accepted to his first-choice college but decided to take a gap year. That created much uncertainty. Then he got a wonderful summer job and went off and was very successful; his parents were very proud. In the fall he returned to face his gap year—no college, no job, and much fighting between son and parents. Then he got a job. His parents were relieved. His father and he did a building project in the house. That was important psychological work for them both. He then went off to college and did beautifully for four years, only to return to live at home with no job. Much angst on the parents' part. This pattern of going off and returning home continued until he was twenty-five, when he really did move out on his own for good (but he continued to take care of the dog when his parents went on vacation).

Eighteen is not the end of your parenting. Twenty-one isn't the end of your parenting. There will be more work to do—briefly, and in the transitions—at twenty-five and thirty. Your experience of parenting your son will never really end. Yes, he will finish college or find a good job. Yes, his brain will finally mature sometime in his mid- to late twenties. Yes, he will build an intimate relationship and become part of a couple and a friendship group of his own. But you will still be there, celebrating the boy he was and the man he is becoming. You may not see him as much, but you will always see his growth (and worry about the ways in which he seems psychologically stuck). The mother of a thirty-two-year-old son who had just made her a grandmother recently told me how excited and proud she was to see what a good father her son was: "He's just totally in love with his little girl."

She should not be surprised, because she was a totally devoted mother for her four boys. Of course, there was that weekend when she and the boys' dad went away and left the boys in charge of the house. They absolutely promised to look out for the youngest brother, the eleven-year-old, and not give a party. Years later, she learned that they had paid the eleven-year-old twenty dollars to keep silent and locked him in the attic for four hours—no bathroom access—so he could not witness the wicked party with girls and drinking that they held in the house. Her wild boys, who looked her in the eye and lied to her about their intentions, are now becoming responsible parents themselves. And so it goes.

One mother of a six-year-old wrote to me about her experience of raising a son. I would like to end this book with her words:

I love my boy. I would not be the mother I am today without him. I used to believe that boys and girls were the same. Equality, equality, equality. I was raised with the belief that a woman can do anything a man can do. Well, after having a son I realize that I was wrong. They are very different. They have different roles and expectations than females. He has taught me so much about men. They do way more than pee differently. I am so lucky to have my boy to hold my hand.

ACKNOWLEDGMENTS

I COULD NOT AND WOULD NOT HAVE WRITTEN *IT'S A BOY!* WITHOUT THE help of many wonderful people. Nancy Miller, our editor, came up with the idea for a book that would tell the whole story of boys, from birth through age eighteen. She is a brilliant editor as well as the mother of three boys; her confidence in the manuscript has sustained me when my own has wavered. Gail Ross, my wise agent, saw the promise in the book and has supported me throughout the writing of it.

A number of people have helped me from the beginning by suggesting ideas and approaches to the book and by reading later drafts of the manuscript. Larry Cohen, Ph.D., my *Best Friends, Worst Enemies* and *Mom, They're Teasing Me* coauthor, has been my lead advisor and has provided me with invaluable guidance with the Eight Lines of Development sections of the book. Martha Bestebreutje, Ph.D., Theresa McNally, Ed.D., Kathleen Fraser, Ed.D., and Professor Gillian McNamee of the Erikson Institute in Chicago have all contributed valuable insights based on their extensive experience with young children in school settings. Johnye Ballenger, M.D., opened the doors of her pediatric practice and invited me to observe her at work. Michelle Anthony and Reyna Lindert, coauthors of *Signing Smart with Babies and Toddlers*, both kept detailed journals of the early months of their sons' lives and shared them with me. Peter Mortola, Ph.D., and his partners in the BAM! Boys Advocacy and Mentoring Program at Lewis and Clark College shared their materials and wisdom. They have all inspired me.

More than five hundred people—parents, teachers, and boys—took the time to answer the extensive questionnaires that I posted on my Web site. I want to thank them for their honesty, their insights into teaching and parenting boys, and their marvelous anecdotes about boy life. I conducted close to one hundred individual interviews with parents and boys, some of them highly personal. I wish I could acknowledge them all by name here; I'll have to settle for saying that I am enormously grateful for their time and their trust.

During the writing of this book I visited forty different school communities and have learned much from the teachers in all of them. Joel Weiss invited me to be the "educator in residence" at the Crane School in Santa Barbara during the academic year 2006–2007, when the faculty was discussing the teaching of boys and experimenting with single-sex classes. The Chestnut Hill School has been experimenting with single-sex classes for a decade; Dr. Greg Blackburn, the headmaster, invited me to interview teachers, students, and families in his community. Fretta Reitzes and Nancy Schulman of the 92nd Street Y in New York shared their wisdom and gave me complete access to their preschool. The American School in Tampico, the Salisbury School, the International School of Prague, Catlin Gabel School in Portland, Oregon, Hiteon Elementary School in Beaverton, Oregon, and the Seven Hills School in Cincinnati were all enormously helpful, as were Chris Wadsworth and Bradley Adams, directors of the International Boys' School Coalition. For the last fifteen years I have been the consulting psychologist to a superb all-boys school outside Boston, the Belmont Hill School. I have learned more than I can say from watching the gifted teachers and administrators work with students, and I have, of course, learned an immense amount from the boys themselves.

At the age of sixty, I still have many of the traits I had as a seventh-grade boy in school. I am disorganized, I procrastinate, I cannot find things in the piles all over the floor of my office, and because I learn through hearing as much or more than by reading, I often cannot recall where I have picked up certain facts. Though I am a fluent writer, I am not a disciplined rewriter. In short, if it were up to me alone, this book never would have gotten written. Four women are responsible for keeping me on track.

My research assistant, Lindsay Garre, has been a gift from the gods. She has located research articles, hunted down facts, found boys and families for me to interview, read every word of the book, and written the Notes at the end of this book. Her organizational and technical skills and work ethic are awe-inspiring; her good cheer always lifts me up.

Elizabeth Diggins, my administrative assistant, has run my office, organized my traveling life, paid my bills for me, and put up with my crankiness with great good humor. I cannot imagine how I ran my life before she came to work for me.

I have been fortunate indeed to coauthor four books with Teresa Barker. She has a deep appreciation for the lives of boys; she also loves the English language and the process of creating books. When I'm lost in the trees, she can always see the whole forest. If I am a writer, it is because she believes in my writing and brings out the best in me. She is my muse, my editor, my coach, my teacher, my therapist, and my dear friend.

Finally, I would like to thank my wife, Theresa McNally, for holding our home life together during the last two years with humor, grace, and love. She patiently read many versions of these chapters and helped to ground them in her wisdom as a psychologist and her experience as a mother. I would also like to thank my children, Joanna and Will, for their patience and their love. I completely underestimated the size and scope of this book and how much time it would take to write. I'm sorry.

One of the great ironies of writing parenting books is that in order to write them you become a stranger in your own family. I am keenly aware that when Benjamin Spock, M.D., died, his two embittered sons had nothing good to say about him to journalists. I am a fortunate man; my family is still speaking to me.

—Michael Thompson

IN ADDITION TO ALL THOSE LISTED ABOVE, I WOULD LIKE TO THANK THE many friends—parents of boys—with whom I have shared the joys and challenges of raising sons over the years, and the boys themselves. Many of them are young men now, pursuing their dreams and thriving in their own distinct ways. These are boys who drove us crazy with their mischief and disorganized ways. The young boy who secretly redesigned the rain gutters on the roof of his parents' home so the water would collect in one muddy splash is about to graduate as an engineer. The boy who always put friends first when they needed to talk, even if it meant the English paper had to wait, is heading for graduate school in counseling psychology. Things work out. To the fathers in that group, to my own father, George Barker, and to those of my friends growing up, I also owe a special debt for showing me the many different ways that men lead lives of emotional connection.

My deep appreciation for Michael Thompson, as a psychologist and advocate for children, an author, a writing partner, and a friend goes beyond words, and extends to his family for sharing him as they have with the work.

Finally, I want to thank my husband, Steve, and our son, Aaron, for teaching me so much about the lives of boys and men; my daughters, Rebecca and Rachel, for their years of rich, articulate field reports on boy behavior; and all four of them for their continued patience and love.

—Teresa Barker

NOTES

Introduction

xiv *Recent research, in part the result of our ability to look inside the brain:* L. Sax, *Why Gender Matters: What Parents and Teachers Need to Know About the Emerging Science of Sex Differences* (New York: Broadway Books, 2006).

xiv *Steven Pinker, a professor:* D. Halpern and S. Pinker, "The Science of Gender and Science: Pinker vs. Spelke: A Debate," *Edge: The Third Culture,* May 16, 2005. www.edge.org/3rd_culture/debate05/debate05_index.html.

xiv *When researchers give boys and girls:* B. A. Shaywitz et al., "Sex Differences in the Functional Organization of the Brain for Language," *Nature,* February 16, 1995, 607–9.

xiv *When we understand that boys:* C. D. Good et al., "Cerebral Asymmetry and the Effects of Sex and Handedness on Brain Structure: A Voxel-Based Morphometric Analysis of 465 Normal Adult Human Brains," *Neuroimage* 14, 3 (2001): 685–700.

xiv *Researchers working with infants:* K. Weinberg, "Infant Affective Reactions to the Resumption of Maternal Interaction after the Still-Face," *Child Development* 67, 3 (1996): 905–14.

xvii *Forty years ago:* U.S. Department of Education, National Assessment of Educational Progress, *The Nation's Report Card* (Washington, D.C.: National Center for Education Statistics, 2006).

xx *They do get toilet-trained:* D. Halpern, "Sex Differences in Intelligence: Implications for Education," *American Psychologist* 52, 10 (1997): 1091–102.

Chapter 1: Imagining a Boy: What Were You Thinking?

5 *Though it may be surprising:* Information on embryo development provided by Dr. Jan L. Shifren, M.D., September 2006.

8 *Parenting advisor T. Berry Brazelton, M.D.:* T. B. Brazelton, *Touchpoints: The Essential Reference: Your Child's Emotional and Behavioral Development* (Reading, Mass.: Perseus, 1992). This classic reference guide mindfully outlines the various "touchpoints" of a child's developmental stages.

Brazelton is a pediatrician at Children's Hospital in Boston, Massachusetts, and has been a guide to parents for decades.

11 *Author Andrea Buchanan:* A. J. Buchanan, *It's a Boy: Women Writers on Raising Sons* (Emeryville, Calif.: Seal Press, 2005). A wonderful collection of women writers discussing their experiences of being pregnant with boys, raising boys, and how it changed their outlook on boys.

23 *That is part of the picture:* J. Deak, *Girls Will Be Girls: Raising Confident and Courageous Daughters* (New York: Hyperion, 2002).

23–24 *That's wonderful when it happens:* W. Farrell, *Father and Child Reunion: How to Bring the Dads We Need to the Children We Love* (New York: Penguin Putnam, 2001).

24 *Indeed, 35 percent of boys:* Centers for Disease Control, Prevention Research Centers, "Boys' Health Risks May Be Reduced by Strengthening Father-Son Bonds," June 30, 2006, http://www.cdc.gov/prc/tested-interventions/promising-interventions/boys-health-risks -reduced-father-son-bonds.htm#backgrnd.

25 *The textbook definition of child development:* M. Cole and S. Cole, *The Development of Children*, 4th ed. (New York: Worth, 2001). This is the best child development text yet, beautifully written.

28 *If you are going to be the parent:* P. Leach, *Your Baby and Child from Birth to Age 5* (New York: Alfred A. Knopf, 2003). This resourceful parenting guide outlines each developmental stage in this period (newborn, settled baby, older baby, toddler, and young child), discussing different topics such as feeding, teeth and teething, crying, sleeping, and everyday care.

Chapter 2: An Essential Love Affair: Your Baby Boy: Birth to Eighteen Months

33 *The English pediatrician and psychoanalyst:* D. W. Winnicott, *The Child, the Family and the Outside World* (Reading, Mass.: Addison Wesley, 1992). Donald Winnicott, pediatrician and psychoanalyst, wrote popular parenting books in the 1960s on child development.

34 *Recent research in human attachment:* R. Karen, *Becoming Attached: First Relationships and How They Shape Our Capacity to Love* (New York: Oxford University Press, 1998).

36 *Infancy is the period of the:* L. B. Ames, F. Ilg, and C. C. Haber, *Your One-Year-Old: 12 to 24 Months, Fun Loving and Fussy* (New York: Dell, 1982).

42 *Research—and simple observation:* K. D. Pruett, "How Men and Children Affect Each Other's Development," *Zero to Three Journal* 18, 1 (1997). This article examines the various roles that fathers play in their child's development, from nurturer to role model. It also discusses the positive effects of male involvement, stereotypes, and expectations that men try to fulfill, and the journey that boys face as they grow into manhood.

43 *This line of research:* J. Bowlby, *The Making and Breaking of Affectional Bonds* (London: Tavistock, 1979).

44 *If you think TV viewing is harmless:* F. Zimmerman, D. Christakis, and A. Meltzoff, "Associations Between Media Viewing and Language Development in Children Under Age 2 Years," *Journal of Pediatrics,* 151, 4 (2007): 364–68.

46 *In another experiment:* A. J. DeCasper and W. P. Fifer, "Of Human Bonding: Newborns Prefer Their Mother's Voices," *Science* 208 (1980): 1174–76.

47 *When you smile, he wants:* D. Siegel and M. Hartzell, *Parenting from the Inside Out* (New York: Tarcher, 2004).

49 *Fifty years ago, pioneering child psychologist:* E. Erikson, *Childhood and Society* (New York: W. W. Norton, 1993). This book reviews the eight unique stages of life of a child and provides developmental insight on each stage.

50 *"Fathers do not mother":* K. Pruett, *Fatherneed: Why Father Care Is as Essential as Mother Care for Your Child* (New York: Broadway Books, 2001).

51 *However, when a baby frequently sees a flat:* K. Weinberg, "Infant Affective Reactions to the Resumption of Maternal Interaction after the Still-Face," *Child Development* 67, 3 (1996): 905–14.

51 *Researchers also have found:* B. Repacholi and A. Meltzoff, "Emotional Eavesdropping: Infants Selectively Respond to Indirect Emotional Signals," *Child Development,* 78, 2 (2007): 503–521.

53 *"Love, and the lack of it:* T. Lewis, F. Amini, and R. Lannon, *A General Theory of Love* (New York: Vintage, 2001), 89.

53 *I'd like to remind you of:* D. W. Winnicott, *Through Paediatrics to Psychoanalysis* (New York: Basic Books, 1958).

54 *When a mother and child cannot:* Karen, *Becoming Attached.*

56 *"Family is the organizing":* H. L. Rich, *In the Moment: Embracing the Fullness of Life* (New York: William Morrow, 2003).

57 *First, research suggests that boys:* Ibid.

57 *It was a majority of the boys who:* Weinberg, "Infant Affective Reactions."

59 *Still, sex differences are apparent:* S. Baron-Cohen, *The Essential Difference: Male and Female Brains and the Truth About Autism* (New York: Basic Books, 2004). Cambridge University professor of psychology and psychiatry Simon Baron-Cohen lays out his theory about male and female brain similarities and differences. Through neurological case studies and the insights of a full research team, he outlines behaviors associated with the brain.

61 *In a well-known experiment:* J. Connellan et al., "Sex Differences in Human Neonatal Social Perception," *Infant Behavior and Development* 23 (2001): 113–18. This study, conducted at the Autism Research Center, found that boys are more interested in objects, whereas girls are more interested in actual faces.

62 *Leonard Sax concludes that:* L. Sax, *Why Gender Matters: What Parents and Teachers Need to Know About the Emerging Science of Sex Differences* (New York: Broadway Books, 2006).

62 *Infant girls hear better than baby boys:* J. Cassidy and K. Ditty, "Gender Differences Among Newborns on a Transient Otoacoustic Emissions Test for Hearing," *Journal of Music Therapy* 38 (2001): 28–35.

62 *These findings fall in line:* Sax, *Why Gender Matters.*

63 *That is, their hemispheres are more:* Baron-Cohen, *The Essential Difference.*

64 *Karen Adolph, an investigator:* D. Halpern and S. Pinker, "The Science of Gender and Science: Pinker vs. Spelke: A Debate," *Edge: The Third Culture,* May 16, 2005, www.edge.org/3rd_culture/debate05/debate05_index.html.

64 *In another classic gender experiment:* L. Cohen, *Playful Parenting* (New York: Ballantine, 2001).

Chapter 3: Boys in Motion: The Excitement of Being a Toddler: Eighteen Months to Three Years

69 *Eighteen-to-twenty-one-month-old children:* L. B. Ames, F. Ilg, and C. C. Haber, *Your One-Year-Old: 12 to 24 Months, Fun-Loving and Fussy* (New York: Dell, 1982).

69 *Erik Erikson declared it to:* E. Erikson, *Childhood and Society* (New York: W. W. Norton, 1993).

76 *Parents often get angrier:* C. Bagley, M. Wood, and L. Young, "Victim to Abuser: Mental Health and Behavioral Sequels of Child Sexual Abuse in a Community Survey of Young Adult Males," *Child Abuse and Neglect* 18 (1994): 683–97.

76 *Boys have higher activity:* L. B. Ames and F. Ilg, *Your Two-Year-Old: Terrible or Tender* (New York: Dell, 1982).

77 *Boys in groups have more:* Ames and Ilg, *Your Two-Year-Old.*

78 *Richard Tremblay, a Canadian researcher:* D. S. Nagin and R. E. Tremblay, "Parental and Early Childhood Predictors of Persistent Physical Aggression in Boys from Kindergarten to High School," *Archives of General Psychiatry* 58 (2001): 389–94.

80 *Thirty-six percent of one-year-olds:* Study by Newson and Newson, 1963, quoted in Z. Luria, S. Friedman, and M. Rose, *Human Sexuality* (New York: Wiley, 1987).

81 *Alan Sroufe, the respected attachment:* R. Karen, *Becoming Attached: First Relationships and How They Shape Our Capacity to Love* (New York: Oxford University Press, 1998).

83 *One researcher wrote that caretakers:* M. S. Mahler, F. Pine, and A. Bergman, *The Psychological Birth of the Human Infant* (New York: Basic Books, 1975). This book examines the role of a mother in trying to balance her presence and support with the baby's individual development.

88 *One of our favorite characters:* A. A. Milne, *Winnie-the-Pooh* (New York: E. P. Dutton, 1954).

97 *Autism, a serious disorder of:* Autism Society of America, "Defining Autism," http://www.autism-society.org/site/PageServer?pagename=about_whatis_characteristics (accessed September 25, 2006).

98 *Indeed, some characteristics that:* S. Baron-Cohen, *The Essential Difference: Male and Female Brains and the Truth About Autism* (New York: Basic Books, 2004).

98 *Between the ages of two:* T. Pelletier, "Who Is Likely to Stutter," revised by C. Spillers, Department of Communication Sciences and Disorders, University of Minnesota, Duluth, December 2000, http://www.d.umn.edu/~cspiller/stutteringpage/incidence.htm (accessed October 19, 2006).

99 *I asked Michelle Anthony:* M. Anthony and R. Lindert, *Signing Smart with Babies and Toddlers: A Parent's Strategy and Activity Guide* (New York: St. Martin's/Griffin, 2005).

102 *At this early age:* L. Cohen, *Playful Parenting* (New York: Ballantine, 2001).

Chapter 4: Wild Thing: Powerful Little Boys: The Three- and Four-Year-Old Boy

105 *I have always thought:* M. Sendak, *Where the Wild Things Are* (New York: HarperCollins, 1988).

106 *The great English pediatrician:* D. W. Winnicott, *The Child, the Family and the Outside World* (Reading, Mass.: Addison-Wesley, 1992).

114 *Louise Bates Ames describes:* Ames and Ilg, *Your Four-Year-Old.*

116 *In a recent New York Times:* P. Brown, "Supporting Boys and Girls When the Line Isn't Clear," *New York Times,* December 2, 2006.

119 *The United States has the highest rate:* Centers for Disease Control, U.S. Department of Health and Human Services, *Youth Violence* (2006), www.cdc.gov/ncipc/dvp/bestpractices/Introduction.pdf.

120 *Researcher Tiffany Field:* T. Field, "American Adolescents Touch Each Other Less and Are More Aggressive Toward Their Peers as Compared with French Adolescents," *Adolescence* 34 (1999): 753–58.

123 *Boys who are going to:* L. B. Ames and F. Ilg, *Your Three-Year-Old* (New York: Dell, 1982).

123 *First, they recognize:* L. B. Ames and F. Ilg, *Your Four-Year-Old: Wild and Wonderful* (New York: Dell, 1982).

125 *Such sex-stereotyped toy:* E. Maccoby, *The Two Sexes: Growing Up Apart, Coming Together* (Cambridge, Mass.: Belknap, 1998).

127 *Eleanor Maccoby, the author:* E. Maccoby, *The Two Sexes: Growing Up Apart, Coming Together* (Cambridge, Mass.: Belknap, 1998). Eleanor Maccoby, a professor of psychology at Stanford University, is the greatest expert in the past thirty years in the field of gender differences. She has conducted landmark work on the topic, and much of the discussion on gender-exclusive groups is based on Maccoby's works.

131 *Professor Tobin said that:* J. Tobin, *Preschool in Three Cultures: Japan, China and the United States* (New Haven: Yale University Press, 1991). Through videotape observations of children playing in three different cultural settings, Joseph Tobin reveals the different attitudes and behaviors that each culture lays upon its children when engaged in social interactions.

132 *In* Tom Sawyer, *Mark:* M. Twain, *Adventures of Tom Sawyer* (Hartford, Conn.: American Publishing Company, 1876).

133 *Preschool boys who viewed violent TV programming:* D. Christakis and F. Zimmerman, "Violent Television Viewing During Preschool Is Associated with Antisocial Behavior During School Age," *Pediatrics* 120 (2007).

136 *Your four-year-old is:* Ames and Ilg, *Your Four-Year-Old.*

142 *Researchers have found that:* Maccoby, *The Two Sexes;* T. Power, "Mother- and Father-Infant Play: A Development Analysis," *Child Development* 56, 6 (1985): 1514–24.

145 *Research shows that fathers:* K. Pruett, *Fatherneed: Why Father Care Is as Essential as Mother Care for Your Child* (New York: Broadway Books, 2001).

Chapter 5: Ready or Not, Here Comes School: Your Son, Five to Seven

150 *By the age of five:* L. B. Ames and F. Ilg, *Your Five-Year-Old: Sunny and Serene* (New York: Dell, 1982).

150 *Girls excel in fine motor:* Cole and Cole, *The Development of Children.*

151 *By the ages of five to seven:* F. Ilg, L. B. Ames, and S. Baker, *Child Behavior: The Classic Child Care Manual from the Gesell Institute of Human Development* (New York: Harper and Row, 1981).

152 *That boys do not talk:* L. B. Ames, C. Gillespie, J. Haines, and F. Ilg, *The Gesell Institute's Child from One to Six: Evaluating the Behavior of the Preschool Child* (New York: Harper and Row, 1979).

155 *No matter how:* W. S. Barnett and D. J. Yarosz, "Preschool Policy Matters: Who Goes to Preschool and Why Does It Matter?" *Preschool Policy Matters* (National Institute for Early Education Research), August 2004.

155 *Research confirms what most:* S. Moore and R. Frost, *The Little Boy Book: A Guide to the First Eight Years* (New York: Crown, 1986).

156 *Many years ago:* M. Konner, *Childhood: A Multicultural View* (Boston: Little, Brown, 1993). Melvin Konner is the author of the single best book about child development viewed through a multicultural perspective, enabling us to see what is universal and unvarying about child development even across cultures.

156 *They now understand that:* M. Cole and S. Cole, *The Development of Children,* 4th ed. (New York: Worth, 2001).

159 *Jane Katch, for thirty:* J. Katch, *Under Dead Man's Skin: Discovering the Meaning of Children's Violent Play* (Boston: Beacon, 2002); J. Katch, *They Don't Like Me: Lessons on Bullying and Teasing from a Preschool Classroom* (Boston: Beacon, 2004). Jane Katch is a gifted kindergarten teacher and author. She was one of the featured teachers in the PBS documentary *Raising Cain.*

161 *The Question "Should we hold our son back?"* L. A. Bates, *Is Your Child in the Wrong Grade?* (Lumberville, Penn.: Modern Learning, 1978).

162 *Most families, however, cannot:* K. Fraser, private conversation.

166 *She published them:* S. Werman, *Notes from Kindergarten* (Lenox, Mass.: Suky Werman, 2007).

169 *By school age:* M. Thompson and D. Kindlon, *Raising Cain: Protecting the Emotional Life of Boys* (New York: Ballantine, 2000).

169 *If he were in kindergarten:* Centers for Disease Control and Prevention. *Attention Deficit Disorder and Learning Disability: United States, 1997–98.* Publication no. (PHS)2002-1534. A: Hyattsville, Md.: U.S. Department of Health and Human Services, Public Health Service, 2002.

173 *There have been a:* D. Christakis, and F. Zimmerman, *The Elephant in the Living Room: Make Television Work for Your Kids* (Emmaus, Penn.: Rodale, 2006).

175 *Cross-cultural research has shown:* M. Thompson, C. O. Grace, and L. Cohen, *Best Friends, Worst Enemies: Understanding the Social Lives of Children* (New York: Ballantine, 2001).

177 *Rudolf Ekstein and Rocco Motto:* R. Ekstein and R. L. Motto, *From Learning for Love to Love of Learning* (New York: Brunner/Mazel, 1969).

178 *This example is extreme:* E. Maccoby, *The Two Sexes: Growing Up Apart, Coming Together* (Cambridge, Mass.: Belknap, 1998).

179 *By contrast, fathers:* Ibid.

180 *Researcher David Finkelhor, in:* D. Finkelhor, *A Sourcebook on Child Sexual Abuse* (New York: Sage, 1986); C. Bagley, M. Wood, and L. Young, "Victim to Abuser: Mental Health and Behavioral Sequels of Child Sexual Abuse in a Community Survey of Young Adult Males," *Child Abuse and Neglect* 18 (1994): 683–97.

181 *Studies show that by age:* A 1993 study by Flanner and Watson, cited in Maccoby, *The Two Sexes.*

183 *Psychologist and play therapist:* Personal interview with Lawrence Cohen.

186 *A significant minority of children:* Reading statistics from National Center for Educational Statistics, Institute of Education Sciences, U.S. Department of Education, using data from "National Assessment of Educational Progress: The Nation's Report Card," 1992, 1994, 2000, and 2003, http://nces.ed.gov/nationsreportcard. Forty-one percent of boys do not read at the basic

level in fourth grade. Gender-based statistics on the breakdown of word meaning and differencing show that girls outperform boys in reading.

186 *What we do know:* Statistics from the U.S. Department of Education, National Center for Education Statistics, May 2006. National Education Longitudinal Study of 1988 First Follow-up: Student Component Data File User's Manual Volume II. Institute of Education Sciences, U.S. Department of Education, http://nces.ed.gov/pubsearch/pubsinfo.asp?pubid=92088.

189 *In the United States today there:* R. Whitmire, "Boy Trouble," *New Republic,* January 23, 2006.

189 *Though academic underachievement:* United Nations Children's Fund, *The State of the World's Children 2004: What About Boys?,* http://www.unicef.org/sowc04 (accessed September 2006); United Nations, Statistics Division, *Demographic Yearbook 1996* (New York: United Nations, 1998); J. Wirt, S. Choy, P. Rooney, S. Provasnik, A. Sen, and R. Tobin, The Condition of Education 2004 (NCES 2004-077). U.S. Department of Education, National Center for Education Statistics (Washington, D.C.: U.S. Government Printing Office, 2004).

Chapter 6: Boys on a Mission: Your Son from Eight to Ten

194 *Erik Erikson described children:* E. Erikson, *Identity Youth and Crisis* (New York: W. W. Norton, 1968).

196 *Whatever he is doing:* E. Erikson, *Childhood and Society* (New York: W. W. Norton, 1993).

196 *In the industrialized world:* M. Konner, *Childhood: A Multicultural View* (Boston: Little, Brown, 1993).

197 *Each stage of life:* Erikson, *Childhood and Society.*

198 *Perhaps the most pressing:* M. Cole and S. Cole, *The Development of Children,* 4th ed. (New York: Worth, 2001).

199 *Boys' preference for gender-exclusive:* E. Maccoby, *The Two Sexes: Growing Up Apart, Coming Together* (Cambridge, Mass.: Belknap, 1998).

200 *Michelene Chi compared the:* Cole and Cole, *The Development of Children.*

201 *Unfortunately, 41 percent of children:* G. R. Lyon, *The NICHD Research Program in Reading Development, Reading Disorders and Reading Instruction,* National Center for Learning Disabilities, New York, 2004.

205 *This disorder is diagnosed:* American Academy of Child and Adolescent Psychiatry Web site, http://www.aacap.org/page.ww?section=Publication+Store&name=Your+Adolescent++Oppositional+Defiant+Disorder.

205 *Noted child psychiatrist:* E. Hallowell and J. Ratey, *Driven to Distraction* (New York: Pantheon, 1994); E. Hallowell and C. Corman, *Positively ADD* (New York: Walker, 2006). Hallowell's books are probably the most useful sources on ADD for parents. A Harvard-trained child psychologist, he writes in a style that is digestible and resourceful.

205 *Researchers have found that in:* K. Dodge et al., "Peer Status and Aggression in Boys' Groups: Developmental and Contextual Analyses," *Child Development* 61 (1990): 1289–1309.

206 *Boys with impulse control:* M. Conlin, "The New Gender Gap: From Kindergarten to Grad School, Boys Are Becoming the Second Sex," *Business Week,* May 26, 2003.

210 *For many boys:* A. Mulrine, "Are Boys the Weaker Sex?" *US News and World Report,* July 30, 2001.

210–211 *Many boys struggle with:* P. Tyre, "The Trouble with Boys," *Newsweek,* January 30, 2006.

211 *In Illinois, after state tests:* The Chicago Tribune, October 31, 2007.

211 *The answer is that we:* Statistics from Center for Educational Statistics, Institute of Education Sciences, U.S. Department of Education, "NAEP: National Assessment of Educational Progress: The Nation's Report Card," 1992, 1994, 2000, and 2003, http://nces.ed.gov/nationsreportcard.

211 *This concern is heartening:* M. Gurian, *The Minds of Boys: Saving Our Sons from Falling Behind in School and Life* (San Francisco: Jossey-Bass, 2005).

212 *Work consists of whatever:* M. Twain, *The Adventures of Tom Sawyer* (New York: Sterling, 2004).

212 *For a more thorough:* American Academy of Pediatrics, http://www.aap.com.

214 *Critics of school culture:* C. H. Sommers, *The War Against Boys: How Misguided Feminism Is Harming Our Young Men* (New York: Simon and Schuster, 2001).

214 *Thomas Newkirk, a professor:* T. Newkirk, *Misreading Masculinity: Boys, Literacy, and Popular Culture* (Portsmouth, N.H.: Heinemann, 2002).

217 *According to Dimitri Christakis and Frederick Zimmerman:* D. Christakis and F. Zimmerman, *The Elephant in the Living Room: Make Television Work for Your Kids* (Emmaus, Penn.: Rodale, 2006).

219 *The National Institute on Media:* TV stats were collected from: The National Institute on Media (http://www.mediafamily.org); TV Turn Off Network (http://www.tvturnoff.org/factsheets .htm); National Institute on Media and the Family Office of Educational Research and Improvement, *National Education Longitudinal Study of 1988* (Washington, D.C.: Government Printing Office, 1988).

220 *It is only common sense:* D. Reinking and J. Wu, "Reexamining the Research on Television and Reading," *Reading Research and Instruction* 29 (1990): 30–43.

221 *When Christakis and Zimmerman:* D. Christakis et al., "Early Television Exposure and Subsequent Attentional Problems in Children," *Pediatrics* 113 (2004): 708–13.

221 *In the Ohio State:* S. Everett, "Mirage Multiculturalism: Unmasking the Mighty Morphin' Power Rangers," *Journal of Mass Media Ethics* 11, 1 (1996): 28–39.

221 *If watching such shows:* E. A. Geist and M. Gibson, "The Effects of Network and Public Television Programs on Four- and Five-Year-Olds' Ability to Attend to Educational Tasks," *Journal of Instructional Psychology* 27, 4 (2000): 250–61.

221 *Researchers also have shown:* R. Anderson et al., "Relationship of Physical Activity and Television Watching with Body Weight and Level of Fatness Among Children: Results from the Third National Health and Nutrition Examination Survey," *Journal of the American Medical Association* 279 (1998): 938–42.

221 *Pediatricians have taken the:* Christakis and Zimmerman, *The Elephant in the Living Room.*

222 *Many video and computer games:* E. G. M. Van Schie and O. Wiegman, "Children and Videogames: Leisure Activities, Aggression, Social Integration, and School Performance," *Journal of Applied Social Psychology* 27: 1175–94.

223 *However, as boys get:* D. Walsh, "Video Game Violence and Public Policy," paper presented at the conference Playing by the Rules: The Cultural Policy Challenges of Video Games, October 26–27, Chicago, http://culturalpolicy.uchicago.edu/conf2001/papers/walsh.html.

223 *Video games accomplish:* "Video Gaming," *The Economist,* April 2005.

225 *Mark Twain reminds us:* Twain, *The Adventures of Tom Sawyer.*

225 *Nine out of ten children:* Centers for Disease Control, "Physical Activity Levels Among Children Aged 9 to 13 Years—United States, 2002," *Morbidity and Mortality Weekly Report,* August 22, 2003.

227 *If the majority of children:* J. Brown, "When Should Children Start Playing Organized Sports?" May 3, 2004, www.southern.usta.com/sportscience/fullstory.sps?iNewsid=59390&itype=3919 &icategoryid=395.

229 *Despite advances in diagnostic:* Hallowell and Ratey, *Driven to Distraction;* Hallowell and Corman, *Positively ADD.*

Chapter 7: Startling Changes: A Time of Extraordinary Physical Change: Ages Eleven to Thirteen

249 *At the end of the:* D. Offer, D. Marcus, and J. Offer, "A Longitudinal Study of Normal Adolescent Boys," *American Journal of Psychiatry* 126 (1970): 917–24.

251 *Boys in adolescence have:* M. Cole and S. Cole, *The Development of Children,* 4th ed. (New York: Worth, 2001).

251 *Psychiatrists today are seeing more:* H. G. Pope Jr. et al., "Muscle Dysmorphia: An Underrecognized Form of Body Dysmorphic Disorder," *Psychosomatics* 38 (1997): 548–57.

252 *Author Willa Cather perfectly:* Katherine Anne Porter quotes Willa Cather in an essay found in the following book: K. A. Porter, *The Collected Essays and Occasional Writings of Katherine Anne Porter* (New York: Delacorte, 1970).

253 *The level of conformity:* T. J. Berndt, "Developmental Changes in Conformity to Peers and Parents," *Developmental Psychology* 15 (1979): 608–16.

254 *It is however, always the case:* R. Taffel, *The Second Family: Reckoning with Adolescent Power* (New York: St. Martin's, 2001).

255 *Although researchers have not:* U.S. Department of Education, National Assessment of Educational Progress, *The Nation's Report Card* (Washington, D.C.: National Center for Education Statistics, 2006).

255 *Research has shown that:* C. Buchanan, J. S. Eccles, and J. B. Becker, "Are Adolescents the Victims of Raging Hormones: Evidence for Activational Effects of Hormones on Moods and Behavior at Adolescence," *Psychological Bulletin* 111, 1 (1992): 62–107.

256 *David Walsh argues that:* Walsh and Bennett, *Why Do They Act That Way?*

256 *Anne Peterson writes:* A. Peterson, *Adolescent Development and the Biology of Puberty* (Washington, D.C.: National Academy Press, 1999).

256 *Research has shown the happiest:* R. Larson and M. Richards, *Divergent Realities: The Emotional Lives of Mothers, Fathers, and Adolescents* (New York: Basic Books, 1994).

256 *When he is in elementary:* L. Kohlberg, *The Psychology of Moral Development* (San Francisco: Harper and Row, 1984).

257 *Eric Erikson believed:* E. Erikson, *Childhood and Society* (New York: W. W. Norton, 1993).

258 *Psychologist Ron Taffel would:* R. Taffel, *Breaking Through to Teens: A New Psychotherapy for the New Adolescence* (New York: Guilford Press, 2005).

262 *An innovative curriculum:* S. Grant, H. Hiton, and P. Mortola, *BAM! Helping Boys Connect Through Physical Challenge and Strategic Storytelling: A Leader's Guide to Facilitating Strength-Based Boys' Groups* (London: Routledge, 2007).

267 *Sadly, in recent years:* Centers for Disease Control, *Adolescent Health: State of the Nation: Mortality Trends, Causes of Death, and Related Risk Behaviors Among US Adolescents,* publication no. (CDC) 099-4112 (Atlanta: U.S. Department of Health and Human Services, Public Health Service, 1993).

270 *I am reminded of the:* D. Walsh with N. Bennett, *Why Do They Act That Way?: A Survival Guide to the Adolescent Brain for You and Your Teen* (New York: Free Press, 2004).

281 *Sadly, more than 35 percent:* W. Horn and T. Sylvester, *Father Facts* (Gaithersburg, Md.: National Fatherhood Initiative, 2002).; U.S. Department of Commerce, Bureau of the Census, Current Population Survey (CPS), October Supplement, selected years 1977–2001, previously unpublished tabulation (December 2003); MSNBC, "Nearly 4 in 10 US Babies Born out of Wedlock," November 2006.

281 *Boys raised in homes:* National Center for Health Statistics, "Plan and Initial Program of the Health Examination Survey," *Vital and Health Statistics* 1, 4 (1965): 1–43.

285 *However, at the end of 2006:* U.S. Department of Education, National Assessment of Educational Progress, *The Nation's Report Card* (Washington, D.C.: National Center for Education Statistics, 2006).

286 *Since girls outperform boys:* R. Whitmire, "Boy Trouble," *New Republic,* January 23, 2006; J. Wirt, S. Choy, P. Rooney, S. Provasnik, A. Sen, and R. Tobin, The Condition of Education 2004 (NCES 2004-077). U.S. Department of Education, National Center for Education Statistics (Washington, D.C.: Government Printing Office, 2004).

286 *After Carol Gilligan wrote:* L. M. Brown and C. Gilligan, *Meeting at the Crossroads: Women's Psychology and Girls' Development* (Cambridge, Mass.: Harvard University Press, 1992).

286 *Advocates for single-sex:* L. Sax, *Why Gender Matters: What Parents and Teachers Need to Know About the Emerging Science of Sex Differences* (New York: Broadway Books, 2006).

287 *Perhaps boys miss reading:* K. Killion, "22 Practices That May Harm Boys," March 2006, Illinois Loop, www.illinoisloop.org/gender.html.

Chapter 8: Mystery Boy: What Is He Thinking? Ages Fourteen and Fifteen

298 *Exercise can vanish from their life:* U.S. Department of Health and Human Services, *The Surgeon General's Call to Action to Prevent and Decrease Overweight and Obesity* (Rockville, Md.: Public Health Service, Office of the Surgeon General, 2001).

300 *Boys become deeply attached:* D. Offer, D. Marcus, and J. Offer, "A Longitudinal Study of Normal Adolescent Boys," *American Journal of Psychiatry* 126 (1970): 917–24.

300 *Psychologist Ron Taffel calls:* R. Taffel, *Breaking Through to Teens: A New Psychotherapy for the New Adolescence* (New York: Guilford, 2005).

300 *Through adolescence, boys:* D. Eder, C. C. Evans, and S. Parker, *School Talk: Gender and Adolescent Culture* (New Brunswick, N.J.: Rutgers University Press, 1995).

302 *One thing over which:* J. G. Johnson, P. Cohen, S. Kasen, and J. S. Brook, "Extensive Television

Viewing and the Development of Attention and Learning Difficulties During Adolescence," *Archives of Pediatric Adolescent Medicine* 161 (2007).

309 *Indeed, boys under the:* American Psychiatric Association, *Diagnostic and Statistical Manual of Mental Disorders, Fourth Edition: Primary Care Version* (Washington, D.C.: American Psychiatric Association, 1995).

309 *He had many risk factors:* J. Wallerstein and S. Blakeslee, *Second Chances: Men, Women and Children a Decade After Divorce* (New York: Houghton Mifflin, 1996).

312 *Fifteen to 20 percent:* American Psychiatric Association, *Diagnostic and Statistical Manual of Mental Disorders, Fourth Edition: Primary Care Version.*

313 *One researcher found that:* R. M. Glass, "Treatment of Adolescents with Major Depression: Contributions of a Major Trial," *Journal of the American Medical Association* 292, 7 (2004): 861–63.

315 *But first it's important:* U.S. Department of Education, National Center for Education Statistics, National Postsecondary Student Aid Studies, 1995–96, 1999–2000, 2003–4, http://nces.ed .gov/npsas.

315 *In high school, as in:* R. Whitmire, "Boy Trouble," *New Republic,* January 23, 2006.

315 *Forty years ago:* U.S. Department of Education, National Assessment of Educational Progress, *The Nation's Report Card* (Washington, D.C.: National Center for Education Statistics, 2006); J. Wirt, S. Choy, P. Rooney, S. Provasnik, A. Sen, and R. Tobin, The Condition of Education 2004 (NCES 2004-077). U.S. Department of Education, National Center for Education Statistics. (Washington, D.C.: U.S. Government Printing Office, 2004).

315 *Two-thirds of the:* Ibid.

315 *Education reporter Richard Whitmire writes:* Whitmire, "Boy Trouble."

315 *There is controversy about:* M. Conlin, "The New Gender Gap: From Kindergarten to Grad School, Boys Are Becoming the Second Sex," *Business Week,* May 26, 2003.

315 *Judith Warner, writing in the:* J. Warner, "What Boy Crisis?" *New York Times,* July 3, 2006.

315 *Ann Hulbert, writing in the:* A. Hulbert, "Will Boys Be Boys? Why the Gender Lens May Not Shed Light on the Latest Educational Crisis," *Washington Post,* February 1, 2006.

316 *Sadly, inequalities associated:* J. Kozol, *Savage Inequalities* (New York: Harper Perennial, 1991).

316 *In 1971, girls lagged:* National Center for Educational Statistics, Institute of Education Sciences, U.S. Department of Education, data from National Assessment of Educational Progress (NAEP), selected years, 1971–2004, "Long-Term Trend Reading Assessments."

316 *In writing, the gap:* T. Newkirk, *Misreading Masculinity: Boys, Literacy, and Popular Culture* (Portsmouth, N.H.: Heinemann, 2002).

316 *The phenomenon of boy:* Organization for Economic Co-operation and Development, *Education at a Glance: OECD Indicators—2006 Edition.* www.oecd.org/dataoecd/32/0/37393408.pdf.

317 *A growing number of studies:* D. Halpern and S. Pinker, "The Science of Gender and Science: Pinker vs. Spelke: A Debate," *Edge: The Third Culture,* May 16, 2005, www.edge.org/3rd _culture/debate05/debate05_index.html.

318 *Between 79 and 98 percent of teachers:* U.S. Census Bureau, Census 2004, special tabulation, www .census.gov/hhes/www/eeoindex/page_c.html?

319 *Women still earn only:* "Women: Earn What You're Worth," CNN.com, June 24, 2005, www.cnn.com/2005/US/Careers/06/23/women.salary/index.html.

319 *Research on motivation shows:* Halpern and Pinker, "The Science of Gender and Science."

320 *When parents and teachers:* T. Jan, "Schoolboy's Bias Suit Argues System Is Favoring Girls," *Boston Globe,* January 26, 2006.

325 *In my book* The Pressured Child: M. Thompson and T. Barker, *The Pressured Child* (New York: Ballantine, 2005).

325 *As he starts high school:* National Center for Educational Statistics, Institute of Education Sciences, U.S. Department of Education, "Dropout Rates in the United States: 2000."

329 *Chinese are so worried:* S. Kershaw, "Hooked on the Web: Help Is on the Way," *New York Times,* December 2005; E. Cody, "Despite a Ban, Chinese Youth Navigate to Internet Cafés," *Washington Post,* February 2007.

329 *Video games play a huge:* NPD Group Inc. (2006, Sept. 19). *Video Gamer Segmentation Report,* September 19, 2006, www.npd.com/press/releases/press_060919a.html; National Institute on Media and TV Turn Off Network, http://www.mediafamily.org/facts/facts_effect.shtml.

330 *David Grossman, a retired:* D. Grossman, *On Killing: The Psychological Cost of Learning to Kill in War and Society* (Boston: Little, Brown, 1995); D. Grossman and G. DeGaetano, *Stop Teaching Our Kids to Kill: A Call to Action Against TV, Movie and Video Game Violence* (New York: Crown, 1999).

330 *Bruno Bettelheim argued that:* B. Bettelheim, *The Uses of Enchantment: The Meaning and Importance of Fairy Tales* (New York: Vintage, 1989).

331 *Harry Jenkins, the director:* H. Jenkins, "Lessons from Littleton: What Congress Doesn't Want to Hear About Youth and Media," *Independent School,* winter 2002, www.nais.org/publications/ismagazinelist.cfm?Itemnumber=145812&sn.ItemNumber=145956&tn.ItemNumber=145958.

334 *However, I do try to:* G. Jones, *Killing Monsters: Why Children Need Fantasy, Super Heroes, and Make-believe Violence* (New York: Basic Books, 2002).

335 *Are boys who love:* Grossman, *On Killing.*

335 *Normal boys, just like:* Grossman and DeGaetano, *Stop Teaching Our Kids to Kill.*

336 *Our public debate about:* H. Jenkins, "Reality Bytes: Eight Myths About Video Games Debunked," from Web site for PBS's *The Video Game Revolution,* www.pbs.org/kcts/videogamerevolution/impact/myths.html.

336 *Let's be honest:* B. Bettelheim, *The Uses of Enchantment: The Meaning and Importance of Fairy Tales* (New York: Vintage, 1989).

337 *In* Raising Cain *we discussed:* W. Pollack, *Real Boys* (New York: Random House, 1998).

341 *How a father and son:* R. Larson and M. Richards, *Divergent Realities: The Emotional Lives of Mothers, Fathers, and Adolescents* (New York: Basic Books, 1994).

343 *And what about:* O. Silverstein and B. Rashbaum, *The Courage to Raise Good Men* (New York: Penguin, 2000).

Chapter 9: On His Own: Ages Sixteen to Eighteen

355 *The single mother of Cedric:* R. Suskind, *A Hope in the Unseen: An American Odyssey from the Inner City to the Ivy League* (New York: Broadway Books, 1999).

355 *Lynn Ponton, M.D., in her book:* L. Ponton, *The Romance of Risk: Why Teenagers Do the Things They Do* (New York: Basic Books, 1998).

356 *Six thousand teenagers:* National Highway Traffic Safety Administration, crash statistics, November 2004, http://www.nhtsa.dot.gov/.

359 *New research suggests:* J. Ratey, *Spark: The Revolutionary New Science of Exercise and the Brain* (New York: Little, Brown, 2008).

359 *In light of the rapidly:* U.S. Department of Health and Human Services, *The Surgeon General's Call to Action to Prevent and Decrease Overweight and Obesity* (Rockville, Md.: Public Health Service, Office of the Surgeon General, 2001).

367 *By the age of seventeen:* W. D. Mosher, A. Chandra, and J. Jones, *Sexual Behavior and Selected Health Measures: Men and Women 15–44 Years of Age, United States, 2002,* National Center for Health Statistics, Centers for Disease Control, publication no. (PHS) 2003-1250, September 2005, www.cdc.gov/nchs/products/pubs/pubd/ad/361-370/ad362.htm.

369 *Americans spend about:* "Study: Children Bombarded with Online Porn," CBSNews.com, February 5, 2007, www.cbsnews.com/stories/2007/02/05/tech/main2431433.shtml.

375 *They are hearing:* J. H. Gagnon and W. Simon, *Sexual Conduct: The Social Sources of Human Sexuality* (Chicago: Aldine, 1973).

376 *The great American psychiatrist:* H. S. Sullivan, *The Interpersonal Theory of Psychiatry* (New York: W. W. Norton, 1968).

380 *Brain research suggests:* S. LeVay, "A Difference in Hypothalamic Structure Between Heterosexual and Homosexual Men," *Science* 254, 5032 (1991): 630.

380 *One study found:* D. H. Hamer et al., "A Linkage Between DNA Markers on the X Chromosome and Male Sexual Orientation," *Science* 261 (1993): 320–26.

380 *Another recent study:* D. A. Puts, C. L. Jordan, and S. M. Breedlove, "O Brother, Where Art Thou? The Fraternal Birth Order Effect on Male Sexual Orientation," *Proceedings of the National Academy of Sciences of the USA* 103, 28 (2006): 10531–2.

381 *The teachers intuitively:* R. Green, *The "Sissy Boy Syndrome" and the Development of Homosexuality* (New Haven: Yale University Press, 1987).

382 *The biggest problems:* National Mental Health Information Center, United States Department of Health and Human Services, "Children's Mental Health Facts: Children and Adolescents with Conduct Disorder," http://mentalhealth.samhsa.gov/publications/allpubs/CA-0010/default.asp.

383 *The three leading causes:* Centers for Disease Control. "Adolescent Health: State of the Nation—Mortality Trends, Causes of Death, and Related Risk Behaviors Among U.S. Adolescents." Atlanta: U.S. Department of Health and Human Services, Public Health Service, 2004, www.cdc.gov/mmwr/.

387 *When a woman asked:* J. Boswell, *The Life of Samuel Johnson* (New York: Penguin Classics, 1979).

388 *Forty percent of:* R. Hingson et al., "Magnitude of Alcohol-Related Mortality and Morbidity Among US College Students Ages 18–24," *Journal of Studies on Alcohol* 136 (2002): 136–44.

398 *As the great:* D. W. Winnicott, *The Child, the Family and the Outside World* (Reading, Mass.: Addison-Wesley, 1964).

BIBLIOGRAPHY

Ablow, K. 2005. Speaking in the Third Person, Removed from Reality. *New York Times,* November 1.

Ainsworth, M. D. S. 1969. Object Relations, Dependency and Attachment: A Theoretical Review of the Infant-Mother Relationship. *Child Development* 40: 969–1025.

Ainsworth, M. D. S., and S. M. Bell. 1970. Attachment, Exploration, and Separation: Illustrated by the Behavior of One-Year-Olds in a Strange Situation. *Child Development* 41: 49–67.

Allis, S. 2006. The Leadership Thing: What They Don't Teach in College Can Hurt Us. *Boston Sunday Globe,* April 23.

Alvarez, L. 2004. Educators Flocking to Finland, Land of Literate Children. *New York Times,* April 9.

American Academy of Child and Adolescent Psychiatry. 2004. Facts for Families: Conduct Disorder. http://aacap.org/page.ww?section=Facts%20for%20Families&name=Conduct%20Disorder.

American Academy of Pediatrics. 2006. New AAP Report Stresses Play for Healthy Development. [Press release.] October 9. www.aap.org/pressroom/play-public.htm.

American Psychiatric Association. 1994. *Diagnostic and Statistical Manual of Mental Disorders, Fourth Edition: Primary Care Version.* Washington, D.C.: American Psychiatric Association.

American Sociological Association. 2006. Affairs of Heart Matter to Boys, Too, Sociologists Find. [Press release.] www.newswise.com/articles/view/520394.

Ames, L. B. 1978. *Is Your Child in the Wrong Grade?* Lumberville, Penn.: Modern Learning.

Ames, L. B., and A. Gesell. 1937. Early Evidences of Individuality in the Human Infant. *Scientific Monthly* 45, 3: 217–25.

Ames, L. B., C. Gillespie, J. Haines, and F. Ilg. 1979. *The Gesell Institute's Child from One to Six: Evaluating the Behavior of the Preschool Child.* New York: Harper and Row.

Ames, L. B., and F. Ilg. 1982. *Your Three-Year-Old.* New York: Dell.

——. 1982. *Your Two-Year-Old: Terrible or Tender.* New York: Dell.

——. 1982. *Your Four-Year-Old: Wild and Wonderful.* New York: Dell.

——. 1982. *Your Five-Year-Old: Sunny and Serene.* New York: Dell.

——. 1979. *Your Six-Year-Old: Loving and Defiant.* New York: Dell.

Ames, L. B., F. Ilg, and C. C. Haber. 1982. *Your One-Year-Old: 12 to 24 Months, Fun-Loving and Fussy.* New York: Dell.

Ames, L. B., and C. C. Haber. 1985. *Your Seven-Year-Old: Life in a Minor Key.* New York: Dell.

Anderson, R., et al. 1998. Relationship of Physical Activity and Television Watching with Body Weight and Level of Fatness Among Children: Results from the Third National Health and Nutrition Examination Survey. *Journal of the American Medical Association* 279: 938–42.

Anthony, M., and R. Lindert. 2005. *Signing Smart with Babies and Toddlers: A Parent's Strategy and Activity Guide.* New York: St. Martin's/Griffin.

Aries, Philippe. 1962. *Centuries of Childhood: A Social History of Family Life.* New York: Vintage.

Auchincloss, L. 1956. *The Rector of Justin.* Boston: Houghton Mifflin Company.

Autism Society of America. n.d. Defining Autism. http://www.autism-society.org/site/PageServer ?pagename=about_whatis_characteristics.

Bagley, C., M. Wood, and L. Young. 1994. Victim to Abuser: Mental Health and Behavioral Sequels of Child Sexual Abuse in a Community Survey of Young Adult Males. *Child Abuse and Neglect* 18: 683–97.

Bailey, B. A. 2000. *I Love You Rituals.* New York: HarperCollins.

Barnett, W. S., et al. *The State of Preschool: 2005 State Preschool Yearbook.* New Brunswick, NJ: National Institute for Early Education Research.

Barnett, W. S., and D. J. Yarosz. 2004. "Preschool Policy Matters: Who Goes to Preschool and Why Does It Matter?" *Preschool Policy Matters* (National Institute for Early Education Research), August.

Baron-Cohen, S. 2004. *The Essential Difference: Male and Female Brains and the Truth About Autism.* New York: Basic Books.

Beitchman, J., et al. 1986. Prevalence of Speech and Language Disorders in 5-Year-Old Kindergarten Children in the Ottawa-Carleton Region. *Journal of Speech and Hearing Disorder* 51: 98–110.

Bell, N., and W. Carver. 1980. A Reevaluation of Gender Label Effects: Expectant Mothers' Responses to Infants. *Child Development* 51, 31: 925–27.

Benveniste, D. 2005. *Psychological Perspectives on Everyday Life.* Caracas, Venezuela: Ediplus.

Berndt, T. J. 1979. Developmental Changes in Conformity to Peers and Parents. *Developmental Psychology* 15: 608–16.

Berndt, T. J., and G. W. Ladd, eds. 1989. *Peer Relationships in Child Development.* New York: Wiley.

Betcher, R. W., and W. S. Pollack. 1993. *In a Time of Fallen Heroes: The Re-Creation of Masculinity.* New York: Guilford.

Bettelheim, B. 1989. *The Uses of Enchantment: The Meaning and Importance of Fairy Tales.* New York: Vintage Books.

Biddulph, S. 1984. *The Secret of Happy Children.* New York: Marlowe.

———. 1997. *Raising Boys.* Berkeley, Calif.: Celestial Arts.

Bigelow, B., T. Moroney, and L. Hall. 2001. *Just Let the Kids Play: How to Stop Other Adults from Ruining Your Child's Fun and Success in Youth Sports.* Deerfield Beach, Fla.: Health Communications.

Blackman, A. 2004. The Gender Gap. *Wall Street Journal,* January 26, 2004.

Blondell, R., M. Foster, and K. Dave. 1999. Disorders of Puberty. *American Family Physician* 60:1.

Blum, D. 1997. *Sex on the Brain*. New York: Viking.

Bordon, J. 2000. *Confucius Meets Piaget: An Educational Perspective on Ethnic Korean Children and Their Parents*. Seoul: Seoul Foreign School.

Boston Institute for the Development of Infants and Parents. 2006. *Part II: I Listen, therefore I AM*. Vol. 21, No. 1. Belmont, Mass.

Bowlby, J. 1979. *The Making and Breaking of Affectional Bonds*. London: Tavistock.

———. 1988. *A Secure Base: Parent-Child Attachment and Healthy Human Development*. New York: Basic Books.

Bowlby, J., and M. Fry. 1965. *Child Care and the Growth of Love*. London: Pelican.

"Boy Trouble." 2006. [Editorial.] *Boston Globe*, October 2.

Brazelton, T. B. 1992. *Touchpoints: The Essential Reference: Your Child's Emotional and Behavioral Development*. Reading, Mass.: Perseus Books.

Bretherton, I. 1992. The Origins of Attachment Theory. *Developmental Psychology* 28: 759–75.

Britt, R. 2006. Girls Much Quicker than Boys at Timed Tasks. April 25. www.livescience.com/humanbiology/060425_boys_girls.html.

Britton, J., H. Britton, and V. Gronwaldt. 2006. Breastfeeding, Sensitivity, and Attachment. *Pediatrics* 118, 5: 1436–43.

Brown, J. 2004. When Should Children Start Playing Organized Sports? May 3. www.southern.usta.com/sportscience/fullstory.sps?iNewsid=59390&itype=3919&icategoryid=395.

Brown, L. M., and C. Gilligan. 1992. *Meeting at the Crossroads: Women's Psychology and Girls' Development*. Cambridge, Mass.: Harvard University Press.

Brown, P. L. 2006. Supporting Boys or Girls When the Line Isn't Clear. *New York Times*, December 2.

Buchanan, A. J. 2005. *It's a Boy: Women Writers on Raising Sons*. Emeryville, Calif.: Seal Press.

Buchanan, C., J. S. Eccles, and J. B. Becker. 1992. Are Adolescents the Victims of Raging Hormones: Evidence for Activational Effects of Hormones on Moods and Behavior at Adolescence. *Psychological Bulletin* 111, 1: 62–107.

Butler, K. 2006. Beyond Rivalry, a Hidden World of Sibling Violence. *New York Times*, February 28.

Caplan, T., and F. Caplan. 1983. *The Early Childhood Years*. New York: Bantam.

Carey, B. 2005. Men and Women Really Do Think Differently. MSNBC, January 20. www.msnbc.msn.com/id/6849058.

Carnegie Council on Adolescent Development, Task Force on Education of Young Adolescents. 1989. *Turning Points: Preparing American Youth for the 21st Century*. New York: Oxford University Press.

Caron, A. F. 1994. *Strong Mothers, Strong Sons*. New York: Harper Perennial.

Carter, A., L. Mayes, and K. Pajer. 1990. The Role of Dyadic Affect in Play and Infant Sex in Predicting Infant Response to the Still Face Situation. *Child Development* 61, 3: 764–73.

Cassidy, J., and K. Ditty. 2001. "Gender Differences Among Newborns on a Transient Otoacoustic Emissions Test for Hearing." *Journal of Music Therapy* 38: 28–35.

Centers for Disease Control. 2003. "Physical Activity Levels Among Children Aged 9 to 13 Years—United States, 2002." *Morbidity and Mortality Weekly Report*, August 22.

Centers for Disease Control. 2004. "Adolescent Health: State of the Nation—Mortality Trends,

Causes of Death, and Related Risk Behaviors Among U.S. Adolescents." Atlanta: U.S. Department of Health and Human Services, Public Health Service. www.cdc.gov/mmwr/.

Centers for Disease Control and Prevention. 1993. *Adolescent Health: State of the Nation: Mortality Trends, Causes of Death, and Related Risk Behaviors Among US Adolescents.* Publication no. (CDC) 099-4112. Atlanta: U.S. Department of Health and Human Services, Public Health Service.

Centers for Disease Control and Prevention. 2002. *Attention Deficit Disorder and Learning Disability: United States, 1997–98.* Publication no. (PHS)2002-1534. A: Hyattsville, Md. U.S. Department of Health and Human Services, Public Health Service.

Chaker, A. M. 2006. Rethinking Recess: As More Schools Trim Breaks, New Research Points to Value of Unstructured Playtime. *Wall Street Journal,* October 10.

Chapman, A. 1997. *A Great Balancing Act: Equitable Education for Girls and Boys.* Washington, D.C.: National Association of Independent Schools.

Christakis, D., et al. 2004. Early Television Exposure and Subsequent Attentional Problems in Children. *Pediatrics* 113: 708–13.

Christakis, D., and F. Zimmerman. 2006. *The Elephant in the Living Room: Make Television Work for Your Kids.* Emmaus, Penn.: Rodale.

Cody, E. Despite a Ban, Chinese Youth Navigate to Internet Cafés, *Washington Post,* February 2007.

Coggins, C. 2006. Are Boys Making the Grade? Gender Gaps in Achievement and Attainment. Rennie Center for Education Research and Policy, October. www.renniecenter.org/research_docs/Are%20Boys%20Making%20the%20Grade%20-%209.29.06.pdf.

Cohen, L. 2001. *Playful Parenting.* New York: Ballantine.

Cole, M., and S. Cole. 2001. *The Development of Children.* 4th ed. New York: Worth.

Condry, J., and S. Condry. 1976. Sex Differences: A Study of the Eye of the Beholder. *Child Development* 47, 3: 812–19.

Conlin, M. 2003. The New Gender Gap: From Kindergarten to Grad School, Boys are Becoming the Second Sex. *Business Week,* May 26.

Connell, D., and E. Gunzelmann. 2004. The New Gender Gap: Why Are So Many Boys Floundering While So Many Girls Are Soaring? *Scholastic Instructor,* March.

Connellan, J., et al. 2001. Sex Differences in Human Neonatal Social Perception. *Infant Behavior and Development* 23: 113–18.

Conrad, J. 1912. *A Personal Record.*

Conroy, P. 1980. *The Lords of Discipline.* New York: Bantam.

Conture, E. G. 1990. *Stuttering and Your Child: Questions and Answers.* Memphis, Tenn.: Speech Foundation of America.

Cooper, E. 2006. *Crawling: A Father's First Year.* New York: Pantheon.

Cormier, R. 1974. *The Chocolate War.* New York: Pantheon.

Dancy, R. B. 1989. *You Are Your Child's First Teacher.* Berkeley, Calif.: Celestial Arts.

Deak, J. 2002. *Girls Will Be Girls: Raising Confident and Courageous Daughters,* New York: Hyperion.

DeCasper, A. J., and W. P. Fifer. 1980. Of Human Bonding: Newborns Prefer Their Mothers' Voices. *Science* 208: 1174–76.

Dee, T. 2006. The Why Chromosome: How a Teacher's Gender Affects Boys And Girls. *Education Next*, September.

Dodge, K., et al. 1990. Peer Status and Aggression in Boys' Groups: Developmental and Contextual Analyses. *Child Development* 61: 1289–309.

Durica, K. 2006. An Unleveled Playing Field: The Ways in Which School Culture Undermines and Undervalues Boys' Writing. *Colorado Reading Journal* 15: 5.

Easterbrook, G. 2006. TV Really Might Cause Autism. *Slate*, October 16. www.slate.com/id/2151538.

Eder, D., C. C. Evans, and S. Parker. 1995. *School Talk: Gender and Adolescent Culture*. New Brunswick, N.J.: Rutgers University Press.

Egeland, B., and E. Farber. 1984. Infant-Mother Attachment: Factors Related to Its Development and Changes over Time. *Child Development* 55: 753–71.

Ekstein, R., and R. L. Motto. 1969. *From Learning for Love to Love of Learning*. New York: Brunner/Mazel.

Elium, D., and J. Elium. *Raising a Son: Parents and the Making of a Healthy Man*. Berkeley, Calif.: Celestial Arts.

Emmons, C. 2003. *His Mother's Son*. Orlando, Fla.: Harcourt.

English, B. 2005. Pornography Is a Mouse Click Away, and Kids Are Being Exposed to It in Ever Increasing Numbers. *Boston Globe*, May 12.

Epstein, D., et al. 1998. *Failing Boys? Issues in Gender and Achievement*. Buckingham: Open University Press.

Erbeck, S. L., and P. Geib. 2006. Hormone's Peak at Birth Affects Brain. *Chicago Tribune*, June 22.

Erickson, B. M. 1998. *Longing for Dad: Father Loss and Its Impact*. Deerfield Beach, Fla.: Health Communications.

Erikson, E. 1968. *Identity: Youth and Crisis*. New York: W. W. Norton.

——. 1993. *Childhood and Society*. New York: W. W. Norton.

Everett, S.-L. 1996. Mirage Multiculturalism: Unmasking the Mighty Morphin' Power Rangers. *Journal of Mass Media Ethics* 11, 1: 28–39.

Farrell, W. 2001. *Father and Child Reunion: How to Bring the Dads We Need to the Children We Love*. New York: Penguin Putnam.

Feller, B. 2006. Study: Teacher's Gender Affects Learning. *Washington Post*, August 27.

——. 2006. Group: Video Games Can Reshape Education. MSNBC.com, October 18. www.msnbc.msn.com/id/15309615.

Field, T. 1999. American Adolescents Touch Each Other Less and Are More Aggressive Toward Their Peers as Compared with French Adolescents. *Adolescence* 34: 753–58.

——. 1999. Preschoolers in America Are Touched Less and Are More Aggressive than Preschoolers in France. *Early Child Development and Care* 151: 11–17.

Finkelhor, D. 1979. What's Wrong with Sex Between Adults and Children? Ethics and the Problem of Sexual Abuse. *American Journal of Orthopsychiatry* 49: 692–97.

Finkelhor, D. 1986. *A Sourcebook on Child Sexual Abuse*. New York: Sage.

Fisher, S., et al. 2006. Teenagers Are Right: Parents Do Not Know Much: An Analysis of Adolescent-Parent Agreement on Reports of Adolescent Substance Use, Abuse and Dependence. *Alcoholism, Clinical and Experimental Research* 30, 10: 1699–710.

Flanagan, C. 2006. *To Hell with All That: Loving and Loathing Our Inner Housewife.* New York: Little, Brown.

Fletcher, R. 2006. *Boy Writers: Reclaiming Their Voices.* Portland, Maine: Stenhouse.

Fraiberg, S. H. 1959. *The Magic Years: Understanding and Handling the Problems of Early Childhood.* New York: Charles Scribner's Sons.

Freud, A. 1965. *The Writings of Anna Freud.* Vol. 6. *Normality and Pathology in Childhood: Assessments of Development.* New York: International Universities Press.

Garbarino, J. 1999. *Lost Boys: Why Our Sons Turn Violent and How We Can Save Them.* New York: Free Press.

Garbarino, J. 2006. *See Jane Hit.* New York: Penguin.

Garry, J., and S. Morrissey. 2000. Team Sports Participation and Risk-Taking Behaviors Among a Biracial Middle School Population. *Clinical Journal of Sports Medicine* 10, 3: 185–90.

Geist, E. A., and M. Gibson. 2000. The Effects of Network and Public Television Programs on Four- and Five-Year-Olds' Ability to Attend to Educational Tasks. *Journal of Instructional Psychology* 27, 4: 250–61.

Ginsburg, K., and the Committee on Communications and Committee on Psychosocial Aspects of Child and Family Health. 2006. The Importance of Play in Promoting Healthy Child Development and Maintaining Strong Parent-Child Bonds. American Academy of Pediatrics, October.

Ginsburg, R., S. Durant, and A. Baltzell. 2006. *Whose Game Is It Anyway?: A Guide to Helping Your Child Get the Most from Sports, Organized by Age and Stage.* New York: Houghton Mifflin.

Giordano, P., M. Longmore, and W. Manning. 2006. Gender and the Meanings of Adolescent Romantic Relationships: A Focus on Boys. *American Sociological Review* 71: 260–87.

Gladwell, M. 2006. No Mercy. *New Yorker,* September 4.

Glass, R. M. 2004. Treatment of Adolescents with Major Depression: Contributions of a Major Trial. *Journal of the American Medical Association* 292, 7: 861–63.

Glennen, S., and M. G. Masters. 2002. Typical and Atypical Language Development in Infants and Toddlers Adopted from Eastern Europe. *American Journal of Speech-Language Pathology* 11: 417–33.

Glennon, W. 2000. *200 Ways to Raise a Boy's Emotional Intelligence.* Berkeley, Calif.: Conari.

Golding, W. 1954. *Lord of the Flies.* New York: Perigee.

Grace, C. O'N. 2006. Family Ties. *Middlebury Magazine* (Middlebury College), Fall.

Grant, S., H. Hiton, and P. Mortola. 2007. *BAM! Helping Boys Connect Through Physical Challenge and Strategic Storytelling: A Leader's Guide to Facilitating Strength-Based Boys' Groups.* London: Routledge.

Green, R. 1987. *The "Sissy Boy Syndrome" and the Development of Homosexuality.* New Haven: Yale University Press.

Grossman, D. 1995. *On Killing: The Psychological Cost of Learning to Kill in War and Society.* Boston: Little, Brown.

Grossman, D., and G. DeGaetano. 1999. *Stop Teaching Our Kids to Kill: A Call to Action Against TV, Movie and Video Game Violence.* New York: Crown.

Gunnar, M., and M. Donahue. 1980. Sex Differences in Social Responsiveness Between Six Months and Twelve Months. *Child Development* 51, 1: 262–65.

Gurian, M. 1994. *Mothers, Sons and Lovers.* Boston: Shambhala.

———. 2005. *The Minds of Boys: Saving Our Sons from Falling Behind in School and Life.* San Francisco: Jossey-Bass.

———. 1996. *The Wonder of Boys.* New York: G. P. Putnam's Sons.

Hallowell, N., and C. Corman. 2006. *Positively ADD.* New York: Walker.

Hallowell, N., and J. Ratey. 1994. *Driven to Distraction.* New York: Pantheon.

———. 1996. *Answers to Distraction.* New York: Bantam.

———. 2005. *Delivered from Distraction.* New York: Ballantine.

Halpern, D. F. 2004. A Cognitive-Process Taxonomy for Sex Differences in Cognitive Abilities. *Current Directions in Psychological Science* 13, 4: 135–39.

Harris, M. 1995. *The Loss That Is Forever.* New York: Plume.

Harrison, H. H. Jr. 2000. *Father to Son: Life Lessons on Raising a Boy.* New York: Workman.

Hartley-Brewer, E. 2001. *Raising Confident Boys.* Cambridge, Mass.: Perseus Books.

Hauser, S. T., S. I. Powers, and G. G. Noam. 1991. *Adolescents and Their Families.* New York: Free Press.

Hawley, R. A. 1993. *Boys Will Be Men: Masculinity in Troubled Times.* Middlebury, Vt.: Paul S. Eriksson.

———. 2004. *Icarus in Our Midst.* Hunting Valley, Ohio: International Boys' School Coalition.

Hays, N. T. 2003. *A Toss of the Dice.* London: Athenaeum.

Hemingway, V. 2004. *Running with the Bulls.* New York: Ballantine.

Herdt, G., ed. 1989. *Gay and Lesbian Youth.* New York: Harrington Park.

Hertsgaard, L., et al. 1995. Adrenocortical Responses to the Strange Situation in Infants with Disorganized/Disoriented Attachment Relationships. *Child Development* 66, 4: 1100–6.

Holmes, J. 1993. *John Bowlby and Attachment Theory.* London: Routledge.

Hopper, J. 2007. Child Abuse: Statistics, Research and Resources. www.jimhopper.com/abstats.

Horn, W., and T. Sylvester. 2002. *Father Facts.* Gaithersburg, Md.: National Fatherhood Initiative.

Hulbert, A. 2003. *Raising America.* New York: Random House.

———. 2006. Will Boys Be Boys? Why the Gender Lens May Not Shed Light on the Latest Educational Crisis. *Washington Post,* February 1.

Hunter, M. 1991. *Abused Boys: The Neglected Victims of Sexual Abuse.* New York: Fawcett Columbine.

Ilg, F., L. B. Ames, and S. Baker. 1981. *Child Behavior: The Classic Child Care Manual from the Gesell Institute of Human Development.* New York: Harper and Row.

Institute of Medicine. 2004. *Preventing Childhood Obesity: Health in the Balance.* Washington, D.C.: Institute of Medicine.

International Boys' School Coalition. 2006. *Ask Me! About My Action Research.* Toronto: International Boys' School Coalition.

Jan, T. 2006. Schoolboy's Bias Suit Argues System Is Favoring Girls. *Boston Globe,* January 26.

Jenkins, H. 2002. Lessons from Littleton: What Congress Doesn't Want to Hear About Youth and

Media. *Independent School,* winter. www.nais.org/publications/ismagazinelist.cfm?Itemnumber
=145812&sn.ItemNumber=145956&tn.ItemNumber=145958.

———. 2004. Reality Bytes: Eight Myths About Video Games Debunked. [From Web site for PBS's
The Video Game Revolution.] www.pbs.org/kcts/videogamerevolution/impact/myths.html.

Jennings, K. 2006. *Mama's Boy, Preacher's Son: A Memoir.* Boston: Beacon Press.

Jones, G. 2002. *Killing Monsters: Why Children Need Fantasy, Super Heroes, and Make-believe Violence.* New
York: Basic Books.

Jones, L., L. Newman, and D. Isay. 1997. *Our America: Life and Death on the South Side of Chicago.* New
York: Scribner.

Jones, M. 2006. Shutting Themselves In. *New York Times,* January 15. www.nytimes.com.

Jordan, T. 2005. *Keeping Your Family Grounded When You're Flying by the Seat of Your Pants.* Chesterfield,
Mo.: Children and Families.

Kagan, J. 1972. The Emergence of Sex Differences. *School Review,* 80, 2: 217–27.

Karen, R. 1998. *Becoming Attached: First Relationships and How They Shape Our Capacity to Love.* New
York: Oxford University Press.

Karr, M. 2006. *Sinners Welcome.* New York: HarperCollins.

Katch, J. 2001. *Under Deadman's Skin: Discovering the Meaning of Children's Violent Play.* Boston: Beacon
Press.

———. 2004. *They Don't Like Me: Lessons on Bullying and Teasing from a Preschool Classroom.* Boston: Beacon Press.

Kellam, S. G., et al. 2000. Erratum: The Effect of the Level of Aggression in the First Grade Classroom on the Course and Malleability of Aggressive Behavior into Middle School. *Development
and Psychopathology* 12, 1: 107.

Kellion, K. 2006. 22 Practices That May Harm Boys. Illinois Loop Web site, March. www.illinoisloop
.org/gender.html.

Kelly, J., and E. Emery. 2003. Children's Adjustment Following Divorce: Risk and Resilience Perspectives. *Family Relations* 52: 352–62.

Kershaw, S. Hooked on the Web: Help Is on the Way. *New York Times,* December 2005.

Kimmel, M. S., and M. Mahler. 2003. Adolescent Masculinity, Homophobia, and Violence: Random
School Shootings. *American Behavioral Scientist* 46: 1439–58.

Kipke, M. D., ed. 1999. *Adolescent Development and the Biology of Puberty: Summary of a Workshop on New
Research.* Washington, D.C.: National Academy Press.

Knowles, E., and M. Smith. 2005. *Boys and Literacy.* Westport, Conn.: Libraries Unlimited.

Kohlberg, L. 1984. *The Psychology of Moral Development.* San Francisco: Harper and Row.

Konner, M. 2001. *Childhood: A Multicultural View.* Boston: Little, Brown.

Koutures, C. 2006. Children and Sports. www.gladstien.com/SportsMedicine/CHILDRENAND
SPORTSguide.shtml.

Kozol, J. 1991. *Savage Inequalities.* New York: Harper Perennial.

Krull, A. 2006. Celebrating the Pity of Brotherly Love. *Newsweek,* August 14.

Lafo, R. R., et al. 2001. *Lighten Up: Art with a Sense of Humor.* Lincoln, Mass.: DeCordova Museum
and Sculpture Park.

LaHoud, S. 2006. Tagged Out. *Sun Chronicle* (Attleboro/North Attleboro, Mass.). October 18. www.thesunchronicle.com/articles/2006/10/18/features/feature37.txt.

Lamott, A. 1995. *Bird by Bird*. New York: Anchor.

Larson, R., and M. Richards. 1995. *Divergent Realities: The Emotional Lives of Mothers, Fathers, and Adolescents*. New York: Basic Books.

Leach, P. 2003. *Your Baby and Child: From Birth to Age Five*. New York: Alfred A. Knopf.

Lefkowitz, B. 1997. *Our Guys*. New York: Vintage Books.

Levant, R. F. 1995. *Masculinity Reconstructed*. New York: Penguin Group.

Levant, R. F., and G. R. Brooks, eds. 1997. *Men and Sex: New Psychological Perspectives*. New York: John Wiley and Sons.

Lewis, M. 2006. The Ballad of Big Mike. *New York Times Magazine*, September 24.

Lewis, P. G., and J. G. Lippman. 2004. *Helping Children Cope with the Death of Parent: A Guide for the First Year*. Westport, Conn.: Praeger.

Lewis, T., F. Amini, and R. Lannon. 2000. *A General Theory of Love*. New York: Vintage.

Lickona, T. 1992. *Educating for Character: How Our Schools Can Teach Respect and Responsibility*. New York: Bantam.

Lillico, I. 2000. *Boys and Their Schooling: A Guide for Parents and Teachers*. Duncraig, Western Australia: Tranton.

———. 2001. *Australian Issues in Boys' Education*. Duncraig, Western Australia: Tranton.

Lobel, T., N. G. Gruber, and S. Mashraki-Pedhatzur. 2001. Children's Gender-Related Inferences and Judgments: A Cross-Cultural Study. *Developmental Psychology* 37, 6: 839–46.

Lubienski, S., and C. Lubienski. 2005. A New Look at Public and Private Schools: Student Background and Mathematics Achievement. *Phi Delta Kappan*, May, 696–99.

Luria, Z., S. Friedman, and M. D. Rose. 1987. *Human Sexuality*. New York: John Wiley and Sons.

Lyon, G. R. 2004. *The NICHD Research Program in Reading Development, Reading Disorders and Reading Instruction. National Institute of Child Health and Human Development*. National Center for Learning Disabilities, New York.

Maccoby, E. 1990. Gender and Relationships: A Developmental Account. *American Psychologist* 45, 5: 513–20.

———. 1998. *The Two Sexes: Growing Up Apart, Coming Together*. Cambridge, Mass.: Belknap.

Maccoby, E., and T. Power. 1985. Mother- and Father-Infant Play: A Development Analysis. *Child Development* 56, 6: 1514–24.

Mahler, M. S., F. Pine, and A. Bergman. 1975. *The Psychological Birth of the Human Infant*. New York: Basic Books.

Manning, W., M. Longmore, and P. Giordano. 2005. Adolescents' Involvement in Non-Romantic Sexual Activity. *Social Science Research* 34: 384–407.

Martin, K. A. 1996. *Puberty, Sexuality, and the Self: Girls and Boys at Adolescence*. New York: Routledge.

McDonald, M. 1998. The Myth of Epidemic False Allegations of Sexual Abuse in Divorce Cases. www.omsys.com/mmcd/courtrev.htm.

McIntosh, A. N. 1995. *Little Doc*. Boone, N.C.: Minors.

Mead, M. 1928. *Coming of Age in Samoa*. New York: Harper Collins.

——. 1993. *Men and the Water of Life.* New York: Harper Collins.

Miedzian, M. 1991. *Boys Will Be Boys: Breaking the Link Between Masculinity and Violence.* New York: Doubleday.

Miller, D. 2003. *Blue Like Jazz.* Nashville, Tenn.: Nelson.

Miller, D., and J. MacMurray. 2006. *To Own a Dragon.* Colorado Springs, Colo.: Navpress.

Millstein, S., A. C. Petersen, and E. O. Nightingale, eds. 1993. *Promoting the Health of Adolescents: New Directions for the Twenty-first Century.* New York: Oxford University Press.

Milne, A. A. 1924. *The House at Pooh Corner.* London: Methuen.

——. 1924. *When We Were Very Young.* London: Methuen.

——. 1927. *Now We Are Six.* New York: E. P. Dutton.

——. 1954. *Winnie-the-Pooh.* New York: E. P. Dutton.

——. 1994. *The Complete Tales of Winnie-the-Pooh.* New York: Dutton.

The Mismeasure of Woman. 2006. *The Economist,* August 5.

Moffatt, M. 1944. *Coming of Age in New Jersey: College and American Culture.* New Brunswick, N.J.: Rutgers University Press.

Moir, A., and D. Jessel. 1992. *Brain Sex: The Real Difference Between Men and Women.* New York: Dell.

Moller, L., and L. Serbin. 2005. Antecedents of Toddler Gender Segregation: Cognitive Consonance, Gender-Typed Toy Preferences and Behavioral Compatibility. *Sex Roles: A Journal of Research* 35: 445-60.

Moore, S., and R. Frost. 1986. *The Little Boy Book: A Guide to the First Eight Years.* New York: Clarkson.

Moran, G. 2005. Attachment in Early Childhood: Comments on van IJzendoorn, and Grossman and Grossmann. *Encyclopedia on Early Childhood Development.* Centre of Excellence for Early Childhood Development, Montreal.

Moran, M. 2006. Boys vs. Girls: Research Finds Girls Have Advantage on Timed Tests. *Vanderbilt Register* (Vanderbilt University), May 7.

Mosher, W., A. Chandra, and J. Jones. 2005. *Sexual Behavior and Selected Health Measures: Men and Women 15–44 Years of Age, United States, 2002.* National Center for Health Statistics, Centers for Disease Control. Publication no. (PHS) 2003-1250. www.cdc.gov/nchs/products/pubs/pubd/ad/361-370/ad362.htm.

MSNBC. *Nearly 4 in 10 US Babies Born Out of Wedlock.* November 2006.

Mulrine, A. 2001. Are Boys the Weaker Sex? *US News & World Report,* July 30.

Nagin, D. S., and R. E. Tremblay. 2001. Parental and Early Childhood Predictors of Persistent Physical Aggression in Boys from Kindergarten to High School. *Archives of General Psychiatry* 58: 389-94.

National Center for Education Statistics. 2006. *The Nation's Report Card.* National Assessment of Educational Progress. Washington, D.C.: U.S. Department of Education.

National Center for Education Statistics. May 2006. National Education Longitudinal Study of 1988 First Follow-up: Student Component Data File User's Manual Volume II. Institute of Education Sciences, U.S. Department of Education. http://nces.ed.gov/pubsearch/ pubsinfo.asp?pubid=92088.

National Center for Education Statistics. Integrated Postsecondary Education Data System

(IPEDS); the 1989–90, 1995–96, and 1999–2000 National Postsecondary Student Aid Study (NPSAS:90, NPSAS:96, NPSAS:2000); the High School and Beyond Longitudinal Study (HS&B:80/92). Washington, D.C.: U.S. Department of Education.

National Center for Education Statistics. 2001. *International Comparisons in Education.* Education Indicators: An International Perspective. Washington, D.C.: U.S. Department of Education.

National Center for Education Statistics. 2000. *Trends in Educational Equity for Girls and Women.* Washington, D.C.: U.S. Department of Education.

National Center for Health Statistics. 1965. Plan and Initial Program of the Health Examination Survey. *Vital and Health Statistics* 1, 4: 1–43.

National Education Longitudinal Study of 1988 (NELS:88/2000); the 1990/94 and 1996/01 Beginning Postsecondary Students Longitudinal Study (BPS:90/94 and BPS:96/01); and the 1993/97 and 2000/01 Baccalaureate and Beyond Longitudinal Study (B&B:93/93 and B&B:2000/01). Washington, D.C.: U.S. Department of Education.

National Institute for Early Education Research. 2004. *Preschool Policy Matters: Who Goes to Preschool and Why Does It Matter?* NIEER Publication. Washington, D.C.: U.S. Department of Education.

National Institute on Media and the Family. 2006. Educating Parents About Video Games. www.mediafamily.org/activitiesandquizzes/decactivity.shtml.

Neufeld, G., and G. Mate. 2005. *Hold On to Your Kids.* New York: Ballantine.

Newkirk, T. 2000. Misreading Masculinity: Speculations on the Great Gender Gap in Writing. *Language Arts* 77, 4.

———. 2002. *Misreading Masculinity: Boys, Literacy, and Popular Culture.* Portsmouth, N.H.: Heinemann.

Newton, N. 1971. Psychological Differences Between Breast and Bottle-Feeding. *American Journal of Clinical Nutrition* 24: 993–1004.

NICHD Early Child Care Research Network. 1997. The Effects of Infant Child Care on Infant-Mother Attachment Security: Results of the NICHD Study of Early Child Care. *Child Development* 68, 5: 860–79.

———. 2001. Childcare and Family Predictors of Preschool Attachment and Stability from Infancy. *Developmental Psychology* 37.

Nunn, D. M. 2006. *Spiraling Out of Control: Lessons Learned from a Boy in Trouble.* Nova Scotia: Nunn Commission.

Odean, K. 1998. *Great Books for Boys.* New York: Ballantine.

Offer, D., D. Marcus, and J. Offer. 1970. A Longitudinal Study of Normal Adolescent Boys. *American Journal of Psychiatry* 126: 917–24.

Organization for Economic Co-operation and Development. *Education at a Glance: OECD Indicators—2006 Edition.* www.oecd.org/dataoecd/32/0/37393408.pdf.

Orlean, S. 2001. *The Bullfighter Checks Her Makeup.* New York: Random House.

Osier, J. L., and H. P. Fox. 2001. *Settle Conflicts Right Now!* Thousand Oaks, Calif.: Corwin.

Paley, V. G. 1984. *Boys and Girls: Superheroes in the Doll Corner.* Chicago: University of Chicago Press.

———. 1988. *Bad Guys Don't Have Birthdays: Fantasy Play at Four.* Chicago: University of Chicago Press.

Palmer, P. J. 2004. *A Hidden Wholeness: The Journey Toward an Undivided Life.* San Francisco, Calif.: John Wiley and Sons.

Pelletier, T. 2000. "Who Is Likely to Stutter." Revised by C. Spillers. Department of Communication Sciences and Disorders, University of Minnesota, Duluth. http://www.d.umn.edu/~cspiller/stutteringpage/incidence.htm

Petras, H., et al. 2004. When the Course of Aggressive Behavior in Childhood Does Not Predict Antisocial Outcomes in Adolescence and Young Adulthood: An Examination of Potential Explanatory Variables. *Development and Psychopathology* 16: 919–94.

Philips, H. 2005. Violent Video Games Alter Brain's Response to Violence. *New Scientist,* December.

Pinker, S., and E. Spelke. 2005. The Science of Gender and Science: Pinker vs. Spelke: A Debate. *Edge: The Third Culture,* May 16. www.edge.org/3rd_culture/debate05/debate05_index.html.

Polis, B. 2004. *Only a Mother Could Love Him: My Life with and Triumph over ADD.* New York: Ballantine.

Pollack, W. S. 1997. New Treatment Models for Men: Crisis, Opportunity and Connection. Department of Postgraduate and Continuing Education, McLean Hospital, Belmont, Mass.

——. 1998. *Real Boys.* New York: Random House.

Pope, H. G. Jr., et al. 1997. Muscle Dysmorphia: An Underrecognized Form of Body Dysmorphic Disorder. *Psychosomatics* 38: 548–57.

Popenoe, D. 1996. *Life Without a Father.* New York: Free Press.

Porter, K. A. 1970. *The Collected Essays and Occasional Writings of Katherine Anne Porter.* Boston: Houghton Mifflin.

Pruett, K. 2001. 1997. How Men and Children Affect Each Other's Development. *Zero to Three Journal* 18, 1.

——. 2000. *Fatherneed: Why Father Care Is as Essential as Mother Care for Your Child.* New York: Broadway Books.

Pruitt, D. B., ed. 1998. *Your Child: What Every Parent Needs to Know About Childhood Development from Birth to Preadolescence.* New York: HarperCollins.

Public Health Agency of Canada. 2003. Infant Attachment—What Professionals Need to Know. September 26. www.phac-aspc.gc.ca/mh-sm/mhp-psm/pub/fc-pc/prof_know.html.

Quimby, B., and K. Wack. 2006. Boys Learn Better by Doing. *Portland Press Herald,* March 29. http://pressherald.mainetoday.com/specialrpts/boys/060329newday4mainb.shtm.

Reinberg, S. 2006. Antidepressants May Up Risk for Attempted, Not Completed Suicide. HealthDay, December 4. www.healthday.com/Article.asp?AID=536417.

Reinking, D., and J. Wu. 1990. Reexamining the Research on Television and Reading. *Reading Research and Instruction* 29: 30–43.

Reuters. 2007. Worldwide Use of ADHD Drugs Nearly Triples. March 9. www.msnbc.msn.com/id/17503743.

Rich, H. 2003. *In the Moment: Embracing the Fullness of Life.* New York: Harper Paperbacks.

Rimas, A. 2006. Her Rx: Equal Parts Humor, Respect. *Boston Globe,* May 15.

Rimer, S. 2006. A Man, a Van, a Plan for Scrappy Baseball. *New York Times,* October 25.

Roffman, D. 2001. *The Thinking Parent's Guide to Talking Sense About Sex.* Cambridge, Mass.: Perseus.

Romeo, R. D., H. N. Richardson, and C. L. Sisk. 2002. Puberty and the Maturation of the Male Brain and Sexual Behavior: Recasting a Behavioral Potential. *Neuroscience and Biobehavioral Reviews* 26, 3: 381–91.

Rowe, K. J. 2001. Equal and Different? Yes, but What Really Matters? Paper presented at the joint conference of the Alliance of Girls' Schools (Australasia) and the International Boys' Schools Coalition (Australian Hub), Southport School, Gold Coast, Queensland. August.

Rubin, R. 1972. Sex Differences in Effects of Kindergarten Attendance on Development of School Readiness and Language Skills. *Elementary School Journal* 38: 325.

Ruhlman, M. 1996. *Boys Themselves.* New York: Henry Holt.

Sadowski, M. 2006. School Readiness Gap. *Harvard Education Letter,* July/August.

Sandberg, J., and S. Hofferth. 2001. Changes in Children's Time with Parents, U.S. 1981–1997. Population Studies Center, University of Michigan. May 2.

Sax, L. 2005. *Why Gender Matters: What Parents and Teachers Need to Know About the Emerging Science of Sex Differences.* New York: Broadway Books.

Schmitz, S. 2004. *Grade Busters: How Parents Can End the Bad Grades Battle.* Baltimore: Bancroft.

Sessions Stepp, L. 2005. Study: Half of All Teens Have Had Oral Sex. *Washington Post,* September 16.

Sheppard K., and H. Brown. 1982. Social Adaptational and Psychological Antecedents in First Grade of Adolescent Psychopathology Ten Years Later. Paper presented at the Research Workshop on Prevention Aspects of Suicide and Affective Disorders Among Adolescents and Young Adults. Harvard School of Public Health, Boston. December 3–4.

Shibley Hyde, J. 2005. The Gender Similarities Hypothesis. *American Psychologist,* September, 581–92.

Siegel, D. J., and M. Hartzell. 2004. *Parenting from the Inside Out.* New York: Penguin.

Silverstein, O., and B. Rashbaum. 2000. *The Courage to Raise Good Men.* New York: Penguin.

Simon, W., and J. Gagnon. 1986. Sexual Scripts: Permanence and Change. *Archives of Sexual Behavior* 15: 97–120.

Sisk, C. L., and J. Zahr. 2005. Pubertal Hormones Organize the Adolescent Brain and Behavior. *Frontiers in Neuroendocrinology* 26, 3–4: 163–74.

Smith, M. W., and J. D. Wilhelm. 2002. *"Reading Don't Fix No Chevys": Literacy in the Lives of Young Men.* Portsmouth, N.H.: Heinemann.

Sommers, C. H. 2001. *The War Against Boys: How Misguided Feminism Is Harming Our Young Men.* New York: Simon and Schuster.

Stamatakis, E., et al. 2005. Overweight and Obesity Trends from 1974 to 2003 in English Children: What Is the Role of Socioeconomic Factors? *Archives of Disease in Childhood* 90: 999–1004.

Stephenson, B. 2004. *Slaying the Dragon: The Contemporary Struggle of Adolescent Boys.* South Lake Tahoe, Calif.: Adolescent Mind.

Stephenson, S. 1998. *The Joyful Child: for Birth to Three Years.* Arcata, Calif.: Michael Olaf Montessori Company.

Stepp, L. 2000. *Our Last Best Shot: Guiding Our Children Through Early Adolescence.* New York: Riverhead Books.

Steyer, J. P. 2002. *The Other Parent.* New York: Atria Books.

Stoltenberg, J. 1993. *The End of Manhood: A Book for Men of Conscience.* New York: Penguin.

Stone, D., and E. Tippett. 2004. *The Essential Guide to Student Life: Real College.* New York: Penguin.

Stovall-McClough, C. 2002. Introduction to Attachment Theory and Research—Bowlby and Attachment Theory. Weill Medical College of Cornell University.

Sturm, R. 2005. Childhood Obesity: What We Can Learn from Existing Data on Societal Trends: Part 2. *Preventing Chronic Disease: Public Health Research, Practice, and Policy* 2, 2. www.cdc.gov/pcd/issues/2005/apr/04_0039.htm.

Sunderland, M. 2006. *The Science of Parenting.* New York: DK Publishing.

Taffel, R. 2005. *Breaking Through to Teens: A New Psychotherapy for the New Adolescence.* New York: Guilford Press.

Thompson, M., and T. Barker. 2005. *The Pressured Child.* New York: Ballantine.

Thompson, M., C. O. Grace, and L. Cohen. 2001. *Best Friends, Worst Enemies: Understanding the Social Lives of Children.* New York: Ballantine.

Thompson, M., and D. Kindlon. 2000. *Raising Cain: Protecting the Emotional Life of Boys.* New York: Ballantine.

Tobin, J. 1991. *Preschool in Three Cultures: Japan, China and the United States.* New Haven: Yale University Press.

Towle, A., ed. 1986. *Fathers.* New York: Simon and Schuster.

Turner, P. J. 1991. Relations Between Attachment, Gender and Behavior with Peers in Preschool. *Child Development* 62, 6: 1475–88.

Twain, M. 2004. *The Adventures of Tom Sawyer.* New York: Sterling.

Tyre, P. 2005. Boy Brains, Girl Brains. *Newsweek,* September 19.

———. 2006. The Trouble with Boys. *Newsweek,* January 30.

United Nations Children's Fund (UNICEF). 2004. *The State of the World's Children 2004,* chapter 5: What About Boys? New York: UNICEF. www.unicef.org/sowc04/sowc04_contents.html.

U.S. Department of Commerce, Bureau of the Census, Current Population Survey (CPS), October Supplement, selected years 1977–2001, previously unpublished tabulation (December 2003).

U.S. Department of Health and Human Services. 2001. *The Surgeon General's Call to Action to Prevent and Decrease Overweight and Obesity.* Rockville, Md.: Public Health Service.

Van Schie, E. G. M., and O. Wiegman. 1997. Children and Videogames: Leisure Activities, Aggression, Social Interaction, and School Performance. *Journal of Applied Social Psychology* 27: 1175–94.

Video Gaming. 2005. *The Economist.* August 4.

Wallerstein, J., and S. Blakeslee. 1996. *Second Chances: Men, Women and Children a Decade After Divorce.* New York: Houghton Mifflin.

Walls, M. E. 1997. Multiple Predictors of Mother-Child Attachment and Peer Competency During Preschool. Ph.D. dissertation, Purdue University.

Walsh, D. 2001. Video Game Violence and Public Policy. Paper presented at the conference Playing by the Rules: The Cultural Policy Challenges of Video Games. Chicago, October 26–27. http://culturalpolicy.uchicago.edu/conf2001/papers/walsh.html.

Walsh, D., with N. Bennett. 2004. *Why Do They Act That Way? A Survival Guide to the Adolescent Brain for You and Your Teen.* New York: Free Press.

Warner, J. 2006. What Boy Crisis? *New York Times,* July 3.

Weil, E. 2006. What If It's (Sort of) a Boy and (Sort of) a Girl? *New York Times,* September 24.

Weinberg, K. 1996. Infant Affective Reactions to the Resumption of Maternal Interaction after the Still-Face. *Child Development* 67, 3: 905–14.

Weinstock, N. 1997. *The Secret Love of Sons: How We Men Feel About Our Mothers, and Why We Never Tell.* New York: Riverhead Books.

Werner, S. 2006. *Notes from Kindergarten.* Pawling: Fethra Press.

West, P. 1984. How the Media Portray Men: A Review of J. R. McNamara's *Media and Male Identity.* www.ualberta.ca.

Whitmire, R. 2006. Boy Trouble. *New Republic,* January 23.

Winnicott, D. W. 1958. *Through Paediatrics to Psychoanalysis.* New York: Basic Books.

——. 1971. *Playing and Reality.* New York: Basic Books.

——. 1992. *The Child, the Family and the Outside World.* Reading, Mass.: Addison-Wesley.

——. 1996. *Thinking About Children.* Reading, Mass.: Addison-Wesley.

Wirt, J., S. Choy, P. Rooney, S. Provasnik, A. Sen, and R. Tobin. 2004. The Condition of Education 2004 (NCES 2004-077). U.S. Department of Education, National Center for Education Statistics. Washington, D.C.: U.S. Government Printing Office.

Wolf, A. E. 2002. *"Get Out of My Life, but First Could You Drive Me and Cheryl to the Mall?" A Parent's Guide to the New Teenager.* New York: Farrar, Straus and Giroux.

Wolff, T. 1989. *This Boy's Life: A Memoir.* New York: Harper and Row.

——. 2003. *Old School.* New York: Vintage.

Your Brain and Psychotherapy: Are There Consistent Underlying Features of Therapeutic Change? *Harvard Mental Health Letter* 23, 2: 1–3.

Zinn, M. B., P. Hondagneu-Sotelo, and M. A. Messner. 2005. *Gender Through the Prism of Difference.* New York: Oxford University Press.

INDEX

MICHAEL THOMPSON, PH.D., is a clinical psychologist, lecturer, consultant, and former seventh-grade teacher. He conducts workshops across the United States and internationally on social cruelty, children's friendships, and boys' development. With Dan Kindlon, Ph.D., he coauthored the *New York Times* bestseller *Raising Cain: Protecting the Emotional Life of Boys,* which was adapted into an acclaimed documentary shown on PBS. With Teresa H. Barker he coauthored *The Pressured Child: Helping Your Child Find Success in School and Life* and *Speaking of Boys: Answers to the Most-Asked Questions About Raising Sons.* With Catherine O'Neill Grace and Lawrence J. Cohen, Ph.D., he coauthored *Best Friends, Worst Enemies: Understanding the Social Lives of Children* and *Mom, They're Teasing Me: Helping Your Child Solve Social Problems.* Dr. Thompson is married and the father of two. He lives in Arlington, Massachusetts, and can be reached at www.michaelthompson-phd.com.

TERESA BARKER, who collaborated with Michael Thompson on *Raising Cain, Speaking of Boys,* and *The Pressured Child,* is a journalist whose other book collaborations include *Girls Will Be Girls: Raising Confident, Courageous Daughters; The Soul of Money: Transforming Your Relationship with Money and Life,* and *In the Moment: Celebrating the Everyday.* Ms. Barker is married and the mother of a son and two daughters. She lives in Portland, Oregon.